The Best
Pub Quiz
Book
EVER! 4

First published in 1997 by
Carlton Books Limited
20 Mortimer Street
London W1T 3JW

Second edition published in 2007

ISBN: 978-1-84442-889-2

Questions set by The Puzzle House

Printed and bound by CPI Group (UK) Ltd, Croydon, CR0 4YY

The Best Pub Quiz Book EVER! 4

SECOND EDITION

CARLTON
BOOKS

Contents

Introduction

Quizzes are strange things. If you were to stroll up to some poor bloke on the street – let's say it's a Saturday lunch time, and he's out with the wife doing the weekly shopping, trying to get it over and done with so he can make it back home for kick-off – and start firing questions at him, one after the other, he'd probably take it pretty badly. He'd be nervous, irritated, and looking for quick ways to escape the maniac who latched on to him. If you take a moment to picture it ("Quick, mate, what would you ride in a velodrome? What colour is an aubergine?"), you'll see how ludicrous it sounds. If he doesn't lamp you one, he'll probably run off screaming in terror.

However, get the same bloke later on the same Saturday, down the pub with his mates after the match, and then you leap up and start firing the same questions at him, at the very least he's going to rise to the challenge and prove he's the equal of your questions. If you've taken the time to sort things out with the landlord in advance, and you're asking the whole pub, you'll have a crowd of people enthralled, hanging on your every word, and not just our bloke. Even if – and this is the best part – there's absolutely no prize at the end of it. We all love glory, after all, and what could be more glorious than proving you've got the keenest mind in the bar? It beats getting on to a horse and charging at a cannon hands down.

This is the fourth volume of *The Best Pub Quiz Book Ever!* and it keeps getting better and better. Inside these hallowed covers, you'll find more than 10,000 questions covering a stunning range of topics, divided into laughably easy, reasonably medium, and brain-shreddingly hard. At the back, you'll also find a comprehensive set of guidelines on how to prepare for and run a successful quiz of your own down the local, and some handy answer sheet templates to photocopy and give out to contestants. There is one important thing you have to remember though, and that is never, ever, under any circumstances, give out your own pens.

More importantly than that though – seriously for a minute – when you are going to be running a quiz, prepare properly beforehand. Don't just take this book along and read out of it (because apart from anything else, some other wise guy might have bought a copy too, and be checking the answers). Note down all the questions and all the answers, and make sure you've got everything. If an answer makes you think "hang on a moment, is that right?" then double-check it to make sure that it is not only correct, but it is the only correct answer. While every possible effort has been undertaken to make absolutely sure that every answer is accurate, there is a slight possibility that an error may have crept in and the answer is wrong. Nothing is more humiliating than telling people who are right that they are wrong, in front of a lot of other people who will remember it and tease you about it mercilessly for the next three years. If you've made sure of your answers, you'll be absolutely 100% safe, not just 99.99% safe.

So, there you go. Wade in, and have fun. After all, that's what it's all about.

Easy Questions

The whole point of these questions is that they are, well, easy. As in not hard. That means that they shouldn't give you, or anyone else who speaks the same language, any problems. If you get these questions right, that's really not much to be proud of. In fact, it's close to the truth that getting these questions wrong is something to be worried about. If you find yourself doing badly on these questions, there are many possible reasons. The first thing to check is that you're looking at the correct answer block. If you've made that mistake, it'll throw your results right out. Alternatively, you may be extremely drunk. If reading this short introduction is proving tricky, that could be the cause. Try again later. Another possible cause is that you might only be three or four years old – again, try again later, only make it much later. Finally, you may have been born in the wilds and have spent your life being raised by a friendly family of otters, in which case you can be forgiven for your ignorance. They're nice creatures, but they're really not much cop when it comes to hits of the 90s.

So, when you're devising a quiz for people, you might like to soften them up with a few of these questions, ease them into the groove, fatten them for the kill, and lots of other clichés that mean you're gently preparing people for something nasty. If nothing else, it'll make sure that even the bloke in the corner who's so hammered he can't stand will get one or two points, and save face. Tomorrow, he may even be grateful enough to buy you a drink for being so considerate. It's worth a shot, so to speak...

1 Which Paddy led the Liberal Democrats?
2 FW De Klerk was President of which country?
3 Which Hussein ruled Iraq during the Gulf War?
4 What were the initials of the US footballer Simpson accused of murdering his wife?
5 Which Gerry was a president of Sinn Fein in 2000?
6 Dr Spock made news in a book about looking after whom or what?
7 In July 2006 which political leader advised people to "hug a hoodie"?
8 Which name was shared by Steel and Owen of the Liberal/Social Democrat Alliance?
9 Which former Chancellor of the Exchequer is the father of TV cook Nigella Lawson?
10 Ferdinand and Imelda Marcos led which country beginning with P?
11 Which Patricia has been health secretary this century?
12 What is the first name of Zimbabwe's President Mugabe?
13 What was the name of Nelson Mandela's wife during the years he was in jail?
14 William Hague was a government minister in which country before leading his party?
15 Benazir Bhutto was Prime Minister of which Asian country?
16 Which Keenan was freed from Beirut after being held hostage for nearly four years?
17 Alex Salmond led which Nationalist Party?
18 In the period 1981–2001, which two US Presidents have had the same surname?
19 Who is Elisabeth Murdoch's media mogul father?
20 In the 1980s who became the USA's oldest President?
21 What was the surname of suffragettes Emmeline, Sylvia and Christabel?
22 Who was the youngest British Prime Minister of the 20th century?
23 Who celebrated fifty years as a monarch in 2002?
24 Which Miss Lewinsky had the so-called "inappropriate relationship" with Bill Clinton?
25 Which Kray died in 2001 after being released from prison after suffering from cancer?
26 Which McGuinness became Northern Ireland's Education Minister after the Good Friday agreement?
27 David Trimble became First Minister in which country of the UK?
28 Which Joseph led the Communist Party in the USSR for over 30 years?
29 Which Arthur led the 1980s miners' strike?
30 Deng Xiaoping was leader of which country?

Answers	TV Soaps *(see Quiz 3)*

1 Ian Beale. 2 5. 3 Coronation Street. 4 Sharon. 5 Eve. 6 Manchester. 7 Police officer. 8 Dixon. 9 George. 10 Grant. 11 Linda. 12 Dingles. 13 Laura. 14 Brown. 15 Brookside. 16 Roy. 17 Battersby. 18 Chester. 19 Alma. 20 Hancock. 21 Coronation Street. 22 Emma. 23 Emmerdale. 24 Red. 25 Tiffany. 26 Coronation Street. 27 Peacock. 28 Nick. 29 Crossroads. 30 Hollyoaks.

Quiz 2

Pot Luck 1

Answers – page 12

1 Which of Durham, Kent and Suffolk is part of East Anglia?
2 What would a Venezuelan do with a Bolivar?
3 Who played Rachel in "Friends"?
4 What does the B stand for in LBW in cricket?
5 Which Spice Girl wore a dress with a Union Jack flag pattern?
6 Which word can be a worker's eating place or a cutlery set?
7 What was President George W Bush's father's first name?
8 Which caped hero flew his way round the city of Metropolis?
9 Which fruit goes in the pudding named after opera diva Nellie Melba?
10 What is a pomegranate?
11 Which was built first – the Eiffel Tower or the Empire State Building?
12 What comes after New South in the name of an Australian state?
13 Which has the most sides – a hexagon, a pentagon or a quadrilateral?
14 Capricorn, Libra, Phoenix – which of these is not a sign of the zodiac?
15 How many faces would a dozen dice have in total?
16 What shape is in the middle of the Japanese flag?
17 In e mail what does the e stand for?
18 What was the name of the bear that belonged to Christopher Robin?
19 In athletics, how many events have taken place when half a decathlon is completed?
20 What is coffee produced from?
21 Where did turkeys originally come from?
22 Who might display, on a British road, a sign worth fifty in Roman numerals?
23 What name is given to buying goods via the Internet?
24 When texting, the word YOU is usually shown by which letter?
25 Which numbers feature in the ads using 1970s-style mustachioed runners?
26 Houston is in which US state?
27 On which continent is the Panama Canal?
28 Which brothers made the first controlled powered flight?
29 Which Mark has managed Blackburn and Wales at soccer?
30 In history the "Marie Celeste" was a type of what?

Answers	People – Stars *(see Quiz 4)*

1 Dance. 2 Elton John. 3 Lennon. 4 Ireland. 5 Scotland. 6 Joely. 7 Reese. 8 Laine. 9 Five. 10 Henshall. 11 Martine. 12 Snooker. 13 Sir Bobby. 14 Wade. 15 Red. 16 Iceland. 17 Jensen. 18 Blanchett. 19 Harry. 20 Honor. 21 Liverpool. 22 Slim. 23 Cruise. 24 Carol. 25 Charlie Dimmock. 26 Sarong. 27 Yorkshire. 28 Bean. 29 Terry. 30 Zinedine Zidane.

1 Jane Collins was lined up to be the fourth bride of which "Eastenders" Ian?
2 On which Channel did "Family Affairs" debut?
3 Which northern soap was the most successful of the 1990s?
4 Which former landlady of the Queen Vic returned to the Square in 2001 after "living in America"?
5 In "Coronation Street" in September 2001 who did Fred marry?
6 Where did Bianca go when she left Albert Square?
7 In "Emmerdale" what responsible job does Angie Reynolds have?
8 Which Ron shot a suspected burglar in the summer of 2001?
9 Which "Straw Dogs" actress Susan joined the Albert Square cast as Terry's love interest?
10 Who was Phil Mitchell's brother as played by Ross Kemp?
11 Who did Mike Baldwin marry after he was divorced from Alma?
12 Which family did Lisa Riley belong to when she starred in "Emmerdale"?
13 Who did Ian Beale marry after his disastrous ceremony with Mel?
14 In "Corrie" what colour did the Battersbys add to the end of their name?
15 In which soap did film actress Anna Friel make her name?
16 Who is Barry Evans' dad in "EastEnders", sharing his name with an ex-Liverpool FC boss?
17 Who were the "Coronation Street" "family from hell", which included Toyah and Janice?
18 Where is "Hollyoaks" set?
19 Which "Coronation Street" character died of cancer in 2001?
20 Which actress Sheila came to Albert Square as Steve Owen's mum?
21 Which soap ran a campaign to free the Weatherfield One?
22 Who did Curly marry after Raquel left him?
23 Which soap features the Lamberts and the Kings?
24 What colour was Rita Sullivan's famous hair?
25 What was the name of the "EastEnders" character played by Martine McCutcheon?
26 Which soap introduced an extra Friday-night instalment in 2001?
27 In "Coronation Street", what was Ashley and Maxine's surname?
28 Who is the evil member of the "EastEnders" Cotton family?
29 Which Midlands soap returned to ITV in 2001?
30 Which teen soap features the Hunters and the Morgans?

Quiz 4

Answers – page 10

1 Michael Flatley was dubbed Lord of the what?
2 Which megastar sang his own song at Princess Diana's funeral?
3 After which Beatle did Liam Gallagher name his son with Patsy Kensit?
4 From where does ex-"Ballykissangel" star Dervla Kirwan hail?
5 In which part of the UK did Madonna marry Guy Ritchie?
6 Which blonde actress Richardson split with Jamie Theakston in 2001?
7 Which Ms Witherspoon starred in "Walk the Line"?
8 Which Cleo is Mrs John Dankworth?
9 How many members of Hear'Say were there?
10 Which Ruthie starred in the musical "Peggy Sue Got Married"?
11 Which Ms McCutcheon played Eliza Doolittle on the London stage?
12 Ronnie O'Sullivan is a star in which sport?
13 Who is Jack Charlton's famous younger brother?
14 Which former tennis star Virginia had a father who was a clergyman?
15 When she was a Spice Girl, Geri Halliwell had what colour hair?
16 Bjork has an emblem from which country on her shoulder?
17 Which DJ David had the name "Kid"?
18 Which actress Cate portrayed Katharine Hepburn in "The Aviator"?
19 Which singer Connick adds Junior to his name?
20 Which Ms Blackman, an ex-Bond girl, has a brown belt in judo?
21 Sir Paul McCartney received the freedom of which city, his childhood home?
22 What does Fatboy Norman Cook add to his name for DJ purposes?
23 Which Tom split with wife Nicole Kidman in 2001?
24 Which first name is shared by TV stars Smillie and Vorderman?
25 Who is the female gardener on "Ground Force"?
26 David Beckham famously wore what normally female garment?
27 Opera star Lesley Garrett hails from which northern county?
28 Which zany Mr is Rowan Atkinson's most famous creation?
29 Who is broadcaster Alan Wogan's famous dad?
30 Which French footballer got his marching orders in the 2006 World Cup Final?

Answers | Pot Luck 1 *(see Quiz 2)*

1 Suffolk. 2 Spend it. 3 Jennifer Aniston. 4 Before. 5 Geri. 6 Canteen. 7 George. 8 Superman. 9 Peach. 10 A fruit. 11 Eiffel Tower. 12 Wales. 13 Hexagon. 14 Phoenix. 15 72. 16 Circle. 17 Electronic. 18 Winnie the Pooh. 19 Five. 20 Beans. 21 North America. 22 A learner driver – L. 23 Shopping on line. 24 U. 25 118 118. 26 Texas. 27 America. 28 Wright. 29 Hughes. 30 Boat/ship.

1 Which equestrian champion was 2006 BBC Sports Personality of the Year?
2 Which zodiac sign of Gemini, Pisces and Taurus represents a human shape?
3 Which Sharon starred in "Basic Instinct" and "Total Recall"?
4 How is a sound produced from a euphonium?
5 What colour is the magic linked with a wicked witch?
6 If you multiply the length of rectangle by the width what do you get?
7 A penny farthing was an early type of bike, but how many farthings made up the value of a penny farthing?
8 What is a nun's head dress called?
9 Which girl band featuring the Appleton girls got back together in 2006?
10 Manx, Marmalade and Tabby are all types of what?
11 In the saying, many what will make light work?
12 Following the gruesome nursery rhyme recipe, how many blackbirds would be baked in two pies?
13 Which fruit of grapes, pears and plums is bought by the bunch?
14 What form of transport is the French TGV?
15 Tortillas are originally from which country?
16 When did Yeovil first play in the Football League – 1973, 1983 or 2003?
17 What was the number of the first Apollo mission to land on the Moon?
18 The Dalai Lama is the spiritual leader of which country?
19 Around which part of your body would you tie a cummerbund?
20 What did the Romans keep in a catacomb?
21 Which object appears on the Canadian flag?
22 What happens to the rows of letters when reading down an eye-test chart?
23 Pevez Musharraf was president of which country?
24 Which of Funny, Grumpy and Happy is not one of Snow White's seven dwarfs?
25 What did David Bowie call his first child?
26 If the first of a month is a Thursday, what day will the eighth be?
27 Cassata is a type of which food?
28 In "The Wombles", which Great Uncle shares his name with a country?
29 Which side of a ship is starboard?
30 Which colour is usually used to show the sea on a map?

Answers | Pot Luck 3 *(see Quiz 7)*

1 New Zealand. 2 Vietnam. 3 English. 4 Sweetcorn. 5 Mick McCarthy. 6 Penguins. 7 Pistol. 8 East. 9 Pierce Brosnan. 10 Cricket. 11 Computer. 12 Madonna. 13 Europe. 14 Nests. 15 Invention. 16 (South) America. 17 Air. 18 Rake. 19 Flags. 20 1992. 21 Autobahn. 22 Vegetative state. 23 Yellow. 24 Fluid ounces. 25 Apples. 26 180. 27 Egg. 28 Throat. 29 General Pinochet. 30 Easter.

1 Which Ian captained Europe to Ryder Cup success in 2006?
2 How many events did Denise Lewis compete in to win her heptathlon Olympic gold?
3 Against which country did England play the first ever Test Match in cricket?
4 Mike Powell beat Bob Beamon's long-standing record in which event?
5 Allan Border made a record number of runs for which international cricketing side?
6 How long does Le Mans's most famous motor race last?
7 In which Greek city were the first modern Olympics held?
8 In which decade did Roger Bannister run his first sub-four-minute mile?
9 Which Czech-born Martina won her ninth Wimbledon singles title in 1990?
10 Gymnast Nadia Comaneci was the first person ever to score what out of 10 at the Olympic Games?
11 In 1988 tennis was re-introduced at which four-yearly sporting event?
12 What colour shirts were England wearing when they won the 1966 World Cup?
13 Eleven athletes from which country were killed at the 1972 Munich Olympics?
14 In which decade did Jesse Owens win four gold medals at the Berlin Olympics?
15 Charismatic gymnast Olga Korbut represented which country?
16 In which city were the 1980 Olympics, boycotted by the Americans?
17 Which cricketer Geoffrey made his hundredth 100 in a 1977 Test Match?
18 Which racehorse was taken from his box in an Irish stud in 1983 and was never seen again?
19 Which German Boris won Wimbledon in 1985?
20 Who, with Jayne Torvill, was awarded a full set of perfect Olympic sixes for ice dancing in 1984?
21 Which Steve was Sebastian Coe's main British rival in middle-distance running in 1980?
22 What was the nickname of James Douglas who beat Mike Tyson in 1990?
23 Who hit six sixes in an over in 1968?
24 Which Manchester side won the European Cup in 1968?
25 Which Second Division team beat Leeds United in the 1973 FA Cup final?
26 What is the nationality of Ballesteros who won the British Open in 1984?
27 How many times did Red Rum win the Grand National?
28 Which England footballer was famous for his tears at Italia 90?
29 Which Briton won gold in the triple jump in the 2001 World Championships?
30 Which English player was sent off against Argentina in the 1998 World Cup?

Answers	New Millennium Movies *(see Quiz 8)*

1 Diary. 2 Cage. 3 Travolta. 4 Pearl Harbor. 5 Ballet. 6 Egypt. 7 Cruz. 8 China. 9 Cruise. 10 Green. 11 Chocolate. 12 Hannibal. 13 Gibson. 14 Harry Potter. 15 Caine. 16 Animation. 17 Desert Island. 18 Croft. 19 Finney. 20 Matt Dillon. 21 Kate Winslet. 22 X. 23 Satellite dish. 24 Low Lifes. 25 Gladiator. 26 St Bernard dog. 27 Ring. 28 Storm. 29 Toy Story 2. 30 Ralph.

1 Maoris were the first settlers in which country?

2 "The Deer Hunter" has which war as its subject matter?

3 What is the main language of North America's two main countries?

4 Which vegetable is produced from the plant maize?

5 Which Mick has managed the Republic of Ireland, Sunderland and Wolves?

6 The animated movie "Happy Feet" is about what kind of creatures?

7 Which weapon is used in Pete Sampras's nickname?

8 Mozambique is on which coast of Africa?

9 Who starred as 007 in "The World is Not Enough"?

10 Which sport is covered by the "Wisden Almanac"?

11 William Henry Gates III became seriously rich through which industry?

12 Which superstar did film producer Guy Ritchie marry in 2000?

13 Which continent is the most crowded and the smallest?

14 Which word describes homes for birds as well as sets of tables?

15 Frank Zappa was leader of the group The Mothers of what – Convention, Intention or Invention?

16 In which continent is the Amazon rainforest?

17 A hovercraft moves along on a cushion of what?

18 Which one of the following tools is pronged – hoe, spade or rake?

19 What does a person hold in their hand when practising semaphore?

20 Which of the following was a leap year –1991, 1992, 1994?

21 What is the German word for a motorway?

22 In medical terms PVS stands for persistent what?

23 What colour does the skin become if someone suffers from jaundice?

24 What does the abbreviation "fl oz" stand for?

25 Which fruit is mainly used when making a strudel?

26 How many degrees are there in a right-angled triangle?

27 What is the main ingredient of mayonnaise other than oil?

28 Laryngitis affects which part of your body?

29 Which former Chilean leader died in December 2006?

30 Lent comes before which Christian festival?

Answers	Pot Luck 2 *(see Quiz 5)*

1 Zara Phillips. 2 Gemini. 3 Stone. 4 By blowing into it. 5 Black. 6 The area. 7 Five. 8 Wimple. 9 All Saints. 10 Cat. 11 Hands. 12 48. 13 Grapes. 14 Train. 15 Mexico. 16 2003. 17 11. 18 Tibet. 19 The waist. 20 Dead bodies. 21 Maple leaf. 22 They get smaller. 23 Pakistan. 24 Funny. 25 Zowie. 26 Thursday. 27 Ice cream. 28 Bulgaria. 29 Right. 30 Blue.

1 What did Bridget Jones write?
2 Which Nicolas starred in "Captain Corelli's Mandolin"?
3 Which John was the counter-terrorist in "Swordfish"?
4 Which 2001 movie was about a Japanese bombing 60 years before?
5 Billy Elliot trained to be what type of dancer?
6 Where is "The Mummy Returns" set?
7 Which Penelope played opposite Johnny Depp in "Blow"?
8 Where was "Crouching Tiger, Hidden Dragon" produced?
9 Which Tom teamed up – both on and off the screen – with Penelope Cruz in the movie "Vanilla Sky"?
10 What colour is Shrek?
11 What type of shop does Juliette Binoche open in "Chocolat"?
12 What was the sequel to "Silence of the Lambs" called?
13 Which Mel read Helen Hunt's thoughts in "What Women Want"?
14 Warner Brothers made a series of movies about which boy wizard?
15 Which Michael co-starred with Sandra Bullock in "Miss Congeniality"?
16 What type of movie was "The Emperor's New Groove"?
17 Where is Tom Hanks trying to survive in "Castaway"?
18 Which Lara was a character in "Tomb Raider"?
19 Which Albert co-starred with Julia Roberts in "Erin Brokovich"?
20 Which Matt starred in "Crash"?
21 Which star of "Titanic" also starred in "Quills"?
22 In which TV "Files" did "Evolution"'s David Duchovny find fame?
23 What is "The Dish" in the title of the movie with Sam Neill?
24 What went with "High Heels" in the movie title?
25 Which Roman epic starred Russell Crowe?
26 Which animal is the hero of "Beethoven's 3rd"?
27 What completes the title – "Fellowship of the ____"?
28 What was "Perfect" in the 2000 movie with George Clooney?
29 What was the sequel to "Toy Story" called?
30 Which Fiennes starred in "The End of the Affair"?

Answers	**Memorable Sporting Moments** *(see Quiz 6)*

1 Ian Woosnam. 2 Seven. 3 Australia. 4 Long jump. 5 Australia. 6 24 hours. 7 Athens. 8 1950s. 9 Navratilova. 10 10. 11 Olympics. 12 Red. 13 Israel. 14 1930s. 15 USSR (Soviet Union). 16 Moscow. 17 Boycott. 18 Shergar. 19 Becker. 20 Christopher Dean. 21 Ovett. 22 Buster. 23 Gary (Garfield) Sobers. 24 United. 25 Sunderland. 26 Spanish. 27 Three. 28 Paul Gascoigne. 29 Jonathan Edwards. 30 David Beckham.

Quiz 9 | Pot Luck 4

Answers – page 19

1 Duplo is a younger version of which favourite toy?
2 What is the name of Mrs Addams in "The Addams Family"?
3 What is a large gathering of Boy Scouts called?
4 What colour car does the Pink Panther drive in his cartoon show?
5 Which politically incorrect adjective is applied to Thomas the Tank Engine's Controller?
6 What's the difference between the highest single dart treble and the lowest single dart treble?
7 What shape is a tambourine?
8 Who has had hits with "Down 4 U" and "Only U"?
9 What is a Barbie's usual hair colour?
10 Which country hosted the last soccer World Cup played in the 20th century?
11 In computing what does O mean in OS?
12 In which Greek city is the Acropolis situated?
13 Chile is on which coast of South America?
14 The edelweiss is a native flower to which mountains?
15 The kiwi fruit is also known as which gooseberry?
16 What did Jodhpur in India give its name to?
17 In which decade of the last century did the Channel Tunnel open to the public?
18 Lebanon is situated at the eastern end of which Sea?
19 A warning of which computer bug was given prior to the start of the year 2000?
20 Which US state is known as the Sunshine State?
21 What are the least number of points needed to win a single game in tennis?
22 Terracotta is made by baking what?
23 What is the abbreviation used for metre?
24 What type of "Sleep" was a classic Bacall and Bogart movie?
25 Which Frenchman gave his name to an item worn by ballet dancers?
26 In 2004, Piers Morgan resigned as editor of which British daily paper?
27 Charlie Chaplin found fame in America but where was he born?
28 Which word means clever and can also be a stinging pain?
29 Which 19th-century American President was murdered in a theatre?
30 Which Kelly got double gold in the 2004 Olympics in Greece?

Answers	Pot Luck 5 *(see Quiz 19)*

1 Argentina. 2 CJ. 3 Washington DC. 4 Children. 5 Long. 6 Watford. 7 Morocco. 8 Plane. 9 Two. 10 Tail. 11 Water. 12 Gown. 13 Peas. 14 Margaret. 15 Monsoon. 16 Raspberry. 17 West Ham. 18 Your family. 19 Polly. 20 Hungary. 21 Top. 22 Cricket. 23 Ritual suicide. 24 Chicago. 25 Wine. 26 India. 27 Radioactivity. 28 Bamber Gascoigne. 29 Cribbage. 30 Tiger.

1 Is Aberdeen to the north or south of Glasgow?
2 Prestwick and Gatwick are both what?
3 The Dales are mainly in which county?
4 On which Devon moor is there a famous prison?
5 Denbighshire is in the north of which country?
6 Who is London's Downing Street's most famous resident?
7 What is the capital of Scotland's Dumfries and Galloway region?
8 Which of Eastbourne, Esher and Eccles is on the coast?
9 In London, Richmond is on which river?
10 In which county is Rutland Water?
11 Where in the UK is Armagh?
12 Dorchester is the county town of which county?
13 Salford is part of which city?
14 Who has their HQ at Scotland Yard?
15 Sherwood Forest is associated with which historical hero?
16 Which food item is associated with London's Smithfield market?
17 Durham is in which part of England?
18 What is Eton's most famous institution?
19 Who has a home at Sandringham?
20 What is the highest mountain in Snowdonia National Park?
21 Which S in central London is an area associated with clubs and nightlife?
22 In which county is Stansted airport?
23 The resort of Aberystwyth is on which coast of Britain?
24 Dudley in the West Midlands is near which major city?
25 Ealing is an area of which city?
26 What is the Savoy in London as well as a theatre?
27 Prince William chose to go to St Andrews university in which part of the UK?
28 What is Salisbury's most famous building?
29 Who are trained at Sandhurst?
30 Who would you be watching if you went to the JJB Stadium?

1 The football team Boca Juniors play in which country?
2 Which initials did Pamela Anderson have in her "Baywatch" role?
3 In which city was Pete Sampras born?
4 UNICEF is an organisation caring for which people?
5 Which jump record was held by Bob Beamon for over 20 years?
6 Did Adrian Boothroyd first manage Watford, Wigan or WBA in the Premiership?
7 Where did athlete Said Aouita come from?
8 In what type of transport did Charles Lindbergh make history?
9 How many people were on the poster for the 1990s movie "Titanic"?
10 Where does a scorpion have its sting?
11 What is most of the Earth's surface covered by?
12 Which word is a type of frock and also an academic robe?
13 Which vegetable goes after The Black Eyed to name a top-selling hip-hop group?
14 What was Mrs Victor Meldrew's first name?
15 What's the weather word linked to an "Absolutely Fabulous" character's surname?
16 Glen Cova and Malling Jewel are types of which fruit?
17 Which football team did TV terror Alf Garnett support?
18 Who do you favour if you are a nepotist?
19 What was the name of the hotel chambermaid in "Fawlty Towers"?
20 Which country beginning with a H joined the European Union in 2004?
21 Q is on which row on a British/US keyboard?
22 In which sport can there be a night watchman?
23 In Japan, what is Hara-Kiri?
24 "ER" is set in which city?
25 Oz Clarke is a TV expert on what?
26 In the 1980s there was a catastrophic chemical accident at Bhopal in which country?
27 What is detected by a Geiger counter?
28 Who was the first presenter of TV quiz show "University Challenge"?
29 In which card game do you peg for cards making 15?
30 Which of scarlet, swine and tiger, is not a type of fever?

Answers	**Pot Luck 4** *(see Quiz 9)*

1 Lego. 2 Morticia. 3 Jamboree. 4 Pink. 5 Fat. 6 57. 7 Round. 8 Ashanti. 9 Blonde. 10 France. 11 Operating. 12 Athens. 13 West. 14 Alps. 15 Chinese. 16 Riding trousers (breeches/britches). 17 1990s. 18 Mediterranean 19 Millennium bug. 20 Florida. 21 Four. 22 Clay. 23 M (m). 24 Big. 25 Leotard. 26 Daily Mirror. 27 England. 28 Smart. 29 Abraham Lincoln. 30 Kelly Holmes.

1 Which country does Ronan Keating come from?
2 The 2006 album "Love" featured which iconic 1960s band?
3 What was the occupation of chart topper Bob?
4 Which number follows S Club in the band's title?
5 How many boys are there in Destiny's Child?
6 How are the Street Preachers described?
7 What is the surname of the two brothers in Oasis?
8 Which "Pie" did Madonna sing about?
9 What did Geri Halliwell say to do "If You Want to Run Faster"?
10 What was Billie's surname when she first topped the charts?
11 Which sporting event did Kylie Minogue close in 2000?
12 Which Craig had a hit with "Fill Me In"?
13 Which Mariah had a hit with Westlife in 2000?
14 Which Robbie was a "Rock DJ"?
15 What was Mel B called during her brief first marriage?
16 What type of music is LeAnn Rimes famous for?
17 "Stop the Clocks" was a compilation of songs from which band?
18 Which teenage Charlotte wowed audiences on both side of the Atlantic?
19 What type of "Coffee" was a chart topper for All Saints?
20 "Never Had a Dream Come True" was the theme song to which children's TV charity?
21 Craig Phillips charted after winning on which Big TV show?
22 Who charted with The Bangles' "Eternal Flame"?
23 Who was "2 Faced" in 2000?
24 Whose third UK No 1 was "Oops I Did It Again"?
25 How many members of Westlife are there?
26 Which band named after a US state were "In Demand" in 2000?
27 Which Jones was a "Sex Bomb" with the Stereophonics in 2000?
28 Which band were formed from the "Popstars" TV show?
29 What is the surname of all the Corrs?
30 How is controversial rapper Marshall Mathers better known?

| **Answers** | **UK Tour** *(see Quiz 10)* |

1 North. 2 Airports. 3 Yorkshire. 4 Dartmoor. 5 Wales. 6 The Prime Minister. 7 Dumfries. 8 Eastbourne. 9 Thames. 10 Rutland. 11 Northern Ireland. 12 Dorset. 13 Manchester. 14 Metropolitan Police. 15 Robin Hood. 16 Meat. 17 North east. 18 School/College. 19 The Queen. 20 Snowdon. 21 Soho. 22 Essex. 23 West. 24 Birmingham. 25 London. 26 Hotel. 27 Scotland. 28 Cathedral. 29 Soldiers. 30 Wigan Athletic.

1 In which sport can Canaries take on Owls?

2 How many colours are there on the German flag?

3 In a limerick which line does the third line rhyme with?

4 Which three initials was the 1960s' US President Johnson known by?

5 Which solo singer sang "Baby One More Time" in 1999?

6 What sort of creature is a shrike?

7 Edmund Hillary became the first man to climb which mountain?

8 Charles Holley became known as which entertainer Buddy?

9 Which word describes sailors as well as medicinal minerals?

10 What was Beijing called immediately before adopting the name Beijing?

11 In which US state is the resort of Orlando?

12 What was the occupation of the hero of the movie "Raging Bull"?

13 What covers most of the Antarctic?

14 Skater Kurt Browning comes from which country?

15 What term is given to a human being's complete set of genes?

16 TE Lawrence became known as Lawrence of where?

17 Carl Lewis found fame running and in which other athletics event?

18 What colour was Marilyn Monroe's hair in most of her movies?

19 Which country does Monaco border?

20 Which way do the stripes on the American flag run?

21 Which country was first to have ten kings all called Rameses?

22 A tsunami is another name for what?

23 Which Kate released the album "Aerial" in 2005, her first in 12 years?

24 Who were the beaten finalists of the 2006 FIFA World Cup?

25 Ellen MacArthur became known for her solo what?

26 What did a sundial used to tell?

27 Which of pink, purple or red is a primary colour?

28 The Wolf Cubs evolved as a junior branch of which organisation?

29 Yasser Arafat led which organisation known by its initials?

30 What was the horse made out of that was delivered to the ancient city of Troy?

Answers | TV Stars *(see Quiz 15)*

1 Yorath. 2 Aspel. 3 Ainsley Harriott. 4 Rolf Harris. 5 The Simpsons. 6 Alistair McGowan. 7 Gloria Hunniford. 8 Chris Tarrant. 9 Sue Barker. 10 Frost. 11 Penguin. 12 Titchmarsh. 13 G. 14 McDonald. 15 Doctor/surgeon. 16 Robin Hood. 17 Vaughan. 18 Davidson. 19 Cilla Black. 20 Rantzen. 21 Lorraine Kelly. 22 History. 23 Cook. 24 Graham Norton. 25 Parkinson. 26 Thaw. 27 David. 28 Smillie. 29 Jeremy. 30 Schofield.

Quiz 14 | Plants and Animals

LEVEL 1

1 What sort of creature is an aardvark?
2 What colour are a daisy's petals?
3 Which of the following dogs is the biggest: Pekinese, Labrador or St Bernard?
4 The dove is a member of which bird family?
5 What is the largest and most powerful land mammal?
6 What sort of feet do antelopes have?
7 A caribou is a type of what?
8 What is a rhododendron?
9 What is a Scots pine?
10 The lynx belongs to which family?
11 What do herbivores eat?
12 Where is a horse's muzzle?
13 How many nostrils does a dog have?
14 In the animal world what is an adder?
15 What colour are rhubarb stalks?
16 In the very early part of which season do snowdrops appear?
17 Which big cat has a mane?
18 What is an antirrhinum?
19 Mushrooms and puffballs are what types of living things?
20 Which of cacti, root vegetables or water lilies can survive in the desert?
21 In plants, pollination is the transfer of what?
22 Where do wetland plants grow?
23 What do carnivorous plants eat?
24 What colour are natural sponges?
25 How many tentacles does a starfish have?
26 Which animal can be field or harvest?
27 Where would an insect have its antenna?
28 In animals what is another name for the backbone?
29 Which is the heaviest of chimpanzee, gorilla or man?
30 Where are a deer's antlers?

Answers	**Pot Luck 7** *(see Quiz 16)*

1 Depp. 2 Australia. 3 USA. 4 Spirits. 5 Suffolk. 6 Wales. 7 Square. 8 Canada. 9 Two. 10 Ear. 11 American Football. 12 Bulls. 13 India. 14 St Francis. 15 14. 16 Thinking Day. 17 Telescope. 18 Scarface. 19 Globe. 20 Abbey. 21 Lines of longitude. 22 Water. 23 Vacuum cleaner. 24 1950s. 25 His manager. 26 Photocopier. 27 Cake. 28 Tenor. 29 Latin. 30 Songs.

1 How was sports commentator Gabby Logan known before her marriage?
2 Which Michael replaced Hugh Scully on the "Antiques Roadshow"?
3 Which chef replaced Fern Britton on "Ready Steady Cook"?
4 Which Australian presents "Animal Hospital"?
5 In which series are Marge and Homer the stars?
6 Who starred in his own show impersonating stars and made a "Big Impression"?
7 Which Irish presenter hosts "Open House" daily on Channel 5?
8 Who hosts the UK version of "Who Wants to be A Millionaire"?
9 Who was the first female presenter of "A Question of Sport"?
10 David Jason starred in the detective series "A Touch of what"?
11 Which animal is the star of "Pingu"?
12 Which Alan succeeded Geoff Hamilton on "Gardener's World"?
13 Which Ali is the alter ego of Sacha Baron Cohen?
14 Which singer Jane found fame on "The Cruise"?
15 What was George Clooney's profession in ER?
16 Jonas Armstrong played which hero Robin?
17 Which Johnny moved from "The Big Breakfast" to the BBC in 2001?
18 Which Jim presented "The Generation Game"?
19 Which Liverpool singer presented "Moment of Truth"?
20 Who is the Esther of "That's Esther"?
21 Which Scottish presenter is the star of GMTV's "LK Today"?
22 Does David Starkey present shows on health, history or house plants?
23 What would you expect Antony Worrall Thompson to do on TV?
24 Who was the star of "So Graham Norton"?
25 Which Michael began his chat shows back in 1971?
26 Which John has played Morse and Kavanagh?
27 Which Attenborough presented "The Blue Planet" about life beneath the sea?
28 Which Carol presented "Changing Rooms"?
29 What is the first name of "Newsnight" interrogators Vine and Paxman?
30 Which Phillip, star of "Dr Doolittle", presented "National Lottery Winning Lines"?

1 Which actor Johnny was in "Sleepy Hollow", "Edward Scissorhands" and "Fear and Loathing in Las Vegas"?
2 Which of Australia, the UK and the USA does not have a large city called Birmingham?
3 The Sears Tower became the tallest skyscraper in which country?
4 Which word means ghosts and also means strong drinks?
5 In which county is Ipswich, the scene of grisly murders at the end of 2006?
6 The Stereophonics come from which part of the UK?
7 Which shape name is given to the area in which Nelson's Column stands?
8 The Great Lakes border the USA along with which other country?
9 How many people usually play a game of chess?
10 Which part of the body can go before the words ache and muff?
11 Jerry Rice and Emmitt Smith are both connected with which sport?
12 In rugby league are Bradford the Bears, the Braves or the Bulls?
13 Mahatma Gandhi was a leader in which country?
14 Which Saint founded the Franciscan order of monks?
15 How many letters are there in the English alphabet between E and T?
16 What kind of Day do Scouts and Guides call the anniversary of their founder's birth?
17 Which instrument did Galileo invent as an aid to study the stars?
18 What was Al Capone's nickname, after he was injured in a knife fight?
19 What name is given to a world map presented in spherical form?
20 Queen Elizabeth II was crowned in what type of building?
21 Which type of lines on a map run north to south?
22 What does a coracle travel on?
23 William Hoover first marketed which household appliance?
24 In which decade did the Mini car first appear on British roads?
25 In the 1990s Macaulay Culkin sacked his dad from which job?
26 Invented as the xerox machine what is this device usually known as today?
27 French Queen Marie Antoinette famously said, "Let them eat" what?
28 Is operatic singer Andrea Bocelli a tenor or a base?
29 Which language was spoken by the ancient Romans?
30 Irving Berlin was famous for writing what?

Answers	**Plants and Animals** *(see Quiz 14)*

1 Mammal. 2 White. 3 St Bernard. 4 Pigeon. 5 Elephant. 6 Hooves. 7 Reindeer. 8 Plant. 9 Tree. 10 Cat. 11 Plants. 12 Head. 13 Two. 14 Snake. 15 Pink. 16 Spring. 17 Lion. 18 Plant. 19 Fungus. 20 Cacti. 21 Pollen. 22 In water. 23 Insects. 24 Yellow. 25 Five. 26 Mouse. 27 Head. 28 Spine. 29 Gorilla. 30 Head.

1 Which sport did Joe Davis play in addition to billiards?

2 Jack Dempsey was a heavyweight what?

3 Which Ramsey took England to be World Cup champions?

4 Which Steve was knighted after the 2000 Olympics?

5 By which name was IVA Richards known?

6 Which country does tennis's Pete Sampras come from?

7 In which decade of the 20th century did Ayrton Senna meet his untimely death?

8 Which club has a commemorative gate in memory of Bill Shankly?

9 In which position did soccer legend Lev Yashin play?

10 Mark Spitz won his seven gold medals in 1972 doing what?

11 Which motor racing star became Sir Jackie in the new millennium?

12 Brian Lara played international cricket for which country?

13 Athlete Frederick Carleton Lewis was better known by which first name?

14 Aussie cricketer Dennis Lillee was a specialist what?

15 Gary Lineker has which Churchillian middle name?

16 In addition to his sporting skill John McEnroe was also famous for what?

17 Diego Maradona led which side to World Cup victory in 1986?

18 Sir Stanley Matthews played for which famous seaside resort town?

19 Which Bobby captained England's World Cup soccer winning side?

20 Which Mr Moss was a successful motor racing legend of the 1950s?

21 Which boxer modestly announced "I am the greatest!", and went on to prove it?

22 Which 1990s football international is nicknamed Gazza?

23 Which US tennis star with 13 Grand Slams to his credit lost to Leighton Hewitt in the 2001 US Open?

24 Which Coe became an adviser to the then Tory Party leader William Hague?

25 In which gambling city did Evander Holyfield become world boxing champion in 1997?

26 In which decade was Arnold Palmer most successful in competition?

27 For which country did Jonah Lomu win his rugby caps?

28 Which British boxer did Mike Tyson beat to become champion in 1996?

29 Whom did Denis Law play international football for?

30 Which childlike first name did baseball's George Herman Ruth have?

Answers	**Movies – Heroes and Heroines** *(see Quiz 19)*

1 Hugh. 2 John. 3 Madness. 4 Grace. 5 Horror. 6 Hamlet. 7 Steel. 8 Forrest. 9 Dr Evil. 10 Cruise. 11 Sundance. 12 Pierce Brosnan. 13 Catwoman. 14 Robin Hood. 15 Doctor. 16 India. 17 Starling. 18 The Mafia. 19 Soldier. 20 Pan. 21 Mel Gibson. 22 Kennedy. 23 Astronauts. 24 Harry. 25 Romeo. 26 Schindler. 27 Irons. 28 Toy Story. 29 Mason "The Line" Dixon. 30 Wayne.

Quiz 18 | Pot Luck 8

Answers – page 28

1 In which quiz show are individual contestants dismissed with Ms Robinson saying "Goodbye"?

2 Where would a spade, a club and a diamond be kept together?

3 King Hussein was ruler of which Middle East country?

4 In which country was John Lennon shot?

5 Which legendary king held court at Camelot?

6 How many letters are not vowels in the word queen?

7 Which trio split in 2005 after having a No 1 with "Thunderbirds"?

8 Standing down as an MP in 2005, Michael Portillo was in which party?

9 Oxford bags were a type of which item of clothing?

10 What can be a musical sound or a short letter?

11 In place-names what can precede England, Hampshire and York?

12 What name is given to the part of a parachute jump before the parachute opens?

13 Shrove Tuesday – or Pancake Day – is celebrated in which month?

14 Caviar is a great food delicacy but what is it?

15 Northern Territory is a "state" in which country in the southern hemisphere?

16 A rhombus is a shape with how many sides?

17 Which word meaning talk is the name of a bird?

18 How many letters are there in the English alphabet before Y?

19 In Monopoly what do you pass, collecting £200, when you complete one circuit of the board and start another?

20 What is the name of the special mark on precious metals to denote their purity?

21 A kilogram is just over how many pounds in imperial weight?

22 Are Leeds Metropolitan and Manchester Metropolitan stations or universities?

23 How many minutes are there in half a day?

24 Dermatitis is the inflammation of what part of the body?

25 In communications, what does P stand for in the initials ISP?

26 Gibraltar is separated from which European country by the Neutral Zone?

27 What sort of transport is a clipper?

28 Which of dog, fish and rat is not a Chinese year?

29 Which Martin became manager of Spurs in November 2004?

30 Is an area around a city designated not to be built on known as a green belt, a life belt or an urban belt?

Answers	Music Charts *(see Quiz 20)*

1 The Builder. 2 Simpsons. 3 Bohemian. 4 Blue. 5 Mariah Carey. 6 Green. 7 50s. 8 In a Bottle. 9 Rush. 10 Boyzone. 11 Rap. 12 Stop. 13 Eminem. 14 Billie. 15 Ronan Keating. 16 911. 17 The Dance Floor. 18 Prodigy. 19 Mel B. 20 1990s. 21 Kylie Minogue. 22 Millennium Prayer. 23 And the Beast. 24 R. 25 Marmalade. 26 Diana Ross. 27 Billie. 28 Spice Girls. 29 1997. 30 Victoria Beckham.

1 Which Grant played the cad in "Bridget Jones's Diary"?
2 What was Jim Belushi's ill-fated elder brother called?
3 What did King George suffer from in the Nigel Hawthorne and Helen Mirren movie?
4 Which Jones starred in "A View to a Kill" in 1985?
5 What type of movies made Boris Karloff famous?
6 Which Prince of Denmark is the hero of Shakespeare's most filmed play?
7 In which industry had the heroes of "The Full Monty", based in Sheffield, worked?
8 Which "Gump" was the hero of a 1994 movie?
9 Which evil doctor was the enemy of Austin Powers?
10 Which Tom starred in "A Few Good Men"?
11 Which Kid was Butch Cassidy's sidekick?
12 Which James Bond actor got married in the summer of 2001?
13 What sort of woman did Michelle Pfeiffer play in "Batman Returns"?
14 Which heroic outlaw was "Prince of Thieves" on the big screen?
15 What was the title of Doolittle who could talk to the animals?
16 "Gandhi" was about a hero of which country?
17 What was the bird-related last name of the agent played by Jodie Foster in "The Silence of the Lambs"?
18 "The Godfather" was the head of which organisation?
19 What was the occupation of Private Ryan in Spielberg's movie?
20 Which Peter was the hero of "Hook" based on the children's story by JM Barrie?
21 Which actor starred in the "Lethal Weapon" movies and "Braveheart"?
22 What was the surname of the subject of "JFK"?
23 "Apollo 13" was about a group of what type of people?
24 Who was the hero who "Met Sally" in the movie with Billy Crystal and Meg Ryan?
25 Leonardo DiCaprio starred in a 1996 movie about which character "and Juliet"?
26 Which hero had a List in a Spielberg movie?
27 Which Jeremy starred in "Reversal of Fortune"?
28 In which "Story" was Woody a hero?
29 Who did 54-year-old Rocky Balboa come out of retirement to fight?
30 Which John landed a best actor Oscar for "True Grit"?

Answers	**Sporting Legends** *(see Quiz 17)*

1 Snooker. 2 Boxer. 3 (Sir) Alf. 4 Redgrave. 5 Viv. 6 USA. 7 1990s. 8 Liverpool FC. 9 Goalkeeper. 10 Swimming. 11 Stewart. 12 West Indies. 13 Carl. 14 Fast bowler. 15 Winston. 16 His temper. 17 Argentina. 18 Blackpool. 19 Moore. 20 Stirling. 21 Cassius Clay/Muhammad Ali. 22 Paul Gascoigne. 23 Pete Sampras. 24 Sebastian. 25 Las Vegas. 26 1960s. 27 New Zealand. 28 Frank Bruno. 29 Scotland. 30 Babe.

1 Which Bob went to No 1 with "Can We Fix It?"?

2 Which family had a hit with "Do the Bartman"?

3 Which "Rhapsody" was a chart topper for Queen?

4 What colour was the name of the boy band who had a No 1 with Elton John?

5 Which female singer went straight to No 1 in the US with "Fantasy"?

6 Which actor Robson had a string of hits in 1995 with Jerome Flynn?

7 In which age group was Cher when she hit No 1 with "Believe"?

8 Where was the "Genie" in the 1999 hit of Christine Aguilera?

9 Which Jennifer sang "The Power of Love" in 1985?

10 Which band's singles include "No Matter What" and "Words"?

11 What type of single was Puff Daddy's "I'll be Missing You"?

12 Which Spice Girls hit put a stop to a run of No 1s?

13 Which controversial rapper's No 1s include "The Real Slim Shady" and "Stan"?

14 Which British teenager's second No 1 was "Girlfriend"?

15 Which Irish group member had a solo No 1 with "Life is a Rollercoaster"?

16 Which US emergency phone number hit No 1 with "A Little Bit More"?

17 The Arctic Monkeys' first No 1 was "I Bet You Look Good on" what?

18 Which band's singles include "Firestarter" and "Breathe"?

19 Which Spice Girl did Missy Misdemeanour Elliott record "I Want You Back" with?

20 In which decade did Wet Wet Wet have their huge No 1 hit "Love is All Around"?

21 Which Australian singer/actress is the most successful ex-soap star in the British pop charts?

22 Which "Prayer" was a millennium chart topper for Cliff Richard?

23 What went with "Beauty" in the title of Celine Dion's first UK chart success?

24 Which Kelly charted with "I Believe I Can Fly"?

25 Which "Lady" was a 1998 chart hit for All Saints?

26 Which ex-member of the Supremes has charted with Marvin Gaye and Lionel Richie?

27 Which future Mrs Evans charted with "Because We Want To"?

28 Whose follow-up to their first No 1 was "Say You'll be There"?

29 In which year did Elton John have the best-ever-selling single?

30 Who was "Not Such an Innocent Girl" in 2001?

Answers | Pot Luck 8 *(see Quiz 18)*

1 The Weakest Link. 2 In a pack of cards. 3 Jordan. 4 USA. 5 Arthur. 6 Two. 7 Busted. 8 Conservative. 9 Trousers. 10 Note. 11 New. 12 Freefall. 13 February. 14 Roe (fish eggs). 15 Australia. 16 Four. 17 Chat. 18 24. 19 Go. 20 Hallmark. 21 Two. 22 Universities. 23 720 minutes. 24 Skin. 25 Provider. 26 Spain. 27 Ship. 28 Fish. 29 Martin Jol. 30 Green belt.

1 Which shredded vegetable goes into sauerkraut?
2 What does the P stand for in the education initials PTA?
3 In 1997 Hong Kong was returned to the rule of which country?
4 Which number puzzle featured in a series of best-selling books in 2005?
5 Which US grunge band shares a name with the Buddhist state of bliss?
6 In film which Doctor could talk to the animals?
7 Which of these celebs has not guested on "Friends" – Duchess of York, George Clooney or Prince Charles?
8 Out of his six wives, how many did Henry VIII have beheaded?
9 Which tennis player's name was given to a 2001 computer virus?
10 Which Scotsman gave his name to a type of raincoat?
11 Which Mel voiced Rooster in "Chicken Run"?
12 Which word is a type of trousers and also means to breathe rapidly?
13 Who or what is a great bustard?
14 Who was the blonde in the movie "Some Like It Hot"?
15 The late politician Dr Marjorie Mowlam was known by which short first name?
16 What is the shape of a pie chart?
17 Which was the second country to send a man into space?
18 What colour is platinum?
19 The caribou is another name for what?
20 If a number is squared what is it multiplied by?
21 The collapse of a star leads to the formation of what type of a hole?
22 Which bone is the longest bone in the human body?
23 What does U stand for in VDU?
24 Southampton left The Dell to go to which stadium?
25 Hr is the abbreviation for what?
26 What type of creature is a mandrill?
27 If you possessed a Canaletto would you own a painting, a small barge or a tin of stuffed olives?
28 What is a fox's tail known as?
29 What did the Russians call their first spacemen?
30 In which decade did Steve Redgrave win his first Olympic gold?

Answers | Pot Luck 10 (see Quiz 23)

1 Bank. 2 Golf. 3 Emma Bunton. 4 Five. 5 Careers. 6 Linford Christie. 7 1980s. 8 Dylan. 9 Yasser Arafat. 10 Two. 11 Kingfisher. 12 Bird. 13 In water. 14 Stripes. 15 Bulb. 16 Private Frazer. 17 Y. 18 Fish and chips. 19 Books. 20 Salmon. 21 Fawlty Towers. 22 West Ham United. 23 Gold. 24 West. 25 Yuppies. 26 France. 27 Tyres. 28 None. 29 Teaching. 30 March.

Quiz 22 | Famous Names

Famous Names

Quiz 22 — Famous Names

Answers – page 32

1 What is Lucy Henman's tennis-playing husband called?
2 What is the Prince of Wales's first name?
3 Which Chris did Billie Piper marry?
4 Who was the first British PM of the new millennium?
5 What is Chelsea Clinton's dad called?
6 What would you ask Anna Ryder Richardson to design?
7 Which Ms Boothroyd was the first lady Speaker of the House of Commons?
8 What is Christine Hamilton's ex-MP husband called?
9 Which Gordon was Tony Blair's first Chancellor of the Exchequer?
10 Which of Paul McCartney's daughters is a dress designer?
11 Which 1960s model took over a morning TV show in September 2001?
12 Which Max acts as publicist to the famous?
13 What is the first name of ex-athlete and William Hague adviser Lord Coe?
14 From which part of the UK does Eamonn Holmes come?
15 Novelist Baroness James is known with which initials?
16 In 2006 Lord Stevens produced a report on the death of which Princess?
17 Under which female name is Paul O'Grady widely known?
18 What is the surname of TV brother celebs David and Jonathan?
19 What is the name of Dame Norma Major's husband?
20 Which Roger was the long-time singer with The Who?
21 Which former runner led Britain's Olympic bid for 2012?
22 Which Miss MacArthur sailed around the world on her own?
23 Vidal Sassoon is famous in which beauty industry?
24 Which country is Ruby Wax from?
25 Who is Tessa Dahl's famous model daughter?
26 Who was Julian Lennon's famous dad?
27 What are the initials of Harry Potter creator Rowling?
28 What is the first name of MEP Glenys Kinnock's husband?
29 Martin Bell is famous for wearing what colour suit?
30 What is Leo Blair's mum called?

Answers | **20th Century News** *(see Quiz 24)*

1 William Hague. 2 Cuba. 3 Wales. 4 France. 5 USSR/Soviet Union. 6 Clothes. 7 Austria. 8 Edward VIII. 9 Somme. 10 Soviet Union. 11 Three. 12 Russian. 13 Scotland. 14 France. 15 WWII. 16 Women. 17 China. 18 Major. 19 1990s. 20 Nellie. 21 Glenn. 22 Iran. 23 Italy. 24 East. 25 Wembley. 26 Mineworkers. 27 Neil. 28 Three. 29 Drink driving. 30 Brighton.

Quiz 23 | Pot Luck 10

Answers – page 29 — LEVEL 1

1 Robert Barclay founded what type of business?
2 For which sport is Jim Furyk famous?
3 Which Emma went from the Spice Girls to "Strictly Come Dancing"?
4 How many people were there in the original line-up of Hear'Say?
5 Which word means vocations and also means moves wildly?
6 Which Briton is the oldest 100m Olympic winner of the 20th century?
7 In which decade of the 20th century was Britney Spears born?
8 What did Michael Douglas and Catherine Zeta Jones call their baby son?
9 Which leader of the Palestine independence movement was buried in November 2004?
10 How many kidneys do humans normally have?
11 What was the name of the boat in which Ellen MacArthur sailed around the world?
12 The now extinct dodo was what type of creature?
13 Where does a hippopotamus spend most of its life?
14 What type of pattern is on a raccoon's tail?
15 What does a hyacinth grow from?
16 In "Dad's Army" which character often declared, "We're doomed"?
17 When texting, the word WHY is usually shown by which letter?
18 What type of food is associated with Harry Ramsden's?
19 What do you fear if you have bibliophobia?
20 A smolt or smelt is a young of which creature?
21 Manuel the waiter appeared in which classic comedy series?
22 Which soccer club has a stand dedicated to the late Bobby Moore?
23 What were the 19th-century Forty Niners searching for?
24 Which is not the name of a sea – Black Sea, North Sea or West Sea?
25 In the 1980s, young upwardly mobile persons became known as what?
26 In which country would you watch Nantes play a home soccer match?
27 What was manufactured by the business set up by Harvey Firestone?
28 How many English kings known as Henry came after Henry VIII?
29 What was Ken Barlow's main career throughout his many years as a "Coronation Street" character?
30 Which month was named after Mars, the god of war?

Answers | Pot Luck 9 *(see Quiz 21)*

1 Cabbage. 2 Parent. 3 China. 4 Su Doku. 5 Nirvana. 6 Dr Doolittle. 7 Prince Charles. 8 Two. 9 Anna Kournikova. 10 Mackintosh. 11 Gibson. 12 Pants. 13 A bird. 14 Marilyn Monroe. 15 Mo. 16 A circle. 17 USA. 18 Greyish white. 19 Reindeer. 20 Itself. 21 Black hole. 22 Thigh (femur). 23 Unit. 24 St Mary's. 25 Hour. 26 Monkey. 27 Painting. 28 Brush. 29 Cosmonauts. 30 1980s.

31

1 Who was Conservative party leader on 31 December 1999?
2 Fidel Castro took power on which island?
3 The tragedy of Aberfan took place in which part of the UK?
4 Charles de Gaulle was President of which European country?
5 Where did the Red Army come from?
6 Yves St Laurent found fame designing what?
7 Oskar Schindler, whose story was told in a Spielberg movie, was from which country?
8 Which former English king did Wallis Simpson marry?
9 Which S is an area of France where there was massive loss of life in WWI?
10 How was the USSR also known?
11 How many children did Tony Blair have when he became Prime Minister?
12 Lenin was a key figure in which revolution?
13 In which country did a Pan Am jumbo jet explode over Lockerbie in 1988?
14 François Mitterrand was a Socialist head of state in which country?
15 The Battle of El Alamein was during which war?
16 The suffragettes campaigned for votes for whom?
17 Mao Tse Tung led the Long March in which country?
18 Which John succeeded Margaret Thatcher as Prime Minister?
19 In which decade of the 20th century did Nelson Mandela become South African president?
20 What was the first name of famous opera star Melba?
21 Which bandleader Miller disappeared over the English Channel during WWII?
22 In 1979 the Shah was deposed in which country?
23 Mussolini led which country in WWII?
24 After WWII, Germany was divided into West Germany and Communist what?
25 Where was the FA Cup Final held during the 1990s?
26 Particularly in the news in the 1980s, the NUM was the National Union of what?
27 Martin Bell beat which Hamilton to take the constituency of Tatton in the 1997 General Election?
28 How many UK Prime Ministers were there in the 1990s?
29 Arsenal soccer player Tony Adams was jailed for what offence?
30 In which seaside location did an IRA bomb explode at a Tory Party Conference in 1984?

Answers | Famous Names *(see Quiz 22)*

1 Tim. 2 Charles. 3 Evans. 4 Blair. 5 Bill. 6 Your house. 7 Betty. 8 Neil. 9 Brown. 10 Stella. 11 Twiggy. 12 Clifford. 13 Sebastian. 14 Northern Ireland. 15 PD. 16 Princess Diana. 17 Lily Savage. 18 Dimbleby. 19 John. 20 Roger Daltrey. 21 Sebastian Coe. 22 Ellen. 23 Hairdressing. 24 USA. 25 Sophie. 26 John. 27 JK. 28 Neil. 29 White. 30 Cherie.

1 Does the B in ASBO stand for bad, behaviour, bully?
2 According to the Manic Street Preachers who were "The Masses Against"?
3 Who carries out their profession routinely wearing a tutu?
4 The UAE stands for which United Emirates?
5 Which word describes both a paragraph and a corridor?
6 What sort of Hat was the title of an elegant Fred Astaire movie?
7 A praying mantis is a type of what?
8 What is the name for a German from Hamburg?
9 The perambulator was an early type of what?
10 In which town is Harvey's Bitter brewed?
11 Which English queen's head was on the first postage stamp?
12 It's no official secret – which Stella became head of MI5?
13 Which character did Joanna Lumley play in "The New Avengers"?
14 In the ancient world what type of Gardens were created at Babylon?
15 Which item can be carriage, grandmother, alarm or digital?
16 In which US state is Miami?
17 Who, in Holland, is known as Zinter Klaus?
18 Ferrari cars were originally manufactured in which country?
19 Which word for a dissolving substance also means financially in the black?
20 Which girl goes with Educating in the title of a play by Willy Russell?
21 In which year was the 60th anniversary of VE Day?
22 Anna Edson Taylor became the first person to travel Niagara Falls in what?
23 What is the traditional colour of the headwear known as a fez?
24 Which fabric is made by worms?
25 What title does the vampire have in the story "Dracula"?
26 How many angles do 12 separate triangles contain in total?
27 On a compass, which direction is directly opposite to Northeast?
28 What does the middle letter stand for as used in HRH?
29 What sort of busters featured in a Sigourney Weaver movie – Blockbusters, Dambusters or Ghostbusters?
30 What did PM Tony Blair call his son, born in 2000?

Answers | **Pot Luck 12** *(see Quiz 27)*

1 Watergate. 2 Wide. 3 11. 4 Japan. 5 Music. 6 Aeronautics. 7 Henry. 8 Golf. 9 Marathon. 10 Temperature. 11 Atlantic. 12 Rink. 13 Three. 14 Bridge. 15 Little John. 16 Scrooge. 17 Nine. 18 Diameter. 19 Cameron Diaz. 20 January. 21 New Orleans. 22 Three. 23 Green. 24 Newcastle. 25 Earl of Sandwich. 26 Wear it on the head. 27 USA. 28 Ash Wednesday. 29 First. 30 Green fingers.

Quiz 26 TV Comedy

1 In which country was "Father Ted" set?

2 How many Friends are there in the series of the same name?

3 Which Steve's alter ego is Alan Partridge?

4 Which two Js featured in the title of Jennifer Saunders' 2006 WI comedy?

5 Which Caroline created Mrs Merton?

6 Who played Sir Humphrey in "Yes Minister"?

7 Which Hancock hosted "They Think It's All Over"?

8 How many teams competed in "Have I Got News for You"?

9 Which animal follows "Drop the Dead" in the show about a newsroom?

10 What is the name of Harry Enfield's revolting teenager?

11 Mrs Bucket had which floral first name?

12 Where is the series "Chambers" set?

13 Which McBeal was a series with Calista Flockhart?

14 What's the main colour in the wardrobe of "Little Britain" character Vicky Pollard?

15 How many main characters were there in "Men Behaving Badly"?

16 What happened to Victor in the final episode of "One Foot in the Grave"?

17 Which US sitcom's cast included Michael Richards and Jerry Seinfeld?

18 Where did the late comedian Dave Allen come from?

19 In which city was "The Liver Birds" set?

20 Which "Two" stars with the same first name began a long-running comedy series in the 1970s?

21 Which June has starred in comedies from "Terry & June" to "Ab Fab"?

22 In "Are You Being Served"? which department along with ladies' fashions was shown?

23 In which series did the late Compo appear?

24 Which Frank was the star character in "Some Mothers Do 'Ave 'Em"?

25 Dawn French was the "Vicar" of where?

26 Which Irish presenter introduces programme of "Auntie's Bloomers", featuring funny and embarrassing outtakes?

27 What was the name of Mrs Wayne Slob played by Kathy Burke?

28 "Two Point" how many children were in the popular sitcom?

29 Which "Ladies" were the subject of a series with Victoria Wood?

30 What colour is Lily Savage's hair?

Answers	Soccer *(see Quiz 28)*

1 Football. 2 Blackburn. 3 Gary Lineker. 4 Northern Ireland. 5 Italy. 6 Southampton. 7 Burley. 8 Gerard Houllier. 9 Mohammed Al Fayed. 10 Petr Cech. 11 Watford. 12 Royle. 13 Sky. 14 1930s. 15 France. 16 Manchester Utd. 17 Shilton. 18 Munich. 19 European Champions Cup. 20 Rapid. 21 1994. 22 Liverpool. 23 Ginola. 24 Air. 25 Middlesbrough. 26 Milan. 27 World Cup. 28 Arsenal. 29 David Beckham. 30 Arsenal.

1 Which building was burgled by aides of President Nixon in 1972?

2 In Internet abbreviations, what does the middle w in www stand for?

3 What is the next prime number after 7?

4 Honda cars were originally manufactured in which country?

5 Napster was developed for downloading what?

6 What does the first A stand for in NASA?

7 Which is the first name to have been used by eight kings of England?

8 Businessman Samuel Ryder initiated a cup that is still contested in which sport?

9 Which name for a long race comes from a battle in the years BC?

10 What do Fahrenheit and Celsius measure?

11 The "Titanic" sank while travelling across which ocean?

12 What is the name for an ice hockey pitch?

13 How many colours appear on the Australian flag?

14 Cantilever, railway, suspension and toll can all go before which word?

15 Who was the tallest person in Robin Hood's gang of merry men?

16 What was the last name of the miser in "A Christmas Carol" by Charles Dickens?

17 In the English alphabet, how many letters are there before J?

18 What is the line across the middle of a circle called?

19 Who played opposite Leonardo DiCaprio in "The Gangs of New York"?

20 The Roman God Janus gives his name to which calendar month?

21 In the traditional song, is the "House of the Rising Sun" in Newcastle, New Orleans or New York?

22 How many angles does an equilateral triangle contain?

23 Which colour links Kermit and Shrek?

24 Shay Given and Scott Parker were together at which Premiership club?

25 Was it the Earl of Burger, the Earl of Pancake or the Earl of Sandwich who gave his name to a popular type of food?

26 What would you do with a deerstalker?

27 Which of these three countries has got the biggest population – USA, Sweden or Greece?

28 What is the special day that follows Shrove Tuesday?

29 In which course is gazpacho usually served?

30 If you are good at growing plants you are said to have what?

Answers | Pot Luck 11 *(see Quiz 25)*

1 Behaviour. 2 The Classes. 3 Ballet dancer. 4 Arab. 5 Passage. 6 Top. 7 Insect. 8 Hamburger. 9 Baby buggy. 10 Lewes. 11 Victoria. 12 Rimington. 13 Purdey. 14 Hanging. 15 Clock. 16 Florida. 17 Santa Claus. 18 Italy. 19 Solvent. 20 Rita. 21 2005. 22 A barrel. 23 Red. 24 Silk. 25 Count. 26 36. 27 Southwest. 28 Royal. 29 Ghostbusters. 30 Leo.

1 What does the second F stand for in FIFA?

2 Which Lancashire club received a record-breaking £15 million when Alan Shearer went to Newcastle?

3 Who is second only to Bobby Charlton as England's greatest goalscorer?

4 Pat Jennings won 119 full international caps for which British side?

5 Which team won the 2006 World Cup?

6 Which club did Glenn Hoddle leave when he rejoined Spurs in 2001?

7 Which manager George led Ipswich Town back to the Premiership in the year 2000?

8 Who was the first Frenchman to manage Liverpool?

9 Which entrepreneur was chairman of Fulham when they went into the Premiership?

10 In 2006, which goalkeeper fractured his skull playing at Reading?

11 Which side did Vialli take on after leaving Chelsea?

12 Which Joe left Manchester City immediately before Keegan took over?

13 Coventry City are nicknamed which shade of blue?

14 In which decade did the World Cup begin?

15 Who did Platini play international football for?

16 Which British football club is the richest in the world?

17 Which Peter is England's most capped goalkeeper?

18 Which major German side has Bayern before its name?

19 How was the UEFA Champions League formerly known?

20 Which quick sounding word precedes Vienna's name?

21 When was the previous World Cup before 1998?

22 Michael Owen was attached to which club when he scored for England in the World Cup in France 1998?

23 Which David then of Spurs was Footballer of the Year in 1999?

24 Dennis Bergkamp refuses to use which form of travel?

25 Which side plays at the Riverside Stadium?

26 AC and Inter are from which Italian city famous for its fashion?

27 The Jules Rimet trophy was the prize for which tournament?

28 Robert Pires left which London club in 2006?

29 Who captained England in their 2001 5–1 win over Germany?

30 Alphabetically which team is first in the Premiership?

Answers	TV Comedy *(see Quiz 26)*

1 Ireland. 2 Six. 3 Coogan. 4 Jam & Jerusalem. 5 Aherne. 6 Nigel Hawthorne. 7 Nick. 8 Two. 9 Donkey. 10 Kevin. 11 Hyacinth. 12 Legal practice. 13 Ally. 14 Pink. 15 Four. 16 Died. 17 Seinfeld. 18 Ireland. 19 Liverpool. 20 Ronnies. 21 Whitfield. 22 Menswear. 23 Last of the Summer Wine. 24 Spencer. 25 Dibley. 26 Terry Wogan. 27 Waynetta. 28 4. 29 Dinner Ladies. 30 Blonde.

Quiz 29 | Pot Luck 13

LEVEL 1

1 Which of these inventions was developed last – lightbulb, motor car or television?
2 How many sides do 13 rectangles have?
3 What sort of beans are used in the manufacture of chocolate?
4 Which band made the albums "Garbage" and "Beautiful Garbage"?
5 Was the great plague of the 14th century known as The Black Death, The Cold Death or The Creeping Death?
6 What is John McEnroe's middle name?
7 What is the favourite food of Popeye?
8 What was spaceman Yuri Gagarin's home town renamed after his death?
9 The "News of the World" is the top-selling paper on which day of the week?
10 With which item of clothing is the name Levi Strauss linked?
11 Who set up a communications system that used dots and dashes?
12 The first atom bomb was dropped on the city Hiroshima, in which country?
13 Mark Spitz won seven gold medals at one Olympic Games doing what?
14 Which Labour MP and former Foreign Secretary Robin died in 2005?
15 Which of Cantonese, German and Spanish is a major language that is spoken in South America?
16 What was the wife of a tsar called?
17 Where does a nun usually live?
18 What is the name of Fred Flintstone's pet?
19 If a number is not an odd number what is it?
20 Which comedian Jack's surname sounds like a letter of the alphabet?
21 How many women in total travelled to the Moon throughout the 20th century?
22 What is the name of the stick used in croquet to strike the ball?
23 Does goalkeeper Tim Howard play for Australia, Austria or the USA?
24 Richard I of England was known as which Heart – Braveheart, Brokenheart or Lionheart?
25 Puri is a bread that originally came from which country?
26 What name is given to a bank of sand near the coastline?
27 A squirrel can be grey and which other colour?
28 What actually gets trapped in a Venus Fly Trap?
29 "Saving All My Love for You" was the first No 1 for which female singer?
30 What is a baked Alaska's outer layer made from?

Answers	**Pot Luck 14** *(see Quiz 31)*

1 California. 2 Maggie. 3 Ghost. 4 Brazil. 5 Biography. 6 Andy Murray. 7 Baker. 8 Gomez. 9 Musical instrument. 10 White. 11 Hawk. 12 Will Young. 13 Boat. 14 White. 15 29th February. 16 Play. 17 Bolivia. 18 Walkman. 19 February/March. 20 Coral. 21 Rope. 22 Eight. 23 Belgium. 24 Alice. 25 Wood. 26 Johnny. 27 London. 28 Moscow. 29 King Kong. 30 Medical treatment.

1 Which Dustin links "Finding Neverland" and "Meet the Fockers"?

2 Which Ford played Han Solo in the original "Star Wars" movie?

3 What is the surname of Susan, star of "Dead Man Walking"?

4 Who played Bridget in "Bridget Jones's Diary"?

5 Which Tom was the voice of Woody in the original "Toy Story"?

6 Which Woody had a son called Satchel Farrow?

7 Which star of "Mary Poppins" has written children's stories under the name Julie Edwards?

8 Which actress Kate announced a split from her husband Jim Threapleton in September 2001?

9 Which Kim married Alec Baldwin?

10 Annette Bening is the first wife of which Hollywood playboy actor director?

11 In which decade was Helena Bonham Carter born?

12 Which actor Richard was once married to supermodel Cindy Crawford?

13 Which Mel starred in "What Women Want"?

14 In which city of Northern Ireland was Kenneth Branagh born?

15 In film journalism, what sort of column did Hedda Hopper write?

16 Which Annette fell for Michael Douglas in "The American President"?

17 Which Tom married TV star Roseanne?

18 Which Liam played Alfred Kinsey in the movie "Kinsey"?

19 Which fantasy creature did Daryl Hannah play in "Splash"?

20 Which singer/actress played a music diva in "The Bodyguard"?

21 Which James Bond producer Cubby shares his name with a vegetable?

22 On which continent was Richard E Grant born?

23 Which Patsy who starred in "The Great Gatsby" was once Mrs Liam Gallagher?

24 Which family includes actors Davis, Patricia, Rosanna and Alexis?

25 What is the name of the actress daughter of John Drew Barrymore?

26 Which Kate is the daughter of Goldie Hawn?

27 "The Crying Game"'s director Neil Jordan hails from where?

28 What was silent star Joseph Keaton's nickname?

29 Tobey Maguire played which web-weaving super hero?

30 Which Jeff did Geena Davis marry?

Answers | Euro Tour (see Quiz 32)

1 Dublin. 2 Danish. 3 Dunkirk. 4 Dublin. 5 Greece. 6 Mediterranean. 7 Winter sports. 8 Rome. 9 Portugal. 10 Italy. 11 France. 12 Czechoslovakia. 13 Paris. 14 Switzerland. 15 Mountains. 16 West. 17 Spain. 18 Car. 19 Limerick. 20 Munich. 21 France. 22 Lisbon. 23 Brussels. 24 Berlin. 25 Spain. 26 France. 27 Hungary. 28 Ireland. 29 Arctic. 30 North.

1 Los Angeles is in which US state?
2 Who is Bart Simpson's youngest sister?
3 A banshee is a type of what?
4 Which is the largest country in South America?
5 What category of book describes the life of another real person?
6 In 2005, which Andy became the youngest male Brit to qualify for the US tennis Open?
7 In fiction, Sherlock Holmes lived in a street named after which type of worker?
8 Who is head of the family in the fiendishly funny "Addams Family"?
9 What is a clavichord?
10 What colour is the Taj Mahal?
11 Which bird is part of the name for a native American Indian's war axe?
12 Which Will produced the 2005 big-selling album "Keep On"?
13 In transport terms a smack is a small type of what?
14 What colour was Tin Tin's dog called Snowy?
15 When were you born if your birthdate occurs only once in four years?
16 In the saying, what will the mice do when the cat's away?
17 Which country along with Brazil in South America begins with a B?
18 What was the first personal stereo called?
19 The zodiac sign Pisces covers which two months?
20 What is the Great Barrier Reef made out of?
21 What is a lasso usually made from?
22 How many kings are there in two packs of playing cards?
23 In which country can you visit the Francorchamps race track?
24 Alice, Elizabeth, Mary and Victoria – which of these has never been the name of a queen of England?
25 What was a totem pole usually made from?
26 What is the name of presenter Zoe Ball's dad?
27 In which city can you visit the Tate Modern and Tate Britain?
28 Which city does a Muscovite come from?
29 Which King returned in 2005 in a big-budget movie?
30 Is acupuncture a form of bicycle tyre repairing, medical treatment or recycling of waste material?

| **Answers** | **Pot Luck 13** *(see Quiz 29)* |

1 Television. 2 52. 3 Cocoa beans. 4 Garbage. 5 The Black Death. 6 Patrick. 7 Spinach. 8 Gagarin. 9 Sunday. 10 Jeans. 11 Morse. 12 Japan. 13 Swimming. 14 Robin Cook. 15 Spanish. 16 Tsarina. 17 Convent. 18 Dino. 19 Even. 20 Dee. 21 None. 22 Mallet. 23 USA. 24 Lionheart. 25 India. 26 Dune. 27 Red. 28 Insects. 29 Whitney Houston. 30 Meringue.

1 In which Irish city is the Abbey Theatre?
2 What is the official language of Denmark?
3 What do the British call what the French call Dunkerque?
4 Dun Laoghaire is the port for which Irish city?
5 Rhodes is an island belonging to which country?
6 The Riviera is on the French/Italian coast on which sea?
7 St Moritz is famous for what type of sports?
8 St Peter's Basilica is in which Italian city?
9 Faro, or the Algarve, is in which country?
10 Rimini is a resort of the Adriatic in which country?
11 The Seine reaches the sea from which country?
12 Slovakia was formerly part of which country?
13 In which French city is the university called the Sorbonne?
14 Which European country is made up of cantons?
15 What are the Alps?
16 County Sligo is on which coast of Ireland?
17 Catalonia, Andalusia and Valencia are parts of which country?
18 The French town of Le Mans hosts what type of race?
19 Which Irish county has given its name to a comic rhyme?
20 Which German city is known locally as München?
21 In which country was the Academie Française founded?
22 Which city do the Portuguese call Lisboa?
23 Which city is also known locally as Bruxelles?
24 Which city replaced Bonn as Germany's capital?
25 Where would you spend pesetas?
26 In which country are baguettes and brioches traditional breads?
27 Which country beginning with H is to the east of Austria?
28 The Shannon is which country's chief river?
29 Lapland is nearest to which ocean?
30 In which part of Europe is the Baltic Sea?

Answers	**Movies Who's Who?** *(see Quiz 30)*

1 Dustin Hoffman. 2 Harrison. 3 Sarandon. 4 Renee Zellweger. 5 Hanks. 6 Allen.
7 Julie Andrews. 8 Winslet. 9 Basinger. 10 Warren Beatty. 11 1960s. 12 Gere.
13 Gibson. 14 Belfast. 15 Gossip. 16 Bening. 17 Arnold. 18 Liam Neeson. 19
Mermaid. 20 Whitney Houston. 21 Broccoli. 22 Africa. 23 Kensit. 24 Arquette. 25
Drew Barrymore. 26 Hudson. 27 Ireland. 28 Buster. 29 Spiderman. 30 Goldblum.

1 The "New York Herald" and the "Washington Post" are types of what?

2 Which letter along with H appears on pencils?

3 According to the legend, which weapon did William Tell use to shoot an apple off his son's head?

4 In a calendar year which is the first month to have exactly 30 days?

5 California is on which coast of the USA?

6 Which Arsenal keeper was Germany's No 1 for the 2006 World Cup?

7 Which West European country beginning with an S is landlocked?

8 Ford cars were originally made in which country?

9 Which word links a chess piece and an ancient soldier?

10 Pisa's famous leaning tower was built to house what?

11 CS Lewis wrote about "The Lion, the Witch and the" what?

12 Hermit and spider are types of what?

13 In which city was John Lennon murdered?

14 Who did France beat in the final of the 1998 FIFA World Cup?

15 How many pairs of ribs does a human have?

16 The game of boules comes from which country?

17 Which gas is believed to be encouraging global warming?

18 Which soul singer Luther died at the age of 54 in 2005?

19 Which word names a conductor's stick and also a small French loaf?

20 What items by Georgia O'Keefe fetch record prices at auctions?

21 What is the second highest mountain in the world called?

22 Which John returned to prominence in the movie "Pulp Fiction"?

23 Which female went to "The Edge of Reason" in a 2004 movie?

24 What do people usually do with a Stradivarius?

25 Which TV show was responsible for the the catchphrase "Pass"?

26 What colour describes the extra-time goal to decide certain football matches?

27 Which item of swimwear is named after an atoll in the Pacific?

28 In the human skeleton, is the fibula below or above the patella?

29 In which street would you have been wise to avoid the premises of a barber named Sweeney Todd?

30 In "Bewitched" which part of her body did Samantha move to cast a spell?

Answers	**Pot Luck 16** *(see Quiz 35)*

1 Buffalo. 2 Pole vault. 3 Pacific. 4 Roald Dahl. 5 Never. 6 Ice. 7 Louis Pasteur. 8 Smith. 9 Mexico. 10 Cos. 11 French. 12 Beavis. 13 Moses. 14 Mozart. 15 Johnny Depp. 16 Justine Henin-Hardenne. 17 52. 18 Oasis. 19 An earthquake. 20 Africa. 21 Motor town. 22 Nobel Prize. 23 Sun. 24 Knife. 25 Beautiful. 26 A will. 27 Clubs. 28 Liverpool. 29 White. 30 Television.

1 Who was Simon's singing partner?
2 By which first name is Roderick David Stewart known?
3 Who has the surname Ciccone?
4 Freddie Mercury led which regal-sounding band?
5 Which superstar singer Barbra starred in the hit movie "Meet the Fockers"?
6 Which Elton John song was reworked and dedicated to Princess Diana?
7 What was the Spice Girls' first album called?
8 Which Elvis hit of 2005 has the line, "You ain't a never caught a rabbit"?
9 Which band's singles include "Country House" and "Beetlebum"?
10 Who made the album "Best of Bob Marley"?
11 Whose "Come On Over" album is a top-selling country album in the US?
12 Which ex-Take That member won a Brit Award for "She's the One" in 2000?
13 Whose hits include "Jesus to a Child" and "Outside"?
14 Which band has had the most gold albums of any band in the UK?
15 Which grandfather was a "Sex Bomb" in 2000?
16 In 2000 U2 received the keys to which city?
17 Which Beatle announced his engagement in 2001?
18 Which band's singles include "Common People" and "Disco 2000"?
19 Which band did Sting front?
20 Which late blue-eyed superstar had the first names Francis Albert?
21 Which "Jagged Little" album was a huge hit for Alanis Morissette?
22 Bjorn Again are a tribute band to which superstars?
23 Which Irish band made the album "By Request"?
24 Which Diana fronted The Supremes?
25 Eric Clapton had a transatlantic hit with "I Shot" who?
26 Who was in the news after the break-up of his marriage to Heather Mills?
27 Which George's early solo single was "Careless Whisper"?
28 Which band's singles include "Australia" and "A Design for Life"?
29 Who had hit albums "True Blue" and "Erotica"?
30 Who had huge hits with "Sacrifice" and "Rocket Man"?

Answers	Technology *(see Quiz 36)*

1 Calculator. 2 Wikipedia. 3 Cars. 4 Nanjing Automobile Company. 5 Sky. 6 Sewing machine. 7 Sun. 8 1970s. 9 1960s. 10 Two. 11 Water. 12 Read. 13 Fax. 14 Car. 15 Camera. 16 Apple Macintosh. 17 Personal. 18 Internet. 19 Stars. 20 Menu. 21 Bar code. 22 Temperature. 23 Camera. 24 Lap top. 25 Ipod. 26 Hearing. 27 Voice mail. 28 1980s. 29 IBM. 30 Hypertext.

1 What went before Bill in the Wild West's William Cody's name?
2 Sergey Bubka broke over 30 world records in which event?
3 What is the largest of the Earth's oceans?
4 Who wrote "The BFG" and "Revolting Rhymes"?
5 How many times did Queen Elizabeth I marry?
6 On which sporting surface did Wayne Gretzky find fame?
7 Which scientist pioneered the pasteurisation process to purify milk?
8 In the UK and the USA what is the most common surname for people?
9 The Aztecs came from which part of the world?
10 Which word names a Greek Island and a lettuce?
11 Other than English, which language is spoken in Canada?
12 Who went with Butthead in the TV series?
13 In the Bible which infant was hidden in bulrushes for his own safety?
14 Which famous composer had the first names Wolfgang Amadeus?
15 Which Johnny was in the movies "Chocolat" and "Charlie and the Chocolate Factory"?
16 Which Justine was the first Belgian to win a tennis Grand Slam tournament?
17 How many fortnights are there in two years?
18 Which band's album title advised "Don't Believe the Truth"?
19 The Richter scale measures the strength of what?
20 On which continent is the world's largest desert?
21 Detroit's nickname is Motown – what does Motown stand for?
22 Masters Trophy, Nobel Prize and Oscar – which of these awards links with science?
23 Earth takes 365 days to travel round what?
24 What type of weapon is a kukri?
25 What kind of "Day" gave U2 a No 1 hit?
26 What does a testator make?
27 In whist, which trumps usually follow on after Hearts in descending order?
28 The late David Sheppard was Bishop of which city from 1975 to 1997?
29 What colour are the stars on the American flag?
30 Paper, soap and television – which of these items could not have been found in a house in 1901?

| **Answers** | **Pot Luck 15** *(see Quiz 33)* |

1 Newspaper. 2 B. 3 Crossbow. 4 April. 5 West. 6 Jens Lehmann. 7 Switzerland. 8 USA. 9 Knight. 10 Bells. 11 Wardrobe. 12 Crab. 13 New York. 14 Brazil. 15 Twelve. 16 France. 17 Carbon dioxide. 18 Vandross. 19 Baton. 20 Paintings. 21 K2. 22 Travolta. 23 Bridget Jones. 24 Play it. 25 Mastermind. 26 Golden goal. 27 Bikini. 28 Below it. 29 Fleet Street. 30 Her nose.

1 An abacus was an early type of what?
2 Which W is the most visited on-line encyclopaedia?
3 What did engineer Louis Renault manufacture?
4 Which car manufacturer built the first Chinese-made MG?
5 Which of the following is a UK satellite TV company – Sky, Sun, Mars?
6 Which needlework machine did Isaac Singer invent?
7 What provides solar power?
8 In which decade did Apple computers first appear?
9 In which decade did man first land on the Moon?
10 A stereo music system has a minimum of how many speakers?
11 An aqueduct was constructed to carry what?
12 In CD-ROM what does the letter R stand for?
13 What is the more common name for a facsimile telegraphy machine?
14 The Ford Model T was an early model of what form of transport?
15 Which of these inventions was developed first – the camera, the modem or satellite television?
16 What make is a computer which has an apple symbol on it?
17 What does P refer to in PCs?
18 Which system of communication developed from ARPANET?
19 Astronomy is the study of what?
20 What's the name for the selection bar at the top of a computer monitor?
21 What kind of code is scanned at a supermarket?
22 What does a thermostat control?
23 Polaroid is a type of what?
24 What name is given to a portable computer?
25 Nano and Shuffle were second-generation versions of which portable media device?
26 Audio refers to which of the senses?
27 Which mail is a type of telephone answering machine?
28 In which decade were PCs invented?
29 Which company manufactured the first generally available PC?
30 What does H stand for in HTTP?

Answers	**Music Superstars** *(see Quiz 34)*

1 Garfunkel. 2 Rod. 3 Madonna. 4 Queen. 5 Streisand. 6 Candle in the Wind. 7 Spice. 8 Hound Dog. 9 Blur. 10 Bob Marley. 11 Shania Twain. 12 Robbie Williams. 13 George Michael. 14 Queen. 15 Tom Jones. 16 Dublin. 17 Paul McCartney. 18 Pulp. 19 Police. 20 Sinatra. 21 Pill. 22 Abba. 23 Boyzone. 24 Ross. 25 The Sheriff. 26 Sir Paul McCartney. 27 George Michael. 28 Manic Street Preachers. 29 Madonna. 30 Elton John.

1 Which L is a country on the south-eastern frontier of Belgium?
2 Which was developed last – space flight, television or the telephone?
3 Born in Yugoslavia, Monica Seles eventually played for which country?
4 The movie "Vera Drake" was set in which European capital city?
5 Which sauce is eaten with turkey at Thanksgiving in the USA?
6 Which word names a mobile home and also a line of camels?
7 Which young blonde is a "Vampire Slayer" on TV?
8 How is Uluru also known?
9 Which sport is governed by FIFA?
10 In which war-torn country is the city of Baghdad?
11 What was the first name of the Queen of Scots, beheaded in 1587?
12 What breed of dog was film and TV star Lassie?
13 Which anniversary of the Gunpowder Plot was celebrated in 2005?
14 What main colour goes with white on the flag of Argentina?
15 Carragher and Kewell were together in which club soccer side?
16 Cleopatra's Needle now standing in London came from which country?
17 How many letters appear in the English alphabet before Q?
18 If Albert is the dad and Harold is the son what is the famous TV sitcom?
19 Brass was originally made from copper and which other metal?
20 The star sign Gemini is represented as what?
21 What is the French word meaning yellow?
22 How many straight lines are needed to make a plus sign?
23 Who won the first FA Cup Final played in Cardiff?
24 The coast of Belgium is on which Sea?
25 What is the colour of the cheapest property on a Monopoly board?
26 The most common pub name in the UK is the Red what – Giraffe, Lion or Elephant?
27 Which place name can go before Triangle and shorts?
28 Which initials are linked with genetic fingerprinting?
29 Diwali is an important feast in which religion?
30 How many individual squares are there on a chess board?

1 Mario Andretti found fame in which sport?

2 Which sisters fought out the US Open tennis final in 2001?

3 By which first name was cricketer Sir Garfield Sobers known?

4 Who was England's youngest player in the 2006 World Cup tournament squad?

5 Decathlete Dean Macey competes in how many events?

6 How was athlete James Cleveland Owens better known?

7 Clive Lloyd captained which international cricket side?

8 Which young golfer was "Sports Illustrated"'s sportsman of the year in 1996?

9 Which sport did Michael Jordan play professionally for more than 12 years?

10 Which Phil won the US Masters in 2004 and again in 2006?

11 Whom did the late Don Bradman play international cricket for?

12 Which country does racing driver Riccardo Patrese come from?

13 How did golfer Payne Stewart meet his tragic death in 1999?

14 What type of sporting competitor was Lammtarra?

15 Which Mr Fallon is a top money-winning jockey?

16 Which national side did rugby's Rob Andrew play for?

17 Czech-born Martina Hingis represents which country?

18 In which sport did Shaquille O'Neal make his name – and a fortune?

19 In which sport did Australian Dawn Fraser find fame?

20 World record holder Zola Budd originally came from which country?

21 What is the first name of South African rugby star Pienaar?

22 Novelist Dick Francis had a successful career as what type of sportsman?

23 Which Champion rode the Grand National winner Aldaniti in 1981?

24 Jockey Lester Piggott served a prison sentence for what evasion?

25 Will Carling captained which national rugby side?

26 Franz Klammer and Jean-Claude Killy are famous names in which winter sport?

27 What is the first name of Finnish F1 driver Hakkinen?

28 Graham Gooch is from which English county?

29 Which Caribbean island did Merlene Ottey compete for?

30 Maurice Greene sprints for which country?

Answers	Pot Luck 18 *(see Quiz 40)*

1 Pretty Woman. 2 Wall. 3 I. 4 Rome. 5 Robert. 6 Writing. 7 India. 8 Osama Bin Laden. 9 America. 10 Lockerbie. 11 Round. 12 Four. 13 Emperor. 14 Silver. 15 March. 16 Madison. 17 Katherine Jenkins. 18 Destiny's Child. 19 Waterfall. 20 16.45. 21 Red. 22 Green. 23 Mount Everest. 24 Japan. 25 Africa. 26 Braille. 27 Pear. 28 In the sea. 29 Temple. 30 Alan Pardew.

Quiz 39

Quiz and Game Shows

Answers – page 45

1 How long does the contestant have to answer the question in "Who Wants to be a Millionaire?"?

2 Who asked the questions in the US version of "The Weakest Link"?

3 How many teams take part in one episode of "University Challenge"?

4 Which Swedish-born personality first presented "Dog Eat Dog"?

5 What is "Ready Steady Cook" with famous stars providing the ingredients called?

6 Lea Kristensen helped Jim Davidson on which Saturday-night family show?

7 Which Phillip hosted "National Lottery: Winning Lines"?

8 Which snooker player led a team opposite Ally McCoist on "A Question of Sport"?

9 On which Channel was the afternoon show "Number One" shown?

10 Which actress Penelope presented a later series of "What's My Line?"?

11 Annabel Croft was what type of sportswoman before taking part in the 1980s "Treasure Hunt"?

12 In "Strike It Rich", was a hotspot lucky or unlucky?

13 If Vic was Reeves who was Bob in "Shooting Stars"?

14 On which show did Leslie Crowther invite contestants to "come on down"?

15 What did Bruce Forsyth invite contestants to "Play Right"?

16 Which means of communication replaced postal votes on "Opportunity Knocks"?

17 What was the chair covering made from on the original "Mastermind"?

18 Which show shared its name with Roman fighters?

19 Whose "Moment of Truth" was a family quiz show?

20 What was the prize in "The Krypton Factor"?

21 Which Noel fronted "Deal or No Deal"?

22 In which long-running show did a Des take over from a Des?

23 Which future TV star Carol was a hostess on "Wheel of Fortune"?

24 Which Des presented the 1990s "Take Your Pick"?

25 What receptacle was the booby prize on "3–2–1"?

26 Which student show has the phrase, "Your starter for 10"?

27 Was the first "Who Wants to be a Millionaire?" millionaire, a man or a woman?

28 Which sports quiz always ends with the end of the famous sporting quote, "It is now"?

29 What was the trophy usually made from on "Mastermind"?

30 Which Saturday-night prime-time quizman Chris split from his wife in 2006?

| **Answers** | Pot Luck 17 *(see Quiz 37)* |

1 Luxembourg. 2 Space flight. 3 USA. 4 London. 5 Cranberry. 6 Caravan. 7 Buffy. 8 Ayers Rock. 9 Football. 10 Iraq. 11 Mary. 12 Collie. 13 400th. 14 Light blue. 15 Liverpool. 16 Egypt. 17 16. 18 Steptoe & Son. 19 Zinc. 20 Twins. 21 Jaune. 22 Two. 23 Liverpool. 24 North. 25 Brown. 26 Lion. 27 Bermuda. 28 DNA. 29 Hindu. 30 64.

Quiz 40 | Pot Luck 18

Answers – page 46

1 For which movie with "Woman" in the title was Julia Roberts nominated for an Oscar?

2 What would a mural be painted on?

3 Which of these is not the name of a note in music – E, G or I?

4 Nero was the Emperor of which ancient empire when its main city was destroyed?

5 What was the first name of Boy Scouts founder Baden-Powell?

6 Lazlo Biro's most famous invention was used for what?

7 Mother Teresa was particularly noted for her work with the poor of which country?

8 Who founded Al Qaeda in the late 1980s?

9 Did the Grunge movement begin in Australia or America?

10 In the 1980s, over 250 died after a terrorist bomb exploded a plane over which town in Scotland?

11 Christopher Columbus became convinced that the Earth was what shape?

12 In Spanish, what is the number quatro?

13 What is the name of the largest species of penguin?

14 In heraldry, what is argent?

15 In which month is St David's Day?

16 Which of Madison, Maryland or Montana is not a state of the USA?

17 "Second Nature" was which singer's second album?

18 Who had a hit single with "Independent Woman"?

19 The Angel, in Venezuela, is the world's highest what?

20 In digits, what time is quarter to five in the afternoon on a 24-hour clock?

21 What is the top colour on a rainbow?

22 What colour goes before land to name the world's largest island?

23 What is named after George Everest who was a Surveyor General of India?

24 The Sony company originally developed in which country?

25 Nigeria is the largest country in which continent?

26 Who gave his name to a reading system designed for people who are visually impaired?

27 Which of the following is not a citrus fruit – lemon, lime or pear?

28 "The Blue Planet" was a TV documentary series about life where?

29 A pagoda is a type of what?

30 Which boss Alan took West Ham to their first FA Cup final this century?

Answers	Sporting Who's Who? *(see Quiz 38)*

1 Motor racing. 2 Venus and Serena Williams. 3 Gary. 4 Theo Walcott. 5 Ten. 6 Jesse. 7 West Indies. 8 Tiger Woods. 9 Basketball. 10 Phil Mickelson. 11 Australia. 12 Italy. 13 His Lear Jet suffered decompression, killing all on board, and later crashed. 14 Horse. 15 Kieren. 16 England. 17 Switzerland. 18 Basketball. 19 Swimming. 20 South Africa. 21 Francois. 22 Jockey. 23 Bob. 24 Tax. 25 England. 26 Skiing. 27 Mika. 28 Essex. 29 Jamaica. 30 USA.

1 Which ex-soccer manager of Nottm Forest died aged 69 in September 2004?
2 The Good Friday Agreement was drawn up to help solve problems in which part of the UK?
3 In which decade did Queen Elizabeth II come to the throne?
4 In which month of 2005 was London first bombed?
5 Which island has a political party called Sinn Fein?
6 Which Princess did the future Lord Snowdon marry in 1960?
7 How was the trades union Solidarnosc known in English?
8 Which Maxwell disappeared off his yacht in 1991 before news about misappropriation of pension funds?
9 Marilyn Monroe is thought to have died due to an overdose of what?
10 Which Louis was killed by an IRA bomb in 1979?
11 BSE was also called mad what disease?
12 Which African country entertained only rebel cricket tours because its policy on apartheid meant no official tours could be made?
13 Ken Russell was a controversial name in which area of the arts?
14 Which Act affecting foxes and hares came into force in February 2005?
15 Which tax, also called community charge, was the cause of riots in the 1990s?
16 1990's round-the-world yacht "Maiden" had a crew made up entirely of who or what?
17 Sir Ranulph Fiennes hit the headlines in what capacity?
18 In the 1970s the Americans withdrew troops from which V?
19 Which country has had most experience of spaceflight?
20 The campaign to ban which weapons was supported by Princess Diana?
21 Which O in Northern Ireland was the scene of a horrific bomb in 1998?
22 Which Royal ship ceased service at the end of the 1990s?
23 Apartheid was most well known in which African country?
24 Which television dolls virtually walked off the shelves in a 1990s Christmas buying frenzy?
25 Which sculpture of the North was erected near Gateshead?
26 Which meat did the government ban from being eaten on the bone during the crisis concerning BSE?
27 Princess Anne's daughter Zara hit the headlines with a pierced what?
28 In which decade did Edmund Hillary climb Everest?
29 Salman Rushdie hit the headlines with a controversial what?
30 How many goals did France score when they beat Brazil to win the World Cup?

Answers	**Gardening** (see Quiz 43)

1 Yellow. 2 Wood. 3 Monty Don. 4 Leaves. 5 Artichokes. 6 Over plants. 7 Bulbs. 8 Cut. 9 Cooking. 10 Lawnmower. 11 Compost. 12 Beans. 13 Hedge. 14 Holly. 15 Lavender. 16 Brownish/black. 17 One. 18 Small. 19 Roses. 20 Rockery. 21 Blue. 22 Sweet. 23 Cones. 24 Greenhouse. 25 Apples. 26 William. 27 Mowing. 28 Bulbs. 29 Blue. 30 Elderberries.

Quiz 42 | Pot Luck 19

1 Tony Blair visited the Faisal mosque in which country in November 2006?
2 Which Niall took over as Sunderland chairman and manager?
3 Who is in the title with the Owl in Edward Lear's poem?
4 What went with Hide in the title of a 2005 Robert de Niro movie?
5 How many people are involved in a fencing match?
6 Which British PM during the 1970s "winter of discontent" died in 2005?
7 What are the sides of a stage called?
8 In music, the lines on which notes are written go in which direction?
9 Which people used C, D, L and M in their counting system?
10 John Glenn became the first person over 70 to do what?
11 What is the first name of Ms Hill who sang with the Fugees?
12 Which Texan gave his name to a tall hat – was it Homburg, Stetson or Tengallon?
13 A Bruxellois is a person coming from which city?
14 Marmite yeast extract is rich in which vitamin?
15 Which of these three spoons is the largest – a coffeespoon, a dessertspoon or a tablespoon?
16 What is the piece of the mushroom above the stalk called?
17 What were the pyramids made out of?
18 In the past, Kampuchea was known by which of these names: Cambodia, Sri Lanka or Thailand?
19 Which common kitchen item can also be a type of drum?
20 Which girl band made a movie called "Honest"?
21 Jonathan Edwards won an Olympic gold medal in which event?
22 What job did Peter and Andrew do before becoming disciples of Jesus?
23 Geometry is a branch of which subject?
24 Coal, diamonds, leather – which of these three items is not mined from underground?
25 What is the first of the three letters that invites you to turn over a piece of paper?
26 How many spaces are contained in a frame for noughts and crosses?
27 On a camera, what opens and closes to allow light in?
28 Is a kayak a type of currency, a hairy animal or a sailing craft?
29 Whose first No 1 hit was "Because We Want to"?
30 In the nursery rhyme "Hey Diddle Diddle", who did a runner with the dish?

Answers	Music Who's Who? (see Quiz 44)

1 Duran Duran. 2 Andrew Lloyd Webber. 3 Madonna. 4 Michael Jackson. 5 Ireland. 6 Suede. 7 Enrique. 8 U2. 9 Michael. 10 Robbie Williams. 11 Lopez. 12 Phil. 13 Noel. 14 Spice Girls. 15 Britney Spears. 16 Eternal. 17 Kylie Minogue. 18 Adams. 19 Take That. 20 Eva. 21 US. 22 Barbie. 23 Canada. 24 Martin. 25 Sonny. 26 Kitten. 27 Five. 28 Eminem. 29 Stephen. 30 Sinatra.

Quiz 43 | Gardening | Answers – page 49 | LEVEL 1

1 What is the most common colour for a daffodil?
2 What is decking usually made from?
3 Which Monty took over on BBC's "Gardener's World"?
4 What is a plant's foliage?
5 Which vegetables can be globe or Jerusalem?
6 Where does a cloche go?
7 What are tulips grown from?
8 What do secateurs do?
9 What are culinary herbs used for?
10 Which piece of garden equipment can be hover or rotary?
11 Which heap provides fertiliser for the garden?
12 Which vegetables can be French or broad?
13 If you grew a box in your garden what would it be?
14 Which prickly green shrub with red berries is a Christmas decoration?
15 Which purple aromatic plant takes its name from the Latin Lavo, meaning I wash?
16 What colour is peat?
17 How many wheels does a wheelbarrow usually have?
18 What is significant about bonsai plants?
19 Hybrid tea and floribunda are types of what?
20 Which part of the garden has decorative stones?
21 What is the most common colour of a cornflower?
22 Which Peas are decorative flowers?
23 What do conifers produce?
24 Which house is used for rearing delicate plants?
25 What sort of fruit do you grow if you grow Cox's Orange Pippin and Bramley?
26 Which princely name follows Sweet in a cottage garden plant?
27 Which word describes cutting a lawn?
28 What do lilies grow from?
29 What is the most common colour for a delphinium?
30 Which fruits follow elderflowers?

1 Which 1980s band led by Simon Le Bon were back in the top five in 2004?
2 Who is Timothy Miles Bindon Rice's most famous musical collaborator?
3 Who won the MTV Best Video for "Ray of Light"?
4 Who recorded the album "Thriller"?
5 Where do The Corrs come from?
6 Which band's singles include "Trash" and "Stay Together"?
7 Which Iglesias made the albums "Bailamos" and "Cosas El Amor"?
8 Which Irish band made the album "The Joshua Tree"?
9 Which Jackson has had the most platinum albums in the UK?
10 Which ex-Take That member won a Brit Award for "Angel" in 1999?
11 Which Jennifer's name was linked to that of rapper Puff Daddy?
12 Which Collins, formerly of Genesis, won awards for his songs for the movie "Tarzan"?
13 Who is the oldest Gallagher brother?
14 Which band's singles include "2 Become 1" and "Too Much"?
15 Which teen queen charted with "Born to Make You Happy"?
16 Louise, aka Mrs Jamie Redknapp, belonged to which all-girl band?
17 Which Aussie songstress got to No 1 on both sides of the Atlantic with "Spinning Around"?
18 What was Victoria Beckham's maiden name?
19 Which band's singles included "Relight My Fire" and "Back for Good"?
20 Which Cassidy had a posthumous hit with "Over the Rainbow"?
21 Do Destiny's Child come from the UK or the US?
22 Which toy "Girl" was a hit for Aqua?
23 Which country does Celine Dion come from?
24 Which Ricky had the top-selling album "Vuelve" in 1999?
25 Who was Cher's singing partner on her very first UK hit?
26 Which Atomic band had a hit with "Eternal Flame"?
27 How many members of Boyzone are there?
28 Which rapper recorded the albums "Encore" and "The Eminem Show"?
29 What is the first name of songwriter Sondheim?
30 Which Frank was 70 when he had a single in the top ten?

Answers	Pot Luck 19 *(see Quiz 42)*

1 Pakistan. 2 Quinn. 3 The Pussy Cat. 4 Seek. 5 Two. 6 James Callaghan. 7 Wings. 8 Horizontally. 9 Romans. 10 Travel in space. 11 Lauryn. 12 Stetson. 13 Brussels. 14 B. 15 Tablespoon. 16 Cap. 17 Stone. 18 Cambodia. 19 Kettle. 20 All Saints. 21 Triple jump. 22 Fishermen. 23 Mathematics. 24 Leather. 25 P. 26 Nine. 27 Shutter. 28 Sailing craft. 29 Billie. 30 The spoon.

1 The Appleton girls were in which pop band?
2 What were the initials of foodmaker Mr Heinz?
3 Who were the beaten finalists in the 2002 FIFA World Cup?
4 Orly airport is in which country?
5 VSO stands for what type of charitable service overseas?
6 Who did Thumbelina marry?
7 What is the dog called in a Punch and Judy show?
8 In Enid Blyton's stories, what colour is Noddy's hat?
9 When texting, what does a letter l, a number 8 and a letter r stand for?
10 Queen Nefertiti ruled in which country?
11 In song, Nancy Sinatra had boots that were made for doing what?
12 In which country would you watch Real Sociedad play a home soccer match?
13 Joey Barton and Richard Dunn were together at which Premiership club?
14 In military diplomacy SALT involves what kind of limitation talks – Secret Arms, Specialist Arms or Strategic Arms?
15 What did a spinet make?
16 What is the occupation of Phil, David and Tony Archer in the radio soap?
17 What type of map indicates areas of high and low ground?
18 What is the pattern on a bumblebee?
19 The port of Plymouth is in England and which other country?
20 Is Terry Wogan's radio show in the morning or the evening?
21 Which is the last month in a calendar year to have exactly 30 days?
22 In the signs of the zodiac, Pisces represents which creature?
23 What can be a sheet of paper or part of a plant?
24 How is the famous French lady Jeanne d'Arc known in English?
25 Which animal's "eyes" did Percy Shaw invent to help motorists?
26 Thomas Barnardo set up homes for what type of people?
27 Which word completes the Shania Twain album title "Come On ____"?
28 What shaped puzzle did Mr Rubik invent?
29 Does the letter P in OPEC stand for – petroleum, plastic or price?
30 In which country is the musical "Cabaret" set?

Answers	Pot Luck 21 *(see Quiz 47)*

1 Geoff Ogilvy. 2 None. 3 Patrick Moore. 4 Friendly. 5 Germany. 6 Leaves (vegetation). 7 Blood. 8 On land. 9 Nocturnal. 10 Change colour. 11 Vacuum cleaner. 12 The X Files. 13 Calorie. 14 Abacus. 15 Russia. 16 Yellow. 17 Japan. 18 Ballet. 19 Ginger. 20 Thomas. 21 Silver. 22 Drew Barrymore. 23 Little. 24 Fat. 25 USA. 26 China. 27 Second. 28 Kingdom. 29 Metals. 30 Steam.

1 Which bird's name goes between "Where" and "Dare" in the Richard Burton/Clint Eastwood film?

2 Which director Alfred's first Hollywood movie was "Rebecca"?

3 In which country is "The Sound of Music" set?

4 Which TV canine star was originally a male called Pal?

5 Where did Tarzan live?

6 On which night of the week was there "Night Fever"?

7 What went after "White" in the seasonal song from the movie "Holiday Inn"?

8 In which decade was "Gone with the Wind" made?

9 How many "Commandments" were in the title of the 1950s classic?

10 Which 1940s classic had the Ugly Sisters among its characters?

11 In how many days did David Niven travel "Around the World" in 1956?

12 Where was "An American" in the 1950s movie?

13 The action for "Bridge on the River Kwai" was set in which war?

14 Which musical movie was based on Dickens' "Oliver Twist"?

15 Which "High" time of day was an award-winning movie with Gary Cooper?

16 Where was Gene Kelly "Singin'" in 1952?

17 Which Walt directed the first eight Oscar-winning animation films?

18 What sort of animal was Bugs?

19 Who was the hero of "Goldfinger"?

20 What were the first movies with speech called?

21 What was the first name of movie star Ms Swanson?

22 "All Quiet" on which "Front" was a classic of the 1930s?

23 Which "Man" was a post-war thriller set in Vienna?

24 John Wayne was famous for playing what type of character?

25 Which future US President starred in "Stallion Road" in the 1940s?

26 Which convenient initials did the grumpy actor Fields have?

27 What type of "Encounter" did Celia Johnson and Trevor Howard have?

28 What was the name of the "Citizen" in the all-time classic with Orson Welles?

29 What colour Brick Road was followed in "The Wizard of Oz"?

30 "Born Free" was about which African cats?

Answers	Celebs *(see Quiz 48)*

1 Alex Curran. 2 Andrew Lloyd Webber. 3 Sophie. 4 Red. 5 Frankie. 6 Feltz. 7 Emma Bunton. 8 Jules. 9 Madonna. 10 Nigella. 11 Cooking. 12 Wogan. 13 Wales. 14 Turner. 15 Butler. 16 Windsor. 17 Vet. 18 Jonathan. 19 Brad Pitt. 20 Scotland. 21 David. 22 Swansea. 23 Harrison. 24 Cricketer. 25 Michael. 26 Hervey. 27 Clarissa. 28 Hurley. 29 Luciano Pavarotti. 30 Pete Doherty.

1 Which Geoff won golf's US Open in 2006?
2 How many teeth do most human babies have at birth?
3 Which Patrick has presented TV's "The Sky at Night" for 50 years?
4 In comic books and movies what word describes Casper the ghost?
5 Supermodel Claudia Schiffer comes from which country?
6 A giraffe's diet consists mainly of what?
7 What contains red and white corpuscles?
8 Where did George Stephenson's Rocket travel – on land, on sea or in space?
9 A creature that is more active at night is said to be what?
10 What does a chameleon do to disguise itself?
11 What kind of machine did William Hoover develop?
12 Which TV series had the line "The truth is out there"?
13 Which of these terms is a measure of energy in food, calorie, fat, cholesterol?
14 Which ancient counting device uses beads and string?
15 Anna Kournikova is originally from which country?
16 What colour is Nintendo's Pikachu?
17 The first Disneyland in Asia was built in which country?
18 An entrechat and a glissade appear in what type of dancing?
19 Who made up the original Spice Girls along with Baby, Posh, Sporty and Scary?
20 The Rev. Awdry wrote about which Tank Engine?
21 Which precious metal is associated with the Lone Ranger?
22 How is movie star Andrew Blyth Barrymore better known?
23 What did Stevie Wonder have before his name when he was a young performer?
24 What does a camel keep stored in its hump?
25 What is Britney Spears' home country?
26 Life-size figures in terracotta of an army were found in which country?
27 Did World War I begin in the first, second or third decade of the 20th century?
28 A king rules a kingdom but what does a queen rule?
29 An alloy is a combination of two different what?
30 What powered James Watt's engine built in 1777?

Answers | Pot Luck 20 *(see Quiz 45)*

1 All Saints. 2 HJ. 3 Germany. 4 France. 5 Voluntary. 6 Prince Cornelius. 7 Toby.
8 Blue. 9 Later. 10 Egypt. 11 Walking. 12 Spain. 13 Man City. 14 Strategic Arms.
15 Music. 16 Farmers. 17 Relief map. 18 Stripes. 19 America. 20 Morning. 21
November. 22 Fish. 23 Leaf. 24 Joan of Arc. 25 Cat's. 26 Children. 27 Over. 28
Cube. 29 Petroleum. 30 Germany.

1 Which Ms Curran is the other half of footballer Steve Gerrard?

2 Sarah Brightman was married to which big theatre name?

3 Which Ms Dahl is famous in the modelling world?

4 What colour is Charlie Dimmock's hair?

5 How is Lanfranco Dettori better known?

6 Which Vanessa was in the celebrity "Big Brother" House?

7 Who was the first ex-Spice Girl to appear on "Strictly Come Dancing"?

8 What is Jamie Oliver's wife called?

9 Guy Ritchie married which US megastar in 2000?

10 Which Lawson was dubbed "a domestic goddess"?

11 What were the Two Fat Ladies famous for on TV?

12 Which Radio 2 star Terry's autobiography was called "Is It Me"?

13 From which part of the UK does Catherine Zeta Jones hail?

14 What is the surname of TV sister celebs Anthea and Wendy?

15 What was the position of the ex-employee of Princess Diana who was arrested for theft of some of her property?

16 Which Barbara went from "Carry On" films to "EastEnders"?

17 Trude Mostue found TV fame in which profession?

18 Who is Paul Ross's famous younger brother?

19 Angelica Jolie linked up with which actor Brad?

20 The name of which country does Sean Connery have tattooed on his arm?

21 Which Mellor was dubbed the Minister of Fun?

22 Prince Charles received the freedom of which city, which has a link with his title?

23 Which Ford split with wife Melissa Mathison in 2001?

24 Jemima Khan married what type of sportsman in Imran Khan?

25 Which actor is ex-beauty queen Shakira Caine married to?

26 What is the surname of tabloid celeb Lady Victoria?

27 What is the first name of Ms Dickson Wright, famous for her cooking and country pursuits?

28 Which Elizabeth ceased to be the main face of Estee Lauder in 2001?

29 Who was the heaviest of the Three Tenors?

30 Which Pete is the frontman of Babyshambles?

| **Answers** | **Movies: Golden Oldies** *(see Quiz 46)* |

1 Eagles. 2 Hitchcock. 3 Austria. 4 Lassie. 5 Jungle. 6 Saturday. 7 Christmas. 8 1930s. 9 Ten. 10 Cinderella. 11 80. 12 Paris. 13 WWII. 14 Oliver!. 15 Noon. 16 In the Rain. 17 Disney. 18 Bunny. 19 James Bond. 20 Talkies. 21 Gloria. 22 Western. 23 Third Man. 24 Cowboy. 25 Ronald Reagan. 26 WC. 27 Brief. 28 Kane. 29 Yellow. 30 Lions.

Quiz 49 | Pot Luck 22

Answers – page 59

LEVEL 1

1 Which sprinter Michael won 200m and 400m gold at the Atlanta Olympics?
2 Which group included two girls with the same name but differentiated by letters of the alphabet?
3 Which W is a jacket that has no sleeves?
4 Which form of transport is Christopher Cockerell famous for developing?
5 What is the name for the place where coins manufactured?
6 Who was Gilbert's partner in writing comic operas?
7 What do you do if you dawdle – do you idle, do you run or do you rinse your mouth out?
8 In rhyme, what precedes "paddywack, give the dog a bone"?
9 Kissing the Blarney Stone is supposed to gift you the power to do what?
10 What is the usual colour of healthy parsley?
11 Which type of puzzle requires a grid to be filled in so that every row, every column and every 3 x 3 box contains the numbers 1 to 9?
12 What sort of pit do athletes jump into during a triple jump?
13 "Revenge of the Sith" was one of which series of movies?
14 Which swimming stroke is named after an insect?
15 Which ex-England football captain was a manager at Middlesbrough and WBA?
16 Which fabric is made from flax?
17 Korea is divided into how many countries?
18 Algeria is in which part of Africa?
19 Which classical composer had the names George Frederick?
20 According to the TV programme title "Sabrina is the Teenage" what – Doctor, Vampire or Witch?
21 In the "Shrek" movies did Eddie Murphy voice Cat, Donkey or Elephant?
22 In which Disney classic movie does Jiminy Cricket appear?
23 Which of these musical instruments does not use a reed when being played – clarinet, guitar or oboe?
24 Lourdes Maria was the first daughter of which pop superstar?
25 In the wartime song what do you pack up in your old kit bag?
26 Which of black, purple and yellow is a primary colour?
27 In fiction, what did Oliver Twist ask for after he had eaten all his food in the workhouse?
28 Attila was a leader of which tribe of which group of people?
29 Which B is the second largest city in Spain?
30 In which country is the musical "Evita" set?

Answers	Pot Luck 23 *(see Quiz 51)*

1 Iraq. 2 Jet engine. 3 First Lady. 4 Isaac. 5 Uma Thurman. 6 Ryder. 7 Egyptians. 8 Pins & needles. 9 Dance. 10 Dark blue. 11 Two. 12 Nappy. 13 Portugal. 14 Romans. 15 It boils. 16 Software. 17 Comet. 18 Countess. 19 Travellers. 20 Ten. 21 Jack. 22 Under the sea. 23 Yarn. 24 Guillotine. 25 2000. 26 General Custer. 27 Face. 28 Iced. 29 Blue. 30 Andre.

Quiz 50 | TV Classics

1 Who is Tracey's sister in "Birds of a Feather"?
2 Which series set in a prison shared its name with a breakfast food?
3 Who was Tom's wife in "The Good Life"?
4 What is British TV's longest-running children's show?
5 Which BBC show ended its Saturday-night run in 2001 when Premiership football moved to ITV?
6 On which night of the week is "Songs of Praise" usually shown?
7 Which "Team" included Mr T?
8 Which series with John Cleese was set in a hotel in Torquay?
9 Who was Inspector Morse's sidekick?
10 What was the occupation of Perry Mason?
11 Sergeant Wilson and Captain Mainwaring were in which "Army"?
12 In Morecambe & Wise, what was Morecambe's first name?
13 What was the nickname of Simon Templar, first played by Roger Moore?
14 Which "Challenge" was first presented by Bamber Gascoigne and later by Jeremy Paxman?
15 Which "Cars" were an early police drama?
16 Which "Doctor" first appeared in the 1960s in a phone box?
17 Which "Roundabout" became a children's classic?
18 Which type of workplace gave Ricky Gervais his first hit series?
19 "Jeux Sans Frontières" was also called "It's a" what?
20 Which Prime Minister's father-in-law was in "Till Death Us Do Part"?
21 Which weapon was used in the game show "The Golden Shot"?
22 Where did singer Val Doonican hail from?
23 Which puppet bear had friends called Sweep and Soo?
24 Which show was associated with a "Flying Circus"?
25 Who presented "The Generation Game" back in the 1970s?
26 What was the favourite item of footwear of Compo as played by the late Bill Owen?
27 Barry Norman began the first of many review programmes on which subject in 1972?
28 John Craven pioneered a "Newsround" programme for whom?
29 What colour was the chair in "Mastermind"?
30 Which Ricky appeared in "The Royle Family"?

Answers | **Science and the Natural World** *(see Quiz 52)*

1 Heel. 2 Cows/cattle. 3 Bee. 4 Temperature. 5 Tropical. 6 Orange/yellow. 7 Cold-blooded. 8 Rib cage. 9 Red. 10 Eating. 11 Asia. 12 Mouth. 13 Slime. 14 Your voice. 15 Back. 16 Needles. 17 Cat. 18 Spider. 19 Africa. 20 Blood. 21 Man. 22 Snake. 23 Sheep. 24 Plus. 25 Red. 26 Pink. 27 Australia. 28 Ice. 29 Mistletoe. 30 Mercury.

1 In which country is the war-scarred city of Basra?
2 What sort of engine was invented by Frank Whittle?
3 Which unofficial title is given to the wife of a US President?
4 What was the first name of scientist Newton?
5 Which actress Uma featured in the "Kill Bill" movies?
6 Which Winona links the movies "Little Women", "The Crucible" and "Alien: Resurrection"?
7 Isis and Osiris were gods of which ancient people?
8 Which sewing items can also be a sharp pain?
9 A palais glide is a type of what?
10 On a Monopoly board, what colour is the most expensive property?
11 How many players are on court in a game of tennis singles?
12 What do the British call what the Americans call a diaper?
13 Deco, Figo and Pauleta played soccer for which country?
14 Queen Boudicca led a revolt against which people?
15 What happens to water at 100 degrees centigrade?
16 What's the name for the instructions or programs used in computers?
17 Astronomer Edmond Halley gave his name to what?
18 What is the wife of an Earl called?
19 St Christopher is the patron saint of which group of people?
20 How many sides does a decagon have?
21 Which name can go before the words frost and knife?
22 Which part of the Earth was Jacques Cousteau famous for exploring?
23 What can be either a piece of thread or a long story?
24 Which device from the French Revolution is now used to trim paper?
25 What was the first leap year beginning with the numbers 20?
26 Which General made his "last stand" at the Battle of the Little Big Horn?
27 Where on her body would a Muslim woman wear a yashmak?
28 Is a sorbet served hot, iced or warm?
29 What colour blood are you said to have if you have a noble family?
30 Which Peter had No 1s with "Flava" and "I Feel You"?

1 Which part of the body is associated with Achilles?
2 Dairy farming is usually associated with the rearing of which animals?
3 A drone is a type of which insect?
4 What does the Kelvin scale measure?
5 In what sort of climate do rainforests appear?
6 What colour is amber?
7 What charachteristic of reptiles is also a phrase used to describe a callous act?
8 What is the framework of ribs called?
9 What colour is a robin's breast?
10 Anorexia nervosa is what type of disorder?
11 Which continent grows the most rice?
12 Saliva is produced in which part of the body?
13 What sort of trail does a slug leave behind?
14 If you have laryngitis what may you lose?
15 Lumbago causes pain in which part of the body?
16 What is inserted in the body in acupuncture?
17 The Florida cougar is a member of which family?
18 Which eight-legged creature do many people have a phobia about?
19 On which continent are most elephants found?
20 What do arteries in the body carry?
21 Chimpanzee, gorilla and man – present company excepted – which is the most intelligent?
22 What is a black mamba?
23 Cats, dogs and sheep – which of these animals are sheared?
24 Which contains more lines a plus or a minus sign?
25 Mars is called what colour planet?
26 What colour are a flamingo's feathers?
27 Koalas are natives to which country?
28 If water freezes what does it become?
29 Which plant increases in popularity at Christmas when you kiss under it?
30 Which metal is used in thermometers?

Answers	TV Classics *(see Quiz 50)*

1 Sharon. 2 Porridge. 3 Barbara. 4 Blue Peter. 5 Match of the Day. 6 Sunday. 7 A Team. 8 Fawlty Towers. 9 Lewis. 10 Lawyer (barrister). 11 Dad's Army. 12 Eric. 13 The Saint. 14 University. 15 Z Cars. 16 Who. 17 Magic. 18 Office. 19 Knockout. 20 Tony Blair's. 21 Crossbow. 22 Ireland. 23 Sooty. 24 Monty Python. 25 Bruce Forsyth. 26 Wellies. 27 Films. 28 Children. 29 Black. 30 Ricky Tomlinson.

1 Which Oscar-winner was a "Beauty", with Annette Bening and Kevin Spacey?
2 In which country was Warren Beatty's political thriller "Reds" set?
3 Which Juliette won Best Supporting Actress for "The English Patient"?
4 Where was Nicolas Cage "Leaving" in his 1995 winner?
5 Which Julia won for "Erin Brokovich"?
6 Which Ben shared a screenplay Oscar with Matt Damon for "Good Will Hunting"?
7 Which Jennifer did Oscar-nominee Brad Pitt marry?
8 Which English Oscar-winner Emma has a sister called Sophie?
9 In which US city was "The Godfather" set?
10 How old was Jessica Tandy when she won an Oscar for "Driving Miss Daisy", in her 50s, 60s, 70s or 80s?
11 Which English Julie, a 1960s winner, was nominated for "Afterglow" in the 1990s?
12 In which film venue were the first Oscars presented?
13 Which fighter was the subject of the 2001 winner with Russell Crowe?
14 Which blonde American cried all the way through her acceptance speech for "Shakespeare in Love"?
15 What was the nationality of the main character in "Braveheart"?
16 Which Hilary won Best Supporting Actress for "Boys Don't Cry"?
17 Which language was "La vita e bella in"?
18 Which was the highest-grossing Oscar-winner of the 1990s?
19 "Amadeus" was an Oscar-winner about which composer?
20 "Dances with" which animals was the third-best Oscar-winning earner of the 1990s?
21 Which mythical creature follows "Crouching Tiger, Hidden _____" in the movie title?
22 Which United studio had 13 winning films by the end of the millennium?
23 Which 1990s winner has "English" in the title?
24 In which decade was "Cabaret" a winner?
25 What sort of Games was "Chariots of Fire" about?
26 Which John won for "True Grit"?
27 Which Susan played a nun in "Dead Man Walking"?
28 How many Oscars had Julia Roberts won before "Erin Brokovich"?
29 Which Fonda won for "On Golden Pond"?
30 What type of "Foot" won for Daniel Day Lewis?

Answers | **World Tour** (see Quiz 55)

1 Virgin. 2 Switzerland. 3 Texas. 4 Salt. 5 South America. 6 New York. 7 Eskimo.
8 Rockies. 9 Africa. 10 Delhi. 11 Russian. 12 Amazon river. 13 Rhodesia. 14 Oil.
15 America. 16 Europe. 17 Africa. 18 South Africa. 19 New York. 20 Canal. 21
Canaries. 22 Long. 23 Cars. 24 Louisiana. 25 Australia. 26 Northwest. 27 Canada.
28 Cote d'Ivoire. 29 Sydney. 30 Africa.

1 "Lonely" was the first No 1 single for which rapper beginning with an A?
2 Standing down as an MP in 2005, Dr Jack Cunningham was in which party?
3 A skull and what else appeared on the Jolly Roger flag?
4 A bird's feather was used to make what type of old-fashioned pen?
5 Which country in South America is also the name of a nut?
6 What are you said to tread if you act on stage?
7 In mythology, Neptune is the god of what?
8 What type of vegetable would a vampire not eat in a vegetarian restaurant?
9 How many days are there in April and May together?
10 Which part of the egg is used to make meringues?
11 What does a somnambulist do while asleep?
12 Paul Robinson was at which club during the 2006 World Cup?
13 Who or what were druids in Ancient Britain?
14 In song, who looked out on the Feast of Stephen?
15 What is needed for a game of whist?
16 If something is there to mislead it is said to be a red type of which fish?
17 Who were the first people to settle in New Zealand?
18 What was the nationality of the thinker Archimedes?
19 Which continent has the greatest number of people?
20 What does the first C stand for in CCTV?
21 What sort of fingers does a person have who is always dropping things called?
22 How many angles are contained in a pentagon?
23 Which of the following colours is not a type of rice – black, brown or white?
24 What is the maximum number of people who can sit in a rickshaw?
25 Ratatouille is made from what type of food?
26 What does a kilowatt measure?
27 Which Jack, who died in 2001, starred in "The Odd Couple"?
28 In which season is the festival of the Passover?
29 Which popular small car was invented by Alec Issigonis?
30 Who landed on the Moon along with Neil Armstrong?

Answers	Pot Luck 25 *(see Quiz 56)*

1 Gromit. 2 Net. 3 Music. 4 Shilpa Shetty. 5 Sax. 6 University. 7 Snake. 8 The ear. 9 Bucks. 10 Palace. 11 Baseball. 12 Female. 13 Hundred Acre Wood. 14 Friends. 15 Ice hockey. 16 SEGA. 17 Haddock. 18 Virtual. 19 California. 20 Can. 21 Japan. 22 The Great. 23 Four. 24 JK Rowling. 25 1990 World Cup. 26 Billboard. 27 Ronaldo. 28 Three. 29 50. 30 UK.

Quiz 55 | World Tour

Answers – page 61

LEVEL 1

1 Which islands share their name with Richard Branson's airline?
2 Which country beginning with S borders the east of France?
3 Dallas is in which US oil state?
4 What does the Dead Sea taste of?
5 Ecuador is on which continent?
6 In which US city is the Empire State Building?
7 What is another name for Inuit?
8 What is the nickname for the Rocky Mountains?
9 Algeria is to the north of which continent?
10 Which city comprises Old Delhi and New Delhi?
11 What is the official language of Russia?
12 In Spanish it's Rio de las Amazonas, what is it in English?
13 What name did Zimbabwe have in the 1960s?
14 Saudi Arabia is famous for producing which fuel?
15 The Sioux are a native tribe of which continent?
16 Scandinavia is in which continent?
17 Which continent is the next largest after Asia?
18 Soweto is a suburb of Johannesburg in which country?
19 In which harbour is the Statue of Liberty?
20 What type of waterway is at Suez?
21 Gran Canaria is in which islands?
22 What describes the famous Beach resort in California where the "Queen Mary" was brought?
23 Los Angeles suffers from a severe smog problem due to a high percentage of which vehicles?
24 Which is the only US state to begin with L?
25 Aborigines are from which Commonwealth country?
26 In which part of the USA is Alaska?
27 Quebec is a French-speaking part of which country?
28 Which of the following used to be called the Ivory Coast – Cote d'Ivoire, Gold Coast or Rhodesia?
29 What is Australia's largest city?
30 On which continent is Swahili spoken?

Answers	**The Oscars** *(see Quiz 53)*

1 American. 2 Russia/Soviet Union. 3 Binoche. 4 Las Vegas. 5 Roberts. 6 Affleck.
7 Aniston. 8 Thompson. 9 New York. 10 80s. 11 Christie. 12 Hollywood.
13 Gladiator. 14 Gwyneth Paltrow. 15 Scottish. 16 Swank. 17 Italian. 18 Titanic.
19 Mozart. 20 Wolves. 21 Dragon. 22 Artists. 23 The English Patient. 24 1970s.
25 Olympics. 26 Wayne. 27 Sarandon. 28 None. 29 Henry. 30 My Left Foot.

1 Who is the four-legged hero in the movie "The Wrong Trousers"?
2 What is at the end of a stick in lacrosse?
3 What does the letter M stand for in MTV?
4 Which Bollywood actress won "Celebrity Big Brother" in 2007?
5 What was the surname of the inventor of the saxophone?
6 What type of institution in America was named after John Harvard?
7 Which of these has least legs – bird, kangaroo or snake?
8 Where in the body is the smallest bone?
9 Which word names male rabbits and American money?
10 Which type of building did Louis XIV have built at Versailles?
11 Which sport did Hank Aaron play?
12 In pop music is Anastacia female, male or a group?
13 Which Wood is Winnie the Pooh's home?
14 Which TV series includes the characters Phoebe and Chandler?
15 What is the fastest team game in the world?
16 The Dreamcast video game console was developed by which computer company?
17 Which fishy-sounding Captain is in the Tintin stories?
18 What does V stand for in VR?
19 In 2003 Arnold Schwarzenegger became governor of which US state?
20 Which word names a metal container and also means is able to?
21 In which country was the first CD made?
22 What name was given to the English King Alfred – The Awful, The Great or The Lionheart?
23 How many beats to the bar are there in basic rock music?
24 The character Albus Dumbledore was created by which writer?
25 The Three Tenors first sang at which sporting event?
26 What are the US pop charts called – Billboard, Groundhog or Skateboard?
27 Which R was top scorer in the 2002 FIFA World Cup?
28 In a knock-out competition how many games are left – excluding replays or third-place playoffs – after all the quarter finals are completed?
29 About how many countries are there altogether in Europe – 15, 50 or 100?
30 Which country was the first in the world to have a TV service?

Answers	Pot Luck 24 *(see Quiz 54)*

1 Akon. 2 Labour. 3 Cross bones. 4 Quill pen. 5 Brazil. 6 The boards. 7 Sea. 8 Garlic. 9 61. 10 White. 11 Walk. 12 Spurs. 13 Priests. 14 Good King Wenceslas. 15 Pack of cards. 16 Herring. 17 The Maoris. 18 Greek. 19 Asia. 20 Closed. 21 Butterfingers. 22 Five. 23 Black. 24 Two. 25 Vegetables. 26 Electrical power. 27 Lemmon. 28 Spring. 29 Mini. 30 Buzz Aldrin.

Quiz 57 | Classical Music

1 Which is the title of an opera – "The Crying Dutchman", "The Flying Ditchman" or "The Flying Dutchman"?
2 Which composer had the first names Johann Sebastian?
3 Edward Elgar was from which country?
4 What sort of music is "Tosca"?
5 How do you get a sound out of a saxophone?
6 What are the surnames of the Three Tenors?
7 Charlotte Church came from which part of the UK?
8 Which insect follows "Madame" in the title of an opera?
9 Which opera star Andrea had top-selling albums "Romanza" and "Sogno"?
10 In which city is La Scala Opera House?
11 In which venue in London do the Proms take place?
12 Which tenor Russell had a brain tumour removed in 2006?
13 Placido Domingo is particularly famous for which type of music?
14 How many performers are there in a string quartet?
15 In which country is the Sydney Opera House?
16 Which is the highest female voice?
17 What is the first name of conductor Rattle?
18 What was the name of opera singer Callas?
19 What was the nationality of Tchaikovsky?
20 What do you do to a tambourine to get a noise out of it?
21 Where do you hold a flute to play it?
22 Which is the largest of these instruments – violin, viola or double bass?
23 Which musical instrument did Sax invent?
24 Which musical instrument did Yehudi Menuhin play?
25 In which Garden is London's Royal Opera House?
26 Which overture with cannon and bell effects has a date for its title?
27 What night of the week is the Last Night of the Proms?
28 Which country does Kiri Te Kanawa come from?
29 Which is the lowest male voice?
30 "Riverdance" was based on classic, traditional dance from which country?

Answers | 21st Century News (see Quiz 59)

1 September. 2 Poisoned. 3 Labour. 4 London. 5 Conservative. 6 Hussein. 7 John Paul II. 8 Gordon Brown. 9 Rail. 10 Foot & mouth. 11 Swedish. 12 Internet. 13 Farepack. 14 Ships. 15 Alistair. 16 Three. 17 Concorde. 18 Sydney. 19 Asylum. 20 Straw. 21 Venus Williams. 22 Doctor/GP. 23 June. 24 Russia. 25 Labour. 26 Bridget Jones. 27 Florida. 28 Ann. 29 David Cameron. 30 2005.

1 Who won a Bafta for her film portrayal of Queen Elizabeth II?
2 From which country does goulash originate?
3 What can be odd, even or whole?
4 Apart from being a TV programme, what is a Blue Peter?
5 Which country starting with an S did England play in the World Cup 2006?
6 In which US state is Walt Disney World?
7 "Just do it" was featured in ads for which company products?
8 Which Peter had a hit with "Mysterious Girl" in 1996 and 2004?
9 What is a flexible diving board called?
10 The Taliban were a guerrilla group operating in which country?
11 Both World War I and World War II began in which continent?
12 What is French for ten?
13 A clutch is a collection of what?
14 The Beaufort scale identifies different speeds of what?
15 Is "Woman's Hour" on Radio 1, 2, 3 or 4?
16 In the movie title who is described as "International Man of Mystery"?
17 What are the minimum number of notes needed to produce a chord?
18 Which part of a car did John Dunlop invent?
19 In its nickname Chicago is known as what type of city?
20 What type of animal was the first to travel in space?
21 In which country was the first Marathon race run?
22 Josiah Wedgwood found fame making what?
23 What was the first name of the character Dr Lecter in "The Silence of the Lambs"?
24 The emu comes from which country?
25 Tibia and fibula are names of of what?
26 Which English county is part of Superman's secret alias?
27 What is the playing area called in a basketball match?
28 What is Bart Simpson's full first name – is it Bartram, Bartholomew or Stobart?
29 What does Costa Blanca actually mean?
30 In a pack of cards what is the Queen of Spades often known as?

Answers | Pot Luck 27 *(see Quiz 60)*

1 Chris Martin. 2 1950s. 3 61. 4 Bloody. 5 19th March. 6 Orlando Bloom. 7 Sing. 8 A boot. 9 Maize. 10 90. 11 Sloth. 12 Star Wars. 13 Bicycle. 14 Between its shoulders. 15 China's. 16 Zebra. 17 Laura. 18 Peter. 19 Exploring. 20 Tintin. 21 Grimm. 22 Tyres. 23 Bear. 24 Virgin. 25 Spots. 26 Jerzy Dudek. 27 Oz. 28 Hind. 29 Body Shop. 30 Dinosaur.

1 In which month in 2001 was the World Trade Center in New York destroyed by a terrorist attack?
2 In 2006, was the ex-Russian spy Alexander Litvinenko knifed, poisoned or shot?
3 David Blunkett became Home Secretary for which party?
4 In which city did the ill-fated Millennium Dome open?
5 Jailed peer Lord Archer was Deputy Chairman of which political party?
6 Which Saddam led Iraq into the 21st century?
7 Which Pope died in April 2005?
8 Which Chancellor gave the first Budget of the new millennium?
9 What sort of crash at Hatfield caused travel problems for many months?
10 Tony Blair postponed the 2001 General Election because of which farming disaster?
11 What nationality was the full-time England soccer manager who succeeded Kevin Keegan?
12 How did the Kilshaws adopt baby twin girls?
13 Which major Christmas savings club collapsed in 2006?
14 Cammell Laird, which called in the receivers in 2001, manufactured what?
15 Which Campbell was Tony Blair's press secretary?
16 How many children did Madonna have when she married Guy Ritchie?
17 Which supersonic aircraft was grounded in 2000 after crashing outside Paris?
18 Where were the 2000 Olympic Games held?
19 Which seekers were apprehended in the Channel Tunnel?
20 Which Jack replaced Robin Cook as Foreign Secretary?
21 Which sister of Serena won the first two Ladies' Singles Championships of the 21st century at Wimbledon?
22 What was the profession of convicted mass murderer Harold Shipman?
23 In which month did the 2001 UK General Election take place?
24 Vladimir Putin became head of state of which country?
25 Standing down as an MP in 2005, Tony Banks was in which party?
26 Whose film "Diary" broke all box office records when it opened in 2001?
27 Results in which sunshine state held the result of the US Presidential election?
28 Which Shadow Home Secretary Widdecombe published a novel?
29 In 2006 which David took a cycle ride to Westminster, as the chauffeur-driven car followed?
30 In which year did Prince Charles marry Camilla Parker Bowles – 2000, 2003 or 2005?

Answers	**Classical Music** *(see Quiz 57)*

1 The Flying Dutchman. 2 Bach. 3 England. 4 Opera. 5 Blow it. 6 Carreras, Domingo, Pavarotti. 7 Wales. 8 Butterfly. 9 Bocelli. 10 Milan. 11 Albert Hall. 12 Russell Watson. 13 Opera. 14 Four. 15 Australia. 16 Soprano. 17 Simon. 18 Maria. 19 Russian. 20 Shake it. 21 To the side. 22 Double bass. 23 Saxophone. 24 Violin. 25 Covent Garden. 26 1812. 27 Saturday. 28 New Zealand. 29 Bass. 30 Ireland.

1 Which Chris is the lead vocalist for Coldplay?

2 John F Kennedy became President of the USA in which decade?

3 How many days are there in June and July together?

4 What gruesome adjective was given to Mary I?

5 What is the date that is two days after Saint Patrick's day?

6 Which Orlando was Legolas Greenleaf in the "Lord of the Rings" films?

7 If a lady is a soprano what does she do?

8 What is named after the Duke of Wellington – a type of boot, a metal helmet or a breed of dog?

9 What is popcorn made from?

10 A right-angled triangle contains one angle that must be how many degrees?

11 Which creature has a name that means idle and lazy?

12 Which sci-fi movie was Harrison Ford's first film?

13 Miguel Indurain was a record-breaker on what sort of vehicle?

14 Where on a horse are its withers?

15 In 1989 which country's students protested in Tianenmen Square?

16 Which of these is not a member of the cat family – panther, tiger or zebra?

17 What is the first name of President George W Bush's wife?

18 What was the name of the Russian Tsar who founded St Petersburg?

19 Captain James Cook became famous for doing what – cooking, exploring or swimming underwater?

20 Which cartoon young hero did Belgian Hergé create?

21 What was the last name of the fairy tale collecting brothers Jacob and Wilhelm?

22 Charles Goodyear developed what important item for cars?

23 Which animal is included in the nickname of Jack Nicklaus?

24 Which record company was founded by Richard Branson?

25 What type of markings does a cheetah have?

26 Which keeper Jerzy was Liverpool's hero in the 2005 Champions League final?

27 Which land contained a Yellow Brick Road?

28 Explorer Francis Drake had a ship called "The Golden" what?

29 Which environmentally friendly shop did Anita Roddick found?

30 A diplodocus was a type of what – a counting frame, a dinosaur or a steam bath from Roman times?

Answers	Pot Luck 26 *(see Quiz 58)*

1 Helen Mirren. 2 Hungary. 3 A number. 4 Flag. 5 Sweden. 6 Florida. 7 Nike. 8 Peter Andre. 9 Springboard. 10 Afghanistan. 11 Europe. 12 Dix. 13 Eggs. 14 Wind. 15 Radio 4. 16 Austin Powers. 17 Two. 18 Tyres. 19 Windy. 20 Dog. 21 Greece. 22 Pottery. 23 Hannibal. 24 Australia. 25 Bones. 26 Kent. 27 Court. 28 Bartholomew. 29 White Coast. 30 The Black Lady.

1 Judith Keppel was the first million-pound winner of what?
2 What is the Duke of Edinburgh's first name?
3 Which Al Fayed bought Harrods?
4 What is the first name of Lady Archer, wife of the disgraced peer?
5 Which blonde Ball had a baby called Woody?
6 Which Robbie's name was linked with Geri Halliwell?
7 Raymond Blanc is a rich and famous what?
8 Which train service is Richard Branson most associated with?
9 Which Ms Campbell was a supermodel in the 1990s and 2000s?
10 Which Whitney filed for divorce from Bobby Brown in 2006?
11 What is the Countess of Wessex's first name?
12 What is Prince Michael of Kent's wife called?
13 Which Ms Kidd was one of the faces of the Nineties?
14 What is the nickname of Ms Legge Bourke, former "nanny" to Princes William and Harry?
15 Which Peter had to resign from the Cabinet because of the purchase of a house in Notting Hill?
16 Which TV cook Smith has her own on-line service?
17 Which Palmer-Tomkinson has been dubbed the It Girl?
18 What is the first name of Princess Beatrice's mother?
19 Which Catherine did Michael Douglas marry?
20 Which TV interviewer is Lady Carina Frost's husband?
21 Was Nell McAndrew's boy named Devon, Durham or Essex?
22 Ex-King Constantine was King of which European country?
23 Which William led the Conservative Party to defeat in the 2001 election?
24 Who is Prince William's younger brother?
25 Which 007 Roger had a father who was a policeman?
26 Cake-maker and actress Jane Asher has what colour hair?
27 What is the first name of tennis star and product endorser Ms Sharapova?
28 Which was the first of the Williams sisters to win the Wimbledon singles title?
29 Who is Jermaine Jackson's more famous younger brother?
30 Which Elton collected a Disney Legends award in 2006?

Answers	TV Greats *(see Quiz 63)*

1 Attenborough. 2 Thaw. 3 Monk. 4 Keeping Up Appearances. 5 Coltrane. 6 Yorkshire. 7 Square. 8 The Good Life. 9 Three. 10 David Frost. 11 Friends. 12 Dog. 13 French. 14 Flowerpot men. 15 Sybil. 16 ER. 17 Afternoon. 18 Porridge. 19 Doctor. 20 Red. 21 Tell a story. 22 Four. 23 Police. 24 New York. 25 Two. 26 Barker. 27 Perrin. 28 Dibley. 29 Charles. 30 Barrister (lawyer).

Quiz 62 | Pot Luck 28

Answers – page 72

1 Ronaldinho played for which 2006 Champions League final winners?
2 How many kings are there on a chessboard at the start of a game?
3 How many do you score in darts with all three arrows in double top?
4 Which Pole was explorer Amundsen the first to reach?
5 What is the name for plant and animal remains preserved in rock?
6 Which Robert who died in 2006 directed the movie "Gosford Park"?
7 Would you expect an animator to collect beer mats, make cartoon movies or search for jewels?
8 What is the nationality of most Popes?
9 Sally Ride was the first American woman to travel where?
10 What was the surname of Wild West outlaw brothers Frank and Jesse?
11 What was the name of Pierre Curie's scientist wife?
12 Terrell Davis is famous for which sport?
13 How many different vowels are there in the word relieved?
14 How does twenty past six pm appear on a 24-hour clock?
15 What is the Paris's underground railway system called?
16 Which imaginary line goes across the middle of Africa?
17 Which term is used to describe developing countries?
18 What is the sparsely populated region of Australia called?
19 What do you collect if you are a philatelist?
20 In which country is the Ganges a sacred river?
21 Papyrus was an early form of what everyday item?
22 In "Peter Pan", how many hands does Captain Hook have?
23 WHO is the world what organisation?
24 What do you do if you take part in a mazurka?
25 Actors and actresses join which trade union?
26 Which former England soccer boss has also managed Ipswich, Porto, Barcelona and Newcastle?
27 What are dried to make prunes?
28 In the 1960s, "The Shrimp" was the nickname given to a famous what?
29 Channel 4 broadcast a biopic about which Royal in November 2005?
30 How many rings are linked in the symbol for the Olympic Games?

Answers | Pot Luck 29 *(see Quiz 64)*

1 Pie. 2 (South) Yorkshire. 3 Arctic. 4 Walk. 5 Madeleine Albright. 6 Green. 7 Poles. 8 Eating in binges. 9 Panther. 10 East. 11 Giraffe. 12 Herd. 13 Wane. 14 Dan Maskell. 15 Home page. 16 Two. 17 Japan. 18 Monkey. 19 Atlantic. 20 Star Wars. 21 Coach. 22 Pasta. 23 A pole. 24 Earthquakes. 25 Kentucky. 26 Whales. 27 Novelist. 28 Pacific. 29 Green. 30 Lopez.

Quiz 63 | TV Greats

Answers – page 69

1 Which David with a famous brother investigated "The Private Life of Plants"?
2 Which John played Kavanagh QC?
3 What was the profession of Cadfael?
4 In which series might Hyacinth have tried to impress Emmet?
5 Which Robbie found fame as Cracker?
6 The classic "All Creatures Great and Small" was set in which county?
7 What shape was the medallion on a "Jim'll Fix It" badge?
8 Which 1970s sitcom was set in The Avenue, Surbiton?
9 How many Goodies were there?
10 Who fronted "The Frost Report"?
11 Which Channel 4 modern classic featured six New York chums?
12 What was the most famous pet in "Frasier"?
13 Who is the brunette in "French & Saunders"?
14 What type of Men were Bill and Ben?
15 What was the name of Mrs Basil Fawlty?
16 How is the drama set in a US Emergency Room better known?
17 At what time of day was "Emmerdale Farm" first screened?
18 "Going Straight" was the sequel to which hugely popular Ronnie Barker sitcom?
19 In the original "Heartbeat" what was the profession of Nick's wife?
20 What colour was Inspector Morse's Jaguar?
21 What did stars do on "Jackanory"?
22 How many candles are asked for in the classic "Two Ronnies" shop sketch?
23 "Juliet Bravo" was a popular series about someone in which profession?
24 In which city did Kojak work?
25 How many males shared a flat in "Men Behaving Badly"?
26 Which Ronnie played Arkwright in "Open All Hours"?
27 Which Reginald was played by the late Leonard Rossiter?
28 Alice was married by a female Vicar in which village?
29 Which Prince was interviewed by Jonathan Dimbleby in "The Private Man, the Public Role"?
30 What was the profession of TV great Horace Rumpole?

Answers	Rich and Famous (see Quiz 61)

1 Who Wants to be a Millionaire? 2 Philip. 3 Mohammed. 4 Mary. 5 Zoe. 6 Williams. 7 Chef. 8 Virgin. 9 Naomi. 10 Whitney Houston. 11 Sophie. 12 Princess Michael. 13 Jodie. 14 Tiggy. 15 Mandelson. 16 Delia. 17 Tara. 18 Sarah. 19 Zeta Jones. 20 David. 21 Devon. 22 Greece. 23 Hague. 24 Harry. 25 Moore. 26 Red. 27 Maria. 28 Venus. 29 Michael. 30 Elton John.

Quiz 64 | Pot Luck 29

Quiz 64 | Pot Luck 29 | Answers – page 70

1 What sort of chart presents data seen as slices of a circle – a cake chart, a flow chart or a pie chart?
2 In which county was "The Full Monty" set?
3 The Inuit live around which ocean?
4 Aleksey Leonov was the first man to do what in space?
5 Which Madeleine was the first woman US Secretary of State?
6 What colour is a banana before it is ripe to eat?
7 What are the ends of a magnet called?
8 A bulimia sufferer has an urge to do what?
9 What name is given to a leopard that is coloured black?
10 Lake Tanganyika is in which part of Africa – east, north or south?
11 Which of these creatures has its head furthest from the ground – giraffe, gorilla or rhinoceros?
12 What is the term for a group of elephants?
13 The Moon is said to wax and what else?
14 Which late Dan was the BBC's voice of tennis from the 1950s to the 1990s?
15 What is the introductory page of a web site known as?
16 Excluding borders, how many different colours appear on a chess board playing area?
17 In which country were the Winter Olympics held when they were staged in Nagano?
18 A howler is what type of creature?
19 At the beginning of the last century, Marconi sent radio signals across which ocean?
20 Which "Star" movie was the biggest box office success of the 1970s?
21 In the pantomime "Cinderella", what is the pumpkin turned into?
22 Are Conchiglie and Rigatoni types of cheese, types of pasta or famous soccer strikers once of Juventus?
23 What is used to propel a punt?
24 What does a seismologist study?
25 In which state is the Derby, which is part of the USA's thoroughbred Triple Crown, run?
26 Which mammals will expire when stranded on dry land?
27 Was Iris Murdoch, the subject of the movie "Iris", an actress, nurse or novelist?
28 In which ocean is the US state of Hawaii?
29 In board games, what colour is the Reverend in Cluedo?
30 Which Jennifer did a voiceover in "Antz"?

Answers | Pot Luck 28 *(see Quiz 62)*

1 Barcelona. 2 Two. 3 120. 4 North Pole. 5 Fossils. 6 Robert Altman. 7 Make cartoons. 8 Italian. 9 Space. 10 James. 11 Marie. 12 American Football. 13 Two. 14 18.20. 15 Metro. 16 Equator. 17 Third World. 18 Outback. 19 Stamps. 20 India. 21 Paper. 22 One. 23 World Health. 24 Dance. 25 Equity. 26 Bobby Robson. 27 Plums. 28 Model. 29 Princess Margaret. 30 Five.

1 Which Denise won Heptathlon gold in Sydney?
2 How was record-breaking baseball star Henry Louis Aaron better known?
3 Who scored the goal which took England into the 2002 World Cup Finals?
4 Which Jack was the first golfer to win six US Masters titles?
5 Peter Shilton played a record number of soccer matches in which position?
6 In which country was tennis star Greg Ruzedski born?
7 Maurice Greene was part of the gold-medal-winning 4x100m. relay team in Sydney for which nation?
8 The Chicago Cubs and Chicago White Sox are cross-city rivals in which sport?
9 In which country was England's 5–1 win over Germany in 2001?
10 What type of golfers compete for the Solheim Cup?
11 Which country has won soccer's World Cup more than any other?
12 Which American has won the Men's Singles at Wimbledon more than any other man?
13 Merlene Ottey has won 14 World Championship medals in what sport?
14 How is Eldrick Woods better known?
15 Which soccer side won the FA Cup, the Premier League and the European Champions League in 1999?
16 Which Martina is Wimbledon's most successful Ladies' Champion?
17 What did Ed Moses jump over to win world records between 1977 and 1987?
18 How many were in the boat in which Steve Redgrave won his fifth Olympic gold?
19 In 2006 which Frenchman Robert played his last game for Arsenal?
20 Joe Montana and Dan Marino were high-profile stars of which sport in the 1980s and 1990s?
21 Which Chris won the French Open tennis title seven times?
22 Which driver Alain was dubbed "The Professor of the Track"?
23 Was Krisztina Egerszegi cold or wet when she won her five Olympic gold medals?
24 In which decade was the first Rugby League World Cup held?
25 In what colour shirts do India play floodlit cricket matches?
26 Where did the US women's basketball team win Olympic gold immediately after Atlanta?
27 In June 2000, which young American won golf's US Open by 15 strokes?
28 What colour was the ball in the 1966 World Cup?
29 Dawn Fraser won four Olympic gold medals for which Olympic host?
30 The 2006 Ryder Cup was staged at the K Club, in which country?

Answers	Movie Memories *(see Quiz 67)*

1 Arthur. 2 Eastwood. 3 Meg Ryan. 4 Deer. 5 Marilyn Monroe. 6 Grace Kelly. 7 US. 8 Henry VIII. 9 Harrison. 10 Notting Hill. 11 Mrs Robinson. 12 Rosanna. 13 Cat. 14 Ballet. 15 Streetcar. 16 Ghostbusters. 17 Psycho. 18 Disney. 19 Newman. 20 Purple. 21 Shut. 22 Lemmon. 23 Andrews. 24 Ewan. 25 Notting Hill. 26 Paris. 27 Powers. 28 Hairdresser. 29 Natalie Wood. 30 Star Wars.

1 Which country's capital is on the Potomac river?

2 In Italy what is mascarpone?

3 Which Glenn took over from Graeme Souness as Newcastle boss in 2006?

4 Where would you go to visit the Sea of Tranquillity?

5 To get past a portcullis would you go over it, through it or under it?

6 What was the first name of brilliant physicist Einstein?

7 In which of these countries is there not a place called Halifax – Canada, Austria or England?

8 Which creature may be Golden or Bald?

9 What sort of Detective was Ace Ventura?

10 Which colour can be linked with admiral, card and flag?

11 Which spirit was mixed with water to make grog?

12 When texting, how is the word text usually written?

13 Which English city has given its name to a bun and a wheelchair?

14 How old was Marlon Brando when he died in 2004 – 60, 70 or 80?

15 Cape Horn is at the southern tip of which continent?

16 Mandarin is a form of which world language?

17 What was the first No 1 hit on both sides of the Atlantic for the Spice Girls?

18 The English king Alfred was said to have burnt what?

19 What is the most eaten food in Asia?

20 Who went straight to No 1 in the US with "Fantasy"?

21 Which soccer star advertised Brylcreem then had his head shaved?

22 How many years are involved if a silver celebration is two years away?

23 Which part of his own body did painter Van Gogh cut off?

24 Gottlieb Daimler gave his name to what type of transport?

25 Who wrote the children's story "Matilda"?

26 Writer JM Barrie was the central character in which movie?

27 Bill Gates was head of which computer company?

28 What kind of creatures inhabited the Lake in Tchaikovsky's ballet music?

29 Which 1990s champion was named after tennis great Martina Navratilova?

30 Leonardo DiCaprio starred in "The Man in the Iron" what?

Answers | Pot Luck 31 *(see Quiz 68)*

1 Venice. 2 Blow it. 3 X. 4 Spain. 5 Moss. 6 Emergency. 7 Red. 8 Monte Carlo. 9 521. 10 Australia. 11 Shark. 12 Space. 13 Israel. 14 Skiing. 15 Round. 16 Music. 17 Dried fruit. 18 Horse. 19 Cathy Freeman. 20 Peter Jackson. 21 New Zealand. 22 Who's there?. 23 Hay Fever. 24 Mad. 25 Playing cards. 26 Running. 27 Furniture. 28 Golf. 29 Heart. 30 Washington.

1 "Arthur 2: On the Rocks" was the sequel to what?

2 Which Clint appeared in "Coogan's Bluff"?

3 Which actress fakes an orgasm at a diner in "When Harry Met Sally"?

4 Which "Hunter" had the Vietnam war as its subject matter?

5 Who was the famous blonde in "Bus Stop"?

6 Which future movie princess starred in "High Noon"?

7 Which country's Cavalry is John Ford's "Rio Grande" about?

8 "Carry On Henry" was a Carry On spoof about which English King?

9 Which Ford was "The Fugitive" on the big screen?

10 Which part of London, famous for its carnival, shares its name with a Hugh Grant movie?

11 How does Dustin Hoffman always address Mrs Robinson in "The Graduate"?

12 Which Arquette starred in "Pulp Fiction"?

13 What animal goes before "Ballou" in the movie title?

14 What type of shoes were the "Red Shoes"?

15 What was named "Desire" in the movie with Marlon Brando?

16 What sort of busters were the subject of a movie with Dan Aykroyd?

17 In which movie did Janet Leigh play Marion Crane?

18 Which studio made "The Lion King"?

19 Which Paul starred opposite real wife Joanne Woodward in "Mr & Mrs Bridge"?

20 "The Color" was what in the 1985 Steven Spielberg movie?

21 How were "Eyes Wide" in Stanley Kubrick's final movie?

22 Which Jack, who died in 2001, starred in "Missing"?

23 Which Julie starred in two of the top five box office musical successes of the 1960s?

24 Which McGregor played the young Obi-Wan Kenobi in "The Phantom Menace"?

25 Which Hill was trailed as "an equal not a sequel" to "Four Weddings and a Funeral"?

26 Where was Marlon Brando's "Last Tango" in the 1970s?

27 Which Austin was played by Mike Myers?

28 What was Warren Beatty's job in "Shampoo"?

29 Which actress was on the poster for "West Side Story"?

30 Which sci-fi movie was the biggest box office success of the 1970s?

Answers	**Sporting Action Replay** *(see Quiz 65)*

1 Lewis. 2 Hank. 3 David Beckham. 4 Nicklaus. 5 Goalkeeper. 6 Canada. 7 USA. 8 Baseball. 9 Germany. 10 Professional ladies. 11 Brazil. 12 Pete Sampras. 13 Athletics. 14 Tiger Woods. 15 Manchester United. 16 Navratilova. 17 Hurdles. 18 Four. 19 Robert Pires. 20 American football. 21 Evert. 22 Prost. 23 Wet (she is a swimmer). 24 1950s. 25 Blue. 26 Sydney. 27 Tiger Woods. 28 Orange. 29 Australia. 30 Ireland.

1 In which watery city is the Bridge of Sighs?

2 How would you get a note out of a bassoon?

3 Which letter is a Roman numerals and used in grading movies for viewing suitability?

4 The island of Majorca belongs to which country?

5 Which model Kate became the face of L'Oreal in 1998?

6 In a hospital what does E stand for in ER?

7 In the movies what colour is Superman's cape?

8 Which part of Monaco is famous for its car rally?

9 How many weeks are there in ten years?

10 The Murray is the main river of which country?

11 What sort of creature was the villain in the blockbuster movie "Jaws"?

12 Helen Sharman was the first female from the UK to go where?

13 In which country is there a Parliament called the Knesset?

14 Franz Klammer found fame in which sport?

15 What shape is a bagel?

16 In which branch of the creative arts did Stravinsky find fame?

17 What is mincemeat made from?

18 A mustang is a wild what?

19 Which famous Australian lit the Olympic torch in Sydney?

20 Which Peter directed the "Lord of the Rings" series of movies?

21 Which of these countries is the furthest south – India, Japan or New Zealand?

22 What is always the second line of a "Knock knock" joke?

23 People suffer when the pollen count is high if they have which fever?

24 In "Alice in Wonderland" which word is used to describe The Hatter?

25 What is needed for a game of canasta?

26 How did Maurice Greene win gold at Sydney 2000?

27 Thomas Chippendale was famous for making what?

28 Paul Azinger is linked to which sport?

29 In 1967 Christiaan Barnard performed the first transplant of what?

30 Which American city was named after the country's first President?

---

1 What is an anchovy?
2 What would you find in the middle of a damson?
3 Darjeeling is a type of what?
4 Guinness was first made in which Irish city?
5 What is endive?
6 What would you do with a claret?
7 Saffron tinges food what colour?
8 Which vegetable shares its name with a fruit drink?
9 Which village in Leicestershire gives its name to a classic British blue cheese?
10 All citrus fruits are rich in which vitamin?
11 The island of Madeira shares its name with a cake and also what?
12 What colour is root ginger?
13 What are the tops of asparagus called?
14 Which of the following are not types of tomatoes – plum, orange, cherry?
15 What is rocket?
16 What is the most common fuel for a barbecue?
17 Sirloin is which meat?
18 What ingredient is balsamic?
19 What is the most common colour of an aubergine's skin?
20 Which food item is sold at London's Billingsgate market?
21 How is white wine usually served?
22 Mangetout and sugar snaps are types of what?
23 What is feta?
24 If coffee is drunk without milk or cream how is it described?
25 Which Earl gave his name to a type of mild tea?
26 Ciabatta bread originated in which country?
27 What sort of wine is chardonnay?
28 A shallot is a type of what?
29 What shape is the pasta used to make lasagne?
30 Seville is famous for which fruit used to make marmalade?

Answers	Sea Life *(see Quiz 71)*

1 Fish. 2 Skate. 3 Blue whale. 4 Shell. 5 Calf. 6 Sharks. 7 Lobster. 8 Portuguese. 9 Eight. 10 In the sea. 11 None. 12 Osprey. 13 Gills. 14 Herring. 15 10. 16 In the sea. 17 Whale. 18 Milk. 19 97%. 20 Poor. 21 Blubber. 22 Oxygen. 23 Cod. 24 White. 25 12%. 26 Sturgeon. 27 Shark. 28 Gold. 29 Blowhole. 30 Lobster.

1 Which group of people first developed central heating?
2 Which Margaret became Foreign Secretary of the UK?
3 Which country does supermodel Kate Moss come from?
4 In the movie "Beethoven" what sort of animal saves the day?
5 If the first of a month is a Tuesday what day will the tenth be?
6 In a building what can be made from thatch, slates or tiles?
7 Which country in the world has the most computers?
8 How did Marion Jones first win gold at Sydney 2000?
9 In the theatre who stands in for an actor or actress?
10 Which branch of science was Einstein famous for?
11 What colour was Queen Elizabeth I's hair?
12 Which James Bond actor was born on the same day as first man on the moon Neil Armstrong?
13 How many pieces of bread are used to make a club sandwich?
14 What name is given to an extra file sent with an e mail?
15 Who wrote the children's book "Charlotte's Web"?
16 In grammar what sort of word describes another word?
17 What does Giorgio Armani design?
18 Roger Bannister was the first man to run a mile in less than how many minutes?
19 Which bird can go before the words holed and toed?
20 Which Colin played the title role in Oliver Stone's movie "Alexander"?
21 In which month of the year is Father's Day in the UK?
22 The novel "Watership Down" is about a colony of what?
23 What is the lead ballerina in a company called?
24 How many people play in a game of backgammon?
25 What is fi short for in hi-fi?
26 Where are the highest notes on a piano keyboard – to the far left, the far right, or in the middle?
27 What is the the name of the toy dinosaur in "Toy Story"?
28 Mark Antony was in love with which famous queen?
29 What is the currency of Belgium?
30 Which Hilton heiress is named after a European capital city?

1 The whale shark is the largest what?

2 Which fish shares its name with a sports boot?

3 What is the name of the heaviest mammal which lives in the sea?

4 A mollusc's body is covered in what?

5 What is a baby whale called?

6 Great white and hammerhead are types of what?

7 Which one of these creature has pincers – dolphin, lobster or seal?

8 Which nationality Man o' War is a sea creature?

9 The word octo means an octopus has how many tentacles?

10 Where would you find plankton?

11 How many legs does a seahorse have?

12 Which of these is not a fish – cod, osprey or perch?

13 A fish breathes through what?

14 A sardine is a young what?

15 How many tentacles does a squid have?

16 Where does a marine creature live?

17 Blue, fin and humpback are all types of what?

18 What do marine mammals feed their babies on?

19 Approximately how much of the Earth's water is in the oceans – 67%, 87% or 97%?

20 Which term best describes the eyesight of a whale – excellent, outstanding or poor?

21 What is the name for a whale's layer of fat?

22 What do fish absorb through their gills?

23 Which fish was at the centre of the so-called fishing Wars involving Great Britain and Iceland?

24 What colour fur does a baby grey seal have?

25 How much of an iceberg is visible on or above the surface of the sea – 12%, 50% or 90%?

26 Caviar is the name given to which fish's eggs, seen by many as a great delicacy?

27 Nurse and tiger are both types of what?

28 Which of the following is not a type of whale – Blue, Gold or White?

29 Which hole helps a dolphin to breathe?

30 Which of the following is the crayfish related to – lobster, sardine or whale?

Answers	Food and Drink (see Quiz 69)

1 Fish. 2 Stone. 3 Tea. 4 Dublin. 5 Salad plant. 6 Drink it. 7 Yellow. 8 Squash. 9 Stilton. 10 C. 11 A wine. 12 Brown. 13 Spears. 14 Orange. 15 Salad leaf. 16 Charcoal. 17 Beef. 18 Vinegar. 19 Purple. 20 Fish. 21 Chilled. 22 Peas. 23 Cheese. 24 Black. 25 Grey. 26 Italy. 27 White. 28 Onion. 29 Rectangular. 30 Oranges.

1 On which instrument might a roll be played?
2 When was the Ryder Cup first played at an Irish course?
3 Which Emma starred in, and wrote the screenplay for "Nanny McPhee"?
4 Which number on a dartboard is furthest from the ceiling?
5 The zodiac sign of Aquarius covers which two months?
6 Which sport is also a type of shirt collar?
7 What is usually served from a tureen?
8 On a keyboard which letter is directly below 3 and 4?
9 Where would you be if you were on a pommel horse?
10 What was the first name of Bond girl actress Andress?
11 A kilogram is a measure of what?
12 According to the song "Do-Ray-Mi", ray is a drop of what?
13 What is the pattern on gingham material?
14 Which word went before George in the name of the Culture Club lead singer?
15 Cent before a word relates to which number?
16 Near which city did Concorde crash on takeoff in 2000?
17 What does a librettist write?
18 What would you be displaying if you took part in Crufts?
19 In a suit of armour which parts of the body did the visor protect?
20 Noah's Ark was believed to have struck land at which Mount?
21 How many months of the year begin with a letter T?
22 What colour is the inside of a coconut?
23 How is @ pronounced in an e mail address?
24 A scarab, an Egyptian good luck charm, was shaped like which creature?
25 What is the term for a satellite's path round the Earth?
26 What name was given to the practice of kidnapping people to join the navy?
27 How is model Tracey Jane McAndrew better known?
28 What is a group of geese called?
29 Eggplant is another name for what?
30 Which Neil is the voice of Bob the Builder?

Answers | **Pot Luck 32** *(see Quiz 70)*

1 Romans. 2 Margaret Beckett. 3 England. 4 St Bernard dog. 5 Thursday. 6 Roof. 7 USA. 8 Running. 9 Understudy. 10 Physics. 11 Red. 12 Sean Connery. 13 Three. 14 Attachment. 15 EB White. 16 Adjective. 17 Clothes. 18 Four. 19 Pigeon. 20 Colin Farrell. 21 June. 22 Rabbits. 23 Prima ballerina. 24 Two. 25 Fidelity. 26 Far right. 27 Rex. 28 Cleopatra. 29 Franc. 30 Paris.

1 Which group gazed at "Waterloo Sunset"?
2 Which Elvis hit was about a letter without a reply?
3 The Dakotas were not from Dakota; which UK city did they hail from?
4 Elvis's "Wooden Heart" was based on a folk song from which country?
5 Which Gerry & The Pacemakers No 1 became a football anthem?
6 What went with "Needles" in the title of a Searchers hit?
7 How many Beatles were there when they had their very first No 1?
8 Which word followed "Do Wah Diddy" in the title of a Manfred Mann hit?
9 What type of alpine singing featured on Frank Ifield's "I Remember You"?
10 Was Peter Noone 16, 26 or 36 when he fronted Herman's Hermits?
11 Who could get "No Satisfaction" in 1965?
12 Which musical instrument was played by most of The Shadows?
13 How many people were there in Dave Clark's band?
14 Which famous daughter sang "These Boots are Made for Walkin'"?
15 Which US west coast city was the subject of several hippy songs of the mid-1960s?
16 Who wrote Roy Orbison's recording of "Only the Lonely"?
17 What did the Beatles sing they "Want to Hold" in the title of 1964 No 1 single?
18 Which Boys had "Good Vibrations" in 1966?
19 Which Cliff Richard hit became a standard song for celebratory occasions?
20 How many Everly Brothers were there?
21 What sort of "Children" did Billy J Kramer sing about?
22 Which Beatles song about a certain type of writer was released shortly after their last live concert?
23 How many Tops were there?
24 According to Eddie Cochran, how many "Steps to Heaven" were there?
25 What was "My Old Man" according to Lonnie Donegan in 1960?
26 On which fruity label was The Beatles' "Hey Jude" released?
27 Which "bandits" backed Johnny Kidd?
28 Who went to No 1 with "I Heard It Through the Grapevine" in 1969?
29 Which Liverpool lady went to No 1 with "Anyone Who Had a Heart"?
30 What sort of "Women" gave the Rolling Stones their eighth No 1?

Answers	Late Greats *(see Quiz 75)*

1 Barbara. 2 Yates. 3 Esther Rantzen. 4 Sammy. 5 London. 6 Wilde. 7 Sport. 8 Motor cycle. 9 London. 10 Spy. 11 Blyton. 12 Victoria. 13 Hailsham. 14 Shaving accessories. 15 Adam. 16 Charles. 17 Film. 18 Germany. 19 Jane. 20 France. 21 Richard. 22 The Galaxy. 23 Linda. 24 Albert. 25 Children. 26 Clothes. 27 Cello. 28 Paul. 29 Fables. 30 John F Kennedy.

1 "Setting Sun" and "Block Rockin' Beats" were No 1s for which Brothers?
2 In Australia what is a jumbuck?
3 In "The Magic Roundabout" what kind of creature was Dougal?
4 What colour are triple-word squares in Scrabble?
5 What person would be a member of RIBA?
6 Which day of the year is described as Ash?
7 In "Oliver!" which character sings "As Long as He Needs Me"?
8 Who in 2005 became Arsenal's leading league scorer of all time?
9 What used to be sold by an apothecary?
10 Early Giant, Figaro and Nantes are types of which vegetable?
11 How many black cards are there in a standard pack of playing cards?
12 In printing, what are uppercase letters?
13 In which country is Zurich?
14 In the Bible which book follows directly after Genesis?
15 What is mulligatawny – an Irish port, a small owl or a type of soup?
16 What do you withdraw from an ATM?
17 Which French royal family share their name with a biscuit?
18 In the past in a hospital what was ether used for?
19 Is a kumquat a fruit or a vegetable?
20 Aloha means hello and goodbye on which island?
21 Which number upside down looks like an E on a calculator's LCD?
22 What is the term for an empty space from which air is removed?
23 Which word links a seaside confection and stone?
24 Were Luddites machine wreckers or prison reformers?
25 Which Disney fantasy film and stage show featured the song "Be Our Guest"?
26 What do the numbers on one standard die/dice total?
27 In medicine what is the term for the exchange of blood?
28 The feet of zebras take what form?
29 If Christmas Day was a Wednesday on what day would the following New Year's Day fall?
30 Foods do not brown in what type of oven?

Answers	**Pot Luck 35** *(see Quiz 76)*

1 7. 2 John McEnroe. 3 Park Lane. 4 Before. 5 Hoops. 6 Alicia Keys. 7 Game. 8 Horse. 9 Top row. 10 Black. 11 Skull. 12 Three. 13 Gerard Houllier. 14 Magnus Magnusson. 15 Bees. 16 Eleanor Rigby. 17 Turkey. 18 U. 19 Edelweiss. 20 December. 21 New York. 22 Snail mail. 23 1960s. 24 Lion. 25 Diamonds. 26 Modem. 27 Bernie Taupin. 28 South Africa. 29 Vatican City. 30 Shearer.

1 What was the first name of prolific novelist Ms Cartland?
2 Who was the ex-Mrs Geldof Paula?
3 Desmond Wilcox was the husband of which chat show hostess and TV presenter?
4 Which entertainer Davis added Junior to his name?
5 In which British capital city did Lord Olivier have a theatre named after him?
6 Which playwright Oscar is on the cover of The Beatles' "Sgt Pepper" album?
7 Which type of TV show did Helen Rollason present?
8 What type of transport did Jennifer Paterson use in her TV cookery series?
9 In which city was Jill Dando murdered?
10 Kim Philby found notoriety as a what?
11 Which Enid wrote the Noddy books?
12 Which Queen said, "We are not amused"?
13 Which Lord sat in Parliament as Quintin Hogg?
14 King Camp Gillette pioneered which grooming aid?
15 According to Jewish and Christian teaching, who was the very first person?
16 Which Darwin set out his theory of evolution?
17 For which branch of the arts was James Dean famous?
18 In which country was actress Marlene Dietrich born?
19 What was the first name of novelist Miss Austen?
20 In which country did Princess Diana tragically die?
21 What was the first name of the late broadcaster Dimbleby, father of David and Jonathan?
22 The late Douglas Adams wrote about "The Hitch Hiker's Guide" to where?
23 What was the name of Lady McCartney, wife of Sir Paul, who died from breast cancer?
24 Who was Queen Victoria's consort?
25 Roald Dahl mainly wrote stories for whom?
26 Christian Dior was famous for designing what?
27 Jacqueline Du Pré, whose story was told in the movie "Hilary and Jackie", played which musical instrument?
28 Which actor Eddington found fame in "The Good Life" and "Yes Minister"?
29 What did Aesop write?
30 Which assassinated leader of the USA was the first Catholic to be elected as President?

Answers	Sounds of the Sixties *(see Quiz 73)*

1 The Kinks. 2 Return to Sender. 3 Liverpool. 4 Germany. 5 You'll Never Walk Alone. 6 Pins. 7 Four. 8 Diddy. 9 Yodelling. 10 16. 11 Rolling Stones. 12 Guitar. 13 Five. 14 Nancy Sinatra. 15 San Francisco. 16 Roy Orbison. 17 Your Hand. 18 Beach Boys. 19 Congratulations. 20 Two. 21 Little. 22 Paperback Writer. 23 Four. 24 Three. 25 Dustman. 26 Apple. 27 The Pirates. 28 Marvin Gaye. 29 Cilla Black. 30 Honky Tonk.

Quiz 76 | Pot Luck 35

Answers – page 82

1 How many Days were in the title of Craig David's 2000 No 1?
2 Which sportsman said quite seriously, "You cannot be serious"?
3 In Monopoly what makes a set with Mayfair?
4 What does pre mean when it goes before a word?
5 What is the ball hit through in croquet?
6 Which female songwriter/singer won a Grammy Song of the Year for "Fallin'"?
7 Which word can refer to a sporting fixture or a type of meat?
8 Which of these creatures is not in the same family as humans – chimpanzee, gorilla or horse?
9 Where do numbers most usually appear on a computer keyboard?
10 What colour is the nose of a polar bear?
11 Which is the furthest from the ground in the human body – the fibula, the patella or the skull?
12 How many leaves does a clover plant usually have?
13 Which Liverpool manager collapsed at a soccer match in October 2001?
14 Who on TV said, "I've started so I'll finish"?
15 Which creatures are kept in an apiary?
16 Which song by The Beatles mentions Father Mackenzie?
17 In which country would you watch Galatasaray play a home soccer match?
18 Horseshoes resemble which letter of the alphabet?
19 Which "Sound of Music" flower was a hit?
20 In which month is the Jewish feast of Hannukah?
21 The Lincoln Center is in which US city?
22 What do Internet users derisively call postal mail?
23 Bob Dylan's music is particularly associated with which decade of the last century?
24 What type of body does the ancient monument the Sphinx have?
25 Johannesburg is noted for the cutting of which gems?
26 Modulator-Demodulator is usually shortened to which five-letter word?
27 Who wrote the lyrics for "Candle in the Wind"?
28 Which of these countries does not spend dollars – Australia, New Zealand or South Africa?
29 Which city-state within Rome is the centre of the Roman Catholic Church?
30 Which Alan stopped playing soccer in 2006 and became a BBC pundit?

Answers	Pot Luck 34 *(see Quiz 74)*

1 Chemical Brothers. 2 A sheep. 3 Dog. 4 Red. 5 Architect. 6 Wednesday. 7 Nancy. 8 Thierry Henry. 9 Medicine. 10 Carrot. 11 26. 12 Capitals. 13 Switzerland. 14 Exodus. 15 Soup. 16 Money. 17 Bourbon. 18 Anaesthetic. 19 Fruit. 20 Hawaii. 21 3. 22 Vacuum. 23 Rock. 24 Machine wreckers. 25 Beauty and the Beast. 26 21. 27 Transfusion. 28 Hooves. 29 Wednesday. 30 Microwave.

1 Which Spice Girl presented "This is My Moment"?

2 Which group were formed after "Popstars"?

3 What sort of events take place according to the title of the series set in Midsomer Parva?

4 Which "Little Britain" star played Toad in TV's "The Wind in the Willows"?

5 Which series featured Sylvia "Bodybag" Hollamby?

6 What is the first name of the builder on "Ground Force"?

7 Which Denis presented the long-running TV show "It'll be Alright on the Night"?

8 Which chef replaced Loyd Grossman on "Masterchef"?

9 Which Anne presents "The Weakest Link"?

10 Who hosts a "Supermarket Sweep" on daytime TV?

11 Which chocolate makers first sponsored "Coronation Street" in 1996?

12 At what time of day is GMTV broadcast?

13 Which Steve created the comical Portuguese superstar Tony Ferrino?

14 How many people compete against each other in "Countdown"?

15 Which sitcom was set on Craggy Island?

16 What type of "Rescue" does Wendy Turner Webster host?

17 How is "Breakfast" described on Channel 4?

18 Who or what is CBBC aimed at?

19 "TOTP 2" is a rerun of which TV show?

20 What type of Feet were in the title of the series with James Nesbitt and Helen Baxendale?

21 "This is 5" was the first programme shown on which channel?

22 "London's Burning" was about life in which emergency service?

23 On which day of the week was the children's morning show "Live & Kicking" shown?

24 What was ITV1's Saturday-night show about the Premiership called?

25 In which show might tubby toast appear?

26 If Alistair McGowan impersonated David Beckham whom did Ronni Ancona "do"?

27 Whom can you "ask" on "Who Wants to be a Millionaire?"?

28 Did Channel 4 start in the 1960s or 1980s?

29 Which Tory MP Boris has hosted "Have I Got News for You"?

30 What is the first name of the older psychiatrist Dr Crane?

Answers	**Sports Mixed Bag** *(see Quiz 79)*

1 Ben Foster. 2 Round. 3 Tennis. 4 Yearly. 5 Golfers. 6 Motor racing. 7 South Korea. 8 Wrestling. 9 Cricket. 10 Winter. 11 Japan. 12 Horse racing. 13 Eagles. 14 Cambridge. 15 Bobsleigh. 16 Horse. 17 France. 18 10. 19 Birdie. 20 Curved. 21 1970s. 22 Plastic. 23 Racket. 24 Four. 25 Circular. 26 Throw it. 27 Four. 28 Every four years. 29 Liverpool. 30 10,000 Guineas.

1 What is a sudden rush of snow down a mountain known as?
2 In which part of London was the Millennium Dome built?
3 On a plane or a boat a galley is a type of what?
4 Who draws the Doonesbury cartoon strip?
5 What sort of weather occurs in a monsoon?
6 Which groups are linked together through Interpol?
7 Myanmar is a modern name for which country?
8 What is pulped to make paper?
9 What does I stand for in the communications initials ISP?
10 Whose hits this century include "Amazing" and "Flawless"?
11 The society for magicians is called the Magic what?
12 How many miles are there in a marathon to the nearest mile?
13 The Suez Canal joins which continent to Asia?
14 James Beattie and Phil Neville were in which Premiership side together?
15 How was the ancient king Alexander described?
16 War-torn Falluja is situated in which country?
17 If food is cooked au gratin what ingredient does it contain?
18 What colour is pure gold?
19 If a five shows on the top of a die/dice, what number is on the bottom?
20 Glenn Close acted in a movie about "101" dogs of which breed?
21 Which H is Britain's largest international airport?
22 Which material is used to make things in origami?
23 Who is Venus Williams' tennis player sister?
24 What is a person from Tangier called?
25 Who was the US President on 31 December 1999?
26 What did Madonna call her second child?
27 What is the currency of Canada?
28 What was the name of the explosive invented by Alfred Nobel?
29 Chris Boardman was involved in which type of racing?
30 Which of the following is not the name of a real Sea – Blue Sea, Red Sea or Yellow Sea?

Answers | **Pot Luck 37** (see Quiz 80)

1 Cornflakes. 2 Pacific. 3 Dish. 4 Cricket. 5 France. 6 Great Lakes. 7 Lindsay Davenport. 8 Heptathlon. 9 Finland. 10 Pavement. 11 Violin. 12 660. 13 Water. 14 Chess. 15 America. 16 Cartoons. 17 Happy. 18 Famine. 19 Two. 20 Police officers. 21 Estonia. 22 Fencing. 23 10. 24 Brass. 25 Thames. 26 50s. 27 Nine. 28 George W Bush. 29 Eye. 30 Whirlpool bath.

Quiz 79 | Sports Mixed Bag | Answers – page 85 | LEVEL 1

1 Which Watford goalkeeper made his England debut against Spain in February 2007?
2 What shape is a dartboard?
3 In which sport do players compete for the Davis Cup?
4 How often is the Epsom Derby held?
5 Which sportsmen compete for the Ryder Cup?
6 Formula 1 usually refers to which sport?
7 The Seoul Olympics were in which country?
8 Sumo is a type of what?
9 Which sport is played at Lord's?
10 Which season other than summer has an Olympic Games?
11 Which country has won most Olympic gold medals for judo?
12 The Prix de L'Arc de Triomphe is one of Europe's biggest events in which sport?
13 Which birds of prey did Sheffield's Rugby League club add to its name?
14 Who do Oxford compete against in the university boat race?
15 What do you travel in if you compete in a two-man bob event?
16 What type of racing takes place at Ascot?
17 Boules is similar to bowls and originated in which country?
18 How many pins are there in bowling in a bowling alley?
19 Which B is one under par in golf?
20 What shape is a hockey stick?
21 In which decade was Tiger Woods born?
22 What is a table tennis ball made from?
23 What do you use to hit the shuttlecock in badminton?
24 In tennis how many events make up the Grand Slam?
25 If you throw the discus, competitively, what shape is the area you throw it from?
26 If you "put" a shot what do you actually do with it?
27 How many legs or sections are there in an Olympic relay race?
28 How frequently are the Paralympics held?
29 The racecourse at Aintree is near which northern city?
30 Which of the following is not a major horse race in Britain – 1,000 Guineas, 2,000 Guineas, 10,000 Guineas?

Answers | TV Trivia *(see Quiz 77)*

1 Mel B. 2 Hear'Say. 3 Murders. 4 Matt Lucas. 5 Bad Girls. 6 Jonny. 7 Denis Norden. 8 Gary Rhodes. 9 Robinson. 10 Dale Winton. 11 Cadbury's. 12 Morning. 13 Coogan. 14 Two. 15 Father Ted. 16 Pet. 17 Big. 18 Children. 19 Top of the Pops. 20 Cold. 21 Channel 5. 22 Fire brigade. 23 Saturday. 24 The Premiership. 25 Teletubbies. 26 Victoria Beckham. 27 The audience. 28 1980s. 29 Boris Johnson. 30 Frasier.

1 WK Kellogg created which present-day breakfast favourite in the 19th century?
2 The name of which ocean means peace?
3 Which kitchen item is linked to receiving satellite television?
4 Which sport has wooden uprights that are 22 yards apart?
5 Which country did Renault cars originally come from?
6 Lakes Michigan, Erie, Ontario, Huron and Superior are known as what?
7 Which Lindsay staged a tennis comeback to end 2004 as World No 1?
8 Denise Lewis won gold at the 2000 Olympics in which event?
9 Which country has the Finnmark as its currency?
10 What do the British call what the Americans call a sidewalk?
11 Which musical instrument is associated with Vanessa Mae?
12 How many minutes are there in exactly 11 hours?
13 What does a cactus store up inside it?
14 Gary Kasparov was famous for playing which game?
15 The explorer Amerigo Vespucci gave his name to which continent?
16 What did Barbera work with Hanna to create?
17 Which of Snow White's Seven Dwarfs begins with a H?
18 The charity Oxfam was founded to help relieve which world problem?
19 How many members of Oasis were brothers?
20 Which group of law enforcers was set up by Robert Peel?
21 Which of these countries is not included in Scandinavia – Denmark, Estonia or Norway?
22 In which sport is there a foil discipline?
23 How many letters remain in the English alphabet after P?
24 Trumpets and cornets belong to which section of instruments?
25 Vauxhall Bridge, Tower Bridge and Waterloo Bridge all cross which river?
26 Blondie's Debbie Harry was in which decade of her life when "Maria" topped the UK charts?
27 In sayings, how many lives is a cat meant to have?
28 Who was sworn in as US President for a second term in office in 2005?
29 Which part of the body refers to the centre of a storm?
30 What water feature did Roy Jacuzzi invent?

Answers | Pot Luck 36 *(see Quiz 78)*

1 Avalanche. 2 Greenwich. 3 Kitchen. 4 Garry Trudeau. 5 Rain. 6 Police forces. 7 Burma. 8 Wood. 9 Internet. 10 George Michael. 11 Circle. 12 26. 13 Africa. 14 Everton. 15 The Great. 16 Iraq. 17 Cheese. 18 Yellow. 19 Two. 20 Dalmatians. 21 Heathrow. 22 Paper. 23 Serena. 24 Tangerine. 25 Bill Clinton. 26 Rocco. 27 Dollar. 28 Dynamite. 29 Bicycle. 30 Blue Sea.

Quiz 81 | The Universe

Answers – page 91

1 What is the largest planet in our Solar System?

2 In space, what is Mir?

3 What's the name of the explosion that began Universe?

4 A constellation is a group of what?

5 To make a rainbow what weather conditions are needed?

6 In a storm what can be forked or sheet?

7 If the Moon looks like an illuminated circle what is it called?

8 What is a moving sheet of ice called?

9 In which country is the tropical rain forest of Amazonia?

10 Which layer above Antarctica has a hole in it?

11 Which of these is a danger to the environment – heavy rain, acid rain, drizzly rain?

12 The term fauna refers to what?

13 Which ocean is the deepest?

14 Which M is the largest lake in the USA?

15 What type of natural phenomenon is K2?

16 Which is the most valuable metal – gold, platinum or silver?

17 A monsoon is a wind which brings what along with it?

18 Which river is the longest – Amazon, Mississippi or Nile?

19 What is a meteorite made from?

20 In which southern hemisphere country is Ayers Rock?

21 Which Sea is the lowest point on Earth?

22 Reservoirs are man made to hold what?

23 Europe's longest river the Volga flows in which country?

24 Which of these regions has the most glaciers – Antarctica, Asia or Europe?

25 The water in rivers is provided by either melting snow or what?

26 Cumulus and Nimbostratus are types of what?

27 Which is the world's largest desert?

28 Which "effect" is associated with global warming?

29 What colour is linked to caring for nature and the environment?

30 The Yangtze, Congo and Mekong are all types of what?

Answers	Newsworthy *(see Quiz 83)*

1 European. 2 USA. 3 Republican. 4 Edinburgh. 5 DH. 6 John Major. 7 BSE. 8 1940s. 9 Wall. 10 1980s. 11 National Lottery. 12 Prescott. 13 White. 14 Scottish. 15 Italian. 16 Eton College. 17 Cool. 18 Foot and mouth. 19 Portillo. 20 Livingstone. 21 Nanny. 22 £2. 23 George Osborne. 24 Michael Richards. 25 Channel 4. 26 Heath. 27 Ireland. 28 Clinton. 29 Peace. 30 Her children.

1 In which country was Martina Hingis born?
2 Scotsman Mr Macintosh invented what type of fabric – easy clean, see through or waterproof?
3 Which ocean surrounds the North Pole – the Arctic Ocean, the Atlantic Ocean or the Indian Ocean?
4 Where can you purchase two items and still have bought lots?
5 WMDs stands for weapons of mass what?
6 Which invention was developed last – CD, fax or photocopier?
7 Geronimo was a warrior involved in the fight against which government?
8 Which missile did David use to slay Goliath?
9 Which actor John famously danced with Princess Diana at the White House?
10 Is a valise a type of dance, a holdall or a sunken plain?
11 Which Iain lasted only just over half a year as Charlton soccer boss in 2006?
12 Which ball is heaviest among these sports – table tennis, tennis, volleyball?
13 In which card game do you shout out if two cards match?
14 Who played Maximus in "Gladiator"?
15 Which doll is Ken's girlfriend?
16 Which Catherine appeared in the "Zorro" movies of 1998 and 2005?
17 "Simba's Pride" was a sequel to which movie?
18 Daniel Fahrenheit created a device to measure what?
19 Which company launched the Playstation?
20 What colour is a female pheasant?
21 Which of these will not dissolve in water – salt, sand or sugar?
22 How was Louis XIV of France known?
23 What did a troubadour do?
24 What number appears top left on a standard pocket calculator?
25 A fritillary is a type of what?
26 Aromatherapy treats people using what?
27 In 2001, which Corporation was involved in the largest bankruptcy in the US?
28 Which American hero died at the Alamo?
29 Standing down as an MP in 2005, Paul Boateng was in which party?
30 Who definitely said, "I never said 'You dirty rat'."?

Answers | Pot Luck 39 *(see Quiz 84)*

1 5. 2 Piano. 3 Geri Halliwell. 4 Networking. 5 Celtic. 6 Down. 7 Ike. 8 17. 9 Red. 10 December. 11 White. 12 Carnivore. 13 Bat. 14 Chimpanzees. 15 Furniture polish. 16 Space Shuttle. 17 Pink. 18 Murder. 19 Happy Feet. 20 Makelele. 21 Double bass. 22 Rainbow. 23 Mercury. 24 Hover. 25 Eye. 26 Letter o. 27 Julia Roberts. 28 American Football. 29 Asia. 30 Rollercoaster.

Quiz 83 | Newsworthy

Answers – page 89

LEVEL 1

1 What does the first E stand for in EEC?
2 Dwight D Eisenhower was President of which country?
3 Which of the following is a major US political party – Christian Democrat, Republican, Socialist?
4 Where is the HQ of the Scottish parliament?
5 What were the initials of controversial novelist Lawrence?
6 Which former British Prime Minister became a guardian to Princes William and Harry after their mother's death?
7 CJD was the human form of which disease?
8 In which decade was the first atomic bomb dropped on Hiroshima?
9 What was built across Berlin to stop East Germans escaping to the west?
10 In which decade was the disease AIDS identified?
11 Which money-making draw did Camelot control – Football Pools, National Lottery or Premium Bonds?
12 Which John was Tony Blair's first Deputy Prime Minister?
13 What colour is the background of the flag of the Red Cross?
14 What does the S stand for in the British political party the SNP?
15 What nationality were all the Popes between 1522 and 1978?
16 Which school near Windsor did Princes William and Harry attend?
17 How was trendy Britain – Britannia – dubbed in the media in the 1990s?
18 Which animal disease closed down vast rural areas of the UK in 2001?
19 Which Michael was William Hague's last shadow Chancellor of the Exchequer?
20 Which Ken became the first popularly elected London Mayor?
21 In what capacity was Louise Woodward employed when a baby died in her care?
22 Which value coin was introduced in Britain 1998?
23 Which George became Shadow Chancellor under David Cameron?
24 Which actor Michael of "Seinfeld" fame was in a 2006 racist comment storm?
25 Which TV Channel won the right to broadcast Test cricket after the BBC lost out in the bidding battle?
26 Which former Prime Minister Edward left Parliament in 2001?
27 Bertie Ahern and Albert Reynolds were Prime Ministers of where?
28 Which 1990s US President had the first names William Jefferson?
29 Which Nobel Prize did Nelson Mandela win?
30 Whom did Princess Diana leave most of her money to?

Answers | The Universe (see Quiz 81)

1 Jupiter. 2 Space station. 3 Big Bang. 4 Stars. 5 Sun and rain. 6 Lightning. 7 Full moon. 8 Glacier. 9 Brazil. 10 Ozone layer. 11 Acid rain. 12 Animals. 13 Pacific. 14 Michigan. 15 Mountain. 16 Gold. 17 Rain. 18 Nile. 19 Rock. 20 Australia. 21 Dead Sea. 22 Water. 23 Russia. 24 Antarctica. 25 Rain. 26 Cloud. 27 Sahara. 28 Greenhouse. 29 Green. 30 River.

Quiz 84 | Pot Luck 39

Answers – page 90

1 On a calculator's LCD display which number resembles letter S?
2 Which instrument can be upright or a baby grand?
3 Who had her first solo top ten hit in 1999 with "Look at Me"?
4 Which word describes linking computers together?
5 Which was the first Scottish club that Chris Sutton played for?
6 Which direction do you travel when abseiling?
7 What was the nickname of US President Dwight Eisenhower?
8 If you have displayed 35 cards in a game of patience, how many are left to play?
9 What was the colour in the nickname of flying ace Manfred von Richthofen?
10 In the southern hemisphere, Christmas is in which month?
11 What is the main colour of the White House in Washington?
12 Someone whose diet consists exclusively of meat is known as a what?
13 What is the only mammal that can fly?
14 Who are the most intelligent creatures after humans – chimpanzees, elephants or horses?
15 What is beeswax chiefly used for?
16 What was the name of the first reusable spacecraft?
17 What colour is cooked salmon?
18 What sort of crime has been committed in the game Cluedo?
19 In which movie did Nicole Kidman provide the voice for the character Norma Jean?
20 Which Frenchman Claude played the holding midfield role for Chelsea FC?
21 Which is the largest member of the violin family – the cello, the double bass, or the violin?
22 Which word completes the song title, "Somewhere Over the_____"?
23 Which planet is nearest to the Sun?
24 What does a kestrel do while looking for its prey?
25 Where on the body might a cataract appear?
26 When texting, which letter is left out of the word how?
27 Which actress links the movies "Erin Brokovich", "Runaway Bride" and "My Best Friend's Wedding"?
28 The Dallas Cowboys and Washington Redskins play which sport?
29 The giant panda is native to which continent?
30 In his No 1 hit, Ronan Keating thought "Life" was like which fairground ride?

Answers | Pot Luck 38 *(see Quiz 82)*

1 Czechoslovakia. 2 Waterproof. 3 Arctic. 4 Auction. 5 Destruction. 6 CD. 7 American. 8 Stone (rock/pebble). 9 Travolta. 10 Holdall. 11 Iain Dowie. 12 Volleyball. 13 Snap. 14 Russell Crowe. 15 Barbie. 16 Catherine Zeta-Jones. 17 The Lion King. 18 Temperature. 19 Sony. 20 Brown. 21 Sand. 22 The Sun King. 23 Sing. 24 7. 25 Butterfly. 26 Perfumed oil. 27 Enron. 28 Davy Crockett. 29 Labour. 30 James Cagney.

1 Who is the father of Fraser Heston who played baby Moses in his dad's famous movie?
2 In most of her films what colour was Rita Hayworth's hair?
3 Which Sean played Harrison Ford's father in "Indiana Jones and the Last Crusade"?
4 Which Roy had a horse called Trigger?
5 In which country was Brigitte Bardot born?
6 What is the first name of Bridget Fonda's famous aunt?
7 Which Moore starred in "Indecent Proposal"?
8 How was Roscoe Arbuckle better known?
9 What type of movies was Lucille Ball famous for?
10 Where was Ingrid Bergman born?
11 Which comedy star Charlie did Paulette Goddard marry?
12 Who was famous for Goldwynisms such as, "A verbal contract isn't worth the paper it's written on"'?
13 Which Alec played Obi-wan Kenobi in the original "Star Wars"?
14 Which Hepburn starred in "My Fair Lady"?
15 Which Fred's autobiography was called "Steps in Time"?
16 Which actor Tom turned to directing with "That Thing You Do"?
17 Rex Harrison was Oscar-nominated for which ruling part in "Cleopatra"?
18 What condition led directly to Rock Hudson's death?
19 What did Yul Brynner notably shave to play the King in "The King and I"?
20 Which series of comedy films was Bob Hope famous for?
21 Which part of the UK is Anthony Hopkins from?
22 Which actor had the first names Humphrey DeForest?
23 How was Greta Louisa Gustaffson better known?
24 Who sang "Somewhere Over the Rainbow" in "The Wizard of Oz"?
25 Who did Richard Burton marry after the release of "Cleopatra"?
26 What is Samuel Jackson's middle initial?
27 Who married Carole Lombard while making "Gone with the Wind"?
28 Which "blue-eyed" singer did Ava Gardner marry?
29 What is the surname of actors and directors Walter, John and Anjelica?
30 Who wrote "Lauren Bacall by Myself"?

Answers	Sport – the 1950s *(see Quiz 87)*

1 Billiards and snooker. 2 Roger Bannister. 3 Australian. 4 Golf. 5 Moss. 6 Brazil.
7 Grand National. 8 Marciano. 9 Australia. 10 American. 11 Jake. 12 Tennis.
13 Boxing. 14 Helsinki. 15 Czech. 16 Matthews. 17 Knighthood. 18 Derby. 19
The Commonwealth Games. 20 Jim. 21 Manchester United. 22 Munich. 23 Derek.
24 Wimbledon. 25 Billy Wright. 26 Sweden. 27 Cricket. 28 The Marathon. 29
Floodlights. 30 Footballers.

1 Which Irish group were "Breathless" at making No 1 in the year 2000?

2 England keepers David Seaman and Richard Wright were together at which club in September 2001?

3 Which ocean is to the east of South Africa?

4 What part of the body goes after Winged to name golf's 2006 US Open venue?

5 Under which nationality did Navratilova play her final Wimbledon?

6 If an animal has not been sighted for 50 years it is described as what?

7 What kind of game is bridge?

8 Which country beginning with an E joined the European Union in 2004?

9 Which dance was connected with Marlon Brando and Paris?

10 A natural sponge is what colour?

11 What is the sport of Riddick Bowe and Buster Douglas?

12 Which insect carries the disease malaria?

13 In which decade did Wet Wet Wet have their first hit?

14 Which Sir George masterminded the Beatles album "Love"?

15 What is the first word sung in the popular carol "Away in a Manger"?

16 Which is the fastest speed – a gale, a hurricane or a storm?

17 Which country is directly west of southern Spain?

18 In which decade of last century was Thierry Henry born?

19 Suffragettes campaigned so that women had the right to do what?

20 Ornithophobia is a fear of what?

21 Which former US President died in June 2004?

22 Which bird shares its name with a famous nurse?

23 The disease tuberculosis is often abbreviated to which initials?

24 Which letter is the symbol of the euro currency?

25 What colour is a female blackbird?

26 The Marquis of Queensberry established rules relating to what?

27 How many noughts appear when one million is written in figures?

28 How does a venomous snake kill things?

29 A wishbone resembles letter of the alphabet?

30 What is the name of the system that enables humans to breathe?

Answers | Famous Firsts *(see Quiz 88)*

1 Fernando Alonso. 2 Zip fastener. 3 Neil Armstrong. 4 Chelsea. 5 Israel. 6 United States. 7 Space. 8 Psycho. 9 Heart transplant. 10 Severiano Ballesteros. 11 1980s. 12 Lindbergh. 13 Glenda Jackson. 14 Ashe. 15 Al Jolson. 16 Sheep. 17 Soccer World Cup. 18 Fleming. 19 Roald Amundsen. 20 Spice Girls. 21 Sunday. 22 Rev. Ian Paisley and Gerry Adams. 23 Climbing Everest. 24 Edward VIII. 25 My Way. 26 Hovercraft. 27 Alan Shearer. 28 Elvis Presley. 29 Brazil. 30 USSR.

1 Which two table sports was Joe Davis famous for?
2 Which athlete was the first to run a mile in under four minutes?
3 What nationality were tennis stars Lew Hoad and Ken Rosewall?
4 In which sport did Ben Hogan win the British Championship?
5 Which driver Stirling won his first Grand Prix in 1955?
6 Which South American country gave a soccer debut to Pele?
7 In which steeplechase did Devon Loch fall when victory was in sight?
8 Which boxer Rocky retired undefeated in 1956?
9 In which country south of the Equator were the 1956 Olympics held?
10 What was the nationality of boxer Sugar Ray Robinson?
11 What was the first name of boxer La Motta known as the "Bronx Bull"?
12 Which sport did Maureen "Little Mo" Connolly play?
13 In which sport was Freddie Mills a star during the decade?
14 The opening of the 1952 Olympics was in which Finnish city?
15 What was the nationality of athlete Emil Zatopek?
16 Mortensen and which other Stanley helped Blackpool win the FA Cup?
17 Which honour did Gordon Richards receive shortly before his first Derby win?
18 Which race was Lester Piggott the youngest ever winner of in June 1954?
19 What are The Empire and Commonwealth Games known as today?
20 What was the first name of Yorkshire-born Surrey off spinner Laker?
21 Which football team were known as "The Busby Babes"?
22 Where in Germany were this team involved in an air crash in 1958?
23 What was the first name of world mile record holder Ibbotson?
24 In 1957 Althea Gibson became the first black champion at which tennis tournament?
25 Which soccer player received his 100th England cap in April 1959?
26 Heavyweight boxer Ingemar Johansson came from which country?
27 Len Hutton became the first professional to captain which England team?
28 Jim Peters was the first person to run which race in less than 2 hours 20 minutes?
29 What was used for the first time in a Wembley international in 1955?
30 Which sportsmen asked for extra fees for televised matches in 1956?

---

1 Who was Spain's first ever F1 World Champion?
2 C-Curity was the name of the first of what type of fastener?
3 Who was the first man to set foot on the moon?
4 Ruud Gullit became the Premiership's first black manager at which club?
5 Golda Meir was the first female Prime Minister of which country?
6 In which country did the Grunge movement first begin?
7 Helen Sharman was the first British woman to go where?
8 The Bates Motel first appeared in which film?
9 Christiaan Barnard carried out which medical first?
10 Who was the first Spanish golfer to win the British Open?
11 In which decade did the first wheel clamps arrive in Britain?
12 Which Charles first flew non-stop across the Atlantic?
13 Who was the first of Tony Blair's MPs to have won a film Oscar?
14 In 1975, who became the first black Men's Singles champion at Wimbledon?
15 Who starred in the first talkie movie?
16 The first successful cloning of an adult took place with what type of animal?
17 Which major sporting contest first took place in 1930?
18 Which Alexander discovered the first antibiotic?
19 Who was the leader of the first successful expedition to the South Pole?
20 Which chart-topping girls were the first group seen on Channel 5?
21 In January 1974 British professional soccer was played for the first time on which day?
22 Which two Northern Ireland politicians reached an historic accord in March 2007?
23 Which famous first is claimed by Hillary and Tenzing?
24 Which Edward was the first British monarch to abdicate last century?
25 Which Frank Sinatra single was first to spend 100 weeks in the UK charts?
26 Which type of transport was designed by Christopher Cockerell in the 1950s?
27 Who was the first soccer player to score 100 Premiership goals?
28 "A Little Less Conversation" was this century's first No 1 hit for which late, great star?
29 Which country tops the world list in producing coffee?
30 Which country was the first to send a woman into space?

Answers | Pot Luck 40 *(see Quiz 86)*

1 Corrs. 2 Arsenal. 3 Indian. 4 Foot. 5 American. 6 Extinct. 7 Card game. 8 Estonia. 9 Tango. 10 Yellow. 11 Boxing. 12 Mosquito. 13 1980s. 14 Martin. 15 Away. 16 Hurricane. 17 Portugal. 18 1970s. 19 Vote. 20 Birds. 21 Ronald Reagan. 22 Nightingale. 23 TB. 24 E. 25 Brown. 26 Boxing. 27 Six. 28 Poisoning. 29 Y. 30 Respiratory system.

1 What type of festival has become associated with Reading?
2 In which country is an Eisteddfod celebrated?
3 What is the season leading up to Christmas known as?
4 Which Scottish city hosts what is claimed to be the world's largest arts festival?
5 Yom Kippur is the Day of what?
6 Which Hall is the centre for the BBC Proms?
7 Which religion celebrates the festival of Passover?
8 Since the 1940s, Cannes has hosted what type of Festival?
9 The Buddhist festival of Parinirvana is also known as which Day?
10 The celebrated Spalding Flower Festival takes place in which county?
11 The ninth month in the Islamic calendar is a fasting period known as what?
12 Which C is the Essex venue for the annual rock and pop Festival?
13 The Golden Gate Prize is awarded at which Californian film festival?
14 Which flower features in the Royal British Legion's Festival of Remembrance?
15 Does Rosh Hashanah celebrate the beginning or end of the Jewish New Year?
16 Which music festival is staged at Pilton near Shepton Mallet?
17 Does the Edinburgh Fringe Festival take place in summer or winter?
18 Holi is the Hindu festival marking the coming of which season?
19 The G & S Festival at Buxton celebrates which Victorian writers of comic opera?
20 Is Thanksgiving Day in the USA in February or November?
21 Did the Woodstock festival take place in the 1950s, 1960s or 1980s?
22 What does the festival of Diwali celebrate?
23 The Aldeburgh Festival takes place in which Eastern county of England?
24 The 1951 Festival of Britain saw the opening of the Festival Hall in which city?
25 In Christianity, what is the name for the period of six weeks before Easter?
26 The Lantern Festival in Japan celebrates the harvesting of which crop?
27 Is Henry Wood linked to a flower festival, folk festival or musical concerts?
28 Which religion celebrates the festival of Hanukkah?
29 How many minutes' silence are observed in the Festival of Remembrance?
30 In the USA, which bird is traditionally eaten at Thanksgiving?

Answers	**Around Ireland** *(see Quiz 91)*

1 Liffey. 2 Knock. 3 Post Office. 4 Boyne. 5 Atlantic. 6 Lagan. 7 Cork. 8 Dublin Bay Prawn. 9 None. 10 Lough Neagh. 11 Book of Kells. 12 Meath. 13 Corrib. 14 Derry. 15 President. 16 Trout. 17 Shopping. 18 Mountains of Mourne. 19 Tweed. 20 North. 21 Liverpool. 22 Atlantic. 23 Kilkenny. 24 Belfast. 25 Enniskillen. 26 Apple. 27 O'Connell Street. 28 Shannon. 29 Patrick Street. 30 North.

1 Which comic David hosted TV's 2006 special "My Life with James Bond"?
2 Which Meryl starred in the movie "The Devil Wears Prada"?
3 What's the lowest total you can get from any single row in a 9 x 9 Sudoku box?
4 Which boy band made the No 1 album "Face to Face"?
5 Michael Owen and Titus Bramble were at which Premiership club together?
6 Which British rock band had the late Syd Barrett among its founders?
7 Which MP Clare has represented the Birmingham constituency of Ladywood?
8 Is the pub frequented by the Archers called The Bull, The Cow or The Dog?
9 Which M is the cheese used on top of pizzas?
10 Which Brad gets a name check in Shania Twain's "That Don't Impress Me Much"?
11 How many angles are there in a trapezium?
12 Which sport does Mike Weir play professionally?
13 Who canoodled with Sam the cowman in "The Archers"?
14 How many correct answers will win a million on "Who Wants to be a Millionaire?"?
15 Which two words are repeated in WYSIWYG?
16 Renee Zellweger and Ewan Mcgregor were in the romance "Down with" what?
17 Which club has had Bobby Robson and Jose Mourinho among its managers?
18 "The Green Green Grass" was a spin-off from which favourite TV show?
19 In what year was the Act of Union signed between Scotland and England?
20 Which London Premiership soccer club had Mohammed Al Fayed as chairman?
21 What type of natural disaster devastated Pakistan in October 2005?
22 Pop star Billie married in May 2001 in which US city?
23 The WI became what type of Girls in the movie where they bared all for charity?
24 What is the name of the Gloucestershire home of Prince Charles?
25 In 2005 Charlotte Church released an album called "Tissues and" what?
26 Which vegetable in recent years has been linked with the word "couch"?
27 "Boys Don't Cry" won the best Supporting Actress for which Hilary?
28 William Hartnell was the first person to play which TV Doctor?
29 By what name is cricketer Mudhsuden Singh Panesar better known?
30 Was David Beckham's first son named after an area in Madrid or New York?

Quiz 91 | Around Ireland | Answers – page 97

1 Which is the main river of Dublin?
2 Which village with a shrine is found in Co. Mayo?
3 What sort of building was the focal point of the Easter Rising?
4 Which river is famous for Tara, home of the Kings of Ireland?
5 Which ocean does Cork border?
6 Which river flows through Belfast?
7 Blarney Castle is in which county?
8 Which shellfish does Dublin give its name to?
9 How many Irish counties are bigger than Co. Cork?
10 What is Ireland's biggest Lough?
11 Which famous 9th-century book is in Trinity College?
12 Which M is the county where Trim Castle is situated?
13 Which C is the river on which Galway stands?
14 Which city of Co. Londonderry is on the river Foyle?
15 Which leader has a home in Phoenix Park?
16 Which freshwater food fish is Lough Conn famous for?
17 Grafton Street is most famous for what?
18 What are the most famous mountains of County Down?
19 Donegal is famous for which fabric?
20 Is Larne to the north or south of Belfast?
21 Which Merseyside city is Dublin linked to by ferry?
22 Are the Aran Islands in the Atlantic or the Irish Sea?
23 Which K is Ireland's only inland city?
24 In which city is Crumlin Road gaol?
25 Which E is the county town of Fermanagh?
26 Armagh, the Orchard County, is known for which fruit?
27 Which is Dublin's main thoroughfare?
28 Which river S has a tidal estuary in Limerick?
29 In which Dublin street is St Patrick's Cathedral?
30 Is Dromore Castle in the north or south of Ireland?

Answers	Festivals (see Quiz 89)

1 Rock festival. 2 Wales. 3 Advent. 4 Edinburgh. 5 Atonement. 6 Albert Hall.
7 Judaism. 8 Film Festival. 9 Nirvana Day. 10 Lincolnshire. 11 Ramadan. 12
Chelmsford. 13 San Franciscan. 14 Poppy. 15 Beginning. 16 Glastonbury. 17
Summer. 18 Spring. 19 Gilbert & Sullivan. 20 November. 21 1960s. 22 Light. 23
Suffolk. 24 London. 25 Lent. 26 Rice 27 Musical concerts. 28 Judaism. 29 Two
minutes. 30 Turkey.

1 Who thought that everyone would be famous for 15 minutes?
2 Who was said to have started the fire in the Reichstag in 1933?
3 Which ex-cabinet minister Jonathan was jailed for 18 months in 1999?
4 Who was manager of The Beatles?
5 Which Russian introduced policies of glasnost?
6 Who became the first woman to lead a British political party?
7 Whose dresses raised £2 million for charity in a June 1997 auction?
8 Which British monarch died in 1901?
9 Which 1960s model was known as "The Shrimp"?
10 Who became king of Spain in the 1970s after General Franco's death?
11 Which GB wrote the play "Pygmalion" that was adapted into "My Fair Lady"?
12 Whose ancient tomb was discovered in Egypt in 1922?
13 Who was the ex-peanut farmer who became US President?
14 Who delivered Labour's first budget of the 1990s?
15 Who was awarded a Nobel Peace Prize for her work with the poor in India?
16 Which Ken was leader of the GLC?
17 Who was the man who created "The Muppets"?
18 Which Scot became Man Utd manager in 1986?
19 Which Screaming Lord stood unsuccessfully in many parliamentary elections?
20 Which pop star in the news in 2006 married Linda Eastman in the 1960s?
21 Who declared he had "a dream" where all Americans would live as equals?
22 Who teamed up with Benny, Bjorn and Anni-Frid to form Abba?
23 Which Christian unveiled the New Look of the late 1940s?
24 Mahatma Gandhi led the non-violent struggle for which country to break free from Britain?
25 Who formulated the theory of relativity early in the century?
26 Who did Pope John Paul II succeed as Pope?
27 Fans visited Graceland to pay homage to which rock legend?
28 Which Yuri made the first human journey into space?
29 Which blonde icon made her name in "Gentlemen Prefer Blondes"?
30 Who was the second Queen of England in the 20th century?

Answers	Pot Luck 41 *(see Quiz 90)*

1 David Walliams. 2 Meryl Streep. 3 6 (1,2,3). 4 Westlife. 5 Newcastle. 6 Pink Floyd. 7 Short. 8 Bull. 9 Mozzarella. 10 Brad Pitt. 11 Four. 12 Golf. 13 Ruth Archer. 14 15 questions. 15 What you. 16 Love. 17 Porto. 18 Only Fools and Horses. 19 1707. 20 Fulham. 21 Earthquake. 22 Las Vegas. 23 Calendar Girls. 24 Highgrove. 25 Issues. 26 Potato. 27 Hilary Swank. 28 Dr Who. 29 Monty Panesar. 30 New York.

1 Which ground did Arsenal play at when Wenger joined the club?
2 Which Dutch star played throughout Wenger's first ten years in charge?
3 Which country does Freddy Ljunberg represent?
4 Sol Campbell joined the Gunners from which London rivals?
5 Which Ian, now a TV presenter, was top scorer in Wenger's first season?
6 In 2006, which England left back made a much publicised move to Chelsea?
7 The first FA Cup final success was against which NE club?
8 Who were the opponents in Arsenal's first Champions League final in 2006?
9 Which Nigerian striker moved on to WBA then Portsmouth?
10 Which England keeper was the regular No 1 when Wenger joined the club?
11 Which legendary French striker scored the final league goal at Highbury?
12 Which London-born centre half was skipper in Wenger's early seasons?
13 Which club was young Theo Walcott signed from?
14 Which Utd were beaten in the 2005 FA Cup final penalty shoot-out?
15 Gilberto Sllva joined after winning the World Cup with which country?
16 Which position did Lee Dixon play?
17 Cygan, Keown and Upson all played which position?
18 Which side managed by Gordon Strachan were beaten in an FA Cup Final?
19 Which Frenchman Nicolas, later of Liverpool, Man City and Bolton, was signed?
20 England's Richard Wright played which position?
21 Which country did Sylvain Wiltord play for?
22 Wenger's second FA Cup triumph was against which London side?
23 Which Patrick had left Arsenal before playing in 2006's World Cup Final?
24 Which keeper was sent off in the 2006 Champions League final?
25 With which West Ham manager did Wenger have a touchline feud in 2006?
26 Which long-serving midfielder Ray moved to Middlesbrough?
27 Fabregas and Reyes both came from which country?
28 How many times did Arsenal lose in winning the 2003–04 Premiership?
29 Which Arsenal star was in his home city Paris for 2006's Champions League final?
30 Who did Wenger succeed as manager – Howe, Pleat or Rioch?

1 Which supermarket used the "Taste the Difference" banner on its foods?

2 What was Take That's first No 1 single of this century?

3 Leaving their mark on America this century, who or what were Katrina and Rita?

4 In December 2005 who sparred with Tony Blair as new leader of the Opposition?

5 Since deregulation all directory enquiry service numbers begin with which three digits?

6 In November 2006, which Andy left the post as head coach of England's rugby team?

7 How is excellent usually abbreviated when texting?

8 Who was sent off playing soccer for England in 1998 and again in 2005?

9 Visiting the UK in November 2006, the "Emma Maersk" was the biggest what in the world?

10 Which "King of Skiffle" Lonnie died in November 2002?

11 Which Agatha wrote the long-running play "The Mousetrap"?

12 Which Zara held European and World equestrian titles at the same time?

13 What does the letter E stand for in the acronym NICE?

14 Who featured on Britney's single "Me Against the Music"?

15 Which season names the Bay provided the location for "Home and Away"?

16 Standing down as an MP in 2005, Tam Dalyell was in which party?

17 What was "For Rent" in the title of Dido's hit album?

18 Prince Rainier III ruled for over 50 years in which place?

19 Puri is a bread that originally came from which country – India or Italy?

20 Which 2005 TV series was about British land bordering the sea?

21 Which Buffalo side lost three Super Bowl finals in a row in the 1990s?

22 Which word completes the title of the farce "No Sex Please We're ____"?

23 Which "Corrie" couple remarried the week Charles and Camilla married?

24 Who presented the first UK government budget of this century?

25 What completes the book title, "Harry Potter and the Chamber of ____"?

26 In which month was New York's World Trade Center destroyed by terrorists?

27 On "Who Wants to be a Millionaire?" how do you contact a friend?

28 Is the name of Tony Blair's eldest child Dylan, Euan or Tory?

29 Which Hal was Burt Bacharach's long-time writing partner?

30 Who was Liberal Democrat leader immediately before Charles Kennedy?

Answers | Leaders *(see Quiz 96)*

1 Australia. 2 Libya. 3 John Major. 4 Marcos. 5 Margaret Thatcher. 6 Fidel Castro. 7 Iron Curtain. 8 Tutankhamen. 9 Ethiopia. 10 Saddam Hussein. 11 Bill Clinton. 12 Pol Pot. 13 1960s. 14 African. 15 Tony Blair. 16 Franco. 17 Italy. 18 Israel. 19 Poland. 20 Chris Patten. 21 Mussolini. 22 Salman Rushdie. 23 Clinton. 24 Tsar. 25 Denis. 26 House of Commons. 27 Boris Yeltsin. 28 Arthur Scargill. 29 Poland. 30 Uganda.

1 Who directed Kenneth Branagh in "Mary Shelley's Frankenstein"?
2 Who, according to the movie, fathered Rosemary's Baby?
3 In which Dracula movie did Anthony Hopkins play Professor van Helsing?
4 What was the sequel to "Scream" called?
5 Who wrote the screenplay of William Peter Blatty's "The Exorcist"?
6 What was the first name of Dracula actor Lugosi?
7 What sort of "Man" was Claude Rains in 1933?
8 Which Stephen's first novel "Carrie" became a hit movie?
9 Who was Transylvania's most famous vampire?
10 Which Tom played a vampire with Brad Pitt in "The Vampire Chronicles"?
11 Which creepy crawlies are the subject of "Arachnophobia"?
12 Which Stanley made "The Shining" featuring Jack Nicholson?
13 What part did Boris Karloff play in the pre-World War II "Frankenstein"?
14 Which 1978 movie shares its name with the spooky 31st October?
15 Which Sissy played the title role in "Carrie"?
16 On which Street was the Nightmare in the 1980s movie series?
17 Was "The Exorcist " first released in the 1950s or 1970s?
18 Which Egyptian terror featured in the Rachel Weisz movies?
19 What was Frankenstein's first name in the Kenneth Branagh version?
20 In which English city was the American Werewolf in the 1981 movie?
21 Which Hitchcock movie featured feathered attackers?
22 Which Anthony directed and starred in "Psycho 3" in 1986?
23 Which British actor won an Oscar for "The Silence of the Lambs"?
24 Which Michelle co-starred with Jack Nicholson in "Wolf"?
25 Which British studios were famous for their horror movies?
26 Which PM's name completes the title "The _____ Witch Project"?
27 Edward Woodward played Sergeant Neil Howie in which cult movie?
28 Sam Raimi directed "The Evil" what?
29 In which US state was there a "Chain Saw Massacre"?
30 Which Vincent was the star of "The House of Wax"?

1 Bob Hawke and Paul Keating were Prime Ministers of which country?

2 In which country did Gadaffi seize power in the 1960s?

3 Who was British Prime Minister at the time of the 1990s Gulf War?

4 What was the last name of Ferdinand and Imelda, leaders of the Philippines?

5 Who was Prime Minister of the UK throughout the 1980s?

6 Who failed to appear for his 80th birthday celebrations in Cuba, 2006?

7 How did Winston Churchill describe the East and West divide in Europe?

8 Which Egyptian pharaoh of the 18th dynasty succeeded Akhnaton?

9 Haile Selassie ruled in which country?

10 Which deposed leader of Iraq was captured by US troops in 2003?

11 Which 1990s leader said, "I did not have sexual relations with that woman"?

12 Who was the leader of the brutal Khmer Rouge government?

13 Was Nelson Mandela sent to prison in South Africa in the 1960s or 1980s?

14 What did the letter A stand for in Mandela's ANC?

15 Who became Britain's youngest Prime Minister of the 20th century?

16 Which General's death led to the restoration of the monarchy in Spain?

17 In the 1990s Silvio Berlusconi won the general election in which country?

18 David Ben-Gurion was the first Prime Minister of which new state?

19 Lech Walesa led the conflict against the government in which country?

20 Which Chris was the last British governor of Hong Kong?

21 Who was known as Il Duce ?

22 Ayatollah Khomeini ordered a death threat on which UK-based writer?

23 Which US President had a daughter named Chelsea?

24 Nicholas II was the last person to hold which title in Russia?

25 What was the name of Margaret Thatcher's late husband?

26 Betty Boothroyd was the first female Speaker in which House?

27 Which Boris succeeded Mikhail Gorbachev?

28 Which Arthur was miners' leader in the 1980s?

29 Which eastern country did Pope John Paul II come from?

30 Idi Amin became president of which country?

Answers	Pot Luck 42 *(see Quiz 94)*

1 Sainsbury's. 2 Patience. 3 Hurricanes. 4 David Cameron. 5 118. 6 Andy Robinson. 7 xlnt. 8 David Beckham. 9 Ship. 10 Lonnie Donegan. 11 Agatha Christie. 12 Zara Phillips. 13 Excellence. 14 Madonna. 15 Summer Bay. 16 Labour. 17 Life. 18 Monaco. 19 India. 20 Coast. 21 Buffalo Bills. 22 British. 23 Ken and Deirdre. 24 Gordon Brown. 25 Secrets. 26 September. 27 Phone. 28 Euan. 29 Hal David. 30 Paddy Ashdown.

1 How many goals were scored in the 1998 World Cup Final?
2 Which football team won the Scottish Cup in 1991?
3 Which far eastern country hosted the 1998 Winter Olympics?
4 Who did Man Utd defeat in the 1999 European Champions Cup Final?
5 Which Nasser captained England's cricket team?
6 Which team dropped Damon Hill the season he became world champion?
7 Albertville and Lillehammer were the two 90s venues for which event?
8 Which was the first team not called United to win the Premiership?
9 Which best-on-the-planet trophy did Francois Pienaar collect in 1995?
10 Which team inflicted West Indies' first home Test series defeat in over 20 years?
11 Which NE team were FA Cup beaten finalists in two consecutive seasons?
12 Where do the Super Bowl-winning Cowboys come from?
13 Which England skipper resigned after allegations about taking cocaine?
14 Which man managed victory in all the tennis Grand Slam titles?
15 Teddy Sheringham joined Man Utd from which London club?
16 Which Mark was captain of the European Ryder Cup team?
17 Which soccer star advertised Adidas and Brylcreem?
18 What did Miguel Indurain win each year from 1991 to 1995?
19 Which Liverpool goalkeeper was charged with match fixing?
20 Which rugby club did Martin Johnson play for?
21 Ganguly and Tendulkar played cricket for which country?
22 Which golfer Nick split from his coach David Leadbetter in 1998?
23 Defeat by which country prompted the Graham Taylor turnip jibes?
24 Which Rugby League team became known as Rhinos?
25 Which England cricketer was accused of ball tampering in a Test?
26 Ronald Coeman was a star international with which country?
27 In 1997, which young golfer recorded the lowest ever US Masters total?
28 Which Brian was a captain of the West Indian cricket team?
29 Which Arsenal and Holland star earned the nickname "The Iceman"?
30 Roberto Baggio was known as The Divine what?

Quiz 98 | Holiday Destinations | LEVEL 1

1 The holiday island of Ibiza belongs to which country?
2 Which European country popular with Brits has the rivers Guadiana and Tagos?
3 In which ocean is Fiji?
4 Is Tasmania to the north or south of Australia?
5 Majorca is part of which island group?
6 In which country is Vigo airport?
7 What is the principal seaside resort of the North Norfolk coast?
8 What name is given to America's most westerly time zone?
9 On which European island is the beach of Mazzaro?
10 The resort of Kuta is on which island – Bali or Malta?
11 What colour flag is awarded to quality beaches in Europe?
12 On which island is North Front airport?
13 The Californian coast fronts which ocean?
14 Which island are you on if you visit Mellieha?
15 In Australia, which state is commonly called the "Sunshine State"?
16 Tenerife is part of which island group?
17 In which country is the much-visited Saumur Castle?
18 The Isle of Tiree is part of which country?
19 In which country is Luxor airport?
20 Did "Captain Corelli's Mandolin" feature a Greek island or an Italian one?
21 What is another name for Tonga?
22 Which famous surfing beach is on the outskirts of Sydney?
23 Ludwig II built a fairytale style castle situated in which European country?
24 What is the largest city of Hawaii?
25 Which Italian island has a famous Blue Grotto?
26 The beautiful city of Florence stands on which river?
27 What is the oldest and largest city in Australia?
28 Salina Bay is on which island?
29 In which country would you find the capital city of Ankara?
30 Which US state are you visiting if you are in Miami?

Answers | **Musical Theatre** *(see Quiz 100)*

1 Hancock. 2 Poppins. 3 Les Miserables. 4 Plant. 5 Poems. 6 Barrowman. 7 The Sound of Music. 8 Elton John. 9 Chicago. 10 The Rocky Horror Show. 11 Jesus Christ Superstar. 12 Skates. 13 Alan Jay Lerner. 14 A Chorus Line. 15 Sunset. 16 Wilkie Collins. 17 The Lion King. 18 Monty Python. 19 Argentina. 20 Dirty. 21 The Wizard of Oz. 22 New York. 23 Motown. 24 Prince of Wales. 25 Bess. 26 Paris. 27 Silent movies. 28 The Woman in White. 29 Dolls. 30 Queen.

1 Which Brit was first ranked in the top 100 tennis stars in 2005?
2 Who was the female lead of the film "Dreamgirls"?
3 Actress Eva Green was the leading lady in which Bond film?
4 Which rugby league side were voted Team of the Year at the 2006 BBC awards?
5 Which pop charity concert took place at the same time as 2005's G8 summit?
6 Tilda Swinton was which Witch in 2005's "The Lion, the Witch and the Wardrobe"?
7 Who had a 2004 No 1 single with "Obviously" – McFly or Oasis?
8 Was the movie "Million Dollar Baby" about boxing or baseball?
9 Which country was invaded by the United States and Britain in March 2003?
10 What did Dionicio Ceron win in London in 1994, 1995 and 1996?
11 David Suchet was famed for playing for which character Hercule?
12 What was Ian Huntley's job when he carried out the Soham murders?
13 What does a BACS system transfer – blood, footballers or money?
14 Martha Huber was killed in which series with Housewives in the title?
15 Is the letter M on the top, middle or bottom row of letters on a keyboard?
16 Martina Navratilova won most of her doubles trophies with which partner Pam?
17 In advertising what is the last name of the brothers Charles and Maurice?
18 "Waterloo" was the first hit for which group who became the subject of a musical?
19 Which Michael starred with Sandra Bullock in the film "Miss Congeniality"?
20 Which name links singers Grace, Howard, Norah and Tom?
21 Robbie Williams made a 2005 album about what sort of "Care"?
22 Stamp duty is normally paid on the sale of what – houses or stamps?
23 Which Ian played Mel Hutchwright in "Coronation Street"?
24 What letter is next to the right of the "Y" on a Qwerty keyboard?
25 Was Cruz Beckham born in England, Scotland or Spain?
26 What did David Walliams swim to raise money for charity in 2006?
27 Was the hero of the Mel Gibson's "Braveheart" English, Scottish or Welsh?
28 Which writer Jaqueline was children's laureate in 2005?
29 Did Nelson Mandela become S. African president in the 1960s, 1970s or 1990s?
30 David Beckham announced he would leave Real Madrid and play in which country?

| **Answers** | Pot Luck 44 *(see Quiz 101)* |

1 Numbers. 2 50 Cent. 3 Johnny Depp. 4 Bernhard Langer. 5 Ian McKellen. 6 Iraq. 7 Petula Clark. 8 Oak. 9 Sender. 10 Sistine Chapel. 11 Lancashire. 12 China. 13 Angel. 14 James. 15 Ireland. 16 Britney Spears. 17 Sean Connery. 18 Cucumber. 19 Madonna. 20 Robert. 21 Oxford. 22 Christopher Eccleston. 23 1990s. 24 Guy Ritchie. 25 Dublin. 26 Thomas. 27 Max Clifford. 28 Steffi Graf. 29 Five. 30 Norah Jones.

1 Which Sheila, widow of John Thaw, starred in the 2006 revival of "Cabaret"?
2 Which movie Mary played by Julie Andrews came to the London stage?
3 What is the full name of the musical known as "Les Mis"?
4 A man-eating what was the subject of "Little Shop of Horrors"?
5 Was the musical "Cats" based on poems or paintings?
6 Which John of "Torchwood" appeared on the musical stage with Elaine Paige?
7 "How Do You Solve a Problem Like Maria" was a TV contest linked to which musical?
8 Which knighted superstar wrote the music for "Billy Elliot"?
9 In which musical about women in jail does "Cell Block Tango" appear?
10 In which musical does Frank N Furter appear?
11 Which show does "I Don't Know How to Love Him" come from?
12 In "Starlight Express" what do the performers wear on their feet?
13 Which Alan wrote the words for "My Fair Lady" and "Camelot"?
14 From which musical does the song "One" come?
15 Which "Boulevard" is the title of a musical?
16 Lloyd Webber's musical "The Woman in White" is based on whose novel?
17 Which musical is about a cub called Simba?
18 "Spamalot" was based on which cult TV show?
19 The story of "Evita" takes place in which country?
20 What sort of Dancing hit the stage nearly 20 years after Patrick Swayze's film?
21 "Wicked" was based on which classic story immortalised by Judy Garland?
22 "The Producers" is set in which city famous for its Broadway theatres?
23 "Dancing in the Streets" is based on which Detroit record label?
24 Which theatre, famed for "Mamma Mia", has a name linked to Prince Charles?
25 Which name links with Porgy in a 2006 Trevor Nunn revival?
26 In "Phantom of the Opera", in which French city is the Opera?
27 Is "Mack and Mabel" about silent movies or 1930s Berlin?
28 Was the West End musical, "The Woman in Black" or "The Woman in White"?
29 In Frank Loesser's classic what links with Guys?
30 "We Will Rock You" was based on the music of which regal-sounding band?

Answers	Holiday Destinations *(see Quiz 98)*

1 Spain. 2 Portugal. 3 Pacific. 4 South. 5 Balearics. 6 Spain. 7 Cromer. 8 Pacific. 9 Sicily. 10 Bali. 11 Blue. 12 Gibraltar. 13 Pacific. 14 Malta. 15 Queensland. 16 Canaries. 17 France. 18 Scotland. 19 Egypt. 20 Greek. 21 Friendly Islands. 22 Bondi beach. 23 Germany. 24 Honolulu. 25 Capri. 26 River Arno. 27 Sydney. 28 Malta. 29 Turkey. 30 Florida.

1 What does the solver have to write into the grid in a kakuro puzzle?
2 Who took "P.I.M.P." into the 2003 charts?
3 The movie "The Brave" was the directorial debut of which actor Johnny?
4 Which German was Europe's captain in the 2004 Ryder Cup?
5 Which Ian has played Gandalf the Grey in film and Widow Twankey on stage?
6 Which country with Q as the last letter has four letters in its name?
7 Who went "Downtown" in the charts in the 1960s and the 1980s?
8 The leaves of which tree feature as the symbol of the National Trust?
9 Where does bounced e mail return to?
10 Which famous building is used for the election of a pope?
11 England cricket skippers Atherton and Flintoff played for which county?
12 In the 2004 Olympics, which country won the most gold medals after the US?
13 Whom did Jane Asher play in the short-lived revival of "Crossroads"?
14 Which one of Thomas the Tank Engine's friends is somewhat vain?
15 In which country beginning with I were Victoria and David Beckham married?
16 Whose second album was called "Oops I Did It Again"?
17 Who was the first non-Englishman to play the role of James Bond?
18 Is a Tokyo Slicer a cucumber, an oriental sword or a word game?
19 Which American sang about "American Life" and "American Pie"?
20 Does the R in R Kelly's name stand for Robert, Roy or Rupert?
21 Where is the Radcliffe Camera?
22 Who first played Dr Who in the 2005 revival of the show?
23 Did the Channel Tunnel open to the public in the 1970s, 1990s or in 2000?
24 Which Guy directed the 2005 movie "Revolver"?
25 The Abbey Theatre is in which Irish city?
26 Which Tank Engine celebrated its 60th anniversary in 2005?
27 Which Max's memoirs were called "Read All About It"?
28 Which tennis player married Andre Agassi early this century?
29 How many "Desperate Housewives" featured in the original series?
30 Ravi Shankar is the father of which album-topping Norah?

| **Answers** | Pot Luck 43 *(see Quiz 99)* |

1 Andrew Murray. 2 Beyoncé Knowles. 3 Casino Royale. 4 St Helens. 5 Live 8. 6 White Witch. 7 McFly. 8 Boxing. 9 Iraq. 10 London Marathon. 11 Hercule Poirot. 12 School caretaker. 13 Money. 14 Desperate Housewives. 15 Bottom. 16 Pam Shriver. 17 Saatchi. 18 Abba. 19 Caine. 20 Jones. 21 Intensive. 22 Houses. 23 Ian McKellen. 24 U. 25 Spain. 26 English Channel. 27 Scottish. 28 Jacqueline Wilson. 29 1990s. 30 USA.

Quiz 102 | Double Take

Answers – page 112

1 Which word can mean to hinder and can be a basket of food?

2 Which word for an aquatic bird can also be an order to take cover?

3 Which word for a money container also means to pucker the lips?

4 Which word for stripes can also mean rock groups?

5 Which word for a female's garment also means to tend a wound?

6 Which word for lazy is the surname of Eric of "Monty Python" fame?

7 Which word can be a chess piece or a cleric?

8 Which word meaning to laze around describes a quantity of bread?

9 Which word for a main performer can also mean a heavenly body?

10 Which fish shares a name with a place for a bird to rest?

11 Which word names a shrub as well as a stiff bristled brush?

12 Which word for financially in the black can also be a dissolving substance?

13 Which flat fish shares a name with part of the foot?

14 Which word describes where someone lives as well as a speech?

15 Which word can mean to drill and to be tiresome and dull?

16 Which word can be a dish or it can mean to send down a delivery in cricket?

17 Which word for a pointed weapon is also part of an asparagus?

18 Which word is a measurement for horses and a dealing of playing cards?

19 Which British Prime Minister of the 1970s also means a large open space?

20 Which word describes a piece of hair or a barrier on a canal?

21 Which word for oars also means to walk through water?

22 Which word for illumination can also mean not heavy?

23 Which borough of London shares a name with the cry of a dog?

24 Which word for grumbling also is the quarry on the Glorious Twelfth?

25 Which name of a bird also means to gulp?

26 Which word for something found on a beach can also be part of an egg?

27 Which word links a chess piece and an ancient soldier?

28 Which word for lightly cooked meat also means infrequent?

29 Which word can be the flow of electricity or mean up to date?

30 Which word for a corpse can also mean fullness of flavour?

Answers	Tiger Woods *(see Quiz 104)*

1 Hoylake. 2 Erin Nordegren. 3 Tom Lehman. 4 California. 5 Earl. 6 US Masters. 7 None. 8 Eldrick. 9 Caddie. 10 Pebble Beach. 11 Jack Nicklaus. 12 St Andrews. 13 Singh. 14 Elin. 15 His father. 16 Roger Federer. 17 Hawaii. 18 Nike. 19 15 strokes. 20 September. 21 21 years. 22 Augusta. 23 US Masters. 24 Gary Player. 25 None. 26 Walter Hagen. 27 The Open. 28 US Masters. 29 2006. 30 US Masters 2006.

1 Prince William graduated from which Scottish university in 2005?
2 Which album by The Beatles was released in 2006?
3 Who is the most well-known employee of cartoon character Mr Burns?
4 In which Australian city is the WACA cricket ground?
5 Which John wrote the book "Mission Song"?
6 Which singer Bob became a Tory Party's adviser on global warming in Nov. 2005?
7 Sam Walton founded which US-based chain of stores?
8 A bruschetta is fried or toasted what?
9 What is the first name of supermodel Ms MacPherson, dubbed "The Body"?
10 Queens is the largest borough in which famous American city?
11 Which David had a No 1 album with "Life in Slow Motion"?
12 Which Colin featured with Al Pacino in the movie "The Recruit"?
13 In "Cats" which showstopper does Grizabella remember to sing?
14 A millennium best seller, what is added to champagne to make Bucks Fizz?
15 In which city is the Dome of the Rock?
16 Which Keanu played the lead in "The Matrix" series of movies?
17 If IC stands for Inter-Continental what does M stand for in ICBM?
18 Pippa and Patrick lived next door to which elderly sitcom couple?
19 Which movie actress links "Gangs of New York" and "In Her Shoes"?
20 A sufferer from alopecia is likely to lose what?
21 Who or what are James M Cox and Norman Manley International?
22 In which programme did Desmond Lynam replace Richard Whiteley?
23 The term alter ego originated from which language?
24 Which Katie is better known as Jordan?
25 In a Sudoku what is usually fitted back into the frame?
26 Max and Dr Russell worked as what in "Inspector Morse"?
27 How is a footpath indicated on a modern map?
28 Who was the Labour Party's youngest ever leader of the 20th century?
29 In Roman Polanski's movie "Oliver Twist" which Ben was Fagin?
30 Who sold No. 32 Smith Square in February 2007?

Answers | Pot Luck 46 *(see Quiz 105)*

1 Helen Mirren. 2 1940s (1948). 3 Adler. 4 Paris. 5 Chester. 6 Bob Mortimer. 7 E. 8 Pete Sampras. 9 Netiquette. 10 Marion Jones. 11 Terry Gilliam. 12 None. 13 The Smiths. 14 Stephen Roche. 15 Billie Piper. 16 David Beckham. 17 Fijian. 18 Computer virus. 19 Tiger Woods. 20 Saddam Hussein. 21 Tony Blair. 22 Ozzy Osbourne. 23 Bayern Munich. 24 Jordan. 25 Muhammad Ali. 26 Fire. 27 1990s. 28 Hanks. 29 Ringgit. 30 Cat.

1 At which course did Tiger win the Open in 2006?
2 To whom did Tiger Woods get married in October 2004?
3 Which Tom was Tiger's captain in the US 2006 Ryder Cup team?
4 Which C is the state in which he was born?
5 Was his father called Earl, Elton or Ethan?
6 What was the first major he won back in 1997?
7 How many players before him had won four consecutive majors?
8 What is Tiger's actual first name?
9 What role did Steve Williams play in the Open in 2006?
10 At which Beach did he run away with the 2000 US open?
11 Before Tiger, which Jack was the youngest player to win a career grand slam?
12 At which Scottish course did Tiger first win the Open?
13 Which Vijay from Fiji won the US Masters to stop Tiger winning all four majors in a year?
14 What is his wife's name?
15 Tiger dedicated his 2006 Open win to the memory of which person?
16 Which tennis player pipped Tiger as BBC Overseas Personality in 2006?
17 The 2006 PGA Grand Slam of Golf was played at Poipu Beach in where?
18 Tiger deals with which sportswear company with four letters, the first one N?
19 Was Tiger's new record in the 2000 US Open a winning margin of 10, 15 or 19?
20 In which month did Tiger play in the 2006 Ryder Cup – May or September?
21 Was Tiger 19, 21 or 24 when he became the youngest US Masters winner?
22 Which A was the venue for his US Masters triumph of 1997?
23 Which major of 2001 gave him his fourth consecutive major?
24 Who is the only Gary to share Tiger's feat of winning all four majors?
25 How many majors did he win in 2003 and 2004?
26 Tiger's eleventh major took him level with which great player Walter of the 1920s?
27 After winning which major in 2006 did he break down and weep at the 18th?
28 Tiger established the lowest ever winning total in which of the majors?
29 In which year did Tiger complete his hat trick of British Open titles?
30 What was the last event that Tiger played when his father was alive?

Quiz 105 | Pot Luck 46

Answers – page 111

1 Which Helen won the Emmy for Best Actress at the 2006 TV Awards?
2 In which decade was Sven Goran Eriksson born?
3 What was Grace's surname in the comedy "Will and Grace"?
4 In which French city did unrest begin on the streets in October 2005?
5 UK soap "Hollyoaks" featured a map of which place in its opening credits?
6 Which Bob introduced "Shooting Stars" along with Vic Reeves?
7 What letter is used for numbers relating to food additives – A, E or X?
8 Who was the first man to claim 13 tennis Grand Slam titles?
9 Is good behaviour on the net known as netiquette or nice-loading?
10 Which lady won gold in the Sydney Olympics in the 100m, 200m and 4 x 4 relay?
11 Which Terry of the Monthy Python team made the movie "The Brothers Grimm"?
12 How many goals did Wayne Rooney score in the 2006 World Cup in Germany?
13 Which band did Morrissey leave to go solo – The Browns or The Smiths?
14 Which Stephen was the first Irishmam to win the Tour de France?
15 Which one-time pop princess was Dr Who's assistant in the 2005 series?
16 Who did Victoria Adams marry in 1999?
17 What is the nationality of golfer Vijay Singh?
18 In May 2000 what sort of virus was the Love Bug?
19 Who in 2000 became the first golfer to hold all majors at the same time?
20 Who was the father of Uday and Qusay Hussein?
21 Which Prime Minister was a witness at the Hutton Inquiry?
22 Which Ozzy had his first No 1 in the UK single charts with "Changes"?
23 Who did Man Utd defeat in the 1999 European Champions Cup Final?
24 The Dead Sea is in Israel and which other country begining with a J?
25 Which ex-boxer appeared at the opening ceremony of the 1996 Olympics?
26 What completes the book title, "Harry Potter and the Goblet of ____"?
27 Was Wet Wet Wet's "Love Is All Around" a huge hit in the 1960s or the 1990s?
28 Which actor Tom's first movie as director was "That Thing You Do"?
29 What is the name of currency of Malaysia?
30 Sabrina the Teenage Witch had a pet what called Salem?

Answers | Pot Luck 45 (see Quiz 103)

1 St Andrews. 2 Love. 3 Homer Simpson. 4 Perth. 5 John Le Carré. 6 Bob Geldof. 7 Wal Mart. 8 Bread. 9 Elle. 10 New York. 11 David Gray. 12 Firth. 13 Memory. 14 Orange juice. 15 Jerusalem. 16 Reeves. 17 Missile. 18 The Meldrews. 19 Cameron Diaz. 20 Hair. 21 Airports. 22 Countdown. 23 Latin. 24 Katie Price. 25 Numbers. 26 Pathologists. 27 A dotted line. 28 Tony Blair. 29 Ben Kingsley. 30 The Conservative Party.

1 Which actress Grace who became a Princess had ancestors in Newport?
2 Which Kennedy became US President?
3 Which tennis player John Patrick was dubbed "Superbrat"?
4 John Ford (born Sean Aloysius O'Feeney), directed what type of movies?
5 Did Ed Sullivan have a famous chat show on TV or radio?
6 Which dancer Gene starred in the movie "Singin' in the Rain"??
7 What was the first name of silent movie actor Keaton?
8 By which first name was singer/actor Harry Crosby better known?
9 Did F Scott Fitzgerald write novels or TV scripts?
10 What was the first name of actor Peck?
11 Did Henry Ford manufacture cars or boats?
12 Eugene O'Neill was the father-in-law of which comedy film star Charlie?
13 Was John F Kennedy's father called Joseph or Bobby?
14 Did William Randolph Hearst find fame in newspapers or shipping?
15 Was Joseph McCarthy in US politics in the 19th or 20th century?
16 Which US President married Nancy?
17 Did John F Kennedy Jr die in a plane or car crash?
18 Grace Kelly became Princess Grace of where?
19 Which comic Kops did Mack Sennet establish?
20 Which Big John starred in John Ford's famous film "The Quiet Man"?
21 Which Davy died at the Battle of the Alamo?
22 How was William Frederick Cody better known?
23 Which James won an Oscar for "Yankee Doodle Dandy"?
24 Which John won the Men's US Open four times between 1979 and 1984?
25 Frank McCourt's book became the film titled "Angela's" what?
26 Which Daniel explored the Wilderness Road?
27 Which Prince did Grace Kelly marry?
28 Was John McCormack famed for painting, singing or writing?
29 Ronald Reagan was Governor of which state before becoming President?
30 What was Gene Kelly's real first name?

1 What type of creature was Lassie?
2 Which series had "Strictly" added to its title in the 21stC version?
3 Which current BBC current affairs programme began in 1953?
4 Ladies and gentlemen! Which programme re-created Old Time Music Hall?
5 Which TV puppet appeared with his creator Harry Corbett?
6 Which much-knocked talent show began its 20-year run in 1956?
7 Which series about astronomy started with Patrick Moore?
8 Which programme surprised its "victims" with a big red book?
9 Which children's series used the phrase, "Here's one we made earlier"?
10 Which BBC sports programme began in 1958?
11 Which long-running series from 1956 looked at the week's press?
12 Gerald Campion played which overweight pupil of Greyfriars school?
13 Which Tony had a Half Hour show?
14 What was the number of the Emergency Ward in the hospital drama?
15 Who played the title role in "I Love Lucy"?
16 What major TV event happened as Grace Archer died on radio?
17 What piece of furniture were you invited to sit in to watch some Theatre?
18 Desmond Morris presented which natural history programme?
19 What type of entertainer was David Nixon?
20 Where was PC George Dixon's "patch"?
21 What were the names of the Flowerpot Men?
22 Which London theatre staged a Sunday-night variety show?
23 Which bandleader's catchphrase was "Wakey Wakey!"?
24 Whose coronation was televised in 1953?
25 What could ITV include with its programmes that BBC could not?
26 Cliff Michelmore presented which nightly information programme?
27 What was the first name of eminent broadcaster of the 1950s Mr Dimbleby?
28 In which show did a celebrity panel try to guess someone's occupation?
29 In which "Game" did a group of National Service soldiers appear?
30 "Laramie" and "Maverick" were what types of series?

Answers	Pot Luck 47 *(see Quiz 109)*

1 Doctor Who. 2 Mads Mikkelsen. 3 Me. 4 Cardiff and Edinburgh. 5 Robin Cook.
6 Martin Clunes. 7 Cliff Richard. 8 The Fast Show. 9 New England Patriots. 10 Phil
Collins. 11 Nanny. 12 Lance Armstrong. 13 Gibb. 14 Martin. 15 Robert Lindsay.
16 Nigella Lawson. 17 Thanks. 18 Nelly. 19 Cheers. 20 Millennium Stadium. 21
Springfield. 22 Oslo. 23 Tam Dalyell. 24 Border. 25 Paul Gascoigne. 26 Kristin
Davis. 27 Venus Williams. 28 Liam Neeson. 29 Hungary. 30 Think.

1 Which Rolling Stone celebrated his 70th birthday in 2006?
2 Who was the late great first vocalist with Queen?
3 Which Pink band re-formed to perform at the 2005 Live 8 concert?
4 Which rocker Rod released "The Great American Songbook" albums?
5 Which musical instrument does Charlie Watts play?
6 Which band has Francis Rossi fronted since the late 1960s?
7 Which Carlos was in his 50s as his band first made the Top Ten with "Smooth"?
8 Ozzy Ozbourne made his name fronting which Black band?
9 Which singer became Sir Mick in 2002?
10 Which US band chose a name to get them last in alphabetical lists?
11 Which Ziggy did Bowie take back in the album charts in 2004?
12 Who recorded "Then and Now! – 1964–2004"?
13 Pink Floyd's "Dark Side of the" what album spent 28 years on the US charts?
14 Which rock veterans embarked on the Forty Licks tour in 2003?
15 Which band are still "Rockin' All Over the World"?
16 Who asked "Da Ya Think I'm Sexy" over a quarter of a century ago?
17 Ian Gillan sang with which Purple heavy rock band?
18 Which guitarist earned the nickname "Slowhand"?
19 Which Syd lived a reclusive life from the late 1960s until his death in 2006?
20 Who has been Mick Jagger's main songwriting partner for over 40 years?
21 "Changes" was a 2003 No 1 single for which veteran with daughter Kelly?
22 Which Roger is the long-time vocalist with The Who?
23 What were Jagger and Bowie doing "In the Street" back in 1985?
24 Members of Status Quo dropped in to which TV soap in 2005?
25 John Deacon and Roger Taylor play in which record-breaking band?
26 Which 1960s trio featuring Ginger Baker played reunion gigs in 2005?
27 Which Mr Stewart was the first solo Brit to top the US album charts this century?
28 Which band sang about "My Generation" over forty years ago?
29 Status Quo claimed that their songs are based on how many chords?
30 Which "Arnold" got a 2006 makeover by David Gilmour and Bowie?

Answers | Irish Americans *(see Quiz 106)*

1 Kelly. 2 John. 3 McEnroe. 4 Westerns. 5 TV. 6 Kelly. 7 Buster. 8 Bing. 9 Novels. 10 Gregory. 11 Cars. 12 Chaplin. 13 Joseph. 14 Newspapers. 15 20th. 16 Reagan. 17 Plane. 18 Monaco. 19 Keystone Kops. 20 John Wayne. 21 Crockett. 22 Buffalo Bill. 23 Cagney. 24 John McEnroe. 25 Ashes. 26 Boone. 27 Rainier III of Monaco. 28 Singing. 29 California. 30 Eugene.

1 Which BBC TV series featured murderous robot Santas?

2 Which actor Madds plays the villain in the 2006 movie "Casino Royale"?

3 What completes the Norah Jones album title "Come Away with __"?

4 Which two cities outside France staged matches in the 2007 Rugby World Cup?

5 Which politician Robin resigned as Leader of the House in 2003?

6 Which Martin played Dr Martin Ellingham on TV?

7 Who had an Xmas hit with "Santa's List", 55 years after his first hit?

8 Which show had the "suits you sir!" catchphrase?

9 Which Patriots won the Super Bowl in 2002 and 2004?

10 "Face Value" was the first solo No 1 album for which long-established singer?

11 On film and in the West End, what was Mary Poppins' job?

12 Which US cyclist was the first to win the Tour de France six successive times?

13 What is the surname of musical brother Barry, Robin and the late Maurice?

14 In "EastEnders", what was the name of Pauline Fowler's younger son?

15 Which actor Robert played Tony Blair in TV's "A Very Social Secretary"?

16 Who wrote "How to Eat "and "How to be a Domestic Goddess"?

17 Thx usually stands for what in a text message?

18 What is the first name of singer Ms Furtado?

19 In which series did Kirstie Alley play Rebecca Howe?

20 Wales played Argentina at Rugby in the inaugural match at which stadium?

21 What was founded by Jebediah Springfield in "The Simpsons"?

22 Which European capital begins and ends with the letter O?

23 Which Tam became Father of the House after the 2001 General Election?

24 Which Allan made a record number of runs for the Aussies at cricket?

25 Which controversial footballer Paul married Sheryl Failes?

26 Which Kirstin played Charlotte York in "Sex and the City"?

27 Which tennis champion had a first name the same as a planet?

28 Which Liam voiced Aslan the lion in the 2005 Narnia film?

29 Which European country has the internet code .hur?

30 Blur's 2003 album was named about what kind of "Tank"?

Answers	TV – the 1950s *(see Quiz 107)*

1 A dog. 2 Come Dancing. 3 Panorama. 4 The Good Old Days. 5 Sooty. 6 Opportunity Knocks. 7 The Sky at Night. 8 This is Your Life. 9 Blue Peter. 10 Grandstand. 11 What the Papers Say. 12 Billy Bunter. 13 Hancock. 14 10. 15 Lucille Ball. 16 First night of ITV. 17 Armchair. 18 Zoo Time. 19 Magician. 20 Dock Green. 21 Bill and Ben. 22 Palladium. 23 Billy Cotton. 24 Queen Elizabeth II. 25 Advertisements. 26 Tonight. 27 Richard. 28 What's My Line?. 29 Army. 30 Westerns.

Quiz 110 | Number Crunching | Answers – page 120

1 What is the highest even number used in a 9 x 9 Sudoku frame?
2 A4 paper is 210 by how many millimetres?
3 What is the fifth Book of the Old Testament?
4 How old was Tony Blair when he became Prime Minister – 33, 43 or 53?
5 How many days make up the celebrations of Chinese New Year?
6 How many Weddings went with a Funeral in the Hugh Grant movie?
7 What is a stitch in time meant to save?
8 Which jailhouse song was Elvis's first No 1 on both sides of the Atlantic?
9 Andy Wharhol thought that everyone would be famous for how many minutes?
10 How many different topics are there in a game of Trivial Pursuits?
11 Which number goes with "Dollar Baby" in an Oscar-winning movie title?
12 How many days are there in the last six months of the year?
13 How many dwarfs did Snow White meet?
14 Which number is represented as M in Roman numerals?
15 Which Shakespeare play has Twelfth in the title?
16 How many winks describe a nap or short sleep?
17 Roger Bannister was the first man to run a mile in how many minutes?
18 How many gold rings are there in the song "The Twelve Days of Christmas"?
19 How many men are on a dead man's chest in the pirate song?
20 Which number appears in the name of Bono's band?
21 How many hills of Rome are there?
22 Which animal is said to have nine lives?
23 How many were in the group where Georgina wanted to be known as George?
24 Which number looks like an S when read upside down on a calculator?
25 What is 4 cubed?
26 What were the "Forty niners" searching for in California?
27 Which sense is intuition or clairvoyance?
28 What bingo number is the politically incorrect two fat ladies?
29 Which number names the motorway that links Manchester and Leeds?
30 What would the Americans call the 6th of May in numbers?

Answers	Healthy Eating (see Quiz 114)

1 Jamie Oliver. 2 Cottage cheese. 3 Five. 4 Green. 5 Without. 6 Calcium. 7 Oats.
8 Blender. 9 Steaming. 10 Lettuce. 11 Chickpea. 12 Italy. 13 High. 14 Orange.
15 Sugars. 16 Saturated. 17 Fibre. 18 0%. 19 Poached. 20 Middle. 21 Turkey
Twizzlers. 22 Vitamin A. 23 Red. 24 Iron. 25 Vitamin C. 26 Seeds. 27 Orange.
28 Carbohydrate. 29 Skimmed. 30 Red.

118

1 How many squares are there in total in a Sudoku grid based on nine numbers?
2 Who had a 2005 No 1 single with "I'll be OK"?
3 What does w/e usually stand for when texting?
4 Which Mr Jacobs is famed for designer handbags?
5 What type of charge did the V&A Museum get rid of in 2001?
6 "Ah, Mr Bond"...how many best actor Oscars did Sean Connery win for that role?
7 What type of friend gave British teenager Billie her second No 1?
8 Is Prince William's second name Andrew, Arthur or Ashley?
9 Dying in November 2005, which horse was a three times winner of the Gold Cup?
10 Michael Ancram was chairman of which political party?
11 Which Jennifer was the star of the movie "Maid in Manhattan"?
12 Craig Phillips hit the pop charts after winning which "Big" TV show?
13 Fitness trainer Carlos Leon was the father of which singer's child?
14 In which sport can Tampa Bay Lightning take on Calgary Flames?
15 Jim and Annie Hacker were characters in which TV series?
16 What's the name of the first Builder to have a No 1 hit single?
17 Which TV soap featured the character Mrs Mangel?
18 In which month was St Patrick's Day in the new millennium year?
19 What colour goes with Simply to name the group who recorded "Stars"?
20 In 1995 which Jacques became president of the European Commission?
21 Which Tess co-hosted "Strictly Come Dancing" with Bruce Forsyth?
22 Which singer Celine recorded the album "A New Day Has Come"?
23 The city of Lincoln gave its name to a shade of what colour?
24 Which actor links "Quills" and an Oscar-winning performance in "Shine"?
25 Which leader has more daughters – George W Bush or Tony Blair?
26 Which Brit band had a hit with the album "This is Hardcore"?
27 Which actress Angelina became a Goodwill Ambassador to the UN?
28 Which Engine had friends called Terence the Tractor and Bertie the Bus?
29 Is County Sligo is on the east or west coast of Ireland?
30 Which novel featured the character Wendy Darling?

1 In which month do the Wimbledon tennis championships begin?
2 How many days of rain are said to follow if it rains on St Swithin's Day?
3 The song "Summer Nights" comes from which musical?
4 The summer solstice is celebrated at which ancient site on Salisbury Plain?
5 Fruit and what are the two main ingredients of a summer pudding?
6 Which V is a starsign for summer months?
7 What is the first name of sultry disco diva Ms Summer?
8 Which US state is called the Sunshine State?
9 Shakespeare wrote the play "A Midsummer Night's" what?
10 In which month is Midsummer Day in the Northern Hemisphere?
11 Which Lovin' Sixties band sang about "Summer in the City"?
12 Which Michael led England to their 2005 summer success in the Ashes?
13 In which city were the summer Olympics of 2000 held?
14 Which Tom starred in the movie "Born on the Fourth of July"?
15 If you were born on 4th July what would your star sign be?
16 Which US state is nicknamed the Sunflower State?
17 Which George wrote the song "Summertime (and the livin' is easy)"?
18 The long hot days between 3rd July and 11th August are known as what days?
19 Eddie Cochran sang "there ain't no cure for the Summertime" what?
20 Which L is a star sign for summer?
21 Which film and stage musical is about taking a bus to Europe for a vacation?
22 In 2005, which worldwide concerts were held to raise awareness of African poverty?
23 Which Prince has a summer birthday in June?
24 What is the least number of days there can be in a calendar month in summer?
25 Which Mungo sang the feel-good, chart-topper "In the Summertime"?
26 St Swithin's Day is the 15th of which month?
27 In which month would you go to watch Trooping the Colour?
28 Which Irish family group had a 2004 hit with "Summer Sunshine"?
29 Which Aussie bowler took his 600th Test wicket in 2005 in England?
30 In which month is Independence Day celebrated in America?

Answers	Number Crunching *(see Quiz 110)*

1 8. 2 297mm. 3 Deuteronomy. 4 43. 5 15 days. 6 Four. 7 Nine. 8 Jailhouse Rock. 9 15 minutes. 10 Six. 11 Million. 12 184 days. 13 Seven Dwarfs. 14 Thousand. 15 Twelfth Night. 16 Forty. 17 Four. 18 Five. 19 15. 20 2. 21 Seven. 22 Cat. 23 Five (Famous). 24 Number 5. 25 64. 26 Gold. 27 Sixth. 28 88. 29 62. 30 5/6.

1 Which legendary Hungarian soccer star passed away aged 79 in November 2006?

2 Which Jamie fronted Sainsbury's Try Something New campaign?

3 Which group reunited in 2006 had 1990s No 1 hits with "Babe" and "Pray"?

4 What type of flu was confirmed in Turkey in October 2005?

5 Which club did Jose Mourinho leave when he came to Chelsea?

6 Standing down as an MP in 2005, Sir Brian Mawhinney was in which party?

7 Jude Law played Lord Alfred Douglas in a movie about which Irish writer?

8 Krotons and Voords have all done battle with which fictional TV traveller?

9 Which great golfer first won the US Amateur Championship in 1994?

10 Which Jimmy was the first male tennis player to win 100 tournaments?

11 Which profession is represented by the union NAS/UWT?

12 On TV, were Bird and Fortune known as the Long Johns or the Wrong Johns?

13 Which Kate was Prince William's girlfriend when he graduated from university?

14 Are Glen Cova and Joy types of perfume, raspberry or rose?

15 In which decade of the 20th century was Bruce Forsyth born?

16 Does the word chassis originate from French, Latin or Russian?

17 Who were the beaten finalists in soccer's Euro 2004?

18 Which Marion was the first female to win five track and field medals at a single Olympics?

19 Is Idaho known as the Gem State or the Gopher State?

20 What colour were the shorts of the home team in Germany 2006 World Cup?

21 Which supermodel Naomi featured in the movie "Miami Rapture"?

22 In TV's "Will and Grace", which Karen was Grace's assistant?

23 Was 142, 911 or 999 the band who had a 1999 No 1 with "A Little Bit More"?

24 Which Northern soccer side did the late John Peel support?

25 In music ENO stands for English National what?

26 Which Elijah made his name by playing Frodo Baggins?

27 Are the trendy animated kids known as Bratz male or female?

28 How many boys were in the original line-up of Destiny's Child?

29 What was the profession of the late Fred Elliott in "Corrie"?

30 In the 2005 Ashes, which Paul of England played in only the final Test match?

Answers	Pot Luck 48 *(see Quiz 111)*

1 81. 2 McFly. 3 Whatever. 4 Marc Jacobs. 5 Entrance charge. 6 None. 7 Girlfriend. 8 Arthur. 9 Best Mate. 10 Conservatives. 11 Lopez. 12 Big Brother. 13 Madonna. 14 Ice Hockey. 15 Yes (Prime) Minister. 16 Bob. 17 Neighbours. 18 March. 19 Red. 20 Jacques Santer. 21 Tess Daly. 22 Celine Dion. 23 Green. 24 Geoffrey Rush. 25 George W Bush. 26 Pulp. 27 Angelina Jolie. 28 Thomas the Tank Engine. 29 West. 30 Peter Pan.

1 Which celeb chef was credited with removing "Turkey Twizzlers" from school menus?

2 Which has most fat, cream cheese or cottage cheese?

3 How many portions of fruit and vegetables a day are recommended?

4 What colour are the bottle tops on semi-skimmed milk?

5 Which has the lower fat content, chicken with skin or chicken without?

6 Which helps to maintain strong bones and teeth, calcium or carbohydrate?

7 Which porridge ingredient helps keep cholesterol levels down?

8 Which B is a piece of equipment used to make a smoothie?

9 Which is the healthier way to cook green vegetables, boiling or steaming?

10 Which salad ingredient can be Iceberg or Little Gem?

11 Which "pea" is an ingredient of houmous or falafels?

12 Mozzarella is a low-fat cheese originally from which country?

13 By eating too much salt do you run the risk of high or low blood pressure?

14 Beta-carotene is responsible for which colour in carrots and sweet potatoes?

15 Glucose and sucrose are types of what?

16 Which is less healthy, saturated or non-saturated fat?

17 Which anagram of brief is an important food element?

18 How much fat is there in watermelon and cucumber, 0% or 50%?

19 Which has a lower fat content, poached eggs or fried eggs?

20 Is it healthier to eat a high-protein meal in the middle of the day or right at the end?

21 Which processed food product did Jamie Oliver campaign to get removed from school menus?

22 Is milk high in Vitamin A or Vitamin C?

23 What colour is the rind on Edam cheese?

24 Which nutrient, the name of a metal, ensures healthy blood and prevents anaemia?

25 Which Vitamin in fruit and vegetables is destroyed by over-cooking?

26 Sunflower, linseed, sesame and pumpkin are all types of what?

27 Which is usually larger, a satsuma or an orange?

28 Carb is an abbreviation of which food term?

29 Which has less fat, skimmed milk or Channel Islands milk?

30 What colour is the salad ingredient radicchio?

Answers | **Summer Breeze** *(see Quiz 112)*

1 June. 2 40. 3 Grease. 4 Stonehenge. 5 Bread. 6 Virgo. 7 Donna. 8 Florida. 9 Dream. 10 June. 11 Lovin' Spoonful. 12 Michael Vaughan. 13 Sydney Australia. 14 Tom Cruise. 15 Cancer. 16 Kansas. 17 George Gershwin. 18 Dog Days. 19 Blues. 20 Leo. 21 Summer Holiday. 22 Live 8. 23 Prince William. 24 30 days. 25 Mungo Jerry. 26 July. 27 June. 28 The Corrs. 29 Shane Warne. 30 July.

1 Which two numbers are missing from a Sudoku line if they total 16?
2 What's the name of the penguin who wants to be a tap dancer in "Happy Feet"?
3 Which boy band made the No 1 album "Turnaround"?
4 Which leader David made a much-photoed 2006 trip to a Norwegian glacier?
5 Which Manhattan store is reckoned to be the world's largest deprtment store?
6 In finance, what does the letter F stand for in IMF?
7 What complete's the Craig David hit title – "Rise and ____"?
8 Alphabetically which word appears first in the acronym WYSIWYG?
9 In the 1990s, which world heavyweight boxing champion was jailed?
10 The character Vesper Lynd appeared in which 2006 blockbuster movie?
11 Which Sue was the first female presenter of "Desert Island Discs"?
12 Tony Blair was MP for which constituency when he first became PM?
13 What is the profession of Raymond Blanc?
14 What completes the book title, "Harry Potter and the Order of the ____"?
15 In which decade was the Brazilian Grand Prix first held?
16 TV's "Heartbreak High" was set in which Australian city?
17 "Eyes Wide Shut" was the final movie directed by which Stanley?
18 Which veteran rock band visited Les Battersby's birthday in "Coronation Street"?
19 Which is the only symbol in the Chinese calendar without legs?
20 What was Billie's surname the first time that she topped the singles charts?
21 Who wrote the play "The Entertainer"?
22 Which Iain was followed as Tory leader by Michael Howard?
23 What is the oldest inn in England?
24 Which Keira played Elizabeth Bennet in the 2005 film of "Pride and Prejudice"?
25 In IVF treatment what does the V stand for?
26 In which country was François Mitterrand a Socialist head of state?
27 In sport, how often is the Super Bowl contested?
28 Which Dale first hosted a "Supermarket Sweep" on daytime TV?
29 Who took "Millennium Prayer" to the top of the charts?
30 Which team went through the 2003–04 Premiership without losing a game?

Medium Questions

For the majority of pub quiz situations, these questions are going to be your primary line of attack. They're tricky enough to make people think about the answer, but they're not so mind-straining that your audience is going to walk off feeling humiliated. And that's important. The majority of folks in the pub are going to know roughly half of the answers to these questions, and where people fall down totally will be in subjects that they know nothing about. If you're setting a quiz for lone contestants, make good use of these questions.

If you're working with teams, you may find that this section is a little on the simple side still. Pick any four people from the bar, and you'll find that between them, they have at least some knowledge of most areas. That means that scores for teams on this sort of material should be around the 75% mark, which leaves plenty of room for doing well or doing badly, but still lets everyone feel good about themselves.

So, either way, use these questions wisely. Rely on their power to help you out of a sticky situation (although that might just be beer on the pub carpet), and you won't go far wrong. They will provide the backbone of your quiz.

Quiz 1

News – Who's Who?

Answers – page 127

1 Which former US President died in December 2006 at the age of 93?
2 Which position did Tony Blair have in the Shadow Cabinet before he became leader of the Labour Party?
3 Barbara Castle became Baroness Castle of which town which was her constituency?
4 Nicolae Ceausescu led which country until 1989?
5 What did Gandhi's title Mahatma mean?
6 Who was George W Bush's first Attorney General?
7 What is the first name of Mrs Al Gore, wife of the former Vice President?
8 Who was Iain Duncan Smith's first Shadow Chancellor?
9 Roy Jenkins became Baron Jenkins of where?
10 How old was Steven Jobs when he developed the first Apple computer?
11 Who was the youngest Kennedy brother, son of ex-Ambassador Joseph Kennedy?
12 Who was the 1st Earl of Stockton?
13 Who left for the Soviet Union with Guy Burgess and Donald Maclean?
14 Richard Beeching is best remembered for his closure of what?
15 Which leader of a Northern Ireland-based party has the first names Ian Richard Kyle?
16 What did John Prescott train to be immediately after leaving school?
17 Which Simon suffered horrendous injuries in the Falklands War?
18 Gitta Sereny caused controversy over her book about which child murderer?
19 Jane Couch became the first woman in Britain to be given a licence to do what?
20 The new British Library was opened near which station?
21 Which Diane won a court case to have the child of her deceased husband using his frozen sperm?
22 Who was in *The Sun*'s 1998 photo headed "Is this the most dangerous man in Britain?"
23 How was Aneurin Bevan familiarly known?
24 Which Eileen was Glenn Hoddle's faith healer during France 98?
25 Which veteran film director left "Celebrity Big Brother" after rowing with Jade Goody?
26 Who is mum to Jayden James Federline?
27 Which Welsh Secretary Ron had a "moment of madness" on Clapham Common?
28 Which world leader has twin daughters called Barbara and Jenna?
29 Who was the first player to make 500 Premiership appearances?
30 George W Bush was Governor of which state before he became President?

Answers	TV – Famous Faces *(see Quiz 3)*

1 Interiors. 2 Sir Alan Sugar. 3 Ainsley Harriott. 4 Nick. 5 Chris. 6 Francesca Annis. 7 Leslie Ash. 8 Oxo. 9 Sam Ryan. 10 The weather. 11 Christopher Eccleston. 12 Sue Johnston. 13 Mariette. 14 Wheel of Fortune. 15 Kathy Staff. 16 Ashley Jensen. 17 Glenda Jackson. 18 Ainsley Harriott. 19 Daniela Nardini. 20 Ronni Ancona. 21 Nesbitt. 22 I'm A Celebrity...Get Me Out Of Here!. 23 Gary Lineker. 24 Christopher Timothy. 25 Bill Oddie. 26 Steve Coogan. 27 Robson Green. 28 Teri Hatcher. 29 Melvyn Bragg. 30 Baxendale.

1 What was the Black day of the week when the stockmarket crashed in 1987?
2 Who was the first England soccer boss to win his first five games?
3 Where in London was the first Virgin record shop?
4 Which E is the driest inhabited country in the world?
5 What is a pachyderm – a briefcase, a thick-skinned animal or a tree?
6 How many teeth does an anteater have?
7 What is the second largest dwarf planet in our Solar System?
8 Which Pope travelled to more countries than any other?
9 The game of mahjong originated in which country?
10 Which former singer with The Mamas and the Papas died in January 2007?
11 Which first name comes from a Latin word that means small?
12 Who was 50 first – Jim Davidson, Angus Deayton or Les Dennis?
13 The city of Salonika is in which country?
14 Tom Rowlands and Ed Simons became which Brothers?
15 In which fictional village was TV drama "Heartbeat" set?
16 A manifest is a detailed list of a ship's what?
17 In which country was the organisation Greenpeace founded?
18 Whom did Tessa Jowell separate from in 2006?
19 What was Billie's follow-up to "Because We Want To"?
20 The Oxford vs Cambridge Boat Race is staged between Putney and where?
21 What does C stand for in the award CBE?
22 Elk, Fox and Wolf can all have which other animal added to their names?
23 Who had his statue removed from Russia's Red Square in 1991?
24 Who featured as the Prince from "Sleeping Beauty" in a 2007 Disneyland campaign?
25 What do frogs and toads not have which other amphibians have?
26 Who is inaugurated on Inauguration Day, 20th January?
27 Bonny Lad, Express and White Windsor are varieties of which vegetable?
28 Which TV detective was based at Denton police station?
29 Which famous clown shares his name with the Royal Family of Monaco?
30 Which co-star also became Brad Pitt's off-screen partner while making the movie "Se7en"?

Answers | Famous Names *(see Quiz 4)*

1 Barnardo. 2 Cardiff. 3 Sculpture. 4 Grantham. 5 Katie Holmes. 6 George Carey. 7 Elstree. 8 Peter Hall. 9 Tea merchant/grocer. 10 Norman Hartnell. 11 Gardens. 12 Ted Hughes. 13 Photographer. 14 Mountaineer. 15 Goran Ivanisevic. 16 1970s. 17 Rebecca. 18 Dance. 19 Hairdressing. 20 McDonalds. 21 Glenn Miller. 22 Monopoly. 23 Circus. 24 Popeye. 25 Ride. 26 Alan Bennett. 27 Fraser. 28 Piano. 29 Tony Banks. 30 Janet.

Quiz 3

TV – Famous Faces

Answers – page 125

LEVEL 2

1 What would Linda Barker design on TV?
2 Who grills the hopeful applicants in "The Apprentice?
3 Who replaced Fern Britton as presenter of "Ready Steady Cook"?
4 Who is Dot's villainous son in "EastEnders"?
5 Which Tate has Peter Amory played in Emmerdale since 1989?
6 Which actress has played opposite Trevor Eve and Robson Green on TV and Ralph Fiennes in real life?
7 Who left "Men Behaving Badly" and moved on to "Where the Heart is"?
8 Lynda Bellingham is famous for which ad?
9 What was the name of Amanda Burton's character in "Silent Witness"?
10 What would Martyn Davies talk about on TV?
11 US drama "Heroes" featured which former Doctor Who?
12 Which actress has had major roles in "Brookside" and "The Royle Family"?
13 Which role did the second Mrs Michael Douglas play in "The Darling Buds of May"?
14 Which TV quiz show did Carol Smillie appear on in the early part of her TV career?
15 Who left "Last of the Summer Wine" to rejoin the new-look "Crossroads"?
16 Which English Ashley featured in US's "Ugly Betty"?
17 Which future MP famously appeared on "The Morecambe & Wise Show"?
18 Which chef presented a series of "Gourmet Express" programmes?
19 Which actress starred in "This Life" and "Undercover Cop"?
20 Who starred with Alistair McGowan and is famed for her impression of Victoria Beckham?
21 Which James played Adam in "Cold Feet"?
22 Tony Blackburn was the first winner of which celebrity reality programme?
23 Which former footballer became presenter of "Match of the Day" in 1999?
24 Which former TV vet plays Dr Mac McGuire in "Doctors"?
25 Which ex-Goodie presented "Springwatch"?
26 Who created the character Pauline Calf?
27 Who starred in "Reckless", "Grafters" and "Touching Evil"?
28 Which former Bond girl starred in "Desperate Housewives"?
29 Who presents "The South Bank Show"?
30 Which Helen starred in "Cold Feet"?

Answers	News – Who's Who? *(see Quiz 1)*

1 Gerald Ford. 2 Home Secretary. 3 Blackburn. 4 Romania. 5 Great Soul. 6 John Ashcroft. 7 Tipper. 8 Michael Howard. 9 Hillhead. 10 21. 11 Edward. 12 Harold Macmillan. 13 Kim Philby. 14 Railways. 15 Paisley. 16 Chef. 17 Weston. 18 Mary Bell. 19 Box. 20 St Pancras. 21 Blood. 22 Tony Blair. 23 Nye. 24 Drewery. 25 Ken Russell. 26 Britney Spears. 27 Davies. 28 George W Bush. 29 Gary Speed. 30 Texas.

1 Which Irish-born Thomas founded his East End Mission for destitute children in 1867?

2 In which Welsh city did Gene Pitney die in 2006?

3 Dame Elisabeth Frink found fame in which field?

4 Where was Margaret Thatcher born?

5 Who is mum to Suri Cruise?

6 Who became Archbishop of Canterbury in 1991?

7 Lew Grade became Baron of which venue associated with the film industry?

8 Who founded the Royal Shakespeare Company?

9 What was the trade of George Harrod who founded the famous London store?

10 Who designed Queen Elizabeth II's coronation gown?

11 What did Gertrude Jekyll design?

12 Which Poet Laureate preceded Andrew Motion?

13 Cecil Beaton was famous for working on "Vogue" magazine in what capacity?

14 How has Chris Bonington found fame?

15 Which Wimbledon champion was called up for military service in 2001?

16 In which decade did Bruce Oldfield display his first collection?

17 What name was Pocahontas given when she was brought to Britain?

18 George Balanchine is a famous name in which branch of the arts?

19 Toni & Guy is what type of famous business?

20 Which famous name in the food world opened in Russia in 1990?

21 Which band leader won the first gold disc?

22 Clarence Darrow modified a board game called The Landlord's Game and renamed it what?

23 Barnum and Bailey together founded what type of entertainment?

24 Who was the first cartoon character to have a statue erected in his honour in the US?

25 Which Sally was the first US woman in space?

26 Who wrote the "Talking Heads" series of monologues?

27 What is the name of the second son of Gordon Brown and wife Sarah?

28 Which musical instrument did Art Tatum play?

29 Which former Labour sports minister died in 2006 aged 62?

30 What is the first name of the opera singer – who became a Dame – Baker?

Answers | Pot Luck 1 *(see Quiz 2)*

1 Monday. 2 Sven Goran Eriksson. 3 Oxford Street. 4 Egypt. 5 Thick-skinned animal. 6 None. 7 Pluto. 8 John Paul II. 9 China. 10 Dennis (Denny) Doherty. 11 Paul. 12 Jim Davidson (2003). 13 Greece. 14 Chemical Brothers. 15 Aidensfield. 16 Cargo. 17 Canada. 18 David Mills. 19 Girlfriend. 20 Mortlake. 21 Commander. 22 Hound. 23 Lenin. 24 David Beckham. 25 Tails. 26 US President. 27 Broad bean. 28 Jack Frost. 29 Grimaldi. 30 Gwyneth Paltrow.

1 Dermatology is concerned with the study of human what?
2 Alistair Cooke became famous for broadcasting his "Letter from" which country?
3 Which country does Nelly Furtado come from?
4 Disney's feature-length cartoon "Pinocchio" was released in which decade?
5 Whose debut album was "Northern Soul" in 1992?
6 Which game was Abner Doubleday credited with inventing?
7 Which of the Kennedy family was involved in the Chappaquiddick incident in the 1960s?
8 Which name was shared by Charlie Chaplin and Diana Princess of Wales?
9 In Hollywood, which Jean was dubbed the first "Blonde Bombshell"?
10 Which describes Rubik's cube – two-dimensional, three-dimensional or four-dimensional?
11 Which stewed item goes into a compote?
12 In which TV series could a patient have been treated by Dr Jack Kerruish?
13 In which country are the Altamira cave paintings?
14 In batik what is painted on to fabric along with dye?
15 "Monty Python's Flying Circus" used which "Bell" as its theme music?
16 What is contained or held in a creel?
17 Dolores O'Riordan fronted which band in the 1990s?
18 Which Alexander discovered penicillin?
19 Who hosted the 1990s revival of TV's "Going for a Song"?
20 Which children's rhyme is linked to the Black Death?
21 What does tempus fugit mean?
22 What do the letters PB indicate by a sporting competitor's name?
23 A pipistrelle is what kind of creature?
24 Which female gymnast won Britain's first gold medal at a World Championship in 2006?
25 In which country could you watch Alaves play a home soccer match?
26 Which Saint is commemorated at Lourdes?
27 What is the compass point name of the Colonel who was the centre of the US Irangate affair?
28 From which city was the first of TV's "Songs of Praise" broadcast?
29 Who did Caroline Quentin play in TV's "Jonathan Creek"?
30 Who was England's main wicket taker in the 2006–07 Ashes?

Answers	Pot Luck 3 *(see Quiz 7)*

1 Blackburn Rovers. 2 Mullet. 3 Samuel. 4 Chelsy Davy. 5 Frisbee. 6 Electrician.
7 Paul Hogan. 8 William Hague. 9 Related. 10 India. 11 Boston. 12 Reading. 13
Iraq. 14 Nicky Campbell. 15 H. 16 Mississippi. 17 Angola. 18 Jester. 19 1930s. 20
A capo. 21 Argentina. 22 Tammy Wynette. 23 Atonement. 24 Mule. 25 Lightning
war. 26 Denzel Washington. 27 Jacob. 28 Lembit Opik. 29 Take That. 30 1974.

1 In London, which famous cathedral is near to the Barbican?
2 Where is the National Exhibition Centre?
3 Which Cross is at the west end of The Strand?
4 Cheddar is in which hills?
5 In which Essex town was Anglia University established?
6 Which area of London is famous for its Dogs' Home?
7 The Bristol Channel is an extension of which river?
8 Where is the University of Kent's main campus?
9 In which season would you see Blackpool's famous illuminations?
10 What is the name of Chesterfield's church with the famous twisted spire?
11 The Cheviot Hills run into which countries?
12 Barrow-in-Furness is on which county's coast?
13 In which county is the Prime Minister's country home?
14 What was Cleveland's county town?
15 On which island is Fingal's Cave?
16 The National Motor Museum is near which stately home?
17 Clydebank was famous for which industry?
18 In which county is the Forest of Dean?
19 What is Antony Gormley's famous sculpture near Gateshead?
20 What is London's second airport?
21 Which racecourse exclusively for flat racing is near Chichester?
22 Which city of south-west England was known to the Romans as Aqua Sulis?
23 In which part of London is the Natural History Museum?
24 Where did the Yvonne Arnaud theatre open in 1965?
25 Where in England is the Scott Polar Research Institute?
26 What is Hull's full name?
27 Which town of north-east Scotland is a terminus of the Caledonian Canal?
28 In which London borough is the National Maritime Museum?
29 What is the UK's electronic surveillance service at Cheltenham called?
30 In which London street are the offices of the Bank of England?

Answers	Sporting Action Replay *(see Quiz 8)*

1 1900. 2 Desert Orchid. 3 Mexico City. 4 Gloucestershire. 5 Worcestershire. 6 35.
7 Mile. 8 Montreal. 9 French. 10 Smith. 11 Joe Davis. 12 Four. 13 Chris Evert.
14 Nick Faldo. 15 Jim Clark. 16 Graf. 17 Florence Griffith Joyner. 18 Gavin Hastings.
19 Evander Holyfield. 20 Dream Team. 21 Bobby Jones. 22 Peter Fleming. 23 US
boycott. 24 12. 25 US. 26 Atlanta. 27 Shoemaker. 28 Seven. 29 Gareth Edwards.
30 Australia.

1 Ray Harford and Roy Hodgson have both managed which soccer club?
2 The name of which fish means a star in heraldry?
3 What was the first name of Mr Ryder of Ryder Cup fame?
4 Which Ms Davy was linked with Prince Harry?
5 The Pluto Platter had changed its name to what when it started to sell to the public?
6 What was the day job of Lech Walesa before he became a Polish leader?
7 Who created the character Mick "Crocodile" Dundee?
8 "No ideas, no experience, no hope" was how Edward Heath spoke of which political person?
9 In finance, what does the letter R in SERPS stand for?
10 Rudyard Kipling was born in which country?
11 In the US, New York and which other north-eastern city stage major marathons?
12 In 2006 who won promotion to the Premiership for the first time in 135 years?
13 Where were thousands of Kurds killed in the 1980s?
14 Who was the first UK presenter of TV's "Wheel of Fortune"?
15 In music, which of the following is not a note, F, G, H?
16 Which major river flows through New Orleans?
17 Which country was formerly known as Portuguese West Africa?
18 In the comic opera "The Yeoman of the Guard", what is the job that Jack Point carries out?
19 She's still going strong but in which decade was Tina Turner born?
20 What is used to raise the natural pitch of a guitar?
21 Aconcagua is the highest peak in which country?
22 Under which name did singer Virginia Pugh find fame?
23 The special Jewish day Yom Kippur is also known as the Day of what?
24 Which animal shares its name with Samuel Crompton's spinning machine?
25 What does Blitzkrieg mean, from which the word Blitz originated?
26 Who was first to a first Best Actor Oscar – Russell Crowe or Denzel Washington?
27 Which J was George Gershwin's original first name?
28 Which Liberal Democrat MP was once engaged to weather presenter Sian Lloyd?
29 Which pop band featured Gary Barlow and Jason Orange?
30 1966 saw Sir Alf Ramsey's finest hour as England manager, but in which year was he sacked?

Answers	Pot Luck 2 *(see Quiz 5)*

1 Skin. 2 America. 3 Canada. 4 1940s. 5 M People. 6 Baseball. 7 Edward. 8 Spencer. 9 Jean Harlow. 10 Three-dimensional. 11 Stewed fruit. 12 Peak Practice. 13 Spain. 14 Wax. 15 The Liberty Bell. 16 Fish. 17 Cranberries. 18 Fleming. 19 Michael Parkinson. 20 Ring-a-ring-a-roses. 21 Time flies. 22 Personal best. 23 Bat. 24 Beth Tweddle. 25 Spain. 26 Bernadette. 27 North. 28 Cardiff. 29 Maddy Magellan. 30 Matthew Hoggard.

1 In which year were women first allowed to compete at the Olympic Games?
2 Which former four times winner of the King George VI Chase died in 2006?
3 Where did Bob Beamon make his record-breaking long jump?
4 Allan Border played county cricket for Essex and which other county?
5 Ian Botham played cricket for Somerset, Durham and which other county?
6 Sergei Bubka has broken in excess of how many world records, 35, 65, 95?
7 In 1981 Sebastian Coe broke the world record in the 800m., 1500m. and what?
8 Where in 1976 did Nadia Comaneci win her perfect 10 in Olympic gymnastics?
9 Which tennis Grand Slam did Jimmy Connors never win?
10 What was Margaret Court's name when she became the first Australian woman to win Wimbledon?
11 Who made the maximum snooker break of 147 in 1955, later acknowledged as a then world record?
12 How many Prix de L'Arc de Triomphe wins did Pat Eddery have in the 1980s?
13 Which American tennis player was undefeated on clay between 1973 and 1979 and had 18 Grand Slam titles?
14 Which Briton first played in the Ryder Cup in 1977 aged 20?
15 Which Scottish driver broke Juan Fangio's record 24 F1 Grand Prix wins?
16 Monica Seles was stabbed on a tennis court because of a supporter's fanatical devotion to which player?
17 Who won the Jesse Owens Award as the outstanding athlete of 1988, the year she broke world records in Seoul?
18 Who captained the British Lions tour of New Zealand in 1993?
19 Out of whose ear did Mike Tyson take a bite during a boxing match in 1997?
20 What was the 1992 US basketball team dubbed?
21 Which golfer was responsible for founding the US Masters in Augusta?
22 Whom did John McEnroe win seven of his eight Grand Slam doubles titles with?
23 What stopped Ed Moses getting a third Olympic gold in 1980?
24 How old was Lester Piggott when he had his first winner?
25 Which Open was Jack Nicklaus' first win?
26 Where did Steve Redgrave win the fourth of his five Olympic gold medals?
27 Which Willie was the first jockey to ride more than 8,000 winners?
28 When Mark Spitz won seven Olympic golds how many world records did he break?
29 Who became Wales's then youngest ever Rugby captain in 1968?
30 Which country was the first to win the ICC Cricket World Cup three times?

Answers | The UK *(see Quiz 6)*

1 St Paul's. 2 (near) Birmingham. 3 Charing Cross. 4 Mendips. 5 Chelmsford. 6 Battersea. 7 Severn. 8 Canterbury. 9 Autumn. 10 All Saints. 11 England/Scotland. 12 Cumbria. 13 Buckinghamshire. 14 Middlesbrough. 15 Staffa. 16 Beaulieu. 17 Shipping. 18 Gloucestershire. 19 Angel of the North. 20 Gatwick. 21 Goodwood. 22 Bath. 23 South Kensington. 24 Guildford. 25 Cambridge. 26 Kingston Upon Hull. 27 Inverness. 28 Greenwich. 29 GCHQ. 30 Threadneedle Street.

Quiz 9   Pot Luck 4

1 Who lost in the final of the women's Australian Open tennis championships in 2007?
2 What type of puzzle requires a grid to be filled in so that each run through of squares adds up to the total in the box above or to the left?
3 Doctors Guy Secretan and Cardine Todd featured in which TV series?
4 What does the term largo mean in music?
5 In cricket, how many bails are on the two sets of wickets?
6 Dying in 2006, who created the famous fictional shark "Jaws"?
7 Who was the first person to have been soccer coach of England and Australia?
8 What did Ben Travers specialise in writing?
9 Joaquin Rodrigo wrote a concerto in the 1930s for which solo instrument?
10 Which movie sequel had the subtitle "Judgment Day"?
11 The composer Sibelius is associated with which country?
12 In Shakespeare's play which king does Macbeth murder?
13 Which P was a country that Paddington bear came from?
14 What did the J stand for in the name of rugby legend JPR Williams?
15 The Golan Heights are on the border of Israel and which other country?
16 Which subject was George Stubbs famous for painting?
17 In the ballroom dancing world, who is married to Darren Bennett?
18 Who goes with Bess in the title of George Gershwin's opera?
19 Which book includes extracts from Jonathan Harker's diary?
20 Which country does snooker's Mark Williams come from?
21 What was Count Basie's actual first name?
22 How many shots does each player get at the target in curling?
23 Susanna Hoffs fronted which band?
24 Where is the Sea of Showers?
25 In which decade did Jesse Owens set a long jump record that would remain unbroken for 25 years?
26 Which musical instrument is Vladimir Ashkenazy famous for playing?
27 The city of Alexandria is in which country?
28 Which Stephen wrote the song "Send in the Clowns"?
29 Ron Atkinson and Danny Wilson have both managed which soccer club?
30 Kayak, rotor and noon are all examples of what type of words?

Answers	Pot Luck 5 *(see Quiz 11)*

1 Ridley. 2 Back to basics. 3 Iceland. 4 The Scarlet Pimpernel. 5 France. 6 All About Eve. 7 Emile Heskey. 8 Die. 9 Kingsley. 10 Judge John Deed. 11 1940s. 12 Birmingham. 13 Martin Scorsese. 14 Ackroyd. 15 Southampton. 16 Conciliation. 17 Greek. 18 Rhapsody. 19 Gary Barlow (2001). 20 Spinach. 21 Whooping cough. 22 Seinfeld. 23 Chile. 24 Jean Alexander. 25 Manchester. 26 Simon Le Bon. 27 Celtic. 28 Parallel Lines. 29 George Gillett and Tom Hicks. 30 Warriors.

1 Who voiced King Harold in "Shrek 2"?
2 "The Libertine" starred which actor as John Wilmot, Earl of Rochester?
3 Who was Meg Ryan's husband in real life when she made "Sleepless in Seattle"?
4 "Just My Luck" and "Mean Girls" starred which actress?
5 Which French actress made her debut in "And God Created Woman"?
6 What was the original nationality of director Milos Forman?
7 Which Oscar-winning actress founded the production company Egg Pictures?
8 Who was Clark Gable's leading lady in his final movie?
9 Who is Kate Hudson's famous actress mother?
10 What are Nick Park's most famous movie characters made from?
11 Which movie shot Quentin Tarantino to prominence?
12 Who played Jack Ryan in "Patriot Games"?
13 Which English playwright scripted "The French Lieutenant's Woman"?
14 In which country was actress Neve Campbell born?
15 Which Steven directed "Sex, Lies and Videotape"?
16 Which star of "Dead Man Walking" was the voice of Ivy in "Cats and Dogs"?
17 Which star of "Batman Returns" and "A View to a Kill" danced on Fatboy Slim's "Weapon of Choice"?
18 Darryl Hannah passed on the role of Shelby in "Steel Magnolias" to whom?
19 Who played the title role in the movie about the US president who resigned in office?
20 What is Penelope Cruz's occupation in "Woman on Top"?
21 Who is the voice of the princess in "Shrek"?
22 Who played the title role in "Miss Congeniality"?
23 Who played Mrs Jack Stanton, wife of the Governor, in "Primary Colors"?
24 Who starred in the original "Thomas Crown Affair" and the 1999 remake?
25 Who played the fitness teacher in "Perfect"?
26 Who was Robin Williams' wife in "Mrs Doubtfire"?
27 In 1999 which Shakespeare play did Kenneth Branagh bring to the big screen in the style of an MGM musical?
28 Who won Best Supporting Actress Oscar for "LA Confidential"?
29 How did Christopher Reeve receive his tragic injuries causing almost total immobility?
30 Which late actor starred with Keanu Reeves in "My Own Private Idaho"?

Answers | Music – Bands *(see Quiz 12)*

1 Bon Jovi. 2 The Rolling Stones. 3 En Vogue. 4 Ace of Base. 5 Appleton. 6 Beatles. 7 Bohemian Rhapsody. 8 I Want to Hold Your Hand. 9 Lordi. 10 Two. 11 Country House. 12 Words. 13 Tsunami. 14 Patience. 15 Prodigy. 16 Def Leppard. 17 Guns N' Roses. 18 U2. 19 Chemical Brothers. 20 REM. 21 The Bangles. 22 Newcastle. 23 Doctor Jones. 24 Mulder & Scully. 25 Northern Ireland. 26 The Great Escape. 27 Creation. 28 Boyzone. 29 Sheffield. 30 Boyzone.

1 In "Coronation Street" what goes with Newton to make the beer for the Rovers' Return?
2 Which John Major campaign urged a return to traditional values?
3 The Althing is the parliament of which country?
4 In fiction, Percy Blakeney was the alias of which hero?
5 In which country was cubism founded?
6 Before "Titanic" what was the last film to win 14 Oscar nominations?
7 Which Emile scored in Sven Goran Eriksson's first game in charge for England?
8 Lester Piggott's first Derby winner was called Never Say what?
9 Which Mr Amis wrote "Lucky Jim"?
10 Martin Shaw played which eponymous TV judge?
11 Still looking Ab Fab, in which decade was Joanna Lumley born?
12 The M1 was originally constructed to link London to where?
13 Harvey Keitel is particularly known for his work with which movie director?
14 Agatha Christie wrote about "The Murder of Roger" who?
15 What was Alan Shearer's first league club?
16 What does the C stand for in ACAS?
17 What was the nationality of fable writer Aesop?
18 What did George Gershwin write "in Blue"?
19 Who was 30 first – Emma Bunton, Gary Barlow or Victoria Beckham?
20 What S is added to pasta to make it green?
21 The illness pertussis is more commonly known as what?
22 Which US sitcom ran to 180 episodes, before finishing in 1998?
23 The southernmost part of South America is owned by which country?
24 Which former soap star became Auntie Wainwright in "Last of the Summer Wine"?
25 The Halle Orchestra is based in which English city?
26 Which pop personality married Yasmin Parvaneh in 1986?
27 Which club did Jock Stein lead to European success?
28 "Sunday Girl" featured on which Blondie album?
29 Who bought Liverpool FC from the Moores family in 2007?
30 In rugby, what was added to Wigan's name in 1997?

1 Whose Best of 1990s album was "Cross Road"?
2 Who embarked on their "Bigger Bang" tour in 2006?
3 Who had a hit with "Don't Let Go"?
4 "Happy Nation" was the debut album of which Scandinavian band?
5 What was the surname of the sisters in All Saints?
6 Which band had 18 consecutive UK Top Ten hits between July 1964 and March 1976?
7 What was Queen's best-selling single?
8 Which Beatles single was their first No 1 in the US?
9 Which band won the 2006 Eurovision Song Contest?
10 How many albums did the Spice Girls release in the 20th century?
11 What was Blur's first UK No 1?
12 Which 1996 Boyzone hit was a previous hit by the Bee Gees?
13 Which 1999 Manic Street Preachers hit shares its name with a natural disaster?
14 What was Take That's first UK No 1 of the 21st century?
15 Whose album "Fat of the Land" debuted at No 1 on both sides of the Atlantic?
16 Joe Elliot was vocalist with which heavy metal band?
17 Who had an "Appetite for Destruction" in 1987?
18 Whose album had some "Rattle & Hum" in 1988?
19 Who had the award-winning 1999 album "Surrender"?
20 Who were "Out of Time" in 1991?
21 Who had the original hit with Atomic Kitten's "Eternal Flame"?
22 Which city did the 1960s band The Animals come from?
23 What was Aqua's follow-up to "Barbie Girl"?
24 Which Catatonia hit shared its name with a TV duo?
25 Which part of the UK did Ash come from?
26 Which Blur album shared its name with a Steve McQueen film?
27 On which label did Oasis have their first Top Ten Hit?
28 Shane Lynch was a member of which band?
29 Arctic Monkeys hail from which city?
30 Which band had 16 consecutive UK Top Ten hits between December 1994 and December 1999?

Answers	**Movies Who's Who?** *(see Quiz 10)*

1 John Cleese. 2 Johnny Depp. 3 Dennis Quaid. 4 Lyndsay Lohan. 5 Brigitte Bardot. 6 Czech. 7 Jodie Foster. 8 Marilyn Monroe. 9 Goldie Hawn. 10 Clay. 11 Reservoir Dogs. 12 Harrison Ford. 13 Harold Pinter. 14 Canada. 15 Soderbergh. 16 Susan Sarandon. 17 Christopher Walken. 18 Julia Roberts. 19 Anthony Hopkins. 20 Chef. 21 Cameron Diaz. 22 Sandra Bullock. 23 Emma Thompson. 24 Faye Dunaway. 25 Jamie Lee Curtis. 26 Sally Field. 27 Love Labour's Lost. 28 Kim Basinger. 29 Fell from a horse. 30 River Phoenix.

1 In France all motorways begin with which letter of the alphabet?
2 What does the Blue Cross Charity provide aid to?
3 Which hypnotist wrote "I Can Make You Thin"?
4 In the song "Rule Britannia" what is Britannia told to rule?
5 Which soccer side won four championships in a row with Johan Cruyff as boss?
6 Did Aaron Copland compose music for "Billy Elliot", "Billy the Kid" or "Billy Liar"?
7 In which western classic did John Wayne play the Ringo Kid?
8 What is the qualification to be Father of the House in the House of Commons?
9 In music, which note is written on the bottom line of the treble clef?
10 The Copacabana beach is in which South American city?
11 Whose first No 1 single used the title of a novel by one of the Brontë sisters?
12 Actor John Savident played which character in "Coronation Street"?
13 How many years before "Star Wars" is the action of "The Phantom Menace", 22, 32 or 42?
14 Which band became the most successful 1990s Scandinavian act on the US singles chart?
15 If you were an LLD what subject would you have studied?
16 What was US President Lyndon Johnson's middle name?
17 Joe Royle and Mike Walker have both managed which soccer club?
18 Green Street and Priory Road are near which London soccer club's stadium?
19 Which Napoleonic battle gave its name to a famous chicken dish?
20 In which decade of last century were BBC TV programmes first broadcast?
21 The Beautiful South were formed after the break-up of which group?
22 What was Hetty Wainthropp's young assistant sleuth called?
23 What was the first name of Eva Peron's husband?
24 Who used Marx Brothers film titles as album titles?
25 When was US hospital drama "St Elsewhere" first screened in the UK?
26 Giovanna Gassion sang under which name?
27 How many states were in the original union of the United States?
28 What would a palaeontologist study?
29 R.E.M. sang about "Shiny Happy" what?
30 What do the words post mortem actually mean?

Answers	Past Times 1900–1950 *(see Quiz 15)*

1 Manhattan Project. 2 Stanley Baldwin. 3 Brussels. 4 Neville Chamberlain. 5 Austria. 6 First. 7 Gestapo. 8 Cost lives. 9 Alexandra. 10 1916. 11 Morris. 12 Birth control. 13 Lenin. 14 1920s. 15 Munich. 16 Queen Mary. 17 Windsor. 18 Dunkirk. 19 Malta. 20 Dresden. 21 Edinburgh. 22 Round. 23 American. 24 Ethel. 25 Sidney Street. 26 Shilling. 27 David Lloyd George. 28 Lady Elizabeth Bowes Lyon. 29 Sydney. 30 George V.

1 What is the main characteristic of the wood of the balsa tree?

2 Plantain is a type of which fruit?

3 What is another name for the blackthorn?

4 Which industry's demands meant that rubber production increased in the last century?

5 What does a berry typically contain?

6 In a biennial plant, when do flower and seed production usually occur?

7 What name is given to small hardy plants ideal for rockeries, such as saxifraga?

8 The name tulip is derived from a Turkish word meaning what type of headgear?

9 What type of soil is vital for growing rhododendrons?

10 What is the most common colour of primula vulgaris or common primrose?

11 Clematis is a member of which family of wild flowers?

12 How many petals does an iris usually have?

13 What nationality was the botanist who gave his name to the dahlia?

14 How is the wild Rosa canina better known?

15 What colour is the rose of York?

16 Antirrhinums are also called what?

17 What is gypsophilia mainly grown for?

18 Which Busy plant has the name Impatiens?

19 Forget Me Nots are usually which colour?

20 Which TV cook Ms Lawson shares her name with the Love in a Mist flower?

21 How are the papery daisy-like flowers of helichrysum better known?

22 In which season do Michaelmas daisies flower?

23 Which best describes leaves of a hosta – scalloped, spiky or very large?

24 Which of the following flowers are not grown from bulbs – pansies, snowdrops and tulips?

25 What sort of bell is a campanula?

26 Muscari are what type of hyacinth?

27 What is used to make a mulch – chemicals, organic material or seeds?

28 What makes the seeds of the laburnum potentially dangerous?

29 What colour are the ripe fruits of the mulberry tree?

30 What is the most common colour for alyssum, often used in borders and hanging baskets?

Quiz 15 | Past Times 1900–1950

Answers – page 137

LEVEL 2

1 What was the code name of the project to develop the atom bomb?
2 Who was Prime Minister during the Abdication of Edward VIII?
3 In which city did Edith Cavell work in WWI?
4 Which Prime Minister declared war on Germany in 1939?
5 The Anschluss concerned Nazi Germany and which other state?
6 In which decade of the 20th century was the Boy Scout movement founded?
7 How was the Geheime Staatspolizei better known?
8 According to the wartime slogan, careless talk does what?
9 What was Tsar Nicholas II's wife called?
10 In which year was the Easter Rising in Dublin?
11 Lord Nuffield founded which car company which originally bore his name?
12 What type of clinic did Marie Stopes open?
13 Which Russian leader died in 1924?
14 In which decade did the Wall Street Crash take place?
15 In which German city was the Nazi Party founded?
16 Which "Queen" left on her maiden voyage across the Atlantic in 1946?
17 Which Duke and Duchess famously visited Hitler in Berlin in 1937?
18 Which French beaches were evacuated in 1940?
19 Which island received a medal for gallantry after WWII?
20 Which city called the German Florence was heavily bombed in 1945?
21 Which now annual arts Festival opened in for the first time in 1947?
22 What shape was the main part of the first AA badge which appeared in 1906?
23 What nationality was Robert Peary who reached the North Pole in 1909?
24 What was Dr Crippen's mistress's first name, with whom he tried to flee to Canada after murdering his wife?
25 Which East End street was the scene of siege by anarchists in 1911?
26 Taking the King's what meant that volunteers had signed up for the army?
27 Who succeeded Kitchener as War Secretary in 1916?
28 Who did the then Duke of York marry in 1923?
29 Which Bridge had the then longest span when it opened in 1932?
30 Which monarch made the first Christmas radio broadcast?

Answers	Pot Luck 6 *(see Quiz 13)*

1 A. 2 Animals. 3 Paul McKenna. 4 The waves. 5 Barcelona. 6 Billy the Kid. 7 Stagecoach. 8 Longest-serving MP. 9 E. 10 Rio de Janeiro. 11 Kate Bush. 12 Fred Elliott. 13 32. 14 Roxette. 15 Law. 16 Baines. 17 Everton. 18 West Ham. 19 Marengo. 20 1930s. 21 The Housemartins. 22 Geoffrey. 23 Juan. 24 Queen. 25 1983. 26 Edith Piaf. 27 13. 28 Fossils. 29 People. 30 After death.

Quiz 16 | Pot Luck 7 | Answers – page 138

1 "BBC Sports Personality of the Year" voted Daniel Anderson top what in 2006?

2 What was Elvis Presley's middle name?

3 In the USA, where is the President's official country home?

4 The Sandanista guerrillas overthrew the government of which country in 1979?

5 Talking about Fred Astaire, Ginger Rogers said "I did what he did but I did it …" in which way?

6 Which board game features a racing car, a top hat and a dog?

7 What was the only hit of one-hit wonders Doop?

8 Which President of the USA had Walter Mondale as Vice President?

9 Cerys Matthews became lead singer with which band in the mid-1990s?

10 The "General Belgrano" was sunk in which conflict?

11 Who won an Oscar for "The Sunshine Boys" at the age of 80?

12 Who took "Promise Me" into the charts in the early 1990s?

13 Which country were the aggressors in the Pearl Harbor attack of the 1940s?

14 Where in Devon did a ship's cargo wash up in January 2007?

15 Whose TV roles have included Arkwright and Fletcher?

16 What was the trade of Charles Lewis Tiffany?

17 In which part of the human skeleton are the metatarsels?

18 Whose last words were reputedly, "Thank God I have done my duty"?

19 Which Tony Di Bart No 1 hit from 1994 is the name of a group?

20 Is the Kandahar region in the north or south of Afghanistan?

21 What was the name of John F Kennedy's brother who predeceased him?

22 IC sounds as if it ought to be Iceland's international vehicle registration but isn't – but what is?

23 The Bass Strait lies between which two islands?

24 Which Pulp single title is also the name of a charity?

25 Who opened the Royal Albert Hall?

26 Presenter Claudia Winkleman is the daughter of which former newspaper editor?

27 For which 1990s film with a prison theme did Johnny Cash contribute to the soundtrack?

28 A sea containing many islands is called what?

29 Who succeeded Queen Victoria?

30 Which gallery displays the "Mona Lisa"?

Answers | **Plants** *(see Quiz 14)*

1 Light. 2 Banana. 3 Sloe. 4 Automobile. 5 Seeds. 6 Second year. 7 Alpines. 8 Turban. 9 Lime free. 10 Yellow. 11 Buttercup. 12 Three. 13 Swedish. 14 Dog rose. 15 White. 16 Snapdragons. 17 Flower arranging. 18 Lizzie. 19 Blue. 20 Nigella. 21 Everlasting flowers. 22 Autumn. 23 Very large. 24 Pansies. 25 Canterbury bell. 26 Grape. 27 Organic material. 28 Poisonous. 29 Dark red. 30 White.

Quiz 17 | TV Trivia | Answers – page 143

1 What was the name of the 1999 BBC series about prehistoric creatures?
2 Where did Mavis leave for when she left "Coronation Street"?
3 Which Nick Berry series was set in the west country?
4 Which drink did Paul Daniels and Debbie McGee advertise singing off key around a piano?
5 What is Betty's culinary speciality in "Coronation Street"?
6 Who played writer Peter Mayle in the ill-fated series "A Year in Provence"?
7 What was the prize to aim for in Cilla's "Moment of Truth"?
8 Zoe Wanamaker and Robert Lindsay starred in which domestic comedy?
9 In which comedy about relationships did Jack Davenport play Steve while Gina Bellman played Jane?
10 Singer Adam Rickitt found fame in which soap?
11 In "Countdown", how many people occupy Dictionary Corner?
12 How long do the cooks have to cook their team members' ingredients in "Ready Steady Cook"?
13 Which ex-"Coronation Street" actress played 1970s TV star Coral Atkins in "Seeing Red"?
14 In 2001 what momentous new purchase did Deirdre make in "Coronation Street"?
15 In "Bargain Hunt", what sort of bargains are being hunted?
16 Which "The O.C." character, played by Micha Baron, was killed off in series three?
17 What is the postcode of Albert Square, Walford?
18 On which show did Hear'Say shoot to stardom?
19 In "Coronation Street", which character killed Charlie Stubbs?
20 In which series would the Skelthwaite Arms feature?
21 Which Tony played the Sheriff in "Maid Marian and Her Merry Men"?
22 Which comedy show was famous for its "Fork handles" sketch?
23 What was the name of Keith Harris's duck?
24 Which "Rainbow" character was pink?
25 Who first hosted "A Question of TV"?
26 Who was the first presenter of "Changing Rooms"?
27 Which comedy show was famous for its "Dead Parrot" sketch?
28 How many contestants start out on the original, BBC2 version, of "The Weakest Link"?
29 Who won the "Best Actor in a TV Drama" award at the 2007 Golden Globes?
30 Who first presented the interactive travel series "Holiday: You Call the Shots"?

Answers	Celebs *(see Quiz 19)*

1 Priscilla. 2 Chicago. 3 Her dogs. 4 Miss Whiplash. 5 Bruce Forsyth. 6 Eight. 7 Denise Van Outen. 8 Playboy. 9 Edward VIII. 10 Gabriela Sabatini. 11 Mary Quant. 12 Newspapers. 13 Prince Andrew. 14 Gilles. 15 Niece. 16 Cambridge. 17 Natasha. 18 Danielle Lloyd. 19 Catherine. 20 Devonshire. 21 Bernie Ecclestone. 22 Andrew Lloyd Webber. 23 Follett. 24 Norway. 25 Barbara. 26 Harrison Ford. 27 Kathleen Turner. 28 Bristol. 29 Shiloh Nouvel. 30 Meet the Fockers.

1 On which day are US elections for the Senate and Congress always held?
2 Which Harris had a huge hit with "Macarthur Park"?
3 In "Bewitched" what was the name of Samantha's mother?
4 On a Monopoly board what is the first station reached after Go?
5 Which franc is the official currency of Liechtenstein?
6 Howard Wilkinson and George Graham have both managed which soccer club?
7 Who played the man in black in the film "Once Upon a Time in the West"?
8 Which female singer performed with the Miami Sound Machine?
9 In 2006 Simon Shepherd dropped out of which musical, days before its opening?
10 Which bass saxophonist released "The "Impulse Story" album in June 2006?
11 Who quite literally took "Trash" into the charts in the mid-1990s?
12 In which war did the Battle of the Bulge take place?
13 In the past which creatures were used by doctors to drain blood?
14 Which Howard discovered Tutankhamun's tomb in the Valley of the Kings?
15 Who sang about "The Good Ship Lollipop"?
16 What was Southern Rhodesia renamed in the 1980s?
17 Who presented the TV series "Sweet Baby James"?
18 Which US First Lady is credited as being the first to use the name?
19 What was the first movie to play John Wayne opposite Maureen O'Hara?
20 "Oh What a Beautiful Morning" comes from which musical?
21 Which river cuts through the Grand Canyon?
22 Who wrote "Nessun Dorma", now regarded as Pavarotti's theme tune?
23 "And I'll cry if I want to" is the second line of the chorus of which song?
24 Ralph McTell wrote and sang about the "Streets of" where?
25 Who was first to be 50 – John Travolta or Martina Navratilova?
26 On which Sea is the Gaza Strip?
27 Roger Waters and Dave Gilmour were members of which long-lasting group?
28 What has the Nursery End and the Pavilion End?
29 In 2006 the FA announced sponsorship of the FA Cup by which energy supplier?
30 How many members of the Righteous Brothers were actual brothers?

Answers	Euro Tour (see Quiz 20)

1 Cork. 2 Porcelain. 3 Paris. 4 Cephallonia. 5 Chamonix. 6 Channel Islands. 7 Connacht (Connaught). 8 Danish. 9 Finland. 10 Estonia. 11 Black Forest. 12 Arc de Triomphe. 13 Sangatte. 14 Paris. 15 Innsbruck. 16 Greece. 17 Kattegat. 18 Mediterranean. 19 Kerry blue. 20 Madrid. 21 Magenta. 22 Stock Exchange. 23 Black. 24 Portugal. 25 Barcelona. 26 Estonia. 27 Leningrad. 28 North Sea. 29 Munich. 30 Pyrenees.

Quiz 19 | Celebs

Answers – page 141

LEVEL 2

1 Who did Elvis Presley sue for divorce on his 38th birthday?
2 In which city did Hugh Hefner open his first Playboy Club?
3 In 1991 Queen Elizabeth II needed medical treatment after breaking up a fight between whom?
4 How did Lindi St Clair, who battled with the Inland Revenue over the nature of her earnings, style herself?
5 Which TV entertainer has a South American wife called Wilnelia?
6 By the end of the 20th century how many times had Elizabeth Taylor been married?
7 Which blonde TV presenter did Jay Kay split with in the new millennium?
8 Which magazine did Hugh Hefner found?
9 Who was the first English king to travel in an aeroplane?
10 Which Argentine tennis player shares her birthdate – 15 years later – with Olga Korbut?
11 Which designer is most associated with the Sixties and the mini-skirt?
12 Lord Beaverbrook is a famous name in which field?
13 Who was the first Royal to visit New York after September 11th 2001?
14 Who is Jacques Villeneuve's famous father?
15 What relation is Bridget Fonda to Jane Fonda?
16 At which university did Vanessa Feltz study?
17 What is the name of Sir Michael Caine's daughter?
18 Who was stripped of the 2006 Miss Great Britain title?
19 What is Mrs Frankie Dettori called?
20 Chatsworth in Derbyshire is owned by the duke of where?
21 Who owned Formula 1 racing when ITV began in 1996?
22 Whose theatre company did Prince Edward join when he left the Royal Marines?
23 What is the surname of Labour stalwart and author Ken and image consultant Barbara?
24 In which country was Mariella Frostrup born?
25 What is Frank Sinatra's widow's first name?
26 Which actor was married to screenwriter Melissa Mathison?
27 Who was the first US star to play "The Graduate"'s Mrs Robinson on a London stage?
28 Which Marquess is the brother of It Girl Victoria Hervey?
29 Brad Pitt and Angelina Jolie's first child was called what?
30 Which 2005 comedy film starred Barbra Streisand and Dustin Hoffman?

Answers	TV Trivia *(see Quiz 17)*

1 Walking with Dinosaurs. 2 Lake District. 3 Harbour Lights. 4 Lager. 5 Hot pot. 6 John Thaw. 7 £20,000. 8 My Family. 9 Coupling. 10 Coronation Street. 11 Two. 12 20 minutes. 13 Sarah Lancashire. 14 Glasses. 15 Antiques. 16 Marissa Cooper. 17 E20. 18 Popstars. 19 Tracy Barlow. 20 Where the Heart is. 21 Robinson. 22 The Two Ronnies. 23 Orville. 24 George. 25 Gaby Roslin. 26 Carol Smillie. 27 Monty Python. 28 Nine. 29 Hugh Laurie. 30 Jamie Theakston.

1 In which county is Bantry Bay in the south of Ireland?
2 What is Italy's Capodimonte famous for?
3 In which city is the Pompidou Centre?
4 Which island is called Kefallinia in Greek?
5 From which resort at the foot of Mont Blanc does the highest cable car in the world rise?
6 What do the British call what the French call Les Iles Normands?
7 Which province of the Irish Republic includes Galway and Sligo?
8 The Amalienborg Palace is the home of which Royal Family?
9 Which Scandinavian country is called Suomi in its own language?
10 The Baltic states are made up of Latvia, Lithuania and where?
11 What is Germany's Schwarzwald?
12 Which monument is at the opposite end of Paris's Champs Elysées from the Place de la Concorde?
13 Where was a refugee camp built for asylum-seekers near the Channel Tunnel?
14 Where is the park called the Bois de Boulogne?
15 What is the capital of the state of the Tyrol?
16 Ithaca is off the west coast of which country?
17 Which Scandinavian strait has a name which means cat's throat?
18 In which Sea are the Balearic Islands?
19 Which breed of dog comes from Kerry in south-west Ireland?
20 In which city is the Prado art gallery?
21 Which town of Lombardy gave its name to a bright reddish mauve dye?
22 What is the Bourse in Paris?
23 On which Sea is Odessa?
24 Which country has the rivers Douro, Tagus and Guadiana?
25 What is the chief city of Catalonia, and Spain's second largest?
26 Which is the farthest north, Belarus, Ukraine or Estonia?
27 What was St Petersburg called for much of the 20th century?
28 Which Sea is to the west of Denmark?
29 Which is the most easterly city, Stuttgart, Munich or Hanover?
30 The Basque country surrounds which mountains?

1 In 2006 which cricketer became England's youngest debut centurion?

2 Who became the first Briton to hold a world javelin record?

3 Where in Germany is a passion play staged once every ten years?

4 Which sport can be played under Australian, Association or Gaelic rules?

5 Which country did the Bay City Rollers come from?

6 Which US president had the middle name Milhous?

7 Ellis Island is in which harbour?

8 What was the rank of Georges Simenon's Maigret?

9 Tommy Docherty quipped that he'd had more what than Jack Nicklaus?

10 Which former athlete announced he would leave TV's "Songs of Praise" in 2007?

11 In American Football which creatures are linked to the Chicago team?

12 Artists Manet and Monet both came from which city?

13 Which star of "Strictly Come Dancing" produced an exercise DVD entitled "Latinasize"?

14 Agatha Christie wrote romantic novels under the pseudonym of Mary who?

15 Which country became the first to legalise abortion?

16 Which early pop classic song begins, "I'm so young and you're so old"?

17 In American college football what can go after Cotton, Orange and Sugar?

18 Navan Fort is in which Irish county?

19 In which country is the oldest angling club in the world?

20 Leonardo Da Vinci, Charles de Gaulle, Jan Smuts have all what named after them?

21 What is the next white note on a keyboard below G?

22 Which actor became a human cartoon in the movie "The Mask"?

23 Which city do the Afrikaaners know as Kaapstad?

24 Which motorway links up with the M25 closest to Heathrow Airport?

25 Which Joplin was one of the originators of ragtime?

26 Which actress starred as Princess Leia in the "Star Wars" trilogy?

27 Who joined Rod Stewart and Sting on the 1994 hit "All for Love"?

28 What does Honolulu mean in Hawaiian?

29 What is the traditional colour of an Indian wedding sari?

30 Which pop group had the last word of the Lord's Prayer as the first word of its name?

Answers | Pot Luck 10 *(see Quiz 23)*

1 Jason. 2 John Barnes. 3 The Rockies. 4 Spanish. 5 Baby. 6 As Time Goes By. 7 Smallpox. 8 Jude. 9 Jeremy Vine. 10 Cop. 11 The Little Mermaid. 12 Christopher Biggins. 13 Atlantic. 14 I Believe. 15 Austria. 16 Hormones. 17 Sol Campbell. 18 Latent. 19 Gabrielle. 20 22. 21 Horse. 22 Thumb. 23 Boombastic. 24 Gianni Versace. 25 Egypt. 26 Colchester. 27 Canterbury. 28 Susan Hampshire. 29 Ealing Comedies. 30 Desert Storm.

1 Which Italian club did Paul Gascoigne play for?
2 Aleksandr Hleb joined Arsenal from which side?
3 Who did Glen Hoddle play for just before he became England manager?
4 Who was Chelsea's top Premiership scorer in the 2005–06 season?
5 In which county was Bobby Charlton born?
6 Which overseas player led Naples to their first ever Italian championship?
7 How old was Stanley Matthews when he made his debut for England?
8 With which club side did Bobby Moore end his career?
9 Whose autobiography was called "My World"?
10 Jaap Stam signed for Manchester United from which club?
11 In the Germany vs England 2001 World Cup qualifier, what was the score at half time?
12 Which club did Chris Sutton join immediately after Blackburn Rovers?
13 Who were the opposition in Gary Lineker's final international when he was taken off by Graham Taylor?
14 Which manager preceded Graeme Souness and Tony Parkes at Blackburn Rovers?
15 In which decade was the European Champions Cup inaugurated?
16 Who won the last FA Cup Final of the 20th century?
17 John Hartson left West Ham for which club in 1999?
18 Who managed Manchester City immediately before Kevin Keegan?
19 The leading goalscorer in the 1998 World Cup finals came from which country?
20 How many goalds did Sunderland score in the FA Cup final of 1973?
21 Doyle and Kitson were joint top scorers as which side made the Premiership?
22 Who was the last side to win the old Division 1?
23 Which London side won the European Cup Winners Cup in 1998?
24 In France 98 who was England's top scorer along with Michael Owen?
25 Who beat Manchester United in their first FA Cup campaign of the 21st century?
26 Who did Scotland play the same day that England beat Germany 5–1?
27 Gary McAllister, Peter Reid and Gordon Strachan have managed which side?
28 Which soccer club did Bobby Charlton manage before becoming a Manchester United director?
29 Who has presented the Footballer of the Year award since 1948?
30 Before Michael Owen in Germany, who was the last England player to score a hat trick in international football?

Answers | Movies – Directors and Producers *(see Quiz 24)*

1 Joel. 2 Baz Luhrmann. 3 Clint Eastwood. 4 Director. 5 James Cameron. 6 Cecil B de Mille. 7 Gilbert & Sullivan (Topsy Turvy). 8 Evita. 9 Mel Brooks. 10 Jordan. 11 Rob Reiner. 12 Tokyo. 13 Nora Ephron. 14 Vincente Minnelli. 15 Mike Nichols. 16 Sylvester Stallone. 17 Tim Robbins. 18 Tchaikovsky. 19 Raging Bull. 20 Tony and Ridley Scott. 21 Nicole Kidman and Tom Cruise. 22 Penny. 23 Nixon. 24 Richard Attenborough. 25 Quentin Tarantino. 26 Apollo 13. 27 Brooklyn. 28 Monty Python's Flying Circus. 29 1970s. 30 Kevin Costner.

Quiz 23 | Pot Luck 10

1 What is the real first name of Jay Kay of Jamiroquai?
2 Who became the first person to wear white boots in an FA Cup Final?
3 In which mountain range is Mount Elbert the highest peak?
4 Which nationality goes with the Riding School in Austria?
5 Who or what was swimming on the cover of Nirvana's album "Nevermind"?
6 On TV, which show's theme song begins, "You must remember this"?
7 Variola is the medical name for which disease?
8 Which name appears in a Beatles song title and in a Thomas Hardy novel title?
9 Who presented "Panorama" when it returned to prime-time TV in 2007?
10 What was the profession of Michael Douglas' character in the movie "Basic Instinct"?
11 Hans Christian Andersen's memorial statue in Copenhagen takes the form of which character?
12 Which actor played Lukewarm in "Porridge"?
13 Which is the saltiest of the major oceans of the world?
14 What was coupled with Robson and Jerome's "Up on the Roof"?
15 German leader Adolf Hitler was born in which country?
16 The pituitary gland controls the production of what in the body?
17 Who scored Arsenal's first goal in a Champions League Final?
18 Which word describes hidden or concealed heat?
19 Which female vocalist featured on East 17's mid-1990s hit "If You Ever"?
20 At what age did Will Carling first captain England at rugby?
21 A Lippizaner is what type of animal?
22 A pollex is another name for which part of the body?
23 What was the second No 1 for Shaggy?
24 In 1997, whose funeral in Milan was attended by Elton John and Naomi Campbell?
25 Which country has the car registration code ET?
26 Blur formed in which East Anglian town?
27 In which city was Orlando Bloom born?
28 Which well-respected actress has been President of the Dyslexia Institute?
29 Which comedies was Michael Balcon responsible for?
30 In the 1990s, the operation to eject Iraqis from Kuwait was codenamed which Operation?

| **Answers** | **Pot Luck 9** *(see Quiz 21)* |

1 Alastair Cook. 2 Fatima Whitbread. 3 Oberammergau. 4 Football. 5 Scotland. 6 Nixon. 7 New York. 8 Inspector. 9 Clubs. 10 Jonathan Edwards. 11 Bears. 12 Paris. 13 Lilia Kopylova. 14 Westmacott. 15 Iceland. 16 Diana. 17 Bowl. 18 Armagh. 19 Scotland. 20 Airports. 21 F. 22 Jim Carrey. 23 Cape Town. 24 M4. 25 Scott. 26 Carrie Fisher. 27 Bryan Adams. 28 Sheltered bay. 29 Scarlet. 30 Amen Corner.

1 Who is Ethan Coen's director brother?
2 Who directed "Moulin Rouge", starring Nicole Kidman and Ewan McGregor?
3 Who directed the film "Flags of Our Fathers"?
4 What was George Lucas's role in the original "Star Wars"?
5 Who directed the movie about the most disastrous disaster at sea in peace time?
6 Who had the middle name Blount but only used his initial?
7 Which musical duo was the subject of a Mike Leigh movie with Jim Broadbent?
8 Which musical did Alan Parker direct before the drama "Angela's Ashes"?
9 How is Melvin Kaminski of "Young Frankenstein" better known?
10 Which Neil was Oscar-nominated as director and also writer for "The Crying Game"?
11 Who was the director of "When Harry Met Sally"?
12 In which city was Akira Kurosawa born?
13 Which lady was the director of the hit movies "Sleepless in Seattle" and "You Got M@il"?
14 Which father of a musical star directed "An American in Paris"?
15 How is the director of "Wolf" and "The Birdcage" born Michael Igor Peschkowsky better known?
16 Which actor directed "Rocky IV"?
17 Who was Oscar-nominated for "Dead Man Walking"?
18 Ken Russell's "The Music Lovers" was about which Russian composer?
19 For which movie with Robert De Niro did Martin Scorsese receive his first Oscar nomination?
20 Which brothers bought Shepperton Studios in 1994?
21 Which then husband and wife were the stars of Kubrick's "Eyes Wide Shut"?
22 What is the name of Garry Marshall's fellow director sibling, formerly married to the director of "When Harry Met Sally"?
23 Which president was the subject of the 1995 movie written and directed by Oliver Stone?
24 Who was the director of "Gandhi"?
25 Who was the subject of the biography "King Pulp"?
26 Which movie about an Apollo moon mission had Ron Howard as director?
27 Where in New York was Woody Allen born?
28 Terry Gilliam was a member of which comedy team?
29 In which decade did Stanley Kubrick direct "A Clockwork Orange"?
30 Which actor directed "Dances with Wolves" and "The Bodyguard?

Answers | Soccer *(see Quiz 22)*

1 Lazio. 2 Stuttgart. 3 Chelsea. 4 Frank Lampard. 5 Northumberland. 6 Diego Maradona. 7 20. 8 Fulham. 9 David Beckham. 10 PSV Eindhoven. 11 1–2. 12 Chelsea. 13 Sweden. 14 Brian Kidd. 15 1950s. 16 Manchester United. 17 Wimbledon. 18 Joe Royle. 19 Croatia. 20 One. 21 Reading. 22 Leeds. 23 Chelsea. 24 Alan Shearer. 25 West Ham. 26 Croatia. 27 Coventry. 28 Preston North End. 29 Football Writers' Association. 30 Alan Shearer.

1 Reba McEntire's best-of album was called "Moments" and what else?
2 Scientist Rene Descartes said "I think therefore ..." what?
3 Florentino Perez resigned as president of which major soccer club in February 2006?
4 An ossicle is a small what?
5 In which decade did Einstein die?
6 Which species of trees and shrubs come from the genus Malus?
7 Approximately how many feet are there in a fathom?
8 Which former Conservative Party Chairman wrote "False Impression"?
9 What was the name of the character played by Harry Enfield when he was in "Men Behaving Badly"?
10 Who said, "Honey I forgot to duck" after a failed assassination attempt?
11 In computing, how many bits are there in a byte?
12 What was the last name of chef Gareth in TV's "Chef!"?
13 A snapper is a type of what when it is red, yellowtail or grey?
14 How many seconds are there in a quarter of an hour?
15 In which country were the world's first known theatres built?
16 Which TV series was set at the Globelink News Office?
17 Terry Butcher and Lawrie McMenemy have both managed which soccer club?
18 Who was known in Australia as "The Crocodile Hunter"?
19 Phidippides was the first runner of which epic race?
20 Which novelist created the character George Smiley?
21 What was the first album from Il Divo to top the charts?
22 Which university is the oldest in the USA?
23 Which actor is on the cover of the "Official Dr Who Annual 2007"?
24 Which Thomas introduced the blue and white pottery known as Willow pattern?
25 The Longmuir brothers were in which teen idol band?
26 The Beeching report led to vast cuts in which service?
27 At Royal Ascot which day is Ladies' Day?
28 In which country would you watch Lokeren play a home soccer match?
29 Which singer called his son Otis in tribute to Otis Redding?
30 In which country did the Sharpeville massacre take place?

Answers | Pot Luck 12 *(see Quiz 27)*

1 Shilpa Shetty. 2 Kinetic energy. 3 Los Angeles. 4 Peas. 5 The phoenix. 6 Twopence. 7 REM. 8 Horizontally. 9 The Elephant Man. 10 Sadat. 11 Mike Ruddock. 12 Fireball XL5. 13 Beirut. 14 McPherson. 15 Anfield. 16 Spungeon. 17 Dutch. 18 Bouvier. 19 Jimi Hendrix. 20 Paul Gascoigne. 21 Woodward. 22 Labour. 23 Skiing. 24 Chess. 25 Orenthal. 26 Ainsley Harriott. 27 One. 28 Poisoned himself. 29 Dame Nellie Melba. 30 Los Angeles.

1 What goes with "Inside In" in the title of The Kooks' first album?
2 Which veteran rockers had a 2005 hit with "The Party ain't Over Yet"?
3 Who sang "I'll be Missing You" with Puff Daddy?
4 Which Mariah Carey single was the first to debut at No 1 in the US, in 1995?
5 What was the title of Corinne Bailey Rae's debut album?
6 Who was the first male rapper to have two solo No 1s?
7 S Club 7's "Never Had a Dream Come True" raised money for which charity?
8 Which was the first band to have seven successive No 1s with their first seven releases?
9 Which British band had the first No 1 of the new millennium?
10 Which girl's name featured in a mega hit for Dexy's Midnight Runners?
11 Which was Wham!'s best-selling Christmas single?
12 Which 2000 Spiller song stopped Victoria Beckham from having her first solo No 1?
13 What was the English title of Sarah Brightman's "Con Te Partiro" which she sang with Andrea Bocelli?
14 Who first made the Top Twenty with "Linger"?
15 In 2000 Oxide & Neutrino charted with a reworking of the theme of which hospital series?
16 Who sang "How Do I Live" in 1998?
17 Whose "Killing Me Softly" was a top seller in 1996?
18 Which song from "Bridget Jones's Diary" did Geri Halliwell have a hit with in 2001?
19 What was Britney Spears' second UK No 1?
20 What was Elton John's first solo No 1 in the US?
21 "Three Lions" charted in which World Cup year?
22 Which family charted with "Mmmbop"?
23 Which Oasis member sang on The Chemical Brothers' "Setting Sun"?
24 What was Michael Jackson's last No 1 of the 20th century?
25 In which decade did Japan have their first Top Ten hit?
26 Who hit No 1 with "Deeper Underground" in 1999?
27 Chef's 1998 No 1 came from which cartoon series?
28 Who charted with "All Right Now" in the 1970s and with a 1990s remix?
29 "Vision of Love" was the first Top Ten hit for which singer?
30 In which decade did smooth soul group the Chi-Lites have most hits?

| **Answers** | Past Times – 1950 on *(see Quiz 28)* |

1 Kenneth Clarke. 2 Germany. 3 Malawi. 4 Cuba. 5 Palestine. 6 1940. 7 Chile. 8 Jacques Chirac. 9 Ronald Reagan. 10 1960s. 11 Barbara. 12 China. 13 Greenham Common. 14 Alexander Gromyko. 15 Salisbury. 16 Erich Honecker. 17 Westminster Abbey. 18 Karadzic. 19 Hampstead & Highgate. 20 Cambodia. 21 Alabama. 22 Charles Manson. 23 Warren. 24 Cricket. 25 Linda Tripp. 26 Humphrey. 27 Chris Evans. 28 Pigs. 29 Althorp. 30 Lisburn.

1 Which Bollywood actress was at the centre of "Big Brother" controversy in 2007?

2 What name is given to the energy produced when something moves?

3 In movies, E.T. arrived in which city of California?

4 What can be Hurst Beagle or Kelvedon Wonder?

5 In legend which bird rose from its own ashes?

6 In "Mary Poppins" how much does it cost for a bag to "Feed the Birds"?

7 Which three initial letters stand for the speedy reactions of the organ of sight?

8 In a window a transom is a bar situated in which way?

9 What type of man was John Merrick known as?

10 Who became the first Egyptian leader to visit Israel?

11 Which Welsh rugby coach resigned for "family reasons" in 2006?

12 Which craft did Steve Zodiac command?

13 Keanu Reeves was born in which war-torn city?

14 What is the surname of Suggs, singer with Madness?

15 At which ground did Bill Shankly suffer his fatal heart attack?

16 Which Nancy was linked with Sid Vicious?

17 What was the nationality of spy Mata Hari?

18 What was Jacqueline Kennedy's surname before her marriage to the future US President?

19 Which rock musician prophetically said, "Once you're dead you're made for life"?

20 Which controversial footballer briefly was the husband of Sheryl Failes?

21 Which journalist was Bernstein's partner in investigating Watergate?

22 TV chat man Robert Kilroy-Silk was an MP for which party?

23 Which activity was Sonny Bono involved in at the time of his accidental death?

24 Bobby Fischer was the first American world champion in which sport?

25 What does O stand for in OJ Simpson's name?

26 Who produced a "Feel-Good Cookbook"?

27 How many of the Beatles were not known by their real names?

28 What final act did Hermann Goering do some hours before his execution?

29 How was Australian singer Helen Porter Mitchell better known?

30 Marilyn Monroe was born and died in which city?

Answers	Pot Luck 11 *(see Quiz 25)*

1 Memories. 2 I Am. 3 Real Madrid. 4 Bone. 5 1950s. 6 Apple. 7 Six. 8 Jeffrey Archer. 9 Dermot. 10 Ronald Reagan. 11 Eight. 12 Blackstock. 13 Fish. 14 900. 15 Greece. 16 Drop the Dead Donkey. 17 Sunderland. 18 Steve Irwin. 19 Marathon. 20 John Le Carre. 21 Il Divo. 22 Harvard. 23 David Tennant. 24 Thomas Turner. 25 Bay City Rollers. 26 Railway. 27 Thursday (third day). 28 Belgium. 29 Bryan Ferry. 30 South Africa.

1 Who was the other final contender for the Tory leadership contest in 1997 when William Hague won?

2 In which country were the Baader Meinhof gang based?

3 Hastings Banda became Prime Minister of which country in 1964?

4 The Bay of Pigs near which island was an area which triggered a missile crisis in 1961?

5 Black September were a terrorist group from which country?

6 In which year did the Battle of Britain begin?

7 Pinochet led a military coup in which country?

8 Who succeeded Mitterrand as President of France?

9 Milton Friedman was policy adviser to which US President in the 1980s?

10 In which decade did Colonel Gaddafi seize power in Libya?

11 What was the name of the first First Lady called Bush?

12 Where was there the "Great Leap Forward" in the 1950s?

13 Which site in Berkshire was the scene of anti-nuclear protests, mainly by women, in the 1980s?

14 Who was Soviet Foreign Minister for almost 30 years in the latter half of the 20th century?

15 What was the former name of Harare?

16 Who was East German leader from 1976 to 1989?

17 In which building was Princess Diana's funeral service held?

18 Who became Bosnian president in 1992?

19 In 1992 Glenda Jackson became MP for which constituency?

20 Where did the Khmer Rouge operate?

21 In which state did Martin Luther King lead the famous bus boycott?

22 Who led the sect which killed actress Sharon Tate?

23 Which Commission was set up to investigate the assassination of John F Kennedy?

24 Kerry Packer set up a rebel sports tour in which sport in the 1970s?

25 Who was Monica Lewinsky's confidante?

26 What was the name of the cat "evicted" from Downing Street as the Blairs moved in?

27 Who bought Virgin Radio from Richard Branson in 1997?

28 Who were the Tamworth Two?

29 Where was Princess Diana buried?

30 Near which town was the former Maze Prison sited?

Answers	Music Charts *(see Quiz 26)*

1 Inside Out. 2 Status Quo. 3 Faith Evans. 4 Fantasy. 5 Corinne Bailey Rae. 6 Eminem. 7 Children in Need. 8 Westlife. 9 Manic Street Preachers. 10 Eileen. 11 Last Christmas. 12 Groovejet. 13 Time to Say Goodbye. 14 Cranberries. 15 Casualty. 16 LeAnn Rimes. 17 The Fugees. 18 It's Raining Men. 19 Born to Make You Happy. 20 Crocodile Rock. 21 1998. 22 Hanson. 23 Noel Gallagher. 24 Blood on the Dance Floor. 25 1980s. 26 Jamiroquai. 27 South Park. 28 Free. 29 Mariah Carey. 30 1970s.

1 The true-life exploits of Harold Abrahams were told in which movie?
2 Who mysteriously vanished off the yacht Lady Ghislaine?
3 In which street did the infamous Rose and Frederick West live in Gloucester?
4 What is actor Michael Caine's real first name?
5 US President Andrew Jackson was nicknamed Old what?
6 In which country could you watch rugby at Ellis Park?
7 Which saint is on the Pope's signet ring?
8 What colour are the stars on the flag of the European Union?
9 Which country had a President with a spouse named Ladybird?
10 Japp Stam left Manchester United to go to which club?
11 Who won Super Bowl XL in 2006?
12 In which country was the scientist Gabriel Fahrenheit born?
13 Who directs and acts in "The Good Shepherd"?
14 What do Harvard Rules govern?
15 In mathematics, the abbreviation HCF stands for what?
16 How many seconds are there in a single round of championship boxing?
17 Whose songs were featured in the movie "Toy Story"?
18 Which actress, famous as a TV detective, was christened Ilynea Lydia Mironoff?
19 Which was the last host nation to have the Olympic Games opened by the country's king?
20 Which aspect of the weather is brontophobia the fear of?
21 Which of these games has the largest playing area – polo, soccer or tennis?
22 How many ribs has the human body?
23 "Grace and Favour" was a sequel to which sitcom?
24 Which England cricketer returned from India in February, and Australia in December 2006?
25 What nationality was mathematician Sir Isaac Newton?
26 What type of creature is equally at home on land and in water?
27 How many oxygen atoms are contained in a molecule of water?
28 PCs Stamp and Quinnan worked at which police station on TV?
29 What is the study of fluids moving in pipes known as?
30 Which band asked, "What's the Frequency Kenneth?"?

Answers Pot Luck 14 (see Quiz 31)

1 Ag. 2 Taggart. 3 Human glands. 4 The sun. 5 The Calypso. 6 Curling. 7 Three. 8 Good Morning Vietnam. 9 Gerald Ford. 10 Nuremberg. 11 Phillip Pulman. 12 France. 13 Tom Cruise. 14 Weightlifting. 15 Vikings. 16 Gone with the Wind. 17 Battles. 18 Boer War. 19 Leicester. 20 Donald Maclean. 21 Time Team. 22 Archery. 23 M6. 24 A roof. 25 London Marathon. 26 Marion. 27 Piccadilly. 28 Robbie Coltrane (2000). 29 Decathlon. 30 July.

Quiz 30 | TV Presenters | Answers – page 156 | LEVEL 2

1 Which "Points of View" presenter wrote an autobiography called "Is It Me?"?
2 Which presenter appeared in the comedy "'Orrible"?
3 Who replaced Loyd Grossman as presenter of "Masterchef"?
4 Who presented "Before They were Famous"?
5 Who preceded Michael Aspel on "The Antiques Road Show"?
6 Which David Attenborough series of 2001 was about life in and under the sea?
7 Who presented and co-devised "Art Attack"?
8 Who moved from "Wheel of Fortune" to a daily show on Radio Five Live?
9 Who was the wine buff on "Food & Drink" when Antony Worrall Thompson and Emma Crowhurst became regular food experts?
10 What would Peter Cockcroft talk about on TV?
11 Who replaced Vanessa on ITV's morning chat show?
12 Which Irish presenter introduced "Animal Hospital" with Rolf Harris?
13 Which daytime show does Gloria Hunniford present regularly on Channel 5?
14 Which former "Mastermind" host died in January 2007?
15 In 2003, Vernon Kay married which TV presenter?
16 Alvin Hall presents programmes about looking after your what?
17 Who presented the reality programme "Space Cadets"?
18 Which ex-"Blue Peter" presenter introduced "The Big Breakfast"?
19 Which actress introduced a "Watercolour Challenge" on daytime TV?
20 Which business programme is presented by Adrian Chiles?
21 Who hosted "Fifteen to One"?
22 Who first presented "The National Lottery: Winning Lines"?
23 Who introduces the "Bloomers" series about BBC TV outtakes?
24 Who replaced the late Jill Dando on "Crimewatch"?
25 Which sport does John McCririck present?
26 Which ex-footballer tested the teams on "Friends Like These"?
27 Alphabetically, who comes first in "Countdown" presenters?
28 Who tested contestants on the comedy game show "Oblivious"?
29 Who replaced Paul Daniels on "Wipeout"?
30 Rachel De Thame offers advice on what?

| **Answers** | **World Tour** *(see Quiz 32)* |

1 Greenland. 2 Indonesia. 3 Argentina. 4 California. 5 Gulf of Finland. 6 Casablanca. 7 Two. 8 Azerbaijan. 9 Bejing. 10 North Africa. 11 Cairo. 12 Manhattan. 13 Saigon. 14 Hawaii. 15 Tigris. 16 Brooklyn. 17 Andes. 18 Cape Horn. 19 Bass. 20 Click. 21 Indonesia. 22 Jodhpur. 23 Johannesburg. 24 Atlantic. 25 Bronx. 26 Iran. 27 Costa Rica. 28 China. 29 Indian. 30 Barbados.

Quiz 31 | Pot Luck 14 | Answers – page 153

1 What is the chemical symbol for silver?
2 Which TV cop show featured DCI Michael Jardine?
3 What are the islets of Langerhans?
4 What does a heliologist study?
5 What was the name of the research ship used by Jacques Cousteau?
6 USA beat Great Britain to a 2006 bronze medal in which Olympic team event?
7 How many pins are there in the front two rows in ten-pin bowling?
8 Which movie gave Robin Williams his first Oscar nomination?
9 Who became US President when Richard Nixon resigned?
10 In which city did trials of major Nazi leaders begin in 1945?
11 Which writer created the character Sally Lockhart?
12 In which country is Satolas international airport?
13 In the movies, who played war veteran Ron Kovic?
14 What are you doing if you carry out a snatch lift and a jerk lift?
15 In American Football which warriors come from Minnesota?
16 In which movie classic was Olivia de Havilland cast as Melanie Wilkes?
17 What do the Sealed Knot Society re-enact?
18 The Siege of Ladysmith took place during which war?
19 Brian Little and Martin O'Neill have both managed which soccer club?
20 Who fled together with Guy Burgess to the USSR in 1951?
21 Tony Robinson presented the long-running history programme "Time" what?
22 In which sport is there a gold-coloured target area worth 10 points?
23 Which motorway takes you south from Carlisle?
24 What is a cupola?
25 Which annual event began in London in 1981?
26 What was John Wayne's less than tough-sounding real first name?
27 Where in London was the first Fortnum & Mason opened?
28 Who was 50 first – Amanda Burton, Keith Chegwin or Robbie Coltrane?
29 In which event did Daley Thompson win Olympic gold?
30 In which month do the French celebrate Bastille Day?

Answers | Pot Luck 13 *(see Quiz 29)*

1 Chariots of Fire. 2 Robert Maxwell. 3 Cromwell Street. 4 Maurice. 5 Hickory. 6 South Africa. 7 St Peter. 8 Yellow. 9 USA. 10 Lazio. 11 Pittsburgh Steelers. 12 Germany. 13 Robert de Niro. 14 American football. 15 Highest common factor. 16 80. 17 Randy Newman. 18 Helen Mirren. 19 Spain. 20 Thunder. 21 Polo. 22 24. 23 Are You Being Served?. 24 Marcus Trescothick. 25 English. 26 Amphibian. 27 One. 28 Sun Hill. 29 Hydraulics. 30 R.E.M.

1 Baffin Island is between Baffin Bay and which island?
2 Bali is a mountainous island of which country?
3 The Falkland Islands are off which country?
4 Which US state is dubbed the Golden State?
5 Helsinki is on which Gulf?
6 Which city, also the name of a film, has the world's largest mosque?
7 How many islands make up Fiji?
8 Baku is the capital of which country on the Caspian Sea?
9 Where is the Forbidden City?
10 The Barbary Coast is the Mediterranean coast of where?
11 Which Egyptian city is Africa's largest city?
12 Greenwich Village is in which borough of New York City?
13 On which river is Ho Chi Minh City?
14 Where is Waikiki Beach?
15 Baghdad is on which river?
16 In which borough of New York City is Coney island?
17 In which mountains is the volcanic Cotopaxi?
18 Where are the Roaring Forties?
19 Which strait separates Australia from Tasmania?
20 What special sound is made in the language of the Hottentots of south-west Africa?
21 Which country was formerly the Dutch East Indies?
22 Which city gave its name to a type of riding breeches?
23 What is South Africa's largest city?
24 In which ocean are the Bahamas?
25 Which part of New York was named after Jonas Bronck?
26 The holy city of Qom is in which country?
27 Which country is between Nicaragua and Panama?
28 K2 is on the border of Pakistan and which country?
29 In which ocean are the Comoros?
30 Which is the most easterly of the Windward Islands in the Caribbean?

1 In which country was Amanda Holden's "Wild at Heart" filmed?
2 Which country gave the Statue of Liberty to the USA?
3 Which word went with "Growing" in the title of Billie Piper's autobiography?
4 What was Mel Gibson's first movie where he was actor, director and producer?
5 In motor racing, what colours are on the flag at the end of a race?
6 Which series with Prunella Scales had three years on radio before transferring to TV?
7 Which racecourse is famous for its Royal Enclosure?
8 Where in the UK is the National Motor Museum?
9 What is the maximum number of pieces that can appear on a chessboard?
10 In Gershwin's song, if it's "Summertime," the living is what?
11 Whereabouts in London did Laura Ashley open her first shop?
12 In credit terms, what does A stand for in an APR?
13 What is the world's biggest-selling copyrighted game?
14 What do the Americans call hockey played outside?
15 In which country did karaoke singing originate?
16 What would be your hobby if you used slip?
17 Lennie Lawrence and Colin Todd have both managed which soccer club?
18 Which 1980s band included Cook, Heaton and Hemingway?
19 What was the first capital of the United States?
20 Which TV series has featured the Kings and the Tates?
21 Which Christian name was shared by former British PMs Winston Churchill and James Callaghan?
22 Who was the first Spice Girl to announce her engagement?
23 What is the name of Andy Murray's tennis-playing brother?
24 In which country could you watch Rennes playing Sedan at soccer?
25 What was the middle name of Ronnie Barker's character Norman Fletcher in TV's "Porridge"?
26 What did Jimmy Carter farm before becoming US President?
27 Coal is composed from which element?
28 What was the profession of Georges Auguste Escoffier?
29 President Mobutu fled in 1997 after more than 30 years in office in which country?
30 What year was the "New York Mining Disaster" according to the Bee Gees?

Answers	Pot Luck 16 *(see Quiz 35)*

1 Big Bang. 2 Sonny Crockett. 3 Gina G. 4 Lesley Garrett. 5 0.54. 6 The eyes. 7 2004. 8 PE teacher. 9 Michelle Pfeiffer. 10 McLaren. 11 Princess Anne. 12 Beirut. 13 Barbara. 14 Paramount Pictures. 15 Sir Matt Busby. 16 Would I Lie to You? 17 Anatomy. 18 Michael Foot. 19 I. 20 The Bodyguard. 21 17th. 22 Variegated. 23 Holly. 24 Fairground. 25 Raisa. 26 Light years. 27 Devon. 28 Desmond Dekker. 29 Bull. 30 1894.

1 In addition to Leicestershire, which county did David Gower play for?
2 Who was the first cricketer to be awarded a knighthood while still playing Test cricket?
3 In which century was the MCC founded?
4 Which country was readmitted to the Test tour in 1992 along with South Africa?
5 On which ground did Brian Lara hit his record 501 not out?
6 Desmond Hayes earned 116 caps for which side?
7 In which decade did Allan Border make the first of his record-breaking 11,174 runs for Australia?
8 In which Gallery at Lord's are the Ashes kept?
9 What is another name for backward point?
10 What did the first C stand for in TCCB?
11 If an umpire raises his index finger in front of his body, or above his head, what does it mean?
12 Which late South African captain was suspended under suspicion of taking bribes?
13 Which country scored the highest single innings total in a Test, in 1997?
14 Which future cricket knight partnered Peter May to a partnership of 411 in 1957?
15 What was the AXA Life League called between 1969 and 1986?
16 Which Test cricketer has regularly captained a team on "They Think It's All Over"?
17 Against which county did Gary Sobers hit his amazing six sixes in an over?
18 Who topped England's batting averages in the 2006/7 Ashes series?
19 Test matches are the highest standard of what type of cricket?
20 How many Tests did Geoff Boycott play for England?
21 In 1986 which southern African-born player was the youngest to make 2,000 runs in a season?
22 Against which side did Ian Botham make his Test debut?
23 What was Graham Gooch's score on his very first Test match?
24 Which was the first English county side to sign Brian Lara?
25 Glenn McGrath played his final Test match in which city?
26 In the 2006/7 Ashes, which English batsman hit a double century?
27 How long are each of the two pieces of wood which make up the bails?
28 In which decade did Gary Sobers first play for the West Indies?
29 In which century did England play its first Test match?
30 Alphabetically, which is the first of the first-class English county sides?

| **Answers** | Movies – 2000 *(see Quiz 36)* |

1 Ewan McGregor. 2 Spielberg. 3 Penelope Cruz. 4 Helen Hunt. 5 Lara Croft. 6 Egg farm. 7 Ridley Scott. 8 Kathy Burke. 9 Meg Ryan. 10 Erin Brokovich. 11 Pierce Brosnan. 12 Penelope Cruz. 13 Julia Sawalha. 14 Swordfish. 15 Thailand. 16 Pistol. 17 Kate Beckinsale. 18 Cats. 19 Mike Myers. 20 Boxing. 21 Jon Voight. 22 Juliette Binoche. 23 Traffic. 24 Albert Finney. 25 Geoffrey Rush. 26 Jurassic Park III. 27 Nicolas Cage. 28 Gemma Jones. 29 Rachel Weisz. 30 Doctor.

1 Which explosive theory explains the formation of the universe?

2 Who did Don Johnson play in "Miami Vice"?

3 Who sang the British Eurovision Song Contest entry the year before Katrina and the Waves won?

4 Who played the Mother Abbess in the 2006 stage revival of "The Sound of Music"?

5 How would 27% doubled be shown as a decimal?

6 Where in the body are there rods and cones?

7 In which year was the 150th University Boat Race?

8 What was the profession of Zoe in the TV sitcom "May to December"?

9 Who was Oscar-nominated for "Dangerous Liaisons" and "The Fabulous Baker Boys"?

10 Which Malcolm was manager of the punk band The Sex Pistols?

11 Who was the first child of a reigning British monarch to be brought before a criminal court?

12 In which war-torn city was Terry Waite kidnapped?

13 In the White House who went after Nancy and came before Hillary?

14 Which movie company did Tom Cruise part company with in 2006?

15 Who was the first manager to win the European Champions Cup with an English club?

16 Which title links the Eurythmics to a Charles and Eddy No 1?

17 Which branch of biology deals with the structure of animals?

18 Who succeeded James Callaghan as leader of the Labour Party?

19 What is the chemical symbol for iodine?

20 Which film featured the song that gave Whitney Houston her fourth UK No 1?

21 In which century was Blaise Pascal working on his calculating machine?

22 What term describes a leaf with two or more colours?

23 Which species of trees and shrubs come from the genus Ilex?

24 What was Simply Red's first UK No 1?

25 What was Soviet leader Mikael Gorbachev's wife called?

26 Which years measure distance in space?

27 Which English county was part of the name of the horse that collapsed in sight of victory in the Grand National?

28 Dying in 2006, who had had his biggest hit with "Israelites"?

29 Which animal name was given to the wild Bronx boxer Jake La Motta?

30 When was Blackpool Tower built – 1834, 1894 or 1924?

Quiz 36 | Movies – 2000 | Answers – page 158

1 Who was Nicole Kidman's co-star in "Moulin Rouge"?
2 Who directed "AI: Artificial Intelligence"?
3 Who played opposite Nicolas Cage in "Captain Corelli's Mandolin"?
4 Who plays Darcy Maguire in "What Women Want", with Mel Gibson?
5 Who was the star of the computer-animated "Tomb Raider"?
6 What sort of farm features in "Chicken Run"?
7 Who directed "Gladiator"?
8 Who co-starred with Harry Enfield in "Kevin and Perry Go Large"?
9 Who became romantically linked with Russell Crowe during the making of "Proof of Life"?
10 For which movie did Julia Roberts win her first Oscar?
11 Who played the title role in Richard Attenborough's "Grey Owl"?
12 Who plays Johnny Depp's wife in "Blow"?
13 Which "Absolutely Fabulous" star was the voice of Ginger in "Chicken Run"?
14 Which movie starred Hugh Jackman as a computer hacker and John Travolta as a counter-terrorist?
15 In which country was "The Beach" filmed?
16 In "The Mexican", what is the Mexican?
17 Who is the female corner of the love triangle in "Pearl Harbor"?
18 In "Meet the Parents" which animals is Robert De Niro particularly fond of?
19 Who was the voice of Shrek?
20 Which classes should Billy Elliot be going to when he is doing ballet?
21 Who played Lara Croft's father in the "Tomb Raider" film and in real life too?
22 Who plays the single mum in "Chocolat"?
23 Which new millennium movie on the drugs trade starred Michael Douglas?
24 Which English actor played the lawyer in "Erin Brokovich"?
25 Who plays the Marquis de Sade in "Quills"?
26 What was the sequel to "The Lost World" in the "Jurassic Park" films?
27 Who is the star of "The Family Man", a remake of "It's a Wonderful Life"?
28 Who played Bridget's mum in "Bridget Jones's Diary"?
29 Which actress is the object of Jude Law's and Joseph Fiennes' affections in "Enemy at the Gates"?
30 What is John Hurt's profession in "Captain Corelli's Mandolin"?

Answers | Cricket *(see Quiz 34)*

1 Hampshire. 2 Richard Hadlee. 3 18th. 4 Zimbabwe. 5 Edgbaston. 6 West Indies.
7 1970s. 8 Memorial Gallery. 9 Gully. 10 County. 11 The batsman is out. 12 Hansie
Cronje. 13 Sri Lanka. 14 Colin Cowdrey. 15 John Player Sunday League. 16 David
Gower. 17 Glamorgan. 18 Kevin Pietersen. 19 First class. 20 108. 21 Graeme Hick.
22 Australia. 23 Duck. 24 Warwickshire. 25 Sydney. 26 Paul Collingwood. 27 Just
under 5 inches. 28 1950s. 29 19th. 30 Derbyshire.

Quiz 37 | Pot Luck 17

Answers – page 163

LEVEL 2

1 Which character in "The Bill" was played by the late Kevin Lloyd?
2 Which branch of physics deals with motion of objects?
3 Which comedian – voted "wittiest living person" – died in 2006 at the age of 48?
4 Who did Nicole Kidman marry in 2006?
5 Eton school is in which English county?
6 In sport, what word can go after Trent and Stamford?
7 How is Mary O'Brien who died in March 1999 better known?
8 In which country is Malpensa international airport?
9 Which great Test cricketer's forename initials are the same as the abbreviation for Information Technology?
10 What does fibrian cause the blood to do?
11 Which late great duetted with kd lang on his mega-hit "Crying"?
12 How would four-fifths be shown as a decimal?
13 Which sport did Marco Van Basten play?
14 Whose life story was re-created in the biopic "Sweet Dreams"?
15 Which country celebrated its bicentenary in 1988?
16 How many stomachs does a cow have?
17 Which country has the car registration code T?
18 Cu is the chemical symbol for which element?
19 Which country was first to host both the Summer and Winter Olympics in the same year?
20 What was the first name of Stephen Tomkinson's character in "Drop the Dead Donkey"?
21 The late Brian Connolly fronted which glam band?
22 What is the name of the cat in "Sabrina the Teenage Witch"?
23 Pop star Billie married in May 2001 in which US city?
24 Who was the body-snatching partner of Hare?
25 Which entertainer said, "George, don't do that"?
26 Which murder victim was mentioned in the trailers for "Twin Peaks"?
27 In which country would you watch Grasshoppers play a home soccer match?
28 Which soccer club has Worcester Avenue and Paxton Road close to the stadium?
29 Which pop superstar's first wife was Cynthia Powell?
30 Patrick Troughton followed William Hartnell to play which character in a long-running TV series?

Answers	Animals *(see Quiz 39)*

1 Monkey. 2 Australia. 3 Chick. 4 Marsupial. 5 Umbilical. 6 India. 7 Dodo. 8 African elephant. 9 Cat. 10 Herbivorous. 11 Squirrel. 12 Trees. 13 40%. 14 Smell. 15 Chimpanzee. 16 Alone. 17 Borneo. 18 Reptiles. 19 Hood. 20 Clawed. 21 Border collie. 22 Tapeworm. 23 Whale. 24 Indian cobra. 25 Spawn. 26 Hare. 27 Starfish. 28 Thumb. 29 Cobra. 30 Grizzly bear.

1 What was on the other side of Boney M's "Brown Girl in the Ring"?
2 Which Dawn single was in the charts for 39 weeks in the 1970s?
3 Which film did "You're the One that I Want" come from?
4 Which 1970s hit by Wings was the first UK single to sell two million copies?
5 Who made the album "Don't Shoot Me I'm Only the Piano Player"?
6 Which solo singer who died in 2001 recorded the album "And I Love You So"?
7 Whom did Elton John have a No 1 single with in 1976?
8 Julie Covington had a UK No 1 with a song from which Andrew Lloyd Webber/Tim Rice musical?
9 Who was the most successful solo star from the group which had a No 1 with "Message in a Bottle"?
10 "Matchstalk Men and Matchstalk Cats and Dogs" was about which artist?
11 With which song did Brotherhood of Man win the Eurovision Song Contest?
12 Who had the original hit with "Seasons in the Sun"?
13 Who had "Breakfast In America"?
14 How many times is Annie's name mentioned in John Denver's "Annie's Song"?
15 Who was the first Beatle to have a solo No 1 in the 1970s?
16 Which member of the cast of "Dad's Army" had a No 1 hit record?
17 Who hit No 1 with "Cum on Feel the Noize"?
18 Who declared that he was the Leader of the Gang?
19 Which star of the stage show "Evita" had a hit with "Hold Me Close"?
20 What was the title of the England World Cup squad's anthem of 1970?
21 On which new record label was Mike Oldfield's "Tubular Bells" released?
22 Which Tony featured on Dawn's "Tie a Yellow Ribbon"?
23 Which instrument did Suzi Quatro play on "Can the Can"?
24 Who had a hit with Nilsson's "Without You" 20 years later?
25 Which band made the super selling "Rumours"?
26 Which band did Roy Wood lead in "Angel Fingers"?
27 Whose "Sailing" was describes by its performer as "one for the terraces"?
28 Which band's very first hit was "Debora"?
29 "I'd Like to Teach the World to Sing" was later used to advertised which drink?
30 Who recorded the album "Arrival"?

Answers | Pot Luck 18 *(see Quiz 40)*

1 Leona Lewis. 2 1896. 3 God. 4 Ballykissangel. 5 Aubretia. 6 16. 7 Nile. 8 Francis Ford Coppola. 9 At a walking pace. 10 Nesta. 11 Hooves. 12 Meridiem. 13 Portugal. 14 16th. 15 Wren. 16 Hedgehunter. 17 1960s. 18 Mr Men. 19 Codes. 20 St Denis. 21 Iron. 22 Swedish. 23 Alan Shearer. 24 Grizabella. 25 1920s. 26 Canada. 27 Busy Lizzy. 28 Violet Wilson. 29 The Three Degrees. 30 Rhubarb.

1 What type of creature is a mandrill?
2 The bandicoot is a marsupial from which country?
3 What is a young penguin called?
4 What sort of creature is a Tasmanian devil?
5 Which cord connects the placenta to the embryo in mammals?
6 Which country has the most Asian elephants in their natural habitat?
7 Which extinct flightless bird has the Latin name Didus ineptus?
8 Which weighs the most – African elephant, hippopotamus or white rhinoceros?
9 What can be Persian long hair, British short hair or Oriental short hair?
10 Which word would describe a wombat's diet?
11 The chipmunk is related to which creature?
12 Where do sloths live?
13 What percentage of all living mammals are rodents?
14 Which of the primates' senses is the weakest?
15 Which is the most intelligent – baboon, chimpanzee or gorilla?
16 How does a tiger hunt?
17 The orang utan in the wild is restricted to Sumatra and where?
18 Who has the most teeth, reptiles, fish or mammals?
19 What is the neck region of the cobra called?
20 What sort of feet do tortoises have?
21 Which is the most intelligent breed of dog?
22 Which of the following animals has the greatest length or height – African elephant, giraffe or tapeworm?
23 What can be minke, grey or bowhead?
24 Which snake is traditionally used by snake charmers?
25 What are the fertilised eggs of amphibians called?
26 Which is the fastest – hare, horse or greyhound?
27 Which fish are members of the class Asteroidea?
28 Which is the only "finger" of a bat that is free from the membrane that forms its wing?
29 Which deadly snakes can be Egyptian, Indian or Forest?
30 Which is the heaviest – black bear, grizzly bear or polar bear?

---

1 Who was the first female winner of "The X Factor"?
2 When were the first Modern Olympic Games held?
3 What are you afraid of if you suffer from theophobia?
4 Father Peter Clifford appeared in which TV series?
5 Which plant was named after Claude Aubriet?
6 How many pawns start off a chess game?
7 The Aswan Dam was built on which river?
8 Who directed all "The Godfather" series of movies?
9 What does the musical term andante mean?
10 What was Bob Marley's middle name?
11 What does an ungulate animal have?
12 What does the letter m in the time abbreviation p.m. stand for?
13 The Azores belong to which country?
14 In which century was William Shakespeare born?
15 Which bird was on the old coin the farthing?
16 Which 2005 Grand National winner started as favourite for the 2006?
17 In which decade did the Victoria line open on the London Underground?
18 Roger Hargreaves created which Men – "The Flowerpot Men", "The Four Just Men" or "Mr Men"?
19 Cryptography is the study of what?
20 Who is the patron saint of France?
21 What do ferrous metals contain?
22 What nationality was chemist Alfred Nobel?
23 Who was the was the first player to score 100 goals in the Premier League?
24 In the musical "Cats" which cat sings "Memory"?
25 In which decade was the first FA Cup Final played at Wembley?
26 As well as being an animal, the Red Deer is a river in which country?
27 How is the plant Impatiens more usually known?
28 She didn't play a Platt, but which character did actress Jenny Platt play in "Corrie"?
29 How were Ferguson, Thompson and Pickney known collectively?
30 Hawk's Champagne and Prince Albert are types of what?

Answers	**Sounds of the Seventies** *(see Quiz 38)*

1 Rivers of Babylon. 2 Tie a Yellow Ribbon. 3 Grease. 4 Mull of Kintyre. 5 Elton John.
6 Perry Como. 7 Kiki Dee. 8 Evita. 9 Sting. 10 LS Lowry. 11 Save Your Kisses for
Me. 12 Terry Jacks. 13 Supertramp. 14 Never. 15 George Harrison. 16 Clive Dunn.
17 Slade. 18 Gary Glitter. 19 David Essex. 20 Back Home. 21 Virgin. 22 Orlando.
23 Bass guitar. 24 Mariah Carey. 25 Fleetwood Mac. 26 Wizzard. 27 Rod Stewart.
28 T. Rex. 29 Coca Cola. 30 Abba.

1 Who defeated Silvio Berlusconi in the 2006 Italian elections?
2 Which country won the 2006 Eurovision Song Contest?
3 Bakelite was the first important what?
4 In which decade did John Logie Baird first demonstrate television?
5 Bangladesh was created from which former territory?
6 Which political leader had a villa retreat at Berchtesgaden?
7 Which Prime Minister suffered the "winter of discontent"?
8 Bill Clinton appointed his wife Hillary to carry out reforms in which social service?
9 What was the Democratic Republic of Congo called between 1971 and 1997?
10 Who did George W Bush defeat to become President in 2000?
11 Inkatha was set up to promote the interests of which South African race?
12 What does the M stand for in IMF?
13 Where in London was a memorial service held three days after the New York and Washington terrorist attacks of September 2001?
14 What does A stand for in IRA?
15 Which Israeli leader was assassinated in 1995?
16 Silvio Berlusconi became which country's Prime Minister in 1994?
17 Who was the first British writer to receive the Nobel Prize for Literature?
18 Who headed the US committee investigating Communist infiltration in public life?
19 Which country has a news agency called TASS?
20 What did Joseph Pulitzer give a Prize for?
21 Who wrote "An Inconvenient Truth" about his concerns about the environment?
22 Which Moors were the scene of the so-called Moors Murders?
23 Where did the Earl and Countess of Wessex marry?
24 Where was the rail crash which caused long delays from 2000 to 2001?
25 In 2001 which country had three kings in as many days when many royals were machine gunned to death?
26 In June 2006 which Oxford college admitted male students for the first time in 113 years?
27 Which Bush family member was Governor of Florida in 2001?
28 Which journalist Diamond, husband of Nigella Lawson, lost his cancer battle in 2001?
29 Peter Mandelson's first Cabinet post was as Secretary for what?
30 What replaced the torch as the Tory party's symbol under David Cameron?

Answers	Families *(see Quiz 43)*

1 Phil Vickery. 2 Mary. 3 George Bush. 4 Siamese twins. 5 Les Dennis. 6 Angie. 7 Rosie. 8 Stella. 9 The Archers. 10 Nigel. 11 Emilia Fox. 12 Philip. 13 Jonathan. 14 Jennifer Saunders. 15 Janet Ellis. 16 David Frost. 17 Hardie. 18 Libby Purves. 19 Wendy Turner. 20 Bobby Brown. 21 Fifi Trixibelle. 22 Joe. 23 Jane. 24 Emma Noble. 25 Zoe Ball. 26 Sarah. 27 Dylan. 28 Kent. 29 Arthur Miller. 30 Mel B.

1 What is petrology the study of?
2 In which decade was the record-breaking "Guinness Book of Records" first published?
3 What number of "Doctor Who" was Tom Baker?
4 Which country did Nana Mouskouri come from?
5 Which former England soccer boss passed away at his Suffolk home in February 2006?
6 Quindeca is a prefix indicating which number?
7 What is the chemical symbol for lead?
8 Which garden fruit has poisonous leaves and edible stems?
9 In the song from "The Music Man", 76 of what type of instrument led the big parade?
10 Which lady's Vineyard is an island off Cape Cod?
11 Who was 50 first – Princess Caroline of Monaco, Adrian Edmondson or Rowan Atkinson?
12 What is the scientific study of inheritance called?
13 Which country did the composer Chopin come from?
14 Which reggae artist starred in the film "The Harder They Come"?
15 What percentage is an eighth?
16 According to the words of a Noel Coward song, who "goes out in the midday sun" with "Mad dogs"?
17 In which London Square is the US Embassy?
18 The movie "Saving Private Ryan" dealt with events in which country?
19 In the 1960s, what was the name of Wayne Fontana's backing group?
20 Photosynthesis is the process by which plants use light to make what?
21 The site of ancient Babylon is today in which country?
22 What was the profession of Anna Politkovskaya, who was shot dead in 2006?
23 Who was the first English rugby union player to play in 50 internationals?
24 Which glands produce white blood cells?
25 Juliette Binoche and Kristin Scott Thomas first co-starred in which movie?
26 Which Derbyshire town is famous for its church with a crooked spire?
27 Which Bells helped launch the Virgin label?
28 The Parthenon in Athens was built as a temple to which goddess?
29 Which daytime show brought Noel Edmonds back into the public eye in 2006?
30 The movie "The Last King of Scotland" is a fictionalised story of which dictator?

1 Which TV chef did Fern Britton marry?
2 What is the first name of Mrs Michael Parkinson?
3 Which US president married Barbara Pierce?
4 Chang and Eng Bunker were famous as what type of siblings?
5 Which TV presenter did Amanda Holden marry?
6 What is the first name of the former Mrs George Best who wrote "George & Me"?
7 What is Lorraine Kelly's young daughter called?
8 Which McCartney became 30 in 2001?
9 On which radio show is Jasper Carrott's daughter a regular voice?
10 Which actor is "This Life"'s Jack Davenport's father?
11 Which actress, who starred in the revival of "Randall & Hopkirk (Deceased)", is the daughter of Joanna David?
12 Which Prince is the grandson of Prince Louis of Battenberg?
13 Which Dimbleby married writer Bel Mooney?
14 Which comedy actress is Mrs Adrian Edmondson?
15 Which former "Blue Peter" presenter is the mother of chart-topping Sophie?
16 Which TV presenter is married to the daughter of the 17th Duke of Norfolk?
17 Which actress Kate is the daughter of Goodie Bill Oddie?
18 Which radio presenter is Mrs Paul Heiney?
19 Which TV presenter with a TV presenter sister married "Minder" actor Gary Webster?
20 Which R & B star married Whitney Houston in 1992?
21 Who is Peaches Geldof's oldest sister?
22 Who is the oldest of the acting McGann brothers?
23 What is Lord Paddy Ashdown's wife called?
24 Which actress/model did ex PM's son James Major marry?
25 Who is Woody Cook's mum?
26 What were Andrew Lloyd Webber's first two wives called?
27 What is the name of the son of Catherine Zeta Jones and Michael Douglas?
28 Lady Helen Taylor is the daughter of which Duchess?
29 Which playwright is Daniel Day Lewis's father-in-law?
30 Which Spice Girl had a daughter called Phoenix Chi?

Answers | Newsworthy *(see Quiz 41)*

1 Romano Prodi. 2 Finland. 3 Plastic. 4 1920s. 5 East Pakistan. 6 Adolf Hitler. 7 James Callaghan. 8 Health. 9 Zaire. 10 Al Gore. 11 Zulus. 12 Monetary. 13 St Paul's. 14 Army. 15 Yitzhak Rabin. 16 Italy. 17 Rudyard Kipling. 18 Senator Joseph McCarthy. 19 Russia. 20 Literature/journalism. 21 Al Gore. 22 Saddleworth. 23 St George's Chapel Windsor. 24 Hatfield. 25 Nepal. 26 St Hilda's. 27 Jeb. 28 John. 29 Trade and Industry. 30 Oak tree.

1 Who were "Just Good Friends"?

2 Who shot to stardom with Jeremy Irons in "Brideshead Revisited"?

3 Which "Coronation Street" character died in his car after a road rage attack?

4 Which detective did Joan Hickson play on TV?

5 Which veteran actress presented "Praise Be!" for many years?

6 What was the surname of Audrey in "To the Manor Born"?

7 Which detective did John Nettles play before becoming involved in "The Midsomer Murders"?

8 Where did Kathy leave for when she first left "EastEnders"?

9 Which dance show's presenters have included Terry Wogan, Angela Rippon and Rosemarie Ford?

10 What was the pattern on Andy Pandy's suit?

11 In which decade was TV panel game "What's My Line?" first shown?

12 What was Beverley Callard's character called in "Coronation Street"?

13 For which event were TV cameras first installed in Westminster Abbey?

14 What was the supposed setting for "The Good Old Days"?

15 Which long-running current affairs programme began in 1953?

16 Which legendary hero played by Richard Greene achieved great success on both sides of the Atlantic?

17 At what time of day was "Crackerjack" broadcast?

18 Who hosted "Double Your Money" throughout its 13-year run?

19 Which famous TV gardener started "Gardening Club"?

20 On "Take Your Pick" what did contestants have to win to open boxes?

21 Which children's show had a masked hero seeking justice in America's wild west?

22 Which travelling journalist with trademark glasses and moustache was famous for presenting his "World"?

23 "All Our Yesterdays" showed film footage of events how many years previously?

24 Which member of "The Goons" presented the zany "It's a Square World"?

25 What number preceded "Sunset Strip" in the US private eye series?

26 Whose catchphrases included "You can't see the join," and "Get out of that!"?

27 Which sitcom was set in Fenners Fashions?

28 Which Dr opened his "Casebook" between 1962 and 1971?

29 Which James Bond played the Saint?

30 In "Coronation Street", who was Mike Baldwin's wife immediately before Linda?

Answers | Pot Luck 19 *(see Quiz 42)*

1 Rocks. 2 1960s. 3 Fourth. 4 Greece. 5 Ron Greenwood. 6 15. 7 Pb. 8 Rhubarb.
9 76 Trombones. 10 Martha's. 11 Rowan Atkinson (2005). 12 Genetics. 13 Poland.
14 Jimmy Cliff. 15 12.5%. 16 Englishmen. 17 Grosvenor. 18 France. 19 The
Mindbenders. 20 Food. 21 Iraq. 22 Journalist. 23 Rory Underwood. 24 Lymph. 25
The English Patient. 26 Chesterfield. 27 Tubular Bells. 28 Athena. 29 Deal or No Deal.
30 Idi Amin.

Quiz 45 | Pot Luck 20

Answers – page 171

1 Which worker gave Ken Barrie a hit – Bob the Builder, Postman Pat or the Singing Postman?
2 Who was the President of Argentina during the Falklands conflict?
3 What is the main island of Japan?
4 Saxifrage is a type of what?
5 On the radio, what is the name of the church in "The Archers"?
6 Which animal was used by Jenner when developing a vaccine against smallpox?
7 The song "I Feel Pretty" comes from which musical?
8 A snake's cast-off skin is known as a what?
9 Where is Britain's National Horseracing Museum?
10 Which group thought it was fun to stay at the "YMCA"?
11 What city is the largest in Nevada?
12 Which club did Robert Pires join when he left Arsenal?
13 Whose albums include "Nothing's Gonna Change My World" and "All for a Song"?
14 Which member of Gianni Versace's family took over his fashion empire after his death?
15 In 1998, who married millionaire hairdresser Stephen Way?
16 Which Brothers were Scott, John and Gary?
17 Where did Peter and Annie Mayle spend a year?
18 If New Year's day was a Thursday what day would Valentine's Day be?
19 Who was first to a first Best Actor Oscar – Nicolas Cage or Kevin Spacey?
20 Ruby is linked to which wedding anniversary?
21 In the traditional song, which herb goes with parsley, rosemary and thyme?
22 Who composed the opera "Norma"?
23 Who was the first member of the Royal Family to be interviewed on British TV?
24 A Blue Orpington is a type of what?
25 Which spirit forms the basis for Pimm's No 1?
26 Who left England as fast-bowling coach in 2006 to go to Australia?
27 Which Prime Minister had a wife who wrote a biography of Joan Sutherland?
28 Which store owner first said, "The customer is always right"?
29 Which group had hits with "The Logical Song" and "Dreamer"?
30 The Sargasso Sea forms part of which ocean?

Answers | Pot Luck 21 *(see Quiz 47)*

1 A. 2 Ear. 3 School. 4 Nut. 5 Trombone. 6 Mrs Beeton. 7 Nervous system. 8 Their feet. 9 Forest Whitaker. 10 Lynda LaPlante. 11 Foxglove. 12 Fiddler on the Roof. 13 Miss Marple. 14 Michel Platini. 15 Common. 16 Rugby. 17 None. 18 Helium. 19 Cawley. 20 The Supremes. 21 Friday. 22 Iraq. 23 Left-handed. 24 Bad breath. 25 Starsky & Hutch. 26 Ice hockey. 27 Eclipse. 28 The Grateful Dead. 29 Football (Shrewsbury Town). 30 Shape.

1 If bread is left to "prove" what does it do?

2 Which initials indicate the highest-quality brandy – AC, RSVP or VSOP?

3 What is a chanterelle?

4 What is aioli flavoured with?

5 What type of sauce was named after the Marquis de Bechamel?

6 What would you be eating if you were served calamari?

7 Enchiladas were originally part of which country's cooking?

8 What shape is the pasta called fusilli?

9 Mozzarella was originally made from which type of milk?

10 Which herb is usually used in gremolata?

11 Which pulses are used to make hummus?

12 Other than tomatoes and onions which is the main vegetable used in moussaka?

13 In which country is the famous wine-growing area of the Barossa valley?

14 Chianti comes from which area of Italy?

15 If a dish is cooked en papillote what is it cooked in?

16 Passata is pureed what?

17 A brochette is another word for what?

18 What is prosciutto?

19 What flavour do ratafia biscuits have?

20 What makes a salsa verde green – celery leaves, herbs or spinach?

21 Schnapps is distilled from what?

22 What type of white wine is Barsac famous for?

23 What type of oven is traditionally used for a tandoori?

24 Which Japanese dish is made from rice, seaweed and raw fish?

25 Which herb is usually used in a pesto sauce?

26 What type of dough is calzone made from?

27 What is a bisque?

28 When would antipasto be served?

29 What does baking powder produce when water is added, which makes dough rise?

30 How is something cooked if it is sauté?

Answers	Motor Sports *(see Quiz 48)*

1 Hungary. 2 500 miles. 3 Automobile. 4 Michael Schumacher. 5 Great Britain. 6 Twice. 7 Luxembourg. 8 Bernie Ecclestone. 9 29. 10 Silverstone. 11 June. 12 Williams. 13 1970s. 14 San Marino. 15 Le Mans 24 Hour race. 16 McLaren. 17 Motorcycling 18 USA. 19 Renault. 20 Never. 21 Twice. 22 Brazil. 23 Michael Schumacher. 24 Monte Carlo. 25 Belgium. 26 May. 27 San Marino. 28 Twice. 29 It was cancelled. 30 Japan.

1 What is the next white note on a keyboard above G?
2 What is examined with an otoscope?
3 Where does the main action of the TV series "Waterloo Road" take place?
4 What type of food is a macadamia?
5 What was Glenn Miller's main instrument?
6 Isabella Mary Mayson became better known as which cook?
7 Which of our body systems controls sight, hearing and touch?
8 For many years the title sequence of "The Bill" featured which part of the police officer's bodies?
9 Who played Idi Amin in the movie "The Last King of Scotland"?
10 Which writer created TV's Jane Tennison?
11 Which plant produce the drug digitalis?
12 "Sunrise, Sunset" comes from which musical?
13 Who was the sleuth in "The Body in the Library"?
14 Which Frenchman was voted European Footballer of the Year three times in a row?
15 L stands for lowest, M stands for multiple, but what does the C stand for in LCM?
16 What are you watching if William Webb Ellis is credited with founding it?
17 How many sides of a scalene triangle are equal?
18 Which element has the atomic number 2?
19 In tennis Miss Goolagong became which Mrs?
20 The late Florence Ballard was a member of which group?
21 The Norse goddess of love gives her name to which day of the week?
22 In which country was British engineer Kenneth Bigley murdered in 2004?
23 Is golfer Phil Mickelson left-handed or right-handed?
24 What do you suffer from if you have halitosis?
25 Dave & Ken were the first names of which TV duo?
26 The American Buffalo Sabres play which sport?
27 What describes the Earth or moon entering the other's shadow?
28 The late Jerry Garcia was the main guitarist with which band?
29 What sport are you watching if you are at Gay Meadow?
30 What changes when something is metamorphosised?

1 In which country did Jenson Button have his first Formula One victory?
2 How long is Indianapolis's most famous race?
3 What does the A stand for in FIA?
4 Which European was the second youngest World Champion of all time in 1994?
5 At the beginning of the new millennium which country had the most Grand Prix wins?
6 How many times was a Finn F1 World Champion in the 1990s?
7 Which Grand Prix was held at the Nurburgring in 1998?
8 Who was the head of F1 at the end of the 20th century?
9 How old was James Hunt when he became World Champion – 24, 29 or 33?
10 Where did Damon Hill drive his first F1 race?
11 In which month does the Isle of Man TT race traditionally take place?
12 Whom did Damon Hill race for when he became World Champion in 1996?
13 In which decade was Barry Sheene world 500cc champion twice?
14 During which Grand Prix did Ayrton Senna meet his death?
15 Which race is run on the Circuit de la Sarthe?
16 Which was Mika Hakkinen's team when he announced in 2001 he was going to take a year out of racing?
17 Which motor sport has the governing body the AMA?
18 Kevin Schwartz from which country was a 1991 World Champion on a Suzuki?
19 Which French constructor raced with Williams and Benetton in the 1990s?
20 How many times did Stirling Moss win the World Championship?
21 How many times was Graham Hill World Champion in the 1960s?
22 Which country was Nelson Piquet from?
23 Which driver was the highest-earning sportsman of 1999?
24 What is the first rally of the World Rally Championship?
25 Where is the Francorchamps circuit?
26 In which month does the Indianapolis 500 take place?
27 Which Grand Prix is held at Imola?
28 How many times was a Briton F1 World Champion in the 1990s?
29 In February 2006 it was announced that what would happen to the year's Belgian Grand Prix?
30 Where is the Suzuka circuit?

Answers	Food and Drink *(see Quiz 46)*

1 Rise. 2 VSOP. 3 Mushroom. 4 Garlic. 5 White sauce. 6 Squid. 7 Mexico. 8 Spirals. 9 Buffalo's. 10 Parsley. 11 Chick peas. 12 Aubergine. 13 Australia. 14 Tuscany. 15 Paper. 16 Tomatoes. 17 Kebab. 18 Ham. 19 Almond. 20 Herbs. 21 Potatoes. 22 Sweet. 23 Clay. 24 Sushi. 25 Basil. 26 Pizza. 27 Soup. 28 Before a meal. 29 Carbon dioxide. 30 Fried.

1 What was Radiohead's first top ten single?
2 In America the Stanley Cup is awarded in which sport?
3 There are 6,080 feet in what?
4 Andy Murray parted company from which coach in April 2006?
5 On radio, what did the A stand for in the programme known as ITMA?
6 In snooker how many reds are there on a table when one-third of them have been potted?
7 Which musical instrument did the late Karen Carpenter play?
8 There are 78 cards in what type of pack?
9 Actor Phil Daniels – who plays Kevin Wicks – is a big fan of which Premiership side?
10 How many edges does a cube have?
11 What was the setting for the TV series "Within These Walls"?
12 On a relief map, which lines connect points of the same height?
13 Gossima was a game that developed into which sport?
14 What green-coloured item goes to the winner of the US Masters?
15 What is family name of the main characters in "Sabrina the Teenage Witch"?
16 What type of word reads the same backwards as forwards?
17 Which American gave her name to an item of underwear?
18 Richard Beckinsale played Godber in which classic sitcom?
19 The final of the US Tennis Open is played at which Meadow?
20 David Beckham scored his final goal for Sven's England against which side?
21 How many letters in our alphabet can be written with one straight line?
22 In which decade were satellite pictures first sent across the Atlantic?
23 In 2005 a European space probe landed on Titan – a moon of which planet?
24 On which island was the TV detective series "Bergerac" set?
25 Which is the biggest planet in our Solar System?
26 Whose leaving Genesis led to Phil Collins becoming the main man for vocals?
27 What type of TV programme was broadcast from Barnsdale?
28 Helvetia features on stamps that come from which country?
29 Which Bob first presented "Blockbusters"?
30 In which decade was Amnesty International established?

Answers	Pot Luck 23 *(see Quiz 51)*

1 High Society 2 Cardigan. 3 15 minutes. 4 Brendan Cole. 5 Feast of Tabernacles. 6 Tennis. 7 Kennedy assassination. 8 Australia. 9 1960s. 10 Vietnam War. 11 Gold. 12 Fraternity. 13 Egypt. 14 Roxy Music. 15 Brother. 16 Julie Walters. 17 Philippines. 18 Eagle. 19 Luddites. 20 George Best (1996). 21 Iran. 22 Horticultural. 23 Badminton. 24 Horror. 25 Peter Andre. 26 Hitler. 27 Genetically. 28 1910s. 29 Teddy Bear. 30 Scott Johnson.

1 How many times in the 20th century did Sean Connery play James Bond?
2 Who played hero Fletcher Reede in "Liar Liar"?
3 Bruno Ganz played Hitler in which 2005 film?
4 Who played the queen to Sid James' King Henry in "Carry On Henry"?
5 In the movie "M*A*S*H" who played the role Alan Alda played on TV?
6 Which Hollywood superstar was the subject of "Mommie Dearest"?
7 In which movie did Tom Hanks play Chuck Noland?
8 Who played Morticia to Raul Julia's Gomez in "The Addams Family"?
9 In what type of place is "The Green Mile" set?
10 Which Tom Cruise movie had the line, "Show me the money!"?
11 Who is Julia Roberts' love rival in "My Best Friend's Wedding"?
12 Jake Gyllenhaal and Jamie Foxx starred in which Gulf War film?
13 Which star of "Singin' in the Rain" appeared with Judy Garland in "Me & My Gal"?
14 Which star of "The Perfect Storm" also starred in "The Thin Red Line"?
15 Which Bridges was "The Big Lebowski"?
16 Who played Estella in the New York-based 1990s version of "Great Expectations"?
17 Which King was played by Leonardo DiCaprio in "The Man in the Iron Mask"?
18 Who plays Annie MacLean in "The Horse Whisperer" with Robert Redford?
19 Who played space hero Harry Stamper in "Armageddon"?
20 Who played Sidney in "Scream" and "Scream 2"?
21 Who plays Gaz in "The Full Monty"?
22 What is Tom Cruise's job in "Mission: Impossible"?
23 Which Redgrave played the astrologer in the life of David Helfgott in "Shine"?
24 Who played airline pilot Steven Hiller in "Independence Day"?
25 Who was the fourth 007?
26 Which historical figure was "Braveheart"?
27 What is the profession of the hero in "The Client", based on John Grisham's novel?
28 What was the name of Andie McDowell's character in "Four Weddings and a Funeral"?
29 In which film did Tom Hanks play a simple hero with a heart of gold?
30 Who played Steve Biko in "Cry Freedom"?

Answers	Science (see Quiz 52)

1 Discovery. 2 Detection. 3 Triangle. 4 Greenwich. 5 Alzheimer. 6 Stereo. 7 Cancer. 8 Great Western. 9 The Church. 10 Marie Curie. 11 HMS Beagle. 12 Better microphone. 13 Radioactivity. 14 Stephen Hawking. 15 English Channel. 16 Parkinson. 17 Heating. 18 Earthquakes. 19 Pollution. 20 Wet. 21 Oxygen. 22 Birth. 23 Two. 24 Vitro. 25 Two years. 26 Carbon dioxide. 27 Antibody. 28 Wind. 29 Anaesthetic. 30 Greek.

1 The song "Who Wants to be a Millionaire?" comes from which musical?
2 Which Earl gave his name to a jacket?
3 Andy Warhol thought that everyone would be famous for how long?
4 Which dancer was runner-up in "Just the Two of Us" with Beverley Knight?
5 How is the Jewish Feast Sukkot also known?
6 What sport does Nicole Vaidisova play?
7 What did the Warren Commission investigate in the 1960s?
8 Composer Percy Grainger came from which country?
9 "Love is All Around" was a huge 1990s hit but in which decade was the original released?
10 The My Lai massacre took place during which war?
11 What was discovered in Rabbit Creek, Klondike in 1896?
12 What goes with Liberty and Equality in the motto adopted by the French republic?
13 Farouk was the last King of which country?
14 The 1996 rerelease of "Love is the Drug" was a remix from which band's 1970s hit?
15 What relation was Edward VIII to George VI?
16 Which actress played Mrs Molly Weasley in "Harry Potter and the Prisoner of Azkaban"?
17 Corazon Aquino was President of which country?
18 In which comic did Dan Dare first appear?
19 In England which protesters smashed spinning and weaving machines in factories?
20 Who was first to be 50 – George Best or Carl Lewis?
21 The Ayatollah Khomeini returned home to take power in which country in 1979?
22 What does the letter H stand for in gardening's RHS?
23 Which sport takes its name from the Duke of Beaufort's House?
24 What type of book does Clive Barker write?
25 "Flava" and "I Feel You" were the first two No 1s for which singer?
26 Which fanatical leader was born with the surname Schicklgruber?
27 What does the G stand for in the GM referring to crops?
28 In which decade was the first non-stop transatlantic flight?
29 What has been named after a nickname of US President Theodore Roosevelt?
30 Which acting rugby coach left Wales in 2006 to join Australia's backroom staff?

Answers	**Pot Luck 22** *(see Quiz 49)*

1 Creep. 2 Ice hockey. 3 A nautical mile. 4 Mark Petchey. 5 Again. 6 10. 7 Drums. 8 Tarot. 9 Chelsea. 10 12. 11 A prison. 12 Contour lines. 13 Table tennis. 14 Jacket. 15 Spellman. 16 Palindrome. 17 Bloomer. 18 Porridge. 19 Flushing Meadow. 20 Ecuador. 21 One. 22 1960s. 23 Around Saturn. 24 Jersey. 25 Jupiter. 26 Peter Gabriel. 27 Gardening. 28 Switzerland. 29 Holness. 30 1960s.

1 Which spacecraft launched the Hubble telescope?

2 What does the letter d stand for in radar?

3 Pythagoras's most famous theorem is about which geometric shape?

4 Which part of London is associated with Mean Time?

5 Which German psychiatrist gave his name to a disease of senile dementia?

6 Famous for demonstrating TV, John Logie Baird also developed what type of sound?

7 The study of oncogenes is crucial in the treatment of which disease?

8 Portsmouth-born Isambard Kingdom Brunel was responsible for the construction of tunnels, bridges and viaducts on which railway's line?

9 Who were the main opponents of Copernicus's assertion that the Sun was at the centre of the Universe?

10 How is the lady born Manya Sklodowska better known?

11 Which dog gave its name to Darwin's explorer ship?

12 What improvement did Edison make to Bell's telephone?

13 What did Geiger's counter measure?

14 Which scientist wrote A Brief History of Time?

15 In 1898 Marconi transmitted radio signals across where – Atlantic, English Channel or the USA?

16 Which physician gave his name to the disease of paralysis agitans?

17 What process is involved in pasteurisation in order to kill bacteria, as researched by Pasteur?

18 Seismologist Charles Richter studied what?

19 What makes acid rain acid – high temperatures, low temperatures or pollution?

20 In what type of atmosphere do algae live – dry, high altitude or wet?

21 Carbohydrates are made up of carbon, hydrogen and what?

22 If a disease is congenital when does it date from?

23 What is the minimum number of species in a hybrid?

24 What does the V stand for in the fertility treatment IVF?

25 A perennial is a plant which lives longer than how long?

26 Dry ice is solid or frozen what?

27 What is a defensive substance produced as a reaction to a foreign body called?

28 Irish naval officer Sir Francis Beaufort gave his name to measurement of what?

29 Sir Humphry Davy discovered that laughing gas has which effect?

30 What was the nationality of Archimedes?

Quiz 53 | Music – Classics | Answers – page 179

1 During which part of Handel's "Messiah" does the audience stand?

2 "Morning" comes from which piece of music by Grieg?

3 Which music by Wagner was used as the theme for "Apocalypse Now"?

4 What was the nationality of Bela Bartok who died at the end of WWII?

5 Rachmaninov wrote a "Rhapsody" on whose theme?

6 What type of work is "Pelleas and Melisande" by Debussy?

7 Which religious song about Jerusalem begins "Last night I lay a sleeping"?

8 Dvorak's famous Symphony No 9 is called what?

9 Mendelssohn's "Fingal's Cave" is from which Overture?

10 About which romantic pair did Berlioz write a symphony?

11 "Take a Pair of Sparkling Eyes" comes from which Gilbert & Sullivan opera?

12 Which birthplace of Handel shares its name with a Manchester-based orchestra?

13 Rodrigo's Concerto d'Aranjuez is played on which instrument?

14 Chopin wrote music almost exclusively for which musical instrument?

15 The music "Crimond" is usually sung to which psalm?

16 What range of voice did Kathleen Ferrier have?

17 Which Gilbert & Sullivan opera is set in the Tower of London?

18 Which of Beethoven's Symphonies is the "Choral Symphony"?

19 "One Fine Day" comes from which Puccini opera?

20 Which words were put to Elgar's "Pomp and Circumstance March No 1 in D Major"?

21 What type of work by Beethoven has the title "Moonlight"?

22 "The Dance of the Sugar Plum Fairy" is from which Tchaikovsky ballet?

23 Which Handel composition about anointing Solomon King is sung at English coronations?

24 "Nimrod" is from which Elgar composition?

25 In which English county was Sir Harrison Birtwistle born?

26 Where was Rossini's famous "Barber" from?

27 Which aria can be translated as "None Shall Sleep"?

28 What type of voice normally sings "O for the Wings of a Dove"?

29 How is Bizet's "Les Pecheurs de Perles" also known?

30 What goes with "Peasant" in the Overture by Suppe?

Answers	Headlines *(see Quiz 55)*

1 Donald Campbell. 2 Kiev. 3 Cuban Missile. 4 Jamaica. 5 Gerald Ford. 6 Anthrax. 7 Pennsylvania. 8 Ayatollah Rafsanjani. 9 Elton John. 10 Lyndon Johnson. 11 Australia. 12 Molly Campbell. 13 November. 14 Oklahoma. 15 Harold. 16 The Philippines. 17 East Sussex. 18 Martin McGuinness. 19 David Cameron. 20 Donald Dewar. 21 The Guardian. 22 President Akihito. 23 Welsh Guards. 24 Tony Banks. 25 Boris Yeltsin. 26 Panorama. 27 Josie. 28 Hyde. 29 Viagra. 30 Battle of Britain.

1 What was Jamiroquai's first UK Top Ten hit?

2 Which of these is a sport that is very similar to ice hockey – bandy, gandy or handy?

3 What does a barometer measure?

4 What was Frank Spencer's daughter called?

5 Who or what was the dauphin?

6 Who retired injured in 2006 leaving Amelie Mauresmo to claim the Australian Open?

7 Copernicus is often cited as being the father of modern what?

8 Which song gave The Shamen their first No 1?

9 Which Wimbledon singles champion was related by marriage to sports tycoon David Lloyd?

10 Chris Patten was the last British Governor of where?

11 Who played bride-to-be Donna in "Doctor Who"?

12 Which household item was developed by Harry Pickup?

13 Fanny Blankers-Koen was the first woman to win how many Olympic gold medals?

14 What was Cherie Blair's maiden name?

15 Which of Queen Elizabeth II's children was the first to marry?

16 What did Clarice Cliff make?

17 In which month of the year is Mother's Day celebrated in America?

18 Cinnamon comes from which part of a tree?

19 What colour is paprika?

20 Which sought-after clothing items went on sale in the UK for the first time in 1941?

21 Who was "Back in the World" according to the title of a 2003 hit album?

22 The Sierra Nevada mountains are in which American state?

23 Which Joe was a world champion at both snooker and billiards?

24 The letters PL show that a car has come from which country?

25 Which politician said, "All babies look like me" – Iain Duncan Smith, William Hague or Winston Churchill?

26 What does the second s mean in the knitting term psso?

27 Roman Romanov was chairman of which soccer club?

28 Hippophobia is a fear of what?

29 Which actress has played Elizabeth II and George III's wife in movies?

30 What was named after Captain Becher?

Answers | Pot Luck 25 *(see Quiz 56)*

1 The moon. 2 Carbon. 3 Prisoner Cell Block H. 4 Sydney. 5 Equilibrium. 6 Barbados. 7 Facsimile. 8 Richard Nixon. 9 Waitangi Day. 10 Sex Pistols. 11 Acute. 12 Dr Livesey. 13 Seaside postcard. 14 Lotus. 15 Quakers. 16 Beach Boys. 17 Patrick Swayze (2002). 18 Queen Victoria. 19 Sopwith. 20 Hobby. 21 Milk. 22 Melbourne. 23 Rossini. 24 US Open. 25 Softer. 26 1950s. 27 Albatross. 28 Alicia Keys. 29 Africa. 30 Tottenham Hotspur.

Quiz 55 | Headlines | Answers – page 177

1 In 2001 whose car was found in Lake Coniston, 30 years after an attempt on the water speed record?

2 Which city of the Ukraine was closest to Chernobyl?

3 Which crisis brought about the hot line between the White House and the Kremlin?

4 On which West Indian island did Bob Woolmer meet his death during the 2007 Cricket World Cup?

5 Who replaced President Nixon after Watergate?

6 In October 2001, the US's Senate Majority leader received what in the post?

7 In the Sept 11th 2001 terrorist attacks on the US, in which state did the plane crash which did not crash into a building?

8 Who succeeded Ayatollah Khomeini as president of Iran?

9 In 1979 who was the first western rock star to visit the USSR?

10 Who succeeded JF Kennedy after his assassination?

11 Paul Keating became Prime Minister of where?

12 What is the British name of Misbah Iram Ahmed, the subject of a 2006 custody battle?

13 In which month did JFK die?

14 Which US city was the scene of a terrorist bomb in 1995?

15 What was spy Kim Philby's real first name?

16 Where did Corazon Aquino become president after being widowed?

17 In which county was Piltdown Man discovered in 1912?

18 Who became Minister of Education after the Good Friday agreement?

19 Which British party leader claimed in 2007 that politicians were entitled to a "private past"?

20 Who was the first leader of the Scottish Parliament?

21 Jonathan Aitken was jailed after a libel case against which newspaper?

22 Which Japanese leader visited Britain amid great controversy in 1998?

23 Simon Weston, who was badly burned in the Falklands War served in which regiment?

24 Who was Tony Blair's first Minister for Sport?

25 Who preceded Vladimir Putin as Russian leader?

26 On which programme did ex-nanny Louise Woodward explain her case on British TV?

27 Which member of the Russell family survived a murderous attack where her mother and sister perished?

28 Where in Greater Manchester did Dr Harold Shipman practise?

29 Which drug was launched in the late 1990s as a cure for impotence?

30 In which Battle did Britain use radar for the first time?

Answers | Music – Classics (see Quiz 53)

1 Hallelujah Chorus. 2 Peer Gynt. 3 Ride of the Valkyries. 4 Hungarian. 5 Paganini. 6 Opera. 7 The Holy City. 8 From the New World. 9 Hebrides. 10 Romeo & Juliet. 11 The Gondoliers. 12 Halle. 13 Guitar. 14 Piano. 15 23, The Lord's My Shepherd. 16 Contralto. 17 Yeomen of the Guard. 18 Ninth. 19 Madame Butterfly. 20 Land of Hope and Glory. 21 Sonata. 22 Nutcracker. 23 Zadok the Priest. 24 Enigma Variations. 25 Lancashire. 26 Seville. 27 Nessun Dorma. 28 (Boy) Soprano. 29 The Pearl Fishers. 30 Poet.

Quiz 56 | Pot Luck 25

LEVEL 2

1 Where does a plaque read: "We came in peace for all mankind. July 1969"?
2 A diamond is made up of which element?
3 Which TV series featured the Wentworth Detention Centre?
4 Michael Hutchence was born in and died in which city?
5 What word describes a state of complete balance?
6 Which West Indian island was host to the 2007 Cricket World Cup final?
7 The word fax is an abbreviation of which word that means a copy?
8 Who was the first US President to resign from office?
9 What is New Zealand's National Day called?
10 Who had a hit with "God Save the Queen" in 1977 and 2002?
11 What name is given to an angle of less than 90 degrees?
12 The adventure yarn "Treasure Island" is narrated by Jim Hawkins and who else?
13 Where would you be most likely to see the artwork of Donald McGill?
14 Which motor racing team has the name of a flower that is sacred in India?
15 Which religious group founded the city of Philadelphia?
16 Carl Wilson of which legendary band died in 1998?
17 Who was 50 first – Tom Hanks, Patrick Swayze or Bruce Willis?
18 Who was the first British monarch to travel by train?
19 Who was the designer of the Sopwith Camel – was it Camel, Sopwith or Sopwith Camel?
20 What can be a small horse or a small falcon?
21 Which everyday food item includes the protein casein?
22 What was Australia's capital before Canberra?
23 Who composed the opera "William Tell"?
24 In which 2006 tournament did Tiger Woods first miss the halfway cut as a professional?
25 If music is diminuendo it gradually becomes what?
26 In which decade were Duke of Edinburgh awards first presented?
27 Which creature provided Fleetwood Mac with a worldwide hit?
28 Who played the character Georgia Sykes in the movie "Smokin' Aces"?
29 Mungo Park is famous for exploration in which part of the world?
30 Gerry Francis and George Graham have both managed which soccer club?

1 Too Young to Die. 2 Bandy. 3 Atmospheric pressure. 4 Jessica. 5 Title of a French prince. 6 Justine Henin-Hardenne. 7 Astronomy. 8 Ebeneezer Goode. 9 Chris Evert. 10 Hong Kong. 11 Catherine Tate. 12 Harpic. 13 Four. 14 Booth. 15 Princess Anne. 16 Pottery. 17 May. 18 Bark. 19 Red. 20 Nylon stockings. 21 Paul McCartney. 22 California. 23 Joe Davis. 24 Poland. 25 Winston Churchill. 26 Stitch. 27 Hearts. 28 Horses. 29 Helen Mirren. 30 The fence at Aintree Becher's Brook.

Quiz 57 The Famous   Answers – page 183 **LEVEL 2**

1 Chad Varah founded which charity?
2 The Queen's residence of Balmoral is on which river?
3 Which Princess is nearest in line to the throne?
4 Who was the only Irish author to win the Nobel Prize for Literature in the 1990s?
5 Which Richard designed the Thrust, the fastest land vehicle of its day?
6 Millvina Dean was the youngest survivor of which ship?
7 What type of radio did Trevor Bayliss invent?
8 Athina Onassis Roussel will inherit millions due to the fortune her grandfather made in what?
9 Sam Walton founded which US-based chain of stores?
10 Which child of a rock star inherited nearly £80 million – Frances Cobain, Sean Lennon or Lisa Marie Presley?
11 Which "Playboy" magazine Playmate of the Year married an 89-year-old oil billionaire?
12 Which religious figure broadcasts regularly on a radio show called "Decision Hour"?
13 What relation is Jemma Redgrave to Vanessa Redgrave?
14 Gwyneth Paltrow and Chris Martin's second child was called what?
15 How was Lesley Hornby better known?
16 Which of the following is not left-handed – Tim Henman, Brian Lara or Martina Navratilova?
17 Alan Ayckbourn famously stages his plays at which seaside resort?
18 Who succeeded Gaby Roslin on Channel 4's "The Big Breakfast"?
19 Who was Tony Blair's first Press Secretary when he became Prime Minister?
20 Jimmy McGovern and Alan Bleasdale are famous names as what?
21 Which First Lady had the maiden name Roddam?
22 What is the first name of Mrs Gordon Brown?
23 How tall was Prince William when he went to university – 6ft 3", 6ft or 5ft 10"?
24 Who named her baby daughter Bluebell Madonna?
25 What do Victor Edelstein and Catherine Walker design?
26 Who was elected to Alan Clark's constituency after his death?
27 Who was inaugurated as President of the USA exactly 32 years after John F Kennedy?
28 What was Tony Blair's first constituency?
29 The Lauder brothers inherited from their mother Estée who made a fortune in what?
30 Which Princess has middle names Elizabeth Mary?

Answers TV Sitcoms *(see Quiz 59)*

1 Chambers. 2 Brabinger. 3 Seattle. 4 Absolutely Fabulous. 5 Victor Meldrew. 6 Tom. 7 Richard Wilson. 8 Sarah Lancashire. 9 Robert Lindsay. 10 Bollinger. 11 Listen very carefully. 12 Calista Flockhart. 13 Are You Being Served?. 14 White. 15 Julia Roberts. 16 Harold Steptoe. 17 Stephen Tomkinson. 18 Paul Eddington. 19 Samantha. 20 Garth. 21 Nurse. 22 Cheers. 23 Captain Mainwaring. 24 Father Jack. 25 Fawlty Towers. 26 Ruby Wax. 27 Draughtsman. 28 Richard. 29 Ivy. 30 North east.

Quiz 58 | Pot Luck 26

Answers – page 184

LEVEL 2

1 James Logan gave his name to a type of what – danceband, fruit or road race?
2 Who beat Andre Agassi in his final singles game at Wimbledon?
3 Which Day was inaugurated by Miss Anna Jarvis in Philadelphia in 1907?
4 What was Walt Disney's first TV programme called?
5 What did William Herschel discover?
6 What term describes a plant created from crossing different species?
7 In which decade of last century was Margaret Thatcher born?
8 Which Brontë wrote the novel "Jane Eyre"?
9 Charles Babbage was involved in the early development of what?
10 Which famous oil trouble-shooter passed away in August 2004?
11 What was tennis player Margaret Smith's married name that was linked to her sport?
12 When was the movie "Enigma" set?
13 Steve Bruce and Nigel Spackman have both managed which soccer club?
14 Princess Anne's second marriage took place near which royal residence?
15 Which group had a hit best-of album "Life Story", almost 50 years after their first hit?
16 What sort of car did "Avenger" Emma Peel drive?
17 What was the real first name of Curly Watts in "Coronation Street"?
18 What would you do with a burrito?
19 What is the English name of the lunar sea Lacus Mortis?
20 Which American state is directly below North Carolina?
21 Warrumbungle is found in Australia, but what is it?
22 Which country established a record Test partnership of 624 runs in 2006?
23 What number does Thomas display on his Tank Engine?
24 Who was UN Secretary-General at the time of the Indian Ocean tsunami of 2004?
25 Which Mr Miller married Marilyn Monroe?
26 What did Grover live in Sesame Street?
27 In which branch of mathematics do letters replace unknown quantities?
28 "The Rose" was a Bette Midler movie based on the life of which singer?
29 Which Diane has been Sean Connery's wife?
30 Del Boy Trotter's catchphrase was "Lovely" what?

Answers | Pot Luck 27 *(see Quiz 60)*

1 911. 2 Boy George. 3 Seattle. 4 Alexander the Great. 5 Cate Blanchett. 6 Channel 5. 7 Limestone. 8 Lleyton Hewitt. 9 Neighbours. 10 Scripts. 11 Lower arm. 12 Golf's US Masters. 13 Ceefax. 14 Kamikaze. 15 60 degrees. 16 Surrey. 17 Colony. 18 Toes and fingers. 19 Hungary. 20 297. 21 Nottingham. 22 Steve Delaney. 23 Rita. 24 Wavelengths of light. 25 Ron Atkinson. 26 Swim the English Channel. 27 Three. 28 Des O' Connor. 29 Processing. 30 Sunday.

182

1 Which series with John Bird was set in a legal practice?
2 In "To the Manor Born" what was the name of Audrey's butler?
3 Where is "Frasier" based?
4 Which show introduced a character called Katy Grin?
5 Whose catchphrase was, "I don't believe it!"?
6 Which character appeared with Linda in "Gimme Gimme Gimme"?
7 Who played opposite Stephanie Cole in "Life as We Know It"?
8 Which ex-"Coronation Street" actress starred in "Blooming Marvellous" with Clive Mantle?
9 Who played Ben to Zoe Wanamaker's Susan in "My Family"?
10 In "Absolutely Fabulous", what was Patsy's favourite champagne?
11 In "Allo Allo", which three words come before "I shall say this only once!"?
12 Who played Ally McBeal?
13 Beane's of Boston was a US version of which UK sitcom set in the retail business?
14 What colour were Seinfeld's shoes?
15 Which 2001 Oscar-winning actress guested on "Friends"?
16 Whose catchphrase was "You dirty old man!"?
17 Which ex "Ballykissangel" star appeared in "Bedtime"?
18 Who found fame as Jerry Leadbetter?
19 Which witch was played by Elizabeth Montgomery in "Bewitched"?
20 Who was Wayne's sidekick in "Wayne's World"?
21 What was Dorothy's profession in "Men Behaving Badly"?
22 Which US programme was the then most watched TV show when it aired for the last time in 1993?
23 Who was in charge of the Walmington on Sea Home Guard?
24 In "Father Ted", which priest was almost permanently drunk?
25 Which sitcom saw Polly, Miss Tibbs and Major Gowen?
26 Which American played the American flatmate in "Girls on Top"?
27 What was Tom Good's job before he gave everything up for "The Good Life"?
28 What was Hyacinth Bucket's husband called?
29 Who was the cafe proprietress in "Last of the Summer Wine"?
30 Where in the UK was "The Likely Lads" set?

Answers The Famous (see Quiz 57)

1 The Samaritans. 2 Dee. 3 Beatrice. 4 Seamus Heaney. 5 Noble. 6 Titanic. 7 Clockwork. 8 Shipping. 9 Wal-Mart. 10 Lisa Marie Presley. 11 Anna Nicole Smith. 12 Billy Graham. 13 Niece. 14 Moses. 15 Twiggy. 16 Tim Henman. 17 Scarborough. 18 Zoe Ball. 19 Alastair Campbell. 20 Playwrights. 21 Hillary Clinton. 22 Sarah. 23 6ft 3". 24 Geri Halliwell. 25 Clothes. 26 Michael Portillo. 27 Bill Clinton. 28 Sedgefield. 29 Cosmetics. 30 Beatrice.

1 In the USA which of these numbers do you ring in an emergency, 999, 606, 911?

2 Which singer received a New York community service order for falsely reporting a break-in?

3 The Seahawks from where were runners-up in Super Bowl XL?

4 Which of the following did Shakespeare not write a play about – Alexander the Great, Julius Caesar or Macbeth?

5 Who co-starred with Judi Dench in the movie "Notes on a Scandal"?

6 Which TV launch was connected with the Spice Girls?

7 Which rock is chiefly made from calcium carbonate?

8 Which top tennis player was once engaged to Kim Clijsters?

9 In which TV show did the kids attend Erinsborough High School?

10 What did Ray Galton and Alan Simpson produce – scripts, shoes or songs?

11 Where in the human body is the ulna?

12 Which of these sporting events is held most frequently – golf's US Masters, golf's Ryder Cup or football's World Cup?

13 What was the BBC's first teletext service called?

14 Which Japanese word actually means "divine wind"?

15 In an equilateral triangle, how many degrees does each angle measure?

16 Wentworth golf course is in which English county?

17 What is the collective name for a group of beavers?

18 What are your phalanges?

19 In which country could you watch Ferencvaros playing Vasas at soccer?

20 A4 paper is 210mm by how many mm?

21 In which city is the Goose Fair held?

22 Which actor and comedian created the character Count Arthur Strong??

23 What was Alf Garnett's daughter called?

24 What does the angstrom unit measure?

25 Who did Alex Ferguson replace at Man Utd?

26 Captain Matthew Webb was the first person to do what?

27 When the prefix kilo is used to describe an amount, how many noughts would be written in digits?

28 Who first presented the 1990s revival of the TV game show "Take Your Pick"?

29 In computing, what does the P stand for in CPU?

30 The Prix de l'Arc de Triomphe is run on which day of the week?

Answers | Pot Luck 26 *(see Quiz 58)*

1 Fruit. 2 Rafael Nadal. 3 Mother's Day. 4 Disneyland. 5 A planet. 6 Hybrid. 7 1920s. 8 Charlotte. 9 The computer. 10 Red Adair. 11 Court. 12 WWII. 13 Sheffield United. 14 Balmoral. 15 The Shadows. 16 Lotus Elan. 17 Norman. 18 Eat it. 19 Lake of Death. 20 South Carolina. 21 National Park. 22 Sri Lanka. 23 1. 24 Kofi Annan. 25 Arthur Miller. 26 Trashcan (dustbin/rubbish bin). 27 Algebra. 28 Janis Joplin. 29 Cilento. 30 Jubbly.

Quiz 61 | Books

Answers – page 187

LEVEL 2

1 Which novel about Hannibal Lecter sets out to explain "the evolution of his evil"?
2 Who wrote the Young Bond series of books?
3 Who wrote the "Mary Ann" series of romantic novels?
4 What was the surname of Richmal Crompton's most famous schoolboy hero?
5 Who wrote "The Day of the Jackal"?
6 Who wrote the book originally published in the UK as "The Diary of a Young Girl"?
7 Nadine Gordimer hails from which country?
8 Who wrote "The Female Eunuch"?
9 Who is the author of "Riders of the Purple Sage"?
10 Which writer famous for her historical fiction wrote "Regency Buck"?
11 What is Ripley's first name in Patricia Highsmith's "The Talented Mr Ripley" and "Ripley Under Water"?
12 In which language did Czech-born Franz Kafka write?
13 Whose "Guns of Navarone" was made into a film?
14 Whose autobiography was called "Learning to Fly"?
15 Which Josephine wrote "Tonight Josephine"?
16 Which ex-jockey wrote "Shattered"?
17 Which thriller writer penned "The Shape of Snakes"?
18 Which word completes the title of Rick Stein's cookery book, "Rick Stein's Seafood ..."?
19 Whose memoir was called "Bad Blood"?
20 What sort of guide did Leslie Halliwell found?
21 In which city was Barbara Taylor Bradford born?
22 Whose "Death in Holy Orders" was set on the coast of East Anglia?
23 Whose autobiography was called "Himoff!"?
24 Who wrote the novels on which the "Touch of Frost" TV character was based?
25 In which Stephen King novel does the character Annie Wilkes feature?
26 In Ruth Rendell's Wexford novels what is Reg's wife called?
27 Which Alfred wrote many books about walks in his beloved Lake District?
28 Which Ian Rankin novel is set in the backdrop of the 2005 G8 conference?
29 Whose cookery book had a title which began with "Happy Days"?
30 Was Richard Branson's autobiography called "Like a Virgin", "Losing My Virginity" or "The Moon's a Balloon"?

Answers | Rugby (see Quiz 63)

1 Australia. 2 Mike Ruddock. 3 Professional. 4 Lebanon. 5 Romania. 6 Prop. 7 Mike Catt. 8 1996. 9 1980s. 10 Lawrence Dallaglio. 11 Paul Newlove. 12 Rugby Union World Cup. 13 Sydney. 14 David Campese. 15 England. 16 Pay (Broken time payments). 17 1920s. 18 South Africa. 19 Pilkington Cup. 20 Llanelli Scarlets. 21 Hunslet. 22 Wales and South Africa. 23 Leeds Rhinos. 24 (Stade de) France. 25 South Africa. 26 Cambridge. 27 Blue Sox. 28 Swalec Cup. 29 Australia. 30 Wigan.

1 Which word describes the brightness of stars?
2 What did Croft and Perry create between them?
3 Which country was first to win soccer's World Cup four times?
4 In which country is La Coruña international airport?
5 Which are there most of – birds, fish or insects?
6 In MODEM, MO stands for Modulator, what does DEM stand for?
7 The Tour of Spain in cycling takes place how often?
8 Before their 2006 triumph, when did Italy last win the FIFA World Cup?
9 After a drugs test Ben Johnson was stripped of Olympic gold in which race?
10 Carbohydrates consist of carbon, hydrogen and which other element?
11 What is the highest number on the Richter scale?
12 In what type of building did the 2004 hostage crisis take place in Beslan, Russia?
13 What shape is a swallow's tail?
14 The Philippines lie in which ocean?
15 147 is a maximum continuous score in which game?
16 What name describes a component that will transmit electricity or heat?
17 How many legs does a flatworm have?
18 Which instrument did jazzman Charlie "Bird" Parker play?
19 The flower edelweiss is what colour?
20 What does C stand for in the abbreviation VCR?
21 Who had hits with "We Belong Together" and "It's Like That"?
22 "Fidelio" was the only opera of which German composer?
23 What type of leaves does a koala eat?
24 Who had chart success with the album "Fever" in 2001?
25 In which country is Rawalpindi?
26 The clock on Big Ben's tower has how many faces?
27 The Channel Island Sark is noted for its ban on what?
28 Which of the Bee Gees is not a twin?
29 What did Lewis E. Waterman invent?
30 What is the name for a camel with two humps?

| **Answers** | Pot Luck 29 *(see Quiz 64)* |

1 Capability Brown. 2 Cats. 3 F. 4 Vicar. 5 Engineering. 6 Turkey. 7 Never Mind the Buzzcocks. 8 Jacques. 9 Al. 10 Bird. 11 Alicia Keys. 12 Three. 13 Corky. 14 Glasgow. 15 Victoria Wood. 16 Brain. 17 Lower arm. 18 Fool's gold. 19 Newcastle. 20 Two. 21 Wolves. 22 Belgium. 23 Two. 24 Harry. 25 Tuesday. 26 New York. 27 The Royle Family. 28 To the Manor Born. 29 Prime Minister. 30 Lawrence Dallaglio.

1 In which country do Parramatta play?
2 Which Mike managed Wales to their first Grand Slam title in 27 years in 2005?
3 What does the P stand for in RFAPC?
4 Hazen El Masri represented which international side?
5 Which side did Philippe Sella face in his first international?
6 What is the usual position played by England and Bath rugby star Matt Stevens?
7 Who scored all of England's points in their 15–15 draw with Australia in November 1997?
8 In what year was the Regal Trophy discontinued – 1986, 1990 or 1996?
9 In which decade of the 20th century did Ireland last win the Five Nations?
10 Who became England captain for the first time in 1997?
11 Who was the youngest League player in an international in the 20th century?
12 What is another name for the Webb Ellis Trophy?
13 Which city's University had the first Rugby Club in Australia?
14 In 1996 which Australian received a UNESCO award as one of the most outstanding sportsmen of the century?
15 By 2000 which country had won the Rugby International Championships outright most times?
16 Rugby League was formed after a dispute with the Rugby Football Union about what?
17 In which decade was the first Challenge Cup Final at Wembley?
18 Who were the third winners of the Rugby Union World Cup after New Zealand and Australia?
19 Which Cup was called the John Player Cup until 1988?
20 Which rugby club did Gareth Jenkins leave to take over as boss of Wales in 2006?
21 Which side became Hawks in the 1990s?
22 Which sides met in the first game at Cardiff's Millennium Stadium?
23 Who won the last Challenge Cup of the 20th century?
24 Which was the only Five Nations side to have its country's name in its home ground?
25 Who joined Australia and New Zealand in the 1998 Tri Nations series?
26 By the end of the millennium, who had won most Varsity matches?
27 What did Halifax add to their name in the 1990s?
28 Which Cup was previously called the Schweppes Welsh Cup?
29 Which was the first team to win the Rugby World Cup twice?
30 Who were the last winners of the Regal Trophy?

| **Answers** | **Books** *(see Quiz 61)* |

1 Hannibal Rising. 2 Charlie Higson. 3 Catherine Cookson. 4 Brown. 5 Frederick Forsyth. 6 Anne Frank. 7 South Africa. 8 Germaine Greer. 9 Zane Grey. 10 Georgette Heyer. 11 Tom. 12 German. 13 Alistair Maclean. 14 Victoria Beckham. 15 Cox. 16 Dick Francis. 17 Minette Walters. 18 Odyssey. 19 Lorna Sage. 20 Film. 21 Leeds. 22 PD James. 23 Richard Whiteley. 24 RD Wingfield. 25 Misery. 26 Dora. 27 Wainwright. 28 The Naming of the Dead. 29 Jamie Oliver. 30 Losing My Virginity.

1 How did Lancelot Brown become better known – Arthur Brown, Capability Brown or James Brown?
2 Allurophobia is a fear of which creature?
3 What is the fourth note in the scale of C?
4 What was the occupation of the sitcom character named Geraldine Grainger?
5 What does Carol Vorderman have a degree in?
6 In which country could you watch Besiktas play a home soccer match?
7 On which TV show did Simon Amstell take over from Mark Lamarr?
8 EC Presidents Delors and Santer both shared which forename?
9 What is the chemical symbol for aluminium?
10 What type of creature is a kookaburra?
11 "Songs in a Minor Key" was the first hit album for which artist?
12 How many different countries did Alfredo di Stefano play international soccer for?
13 Who is Bottle Top Bill's best friend?
14 In which city are you if you walk along Sauchiehall Street?
15 Who wrote the TV sitcom "dinnerladies"?
16 Which part of his body did Einstein leave to Princeton University?
17 Where in the human body is the radius?
18 Iron pyrites are known as what type of gold?
19 Barrack Road goes past the soccer stadium of which club?
20 How many main islands is New Zealand made up of?
21 Graham Taylor and Dave Jones have both managed which soccer club?
22 Waterloo, scene of a famous battle, is in which country?
23 Which number can be typed using only letters on the top row of a keyboard?
24 Which Corbett created Sooty the bear?
25 If the December 1 is a Saturday what day is January 1?
26 Where did the Jumbo jet leave from on its first transatlantic flight?
27 "The Queen of Sheba" was a one-off special of which TV programme?
28 In which sitcom did Richard De Vere marry Audrey?
29 William Pitt became the youngest British what?
30 Which ex-England captain retired from international rugby in 2004 yet came back in 2006?

Quiz 65 Movie Memories

1 Who played Anne Heche's husband in "Donnie Brasco"?
2 Who played Quasimodo in the 1923 version of "The Hunchback of Notre Dame"?
3 How many sound movies did the legendary DW Griffith make?
4 Which category did Disney's "Snow White" have when it first opened?
5 Which wife of Clark Gable was one of Mack Sennett's bathing beauties?
6 Which western with Gary Cooper made Grace Kelly a star?
7 Which 1990s Dreamworks movie is about Moses?
8 What was Quentin Tarantino's first film?
9 Who played Stanley Kowalski in "A Streetcar Named Desire"?
10 What is Nicole Kidman's job in "To Die For"?
11 Who are the musical duo in "Topsy Turvy"?
12 The movie "Thirteen Days" is about which crisis?
13 What was the sequel to "Ace Ventura Pet Detective"?
14 What was the most expensive film of the 20th century?
15 Which sci-fi film of 1999 starred Keanu Reeves?
16 Which of the following movies did not have a dog or dogs as their stars – "Babe", "Beethoven" or "Homeward Bound"?
17 Of the following stars of "Ghostbusters", who did not also write it – Dan Aykroyd, Bill Murray or Harold Ramis?
18 Who plays the widowed hero in "The American President"?
19 Back in the 1960s who was the "Girl on a Motorcycle"?
20 After making "Some Like It Hot", Tony Curtis reputedly said that kissing who was like kissing Hitler?
21 Which Richardson co-starred with Hugh Laurie in "Maybe Baby"?
22 What is Hugh Grant's profession in "Notting Hill"?
23 In which movie did Eddie Murphy play Sherman Klump?
24 How many films did Bogart make with Bacall – was it two, four or six?
25 In which movie did Audrey Hepburn play Holly Golightly?
26 In which city is "Dirty Harry" set?
27 Who does Jack Nicholson play in "The Witches of Eastwick"?
28 In which part of New York is Martin Scorsese's semi-autobiographical movie "Mean Streets" set?
29 What was Wallace & Gromit's first adventure?
30 Which movie classic features Rick and Renault?

Quiz 66 | Pot Luck 30

Answers – page 192

LEVEL 2

1 Which of these words is made from letters on the top row of a keyboard – part, pile or pour?
2 The aria "One Fine Day" comes from which opera?
3 Where were satsumas originally grown?
4 Who was famous for his Theory of Evolution?
5 How many faces does a pyramid with a triangular base have?
6 George Ferris gave his name to which fairground attraction?
7 On which group of islands is Mount Fuji?
8 In music how many lines are there for notes to be written on?
9 Which building was constructed on the orders of Shah Jehan?
10 Which US band had hit singles with "Boulevard of Broken Dreams" and "Holiday"?
11 Which was London's first railway station?
12 Which group of people largely shunned the January 2005 democratic elections in Iraq?
13 In blackjack the maximum score is equivalent to potting how many blacks at snooker?
14 Who was the first Scot to be voted European Footballer of the Year?
15 Where would you find your ventricle and atrium?
16 Which creatures live in a formicary?
17 What does the M stand for in the radio abbreviation FM stand for?
18 What was the first name of the commentator who famously said, "They think it's all over"?
19 The Derby at Epsom is run in which month?
20 Which fellow guitarist joined Brian May for a 1990s version of "We are the Champions"?
21 The movie "The China Syndrome" deals with what type of accident?
22 A male fencer needs how many hits for a victory?
23 Who was 50 first – Robin Williams, Kevin Keegan or Princess Anne?
24 Whose 1990s greatest hits album was modestly called "Modern Classics"?
25 How many bytes are there in a kilobyte?
26 In which country did speed skating originate?
27 Which ship sent out the the first S.O.S.?
28 Richie Richardson captained which country at cricket?
29 Which office machine can be flat-bed or hand-held?
30 What was Keane's first album to top the charts?

Answers	Pot Luck 31 *(see Quiz 68)*

1 Head. **2** Silicon Valley. **3** Haiti. **4** Sir Arthur Conan Doyle. **5** Refraction. **6** 65. **7** Hearn. **8** St Valentine's Day. **9** St Andrews. **10** A Tolkien novel title. **11** Four. **12** Man in Black. **13** Pink Floyd. **14** Nick Leeson. **15** Eskimo. **16** Marzipan. **17** Snake. **18** Coventry. **19** R Kelly. **20** Leeds United. **21** Sandy Lyle. **22** Simnel cake. **23** Isle of Wight. **24** Live and Let Die. **25** Class. **26** Ken Barlow. **27** Cheese. **28** The bereaved. **29** Talk. **30** Ricky Ponting.

Quiz 67 | Natural Phenomena | Answers – page 189

1 What is another name for calcium oxide?
2 What is the next largest body in our solar system after the Sun?
3 What is the only planet to have been discovered by an American – Mars, Pluto or Venus?
4 What is the next deepest ocean after the Pacific?
5 What is the longest river on the American continent?
6 Which is the largest lake on the UK mainland?
7 Which country has the largest area of inland water?
8 In which waters is the EEC's largest island?
9 Which home of the Queen is one of the coldest places in the UK?
10 In December 2006 which natural disaster befell Kensal Rise in North London?
11 The Congo river is in the Democratic Republic of Congo and where else?
12 Which county of mainland England is the warmest?
13 What is the most common element in the universe?
14 Which is the heaviest – plutonium, gold or uranium?
15 What is England's second largest lake?
16 What is the chemical name for chalk?
17 Kaolin is what type of clay?
18 Denmark comprises how many islands – 26, 300 or 500?
19 Which mountain is the highest in the Alaska Range?
20 The Caucasus Mountains divide Georgia and Azerbaijan from where?
21 In which US state is the volcanic mountain of Mount St Helens which erupted in 1980?
22 Which metallic element has its natural occurrence in wolfram?
23 In which country are most of Europe's volcanoes?
24 Where in Japan did a massive earthquake kill over 5,000 people in 1995?
25 What is the most popular form of green beryl called?
26 What was the first name of Richter whose scale measures the intensity of an earthquake?
27 How much of the Earth's area is covered in ice – 5%, 10% or 20%?
28 What colour is the quartz known as citrine?
29 Where is the volcanic island of Sumatra?
30 Which river burst its banks to flood York in 2002?

Answers	Movie Memories *(see Quiz 65)*

1 Johnny Depp. 2 Lon Chaney. 3 Two. 4 A. 5 Carole Lombard. 6 High Noon. 7 The Prince of Egypt. 8 Reservoir Dogs. 9 Marlon Brando. 10 TV weather presenter. 11 Gilbert & Sullivan. 12 Cuban missile. 13 When Nature Calls. 14 Titanic. 15 The Matrix. 16 Babe. 17 Bill Murray. 18 Michael Douglas. 19 Marianne Faithfull. 20 Marilyn Monroe. 21 Joely. 22 Bookshop owner. 23 The Nutty Professor. 24 Four. 25 Breakfast at Tiffany's. 26 San Francisco. 27 The Devil. 28 Little Italy. 29 A Grand Day Out. 30 Casablanca.

Quiz 68 | Pot Luck 31

1 What part of the human body is measured using the cephalix index?
2 What nickname is given to the Santa Clara valley in America?
3 In which country did the private security force the Tontons Macoutes operate?
4 Who was the eponymous Arthur in Julian Barnes's novel "Arthur & George"?
5 What word describes the bending of light passing from one medium to another?
6 How old was singer Gene Pitney at the time of his death – 55, 65 or 75?
7 Which Barry managed snooker's Steve Davis through his winning years?
8 On which special day were seven of Bugs Moran's gang murdered in America?
9 Where could Prince William have a round of golf at the local club for his university?
10 What did the group Marillion base their group name on – a Tolkien novel, Marilyn Monroe or a nightclub?
11 What is the minimum number of times the racket must hit the ball in a tennis game?
12 Darts player Alan Glazier and singer Johnny Cash have been both known as what?
13 Who released the classic "Ummagumma" album?
14 Who was responsible for the crime recounted in the film "Rogue Trader"?
15 From which language does the word anorak – a hooded jacket – come?
16 What is on the outside of a Battenburg cake?
17 A taipan is a type of what?
18 Which of these English cities is the furthest south – Birmingham, Coventry or Leicester?
19 Who had American No 1 albums with "TP-2,Com" and "TP.3 Reloaded"?
20 Eric Cantona joined Manchester United from which club?
21 Who was the first Briton to win golf's US Masters?
22 Which cake was originally made for Mothering Sunday?
23 On which Isle was Queen Victoria's residence Osborne House?
24 In which film did Roger Moore first play James Bond?
25 Pulp's debut album was called "Different" what?
26 Mike Baldwin died in the arms of which "Corrie" character?
27 What is the main ingredient in a traditional fondue?
28 The organisation CRUSE was set up to help who?
29 What was "Happy" in the title of Captain Sensible's only No 1 hit?
30 Who hit Australia's highest score in the 2006–07 Ashes series?

Answers	Pot Luck 30 (see Quiz 66)

1 Pour. 2 Madam Butterfly. 3 Japan. 4 Charles Darwin. 5 Four. 6 Big wheel. 7 Japan. 8 Five. 9 Taj Mahal. 10 Green Day. 11 Euston. 12 Sunnis. 13 Three. 14 Denis Law. 15 Heart. 16 Ants. 17 Modulation. 18 Kenneth. 19 June. 20 Hank Marvin. 21 Nuclear. 22 Five. 23 Princess Anne (2000). 24 Paul Weller. 25 1024. 26 Holland. 27 Titanic. 28 West Indies. 29 Scanner. 30 Hopes and Fears.

1 In which city did Kylie Minogue resume her Showgirl tour in 2006?

2 Which lady sang the soul album "I Never Loved a Man (the Way I Love You)"?

3 Who killed Marvin Gaye?

4 Why was Bob Dylan booed at the Manchester Free Trade Hall in 1966?

5 How many people were on Michael Jackson's "Thriller" album cover?

6 Which Beatle was the first to have a solo No 1 in the US?

7 How old was Elton John when he hit No 1 with the single in memory of Diana Princess of Wales – 46, 51 or 56?

8 Who had a best-selling album "No Jacket Required" in 1985?

9 Which US solo singer had a successful album of "Love Songs" in the 1980s?

10 Which American singer had 35 consecutive UK Top Ten hits.

11 How many years do Cher's No 1 UK hits span – 25, 33 or 39?

12 Which country superstar has had most solo album sales in the USA – Garth Brooks, Dolly Parton or Kenny Rogers?

13 Which superstar band wrote Diana Ross's "Chain Reaction"?

14 In which part of New York was Barry Manilow born?

15 Which superstar played the title role in the 1980s "The Jazz Singer"?

16 Which country singer won a Lifetime Achievement Grammy in 2000?

17 With whom did opera's Monserrat Caballe sing at the Barcelona Olympics?

18 Who recorded "Ten Summoner's Tales" in 1993?

19 Paul McCartney's "Standing Stone" premiered in New York and at which London venue?

20 Who was the first singer to have No 1 hits in five decades?

21 Who wrote the Mariah Carey/Westlife hit "Against All Odds"?

22 Which character in radio's "The Archers" shares her name with a Dolly Parton hit?

23 Which female vocalist duetted with George Michael on "If I Told You That"?

24 Which former Motown star had a new millennium hit with "Not Over Yet"?

25 Which rock star of Scottish parentage was inducted into the Rock and Roll Hall of Fame in 1994?

26 Which James Bond theme did Tina Turner sing?

27 Who is Britain's most successful female chart artist, who became a Dame in 2000?

28 Who sang in a benefit concert following the New York atrocity after suffering her own health problems in 2001?

29 Who was the first major star to make a full album available for downloading?

30 In which year did Cher celebrate her 60th birthday?

Answers	Technology and Industry *(see Quiz 71)*

1 Myspace. 2 Nintendo. 3 Woolwich. 4 Books. 5 Express. 6 London Underground. 7 Colgate. 8 Red. 9 Railtrack. 10 Marks & Spencer. 11 Disneyland Paris. 12 Tesco. 13 Seattle. 14 Mothercare. 15 Honda. 16 Mobile phones. 17 Benjamin Guinness. 18 Apple. 19 Sony. 20 Charles Rolls. 21 Asda. 22 Ginger Productions. 23 Washing machine. 24 Sugar. 25 Sabena. 26 Germany. 27 Henry Royce. 28 Winfield. 29 Airbus A380. 30 Snooker.

Quiz 70 | Pot Luck 32

Answers – page 196

1 Which of the "Monty Python Flying Circus" team was called Michael?
2 Who made the album "Songs from the West Coast"?
3 What did Lord Gyllene win on a Monday in 1997 that would have been on Saturday but for a bomb threat?
4 Robben Island was a prison located near which city?
5 What is the fruit flavour of Cointreau?
6 How old was Billy the Kid when he died?
7 On a computer keyboard where is the letter O in relation to the L – above it, below it or next to it?
8 In rhyme, on what day of the week was Solomon Grundy married?
9 Which "Little" book by Louisa May Alcott became a best seller?
10 Dying in 2006, actress Lynne Perrie had played which TV character for 23 years?
11 Which two colours are most often confused in colour blindness?
12 Which Abba album was No 1 again in 1999 seven years after its release?
13 Who was first to a first Best Actress Oscar – Hilary Swank or Julia Roberts?
14 Which stately home and safari park is owned by the Marquis of Bath?
15 Which ex-Tory MP once said, "Only domestic servants apologise"?
16 Which Spanish club side were the first winners of the European Champions Cup?
17 What type of animal can be Texel and Romney Marsh?
18 The Bee Gees were born on which island?
19 Theatre impresario Bill Kenwright is connected with which soccer club?
20 What was Jemima Khan's maiden name?
21 In the judiciary, what does the D in DPP stand for?
22 Who became the face of Estée Lauder in the mid-1990s?
23 Which is the nearest city to the Tay road bridge?
24 Prime Minister Viktor Yanukovich was defeated in a re-run election in which country?
25 In which decade of last century did Constantinople change its name to Istanbul?
26 In which decade was singer Eva Cassidy born?
27 Which designer was once a partner of Malcolm McLaren?
28 In 2006 it was announced that which country would host cricket's 2019 World Cup?
29 In which century was the last execution at the Tower of London?
30 In which group of islands is Panay?

Answers	Pot Luck 33 *(see Quiz 72)*

1 Four. 2 Chef. 3 The Torrey Canyon. 4 Mackintosh. 5 Justin Gatlin. 6 1930s. 7 M62. 8 Wall Street. 9 USA. 10 Voodoo Chile. 11 Moscow. 12 France. 13 Toad. 14 And That's the Truth. 15 Della Street. 16 West Ham. 17 Grand Hotel. 18 1861. 19 Once. 20 Elizabeth Taylor. 21 Sale of alcohol. 22 Alaska. 23 Francis. 24 Boston. 25 12. 26 Trevor Eve. 27 NBC. 28 Eddie Fitzgerald. 29 Stansted. 30 Witchcraft.

1 Which website gave the space that helped launch the Arctic Monkeys?
2 Which company launched the DS console and the Wii?
3 Which building society merged with Barclays Bank in 2000?
4 What do Amazon.com chiefly sell?
5 Which newspaper did Lord Beaverbrook take over in the 20th century?
6 Ken Livingstone appointed Bob Kiley to oversee the reform of what?
7 Which brand of toothpaste gave its company a huge boost when George W Bush and Tony Blair both admitted using it?
8 What colour was the Vodafone lettering on England cricket shirts?
9 Which UK transport company went into receivership in October 2001?
10 Which retailer introduced the brand Per Una to boost flagging sales?
11 Where was Yves Gerbeau working when he took over as chief executive of the Millennium Dome?
12 Which was the first UK supermarket to achieve profits of more than £1bn?
13 In which city associated with the technology industry was Bill Gates born?
14 Habitat founder Terence Conran has also been involved in the management of which store catering for young families?
15 Which car and motor cycle manufacturer had the first name Soichiro?
16 What did Virgin trains ban from all but designated carriages from the autumn of 2001?
17 Which industrialist, whose name is known all over the world, was the first Lord Mayor of Dublin?
18 Which company did Steven Jobs leave prior to setting up NeXT Inc?
19 Akio Morita and Masaru Ibuka founded which electronics company?
20 Which motor manufacturer made the first non-stop double crossing of the English Channel by plane?
21 Which supermarket chain introduced the fashion label George?
22 What was the name of Chris Evans' company which bought Virgin radio?
23 What type of motor did Sinclair use in his personal transport C5?
24 The donor of the Tate Gallery made his fortune in which commodity?
25 Which Belgian airline effectively went bust after the World Trade Center atrocity?
26 Energy giants e.on. are based in which European country?
27 Which motor manufacturer designed Spitfire and Hurricane engines in WWII?
28 What was Frank Woolworth's middle name which was used for the store's own brand?
29 What is the world's largest passenger plane?
30 888.com sponsored a World Championship in which sport?

Answers	**Music Superstars** (see Quiz 69)

1 Melbourne. **2** Aretha Franklin. **3** His father (Marvin Gaye Sr). **4** He played an electric guitar. **5** One. **6** George Harrison. **7** 51. **8** Phil Collins. **9** Barbra Streisand. **10** Madonna. **11** 33. **12** Garth Brooks. **13** Bee Gees. **14** Brooklyn. **15** Neil Diamond. **16** Willie Nelson. **17** Freddie Mercury. **18** Sting. **19** Albert Hall. **20** Cliff Richard. **21** Phil Collins. **22** Jolene. **23** Whitney Houston. **24** Diana Ross. **25** Rod Stewart. **26** Goldeneye. **27** Shirley Bassey. **28** Mariah Carey. **29** David Bowie. **30** 2006.

1 How many members were in the original line-up of Il Divo?
2 In which profession did Marco Pierre White find fame?
3 Which vessel went down on the Seven Stones reef off Land's End?
4 What was the surname of Scot Charles Rennie of the Art Nouveau movement?
5 Which Justin recorded a 9.77 seconds 100 metres at Doha in 2006?
6 Snooker legend John Spencer died in 2006, but in which decade was he born?
7 Hull and Leeds are linked by which motorway?
8 In which film did Michael Douglas live by the maxim that "Greed is good"?
9 In which country is Peterson Field international airport?
10 Which Jimi Hendrix song hit No 1 a few weeks after the singer's death?
11 The news agency TASS is based in which city?
12 In which country was Edith Cresson PM in the 1990s?
13 Which of the following is not a crustacean – crab, lobster or toad?
14 In the 1990s single title what did Meat Loaf add to "I'd Lie for You"?
15 In fiction, what was the name of Perry Mason's secretary?
16 Which soccer team does Russell Brand support?
17 In which Brighton Hotel did an IRA bomb explode in 1984 at the Tory Conference?
18 When did the Pony Express ride into the sunset and close down its service – was it 1791, 1861 or 1921?
19 How many times did Gagarin orbit the Earth on his first journey into space?
20 Who was the first actress to be paid $1 million for a single film?
21 What did the Falstead Act aim to control in the US?
22 The northern terminus of the Pan American highway is in which state?
23 What is Daley Thompson's first name?
24 In which city did Louise Woodward's trial take place after a baby died in her care?
25 How many faces does a dodecahedron have?
26 Which actor played the TV character Detective Superintendent Peter Boyd?
27 What was the USA's first public television service?
28 What was Fitz's full name in "Cracker"?
29 What is Britain's third largest airport?
30 What is the main subject of the play "The Crucible" – chemistry, snooker or witchcraft?

Answers | Pot Luck 32 *(see Quiz 70)*

1 Palin. 2 Elton John. 3 Grand National. 4 Cape Town. 5 Orange. 6 21. 7 Above it. 8 Wednesday. 9 Little Women. 10 Ivy Tilsley. 11 Green and red. 12 Abba Gold. 13 Hilary Swank. 14 Longleat. 15 Alan Clark. 16 Real Madrid. 17 Sheep. 18 The Isle of Man. 19 Everton. 20 Goldsmith. 21 Director. 22 Elizabeth Hurley. 23 Dundee. 24 Ukraine. 25 1930s. 26 1960s. 27 Vivienne Westwood. 28 England. 29 20th. 30 Philippines.

1 What was Vaclav Havel's profession before he became President of the Czech Republic?

2 In 1985 Oxford University refused to give an honorary degree to which PM?

3 Assassinated Prime Minister Olof Palme led which country?

4 Who called the USSR an "evil empire"?

5 Which Prime Minister of Australia wept on TV when he confessed to marital misdemeanours?

6 Who did John Hinckley Jr shoot?

7 Lord Carrington resigned as Foreign Secretary during which conflict?

8 Which former leader died in jail in March 2006 while on trial for war crimes?

9 Who did Nelson Mandela succeed as head of the ANC?

10 On which day does the US President give his weekly talk to the American people?

11 Who became Secretary of State for Culture Media & Sport after the 2001 election?

12 Betty Boothroyd had which famous position of responsibility?

13 At the turn of the millennium which queen – other than Victoria – had reigned longest?

14 Which of the following Prime Ministers were in their nineties when they died – Clement Attlee, William Gladstone and Harold Macmillan?

15 How many years was Margaret Thatcher British Prime Minister – 9, 11 or 15?

16 Newt Gingrich was a respected politician in which country?

17 Who did Jack Straw replace as Foreign Secretary?

18 In 1999 Ehud Barak became Prime Minister of which country?

19 Who was Bill Clinton's first Vice President?

20 Which former South African prime minister died aged 90 in 2006?

21 Who did Gerhard Schroeder replace as German Chancellor?

22 Who was Mayor of New York at the time of the World Trade Center disaster?

23 Who did Paddy Ashdown replace as Liberal leader?

24 How many leaders did the Conservative Party have in the 1990s?

25 Which British Queen had 17 children?

26 Who did Tony Blair replace as Labour leader?

27 Which monarch succeeded King Hussein of Jordan?

28 Who became French Prime Minister in 1997?

29 Queen Wilhelmina led which country?

30 Who was George W Bush's first Secretary of State?

Answers	TV Drama *(see Quiz 75)*

1 Detective. 2 WWII. 3 Casualty. 4 Emilia Fox. 5 Goodnight Mister Tom. 6 Colin Firth. 7 Peter. 8 Merseyside. 9 This Life. 10 Miss Marple. 11 Forensic. 12 England & USA. 13 Martin Chuzzlewit. 14 Lindsay Duncan. 15 Cardiac Arrest. 16 Bleak House. 17 Sean Bean. 18 Hearts & Bones. 19 Poirot. 20 Bradford. 21 Bergerac. 22 Ewan McGregor. 23 Cherie Lunghi. 24 Northern Exposure. 25 Philadelphia. 26 Jack Frost. 27 Edward VII. 28 Wednesday. 29 Cracker. 30 Earl of Leicester (Robert Dudley).

1 Who played the title character in the first "Doctor Who" movie?
2 In 2007 the isle of Inis Mor held a festival celebrating which TV show?
3 Which Grand National course fence, other than Becher's, contains the name Brook?
4 Stephen Cameron's 1996 death was a tragic first in which circumstances?
5 Which American was the first to achieve tennis's Men's Singles Grand Slam?
6 In song lyrics, where did Billie Jo Spears want to lay her blanket?
7 Which Roger was drummer with Queen?
8 Along with Doric and Corinthian, what is the third Greek order of architecture?
9 Who was the first British woman to win a world swimming title?
10 Which northern city has the dialling code 0113?
11 What nationality is Salman Rushdie?
12 What was the first hit album by The Killers?
13 Which population was devastated by myxomatosis?
14 Which is the brightest planet as seen from the Earth?
15 What do three horizontal lines represent in mathematics?
16 Which English King was the last to die in battle?
17 In rock opera, Tommy was deaf, dumb and what else?
18 How many times does the letter A appear in the first name of singer/actress Streisand?
19 Sale Sharks won the Guinness Premiership title in 2006, beating which team in the final?
20 What is the next prime number above 100?
21 What is a quadrilateral with one pair of opposite sides parallel called?
22 Which telephone link service was established in July 1937?
23 What is lowered by a beta-blocker?
24 Which country has the greatest number of telephone subscribers?
25 In the song "Country Roads", which place is described as "almost heaven"?
26 Who was the most famous inhabitant of the fictitious village St Mary Mead?
27 Which composer's "6th Symphony" is known as the "Pathétique?
28 Who was 60 first – Gloria Hunniford, Cliff Richard or John Major?
29 Boxer Jack Dempsey was nicknamed which Mauler?
30 Which country suffered most loss of life in the Indian Ocean tsunami of December 2004?

Answers	Pot Luck 35 *(see Quiz 76)*

1 France. 2 William Henry. 3 Christmas Day. 4 Breathing. 5 South. 6 The Number of the Beast. 7 Swedish. 8 Virgin Soldiers. 9 Capri. 10 Syd Little. 11 Sweden. 12 London. 13 None. 14 Dodecanese. 15 September 15th. 16 Tony Hancock. 17 Yellowstone Park. 18 Zip fastener. 19 Wes Craven. 20 Goat. 21 Kathy Bates. 22 Sally Lockhart. 23 Mona Lisa. 24 Parish. 25 K. 26 Lloyds of London. 27 George Michael. 28 Ian Millward. 29 Southampton. 30 Setting Sun.

1 What was the occupation of the person in the title role in "Rebus"?
2 Which War did "Foyle's War" deal with?
3 Ian Kelsey left "Emmerdale" for which hospital drama?
4 Who played Jeannie in the revival of "Randall & Hopkirk (Deceased)"?
5 In which drama did John Thaw play an elderly man who takes in a London evacuee?
6 Who was a memorable and different Mr Darcy on the large and small screen?
7 What was the name of the priest played by Stephen Tompkinson in "Ballykissangel"?
8 Where was the classic "Boys from the Blackstuff" set?
9 Which series featured Miles, Anna and Egg?
10 The late Joan Hickson played which famous sleuth on TV?
11 What type of surgeon was Dangerfield?
12 In which two countries was "The Buccaneers" set?
13 Which 1990s Dickens adaptation had Paul Scofield in the title role?
14 Who played Mrs Peter Mayle in the ill-fated "A Year in Provence"?
15 In which series did Helen Baxendale play Claire Maitland?
16 Anna Maxwell Martin won her first "Best Actress" BAFTA for which drama?
17 Who played Mellors in the 1993 TV adaptation of "Lady Chatterley's Lover"?
18 Which "thirtysomething" drama series starred Amanda Holden and Dervla Kirwan?
19 Which sleuth had a secretary called Miss Lemon?
20 Where was "Band of Gold" set?
21 Which TV detective worked for the Bureau des Etrangers?
22 Which future co-star of Nicole Kidman starred in Dennis Potter's "Lipstick on Your Collar"?
23 Which actress, who made a brief appearance in "EastEnders" in 2001, starred as "The Manageress"?
24 Which series had Dr Joel Fleishmann in the Alaskan town of Cicely?
25 In which state was "Thirtysomething" set?
26 Which TV detective was created in the books of RD Wingfield?
27 Which monarch was on the throne at the time "Upstairs Downstairs" was set?
28 Which day of the week was famous for having a weekly play in the late 1960s?
29 In which series did Robbie Coltrane play Fitz?
30 Jeremy Irons played which Earl in 2005's historical drama "Elizabeth"?

Answers	Leaders *(see Quiz 73)*

1 Dramatist. 2 Margaret Thatcher. 3 Sweden. 4 Ronald Reagan. 5 Bob Hawke. 6 Ronald Reagan. 7 Falklands. 8 Slobodan Milosevic. 9 Oliver Tambo. 10 Saturday. 11 Tessa Jowell. 12 Speaker of the House of Commons. 13 Elizabeth II. 14 Harold Macmillan. 15 11. 16 USA. 17 Robin Cook. 18 Israel. 19 Al Gore. 20 Pieter Botha. 21 Helmut Kohl. 22 Rudolph Giuliani. 23 David Steel. 24 Three. 25 Anne. 26 John Smith. 27 Abdullah. 28 Lionel Jospin. 29 Netherlands. 30 Colin Powell.

1 Which was the world's first country to introduce a driving test?
2 What are Bill Gates's two first names?
3 James Brown, "The Godfather of Soul", died on which special day in 2006?
4 What does the letter B stand for in SCUBA?
5 Is Helmand in the north or south of Afghanistan?
6 Which reissue of a 1982 Iron Maiden hit charted again in 2005?
7 Which language does the word ombudsman derives from?
8 Leslie Thomas wrote a novel about what kind of "Soldiers"?
9 Which island lies in the Bay of Naples?
10 Cyril Mead became known as which half of a comic duo?
11 Which country produced the first Miss World contest winner?
12 Florence Nightingale was given the Freedom of which city?
13 How many top ten hits did Kate Bush have in the last decade of the old millennium?
14 Rhodes is the largest of which group of islands?
15 The Battle of Britain is remembered on which date?
16 Which of these comics died the youngest – Tony Hancock, Eric Morecambe or Peter Sellers?
17 Which US national park has a highway called Alligator Alley?
18 Which invention affecting trousers was patented in Chicago in 1913?
19 Which director started off the "Scream" series of movies?
20 What animal appears on the cover of the Beach Boys' album "Pet Sounds"?
21 Who won the Best Actress Oscar for the movie "Misery"?
22 Which character did Billie Piper play in "The Ruby in the Smoke"?
23 How is the painting La Gioconda also known?
24 In the Church of England what is the smallest administrative unit?
25 Which letter identified Tommy Lee Jones' character in the "Men in Black" movie?
26 In which London building does the Lutine Bell hang?
27 Which male singer called his debut solo album "Faith"?
28 Which rugby head coach Ian suffered a 2006 sacking at Wigan?
29 Which of these is furthest south – Bath, Bristol or Southampton?
30 What was the first top ten hit for the Chemical Brothers?

| **Answers** | **Pot Luck 34** *(see Quiz 74)* |

1 Peter Cushing. 2 Father Ted. 3 Valentine's. 4 Road rage attack. 5 Donald Budge. 6 On the ground. 7 Taylor. 8 Ionic. 9 Karen Pickering. 10 Leeds. 11 British. 12 Hot Fuss. 13 Rabbit. 14 Venus. 15 Identically equal to. 16 Richard III. 17 Blind. 18 Twice. 19 Leicester. 20 101. 21 Trapezium. 22 999 service. 23 Heart rate and/or blood pressure. 24 USA. 25 West Virginia. 26 Miss Marple. 27 Tchaikovsky. 28 Gloria Hunniford (April 2000). 29 Manassa. 30 Indonesia.

1 Which company created the computer game Shenmue?

2 In which decade were books issued as CD Roms?

3 Which comic is older, "Beano" or "Dandy"?

4 Which best-selling toys do Steiff make?

5 Where in the UK is the Kelvingrove art gallery?

6 How many counters does each backgammon player have at the start of play?

7 "Roma" and "Tornado" are types of what?

8 Pokemon Yellow was created by which manufacturer?

9 What is a round of play called in a hand of bridge?

10 In which county is Alton Towers?

11 What is the number to aim for in a game of cribbage?

12 In which decade was the first Home Video System produced?

13 What colour are Scrabble tiles?

14 Which computer games can be Red, Yellow and Pikachu?

15 What type of needlework requires aida fabric?

16 Where was shuffleboard originally played?

17 Which company created the Gran Turismo Real Driving Simulator?

18 Ikebana is the art of what?

19 What are satin, stem and lazy daisy?

20 EasyEverything is the world's biggest what?

21 Which colour do Morris dancers predominantly wear?

22 Where in the UK is the Blackgang Chine Clifftop Theme Park?

23 Which special piece of equipment is needed to do crochet?

24 Who wrote the spy thriller "Without Remorse"?

25 How many dice are used in a craps game?

26 Which company produced the first battery-powered cassette recorder?

27 How many packs of cards are used in a game of canasta?

28 What is the world's most widely played board game?

29 Which company created the MS Flight Simulator?

30 In draughts when can a piece move forwards or backwards?

Answers | **Sporting Legends** *(see Quiz 79)*

1 Severiano Ballesteros. 2 Doctor. 3 Manchester United. 4 1970s. 5 Four. 6 Sydney. 7 1950s. 8 Aberdeen. 9 Chelsea. 10 1970s. 11 400m hurdles. 12 14. 13 Stephen Hendry. 14 Tony Jacklin. 15 Barry John. 16 Michael Johnson. 17 Kapil Dev. 18 Chess. 19 Hamburg. 20 Squash. 21 20. 22 Bjorn Borg. 23 452. 24 Australian. 25 Ravel's Bolero. 26 Ipswich Town. 27 Baseball. 28 Refused to do military service. 29 French. 30 Willie Carson.

Quiz 78 | Pot Luck 36

Answers – page 204

1 Usually meaning extra-terrestrial, where is a car from with the registration letters ET?
2 Which football ground has a Matthew Harding Stand?
3 Which method did John Haigh use to dispose of his victims' bodies?
4 Ralph Scheider was an inventor credited with developing which daily used item?
5 What colour were Arsenal's shirts in their first Champions League Final?
6 What does the reference ibid. mean?
7 Which creepy horror movie features the character Jack Torrance?
8 What does the C stand for in COBOL?
9 What is the nationality of Jennifer Lopez's parents?
10 In which city should you "be sure to wear some flowers in your hair"?
11 In which country was the musician Bela Bartok born?
12 In 1918 in Britain women over what age were given the vote?
13 Which Royal first sat in the House of Lords in 1987?
14 Baroness de Laroche was the first woman to be awarded what licence?
15 Leona Lewis was born and bred in which city?
16 In which London street did Selfridge's first open?
17 Michael Steele was in which all-girl group?
18 Which culinary ingredient can be Extra Virgin?
19 On TV, who was the first regular female presenter of "Points Of View"?
20 Who composed the comic opera "The Gondoliers"?
21 Which picnic aid did James Dewar invent?
22 "The Most Beautiful Girl in the World" was the first UK No 1 single for which artist?
23 Which sisters used Bell as a pseudonym?
24 Whose dying words were, "My neck is very slender"?
25 "Goodbye England's Rose" was the first line of which song?
26 Oyster and Morel are both types of which vegetable?
27 Who is the local sporting hero of the city of Oviedo, Spain?
28 What was the title of the first album from the Scissor Sisters?
29 How was designer Laura Mountney better known?
30 ABTA represents which group of people?

Answers | Pot Luck 37 *(see Quiz 80)*

1 Four Tops. 2 Cheltenham. 3 A clove. 4 George VI. 5 Women's Institute. 6 Bikini.
7 Stuart Clark. 8 Colditz. 9 News of the World. 10 Champion Jockey. 11 Michaelmas
Day. 12 Beatrix Potter. 13 Axis. 14 1,000 Guineas. 15 Valencia. 16 Push the Button.
17 Peru. 18 Duke of Bedford. 19 Norfolk. 20 Charterhouse. 21 Walt Disney. 22 The
Duchess of Windsor. 23 Pankhurst. 24 Brazil. 25 Test tube baby. 26 Belgium. 27
Manchester. 28 Julienne. 29 Greek kilt. 30 South Africa.

Quiz 79 | Sporting Legends | Answers – page 201

LEVEL 2

1 Which Spaniard became the youngest golfer to win the British Open in the 20th century?

2 What was Roger Bannister's "day job"?

3 Which English club did George Best join immediately after leaving school?

4 In which decade did Ian Botham make his Test debut?

5 How many times did Will Carling lead England to the Five Nations title?

6 In which city did Shane Warne play his last Test match?

7 In which decade did Henry Cooper win his first British heavyweight championship?

8 Which side did Alex Ferguson manage before he went to Manchester United?

9 For which club did Jimmy Greaves make his Football League debut?

10 In which decade did Wayne Gretzky make his professional debut?

11 What was Sally Gunnell's Olympic gold-medal-winning event?

12 Mike Hailwood won how many Isle of Man TT races in the period 1961–1979?

13 Who was the first snooker player to win all nine world ranking tournaments?

14 Who was the European Ryder Cup team's captain from 1983 to 1989?

15 Which Welsh Rugby player scored a record 90 points for his country between 1966 and 1972?

16 Who was the first man to hold the world record at 200m and 400m simultaneously?

17 Who led India to victory in the Cricket World Cup in 1983?

18 Anatoli Karpov was world champion in what?

19 Which team on the European mainland did Kevin Keegan play for?

20 Which sport did Jahangir Khan play?

21 How many Wimbledon titles did Billie Jean King win?

22 Who broke Fred Perry's record of three consecutive Wimbledon titles?

23 To the nearest 50 how many runs did Don Bradman make on his first innings for New South Wales?

24 In 1990 John McEnroe was expelled from which Grand Slam Open for swearing?

25 Which music did Torvill & Dean use when they scored a full hand of perfect scores at the 1984 Olympics?

26 Which team did Alf Ramsey take to the First Division Championship?

27 Which sport did Hank Aaron play?

28 Why was Muhammad Ali stripped of his World Heavyweight tile in 1967?

29 Which was the only Grand Slam title Pete Sampras has not won?

30 Which former Scottish jockey has the first names William Hunter Fisher?

Answers | Hobbies *(see Quiz 77)*

1 Sega. 2 1990s. 3 Beano. 4 Teddy bears. 5 Glasgow. 6 15. 7 Tomato. 8 Nintendo Game Boy. 9 Trick. 10 Staffordshire. 11 31. 12 1970s. 13 Cream/white. 14 Pokemon. 15 Embroidery. 16 On board ship. 17 Sony Play Station. 18 Flower arranging. 19 Embroidery stitches. 20 Internet cafe. 21 White. 22 Isle of Wight. 23 Hook. 24 Tom Clancy. 25 Two. 26 Philips. 27 Two. 28 Monopoly. 29 Microsoft. 30 When it becomes a king.

1 Levi Stubbs was lead singer with which Tamla Motown group?
2 Which Gloucestershire town had the first public school for girls?
3 What is a small segment of garlic called?
4 Who was the first reigning monarch to visit the USA?
5 Which women's organisation was founded by Mrs Hoodless in 1897?
6 Which fashion statement was created by Louis Reard in 1946?
7 Who topped the Australian bowling averages for the 2006–07 Ashes series?
8 How was the prison camp Oflag IVC better known?
9 Which Queen album had the name of a national newspaper?
10 What did Gordon Richards become a record 26 times between 1925 and 1953?
11 On a calendar, what is the third quarter day in England?
12 Who lived at "Hill Top" near Sawrey, Ambleside?
13 What was the name of the alliance between Germany and Italy in World War II?
14 Which Classic horse race was the first to be run on a Sunday in England?
15 Which club did Fernando Morientes join when he left Liverpool?
16 Which title links a No 1 album by The Chemical Brothers and a Sugababes' No 1 single?
17 In which country does the Amazon begin?
18 Which Duke has an ancestral home at Woburn Abbey?
19 In which county is the Queen's home Sandringham House?
20 All the members of Genesis were ex-pupils of which school?
21 Who said, "I love Mickey Mouse more than any woman I've ever known"?
22 Who said, "No woman can be too rich or too thin"?
23 What was Emmeline Goulden's married name?
24 Which country does supermodel Gisele Bundchen come from?
25 Why was Louise Joy Brown's birth a first in 1978?
26 In which country was the first beauty contest held?
27 In which city did the first Marks & Spencer store open?
28 What term describes thinly cut vegetables slowly cooked in butter?
29 What sort of garment is a fustanella?
30 In which country is the Humewood Golf Club?

Answers | Pot Luck 36 *(see Quiz 78)*

1 Egypt. 2 Stamford Bridge. 3 Acid bath. 4 Credit card. 5 Yellow. 6 In the same place. 7 The Shining. 8 Common. 9 Puerto Rican. 10 San Francisco. 11 Hungary. 12 30. 13 Prince Andrew. 14 Pilot's licence. 15 London. 16 Oxford Street. 17 The Bangles. 18 Olive oil. 19 Anne Robinson. 20 Gilbert & Sullivan. 21 Thermos flask. 22 Prince. 23 Brontë Sisters. 24 Anne Boleyn. 25 Candle in the Wind 97. 26 Mushroom. 27 Fernando Alonso. 28 Scissor Sisters. 29 Laura Ashley. 30 Travel agents.

1 What are the initials for the human form of BSE?
2 Which letter is used to denote the bird flu virus?
3 A hysterectomy involves removal of what?
4 Osteoporosis is a weakness and brittleness of what?
5 In which decade did a report first appear in the US saying smoking could damage health?
6 What was the nationality of the founder of the Red Cross?
7 Penicillin was the first what?
8 Ebola is also known as which disease?
9 What does S stand for in AIDS?
10 Appendicitis causes pain where?
11 Which insects cause bubonic plague?
12 Which disease – more common in children – is also called varicella?
13 What causes cholera – contaminated water, insects or malnutrition?
14 Which part of the body is affected by conjunctivitis?
15 The infection of wounds by what can bring on tetanus?
16 Which of the following is not a blood group – AB, O or T?
17 What sort of flies transmit sleeping sickness?
18 Cranial osteopathy involves the manipulation of which bones?
19 Reflexologists massage which part of the body?
20 Shiatsu is a massage technique from which country?
21 Anabolic steroids are used to repair or build what?
22 What does an analgesic drug do?
23 What does the H stand for in HIV?
24 In which part of the body is the human's longest bone?
25 Hypertension is another name for what?
26 What is the most common element in the human body?
27 After the skin, what is the next largest human organ?
28 What is another name for the sternum?
29 Which impotence drug was used to strengthen a premature baby in 2006?
30 Where was the first ambulance used?

Answers	The Oscars (see Quiz 83)

1 Rachel Weisz. 2 Seven. 3 Gwyneth Paltrow. 4 Charlize Theron. 5 American Beauty. 6 Boys Don't Cry. 7 Tommy Lee Jones. 8 The Cider House Rules. 9 The Piano. 10 March. 11 James Whale. 12 Julia Roberts. 13 Ang Lee. 14 Creature Comforts. 15 John Williams. 16 The Madness of King George. 17 As Good As It Gets. 18 Tom Hanks. 19 Sally Field. 20 Moonstruck. 21 Shirley MacLaine. 22 American Civil War. 23 Oliver Reed. 24 Jane Fonda. 25 Jon Voight. 26 Hayley Mills. 27 Geoffrey Rush. 28 Jeremy Irons. 29 New York. 30 Sam Mendes.

Quiz 82 | Pot Luck 38

Answers – page 208

1 In which country did the Women's Institute begin?
2 On TV who became a "hunter gatherer" searching out food from the wild?
3 The French President occupies which official residence?
4 In which country is Archangel international airport?
5 Which Lawrence and Jacqueline wrote the guide to being civilised called "A Pinch of Posh"?
6 Who was backed by The Dakotas?
7 In which ocean is the Sargasso Sea – Atlantic, Indian or Pacific?
8 French designer Christian Dior created what kind of Look in the late 1940s?
9 Which band have had hits with "Getaway" and "Inner Smile"?
10 The Fosse Way links which two English cities?
11 In which capital city was jazz's Hot Club?
12 Prince Edward resigned from which branch of the services in 1987?
13 Who is the oldest of The Three Tenors?
14 In which song were "them good old boys drinkin' whisky & rye"?
15 How is Formosa now known?
16 Who introduced the very first edition of "Countdown" on TV?
17 Lowfields Road goes past which famous soccer stadium?
18 In what year did "Blue Peter" first set sail on the airwaves of TV?
19 Viscount Linley was the first British Royal to be banned from doing what?
20 Peter Sutcliffe became better known under which graphic name?
21 Which month was in hit titles by Pilot and Barbara Dixon?
22 In which mountain range is the Simplon Pass?
23 Marie Curie was the first woman to win which notable prize?
24 Who had an instrumental hit with "Don't Cry for Me Argentina"?
25 In which year did Queen Elizabeth and the Duke of Edinburgh celebrate their Golden Wedding?
26 What is the chief shopping street in Edinburgh?
27 In 2006, who clocked up 20 years as editor of "Private Eye"?
28 René Lalique used which material when making ornaments?
29 Which city is named after US frontiersman Kit Carson?
30 Kurt Cobain's farewell note in 1995 read, "It's better to burn out than" do what?

Answers	Pot Luck 39 *(see Quiz 84)*

1 Ellis. 2 Chile & Argentina. 3 10th. 4 Hat. 5 Pile it high, sell it cheap. 6 Hannah Waterman. 7 Jimmy Carter. 8 Stevens. 9 Queensland. 10 Bradford. 11 Victoria. 12 Glenys. 13 The Cheeky Girls. 14 Chicago. 15 Safety pin. 16 Clooney. 17 Cream. 18 Jack. 19 And now. 20 Grease. 21 Whole Again. 22 Skull. 23 Albert. 24 Woolworth's. 25 Ulrike Meinhof. 26 Kenya. 27 Banana and toffee. 28 Victoria. 29 Leeds United. 30 Simon Jordan.

Quiz 83 | The Oscars

LEVEL 2

Answers – page 205

1 Who won the only Oscar for "The Constant Gardener"?
2 How many Oscars did "Schindler's List" win?
3 Who played Viola in "Shakespeare in Love"?
4 Who won an Oscar for her role in "Monster"?
5 Which movie was the last Best Picture winner of the 1990s?
6 For which movie did Hilary Swank win her first Oscar?
7 Who played the marshal in an Oscar-winning performance in "The Fugitive"?
8 For which movie did Michael Caine win his second Oscar?
9 For which movie did the 11-year-old Anna Paquin win an Oscar in 1993?
10 In which month does the Oscars ceremony usually take place?
11 Which director is the subject of "Gods and Monsters"?
12 Who won the Best Actress Oscar in 2001?
13 Who directed "Crouching Tiger Hidden Dragon"?
14 For which movie did Nick Park win his first Oscar?
15 Who wrote the music for "Jaws"?
16 Which Nicholas Hytner movie had Nigel Hawthorne in the title role?
17 Which 1997 movie with Oscar-winning performances had the ad line, "Brace yourself for Melvin!"?
18 Who "outed" his drama teacher at an Oscars ceremony where he won for the AIDS issue movie "Philadelphia"?
19 Who played Oscar-nominated Julia Roberts' mother in "Steel Magnolias"?
20 For which movie did Cher receive her Oscar in a dress which caused more uproar than the film?
21 Which actress, who had her 67th birthday in 2001, said "I deserve this" on receiving her Oscar in 1983?
22 Against which conflict is "Dances with Wolves" set?
23 Which actor died during the making of the Oscar-winning "Gladiator"?
24 Between Glenda Jackson's two Best Actress Oscars, Liza Minnelli and who else won?
25 Which father of Angelina Jolie won an Oscar for "Coming Home"?
26 Which English actress won an Oscar as a child in 1960?
27 Which star of "Quills" won an Oscar for "Shine"?
28 Who was the only English Best Actor of the 1990s?
29 Where did Woody Allen set "Hannah and Her Sisters"?
30 Which British director directed "American Beauty"?

Answers	Medicine and Health *(see Quiz 81)*

1 CJD. 2 H. 3 Womb. 4 Bones. 5 1960s. 6 Swiss. 7 Antibiotic. 8 Legionnaire's.
9 Syndrome. 10 Abdomen. 11 Fleas. 12 Chicken pox. 13 Contaminated water. 14 Eyes. 15 Soil. 16 T. 17 Tsetse flies. 18 Skull. 19 Feet. 20 Japan. 21 Muscles. 22 Alleviate pain. 23 Human. 24 Thigh. 25 High blood pressure. 26 Oxygen. 27 Liver. 28 Breastbone. 29 Viagara. 30 France.

1 Which Ruth was the last woman to be hanged in British history?
2 The Transandine railway tunnel links which two countries?
3 Which wedding anniversary is linked to tin?
4 Who or what was Dolly Varden?
5 What was the motto of Tesco founder Sir Jack Cohen?
6 Which actress won "Just the Two of Us" with Marti Pellow?
7 Which US President was married to Rosalynn Smith?
8 Which Cat sang that he loved his dog?
9 The Great Barrier Reef is off which Australian state?
10 Heroic PC Sharon Beshenivsky was murdered in which city in 2005?
11 Which British monarch's name does Princess Eugenie have?
12 What is the first name of MEP Mrs Kinnock?
13 Gabriela Irimia was a member of which group?
14 Ruthie Henshall and Ute Lemper were the first West End stars of which musical?
15 Which Walter Hunt invention of 1849 has Liz Hurley used as a fashion statement?
16 Which 1950s singer Rosemary is aunt of a popular actor George with the same surname?
17 Baker, Bruce and Clapton made up which group?
18 What was the most popular baby boy name in England and Wales from 2000 to 2006?
19 What are the first two words of "My Way"?
20 "Hopelessly Devoted to You" comes from which musical?
21 What was the first UK No 1 for Atomic Kitten?
22 Which part of the body is studied by a phrenologist?
23 What was Frank Sinatra's middle name?
24 Which shopping chain advertised "nothing over sixpence"?
25 Who was the female leader of the Baader Meinhof terrorist group?
26 Where is the Masai Mara game reserve?
27 What are a banoffee pie's main two ingredients?
28 Who was the first British monarch seen on a moving picture?
29 Jack Charlton played all his League football with which club side?
30 Who was Crystal Palace chairman when manager Iain Dowie left "by mutual consent"?

Answers	Pot Luck 38 *(see Quiz 82)*

1 Canada. 2 Ray Mears. 3 Elysee Palace. 4 Russia. 5 Llewelyn Bowen. 6 Billy J Kramer. 7 Atlantic. 8 New Look. 9 Texas. 10 Lincoln & Exeter. 11 Paris. 12 Royal Marines. 13 Luciano Pavarotti. 14 American Pie. 15 Taiwan. 16 Richard Whiteley. 17 Elland Road (Leeds). 18 1958. 19 Driving. 20 The Yorkshire Ripper. 21 January. 22 Alps. 23 Nobel Prize. 24 The Shadows. 25 1997. 26 Princes Street. 27 Ian Hislop. 28 Glass. 29 Carson City. 30 Fade away.

1 Which female band had a No 1 with "Independent Women Part 1"?
2 Who wrote the "Liverpool Oratorio" with Paul McCartney?
3 Whose album had the invitation "Come On Over" in 1998?
4 Who sang "I Walk the Line" and "A Boy Named Sue"?
5 What did Leo Fender make?
6 Which Australian had 13 consecutive UK Top Ten hits between January 1988 and June 1991?
7 Which duo had a multi-million seller with "Unchained Melody" in 1995?
8 Whose best-selling posthumous album was called "Legend"?
9 Who made the solo albums "Watermark" and "Shepherd Moons"?
10 How were John McDermott, Anthony Kearns and Ronan Tynan styled?
11 Whose albums include "Sogno", "Romanza" and "Sueno"?
12 What type of musician was conductor Daniel Barenboim's wife Jacqueline?
13 How was Nathaniel Adams Coles better known?
14 Which Harry won a Lifetime Achievement Grammy in 2000?
15 Which "title" did bandleader Basie have?
16 Which Harry made the albums "We are in Love" and "Blue Light, Red Light"?
17 With which orchestra did Simon Rattle make his name?
18 Which veteran country singer had two best-selling albums recorded in prisons?
19 Who featured in the movie "Purple Rain"?
20 Who sang the theme song from the Bond movie "Tomorrow Never Dies"?
21 Who won a Grammy in 1992 for "Tears in Heaven"?
22 Who wrote the musical "Oliver!"?
23 Which instrument did Stan Getz play?
24 How many members of boy band A1 are there?
25 Which country do the band Modjo come from?
26 Which English city does Craig David come from?
27 Who recorded the song which the Labour Party used in their 1997 campaign?
28 Who played keyboards with the Strawbs and Yes?
29 Selling well in 2006, who recorded the "The Love Album"?
30 Who made the 2006 debut album "Alright, Still"?

Answers | Folk Music (see Quiz 87)

1 Liege & Life (Fairport Convention). 2 Modern Times. 3 Renbourn. 4 Village Green Preservation Society. 5 Norma Waterstone. 6 Thyme. 7 Folk Britannia. 8 Derbyshire. 9 Tom Paxton. 10 Northumberland. 11 Bob Dylan. 12 Drum. 13 Wilson. 14 Kate Rusby. 15 Judy Dyble. 16 Bagpipes. 17 Steeleye Span. 18 Pentangle. 19 Tony Allen. 20 Streets of London. 21 Guitar. 22 Jim Moray. 23 Martin Carthy. 24 Strings. 25 Strawbs. 26 Johnny Cash. 27 Clancy. 28 Kate Rusby. 29 Kathryn Tickell Band. 30 2007.

1 Which European city has the same name as an archer in mythology?
2 Which month comes after the month containing Saint Andrew's Day?
3 Which fruit includes the variety Ellison's Orange?
4 Tyskie is a brand of beer from which country?
5 Aduki, borlotti and cannellini are all types of what?
6 Where would a Spanish lady wear her mantilla?
7 Who was 50 first – Geena Davis, Nigel Kennedy or Annie Lennox?
8 Who was the first woman General of the Salvation Army?
9 Who was the first singer to have seven consecutive singles reach No 1 in the US?
10 Which English cricket captain had a bust-up with umpire Shakoor Rana in Faisalabad?
11 "Rhythm of Life" comes from which musical?
12 Svetlana Savitskaya was the first woman to walk where?
13 Who had UK hits with "Down 4 U" and "Only U"?
14 The frittata is an Italian version of what popular egg dish?
15 What was the highest-ranking job that the fictitious Jim Hacker achieved?
16 How many beats to the bar does a traditional waltz have?
17 Which sweet delicacies have a name meaning "little ovens"?
18 Which title did Hillary Clinton prefer to First Lady?
19 In France what would you buy if you asked for pamplemousses?
20 Which Royal's motto is "Ich dien" or "I serve"?
21 Which flavouring used in tonic water is taken from a cinchona tree?
22 Why might you be embarrassed by your lentigines?
23 Which jazz singer is Mrs Johnny Dankworth?
24 What colour is the background of the flag of the European Union?
25 Kim Carnes sang about which film star's eyes?
26 Who was Fred Elliott about to marry when he died in "Coronation Street"?
27 How many sharps and flats are there in the key of C major?
28 Sven Goran Eriksson first won the Italian Cup as boss of which side?
29 How is the volcanic Mongibello also known?
30 At which English club did Ian Wright end his soccer playing career?

Answers	21st Century Fifa World Cup *(see Quiz 88)*

1 1-1. 2 Right foot. 3 Marco Materazzi. 4 Costa Rica. 5 Group B. 6 Michael Owen (Two). 7 Tim Cahill. 8 Fabio Cannavaro. 9 Ukraine. 10 Robert Green. 11 Trinidad & Tobago. 12 David Beckham. 13 Nine men. 14 Angola. 15 S. Korea. 16 Sweden. 17 White. 18 Germany. 19 David Trezeguet. 20 France (v. Brazil). 21 Gelsenkirchen. 22 Portugal v. Holland. 23 Marcello Lippi. 24 Miroslav Klose (5 goals). 25 No 9. 26 Fabio Grosso. 27 Switzerland. 28 Guus Hiddink. 29 Cristiano Ronaldo. 30 Six.

1 What was voted most influential folk album of all time in a 2006 BBC ballot?

2 Which Bob Dylan album namechecks Alicia Keys?

3 Which guitarist John of Pentangle in the 1960s, reached his 60s in 2004?

4 TV's "Jam & Jerusalem" had Kate Rusby singing which song by The Kinks?

5 Who is Eliza Carthy's famous folk-singing mum?

6 In song, what goes with parsley, sage and rosemary?

7 Which 2006 Barbican concert series was covered by the BBC?

8 Which county does singer John Tams come from?

9 Who wrote the folk club favourite "The Last Thing on My Mind"?

10 Kathryn Tickell comes from which English county?

11 Which Minnesota-born star was inducted into the UK Music Hall of Fame in 2005?

12 A bodhran is what type of instrument?

13 What was the middle name of folk pioneer Woody Guthrie?

14 Who charted in 2006 with "All Over Again", a duet with Ronan Keating?

15 Who was Fairport Convention's first female singer?

16 Uillean pipes are a type of what?

17 Womble producer Mike Batt took which folk band into the pop charts?

18 Which five-piece group recorded the influential "Light Flight"?

19 Who forms a duo with accordionist Mike Foster?

20 "In our winter city the rain cries a little pity" is in which Ralph McTell song?

21 Which instrument is associated with Bert Jansch?

22 Which Jim made the album "Sweet England"?

23 Which folk veteran Martin was BBC 2's Folk Singer of the Year in 2005?

24 What produces the sound in an Irish bouzouki?

25 Which band featured singer/songwriter Dave Cousins?

26 Which country star featured with Bob Dylan on "Nashville Skyline"?

27 Tommy Makem featured with which Brothers in the 1960s?

28 Who recorded the album "The Girl Who Couldn't Fly"?

29 Which female's folk band featured in "Last Night of the Proms" in 2001?

30 Which year marks Fairport Convention's fortieth anniversary?

---

1 What was the 90-minute score in the 2006 World Cup Final?
2 Ahead of Germany 2006, Wayne Rooney fractured metatarsels in which foot?
3 Which Italian was involved in the sending-off incident with Zinadine Zidane in 2006?
4 Who did Germany play in the opening game in 2006?
5 Which Group were England in for Germany 2006?
6 Who was England's top scorer in the 2002 finals?
7 Who scored two goals as Australia beat Japan in 2006?
8 Who was the Italian captain in Germany 2006?
9 Which team lost their opener 4-0 yet still made the last eight of Germany 2006?
10 Which keeper missed Germany after a groin injury while playing for England B?
11 Against which opponents did Wayne Rooney first play in Germany 2006?
12 Which English player scored in both 2002 and 2006 World Cup tournaments?
13 In 2006, how many players did USA have at the end of the 1-1 with Italy?
14 Which A claimed their first point in a final tournament in Germany 2006?
15 Which team finished fourth in the 2002 tournament?
16 Against which team did Michael Owen damage his knee in Germany 2006?
17 What colour shirts did the French wear in the 2006 Final?
18 Which team was the first to progress to the quarter finals in 2006?
19 Who missed a penalty in the 2006 Final shoot-out?
20 Which country knocked out the defending champions in 2006?
21 Where was England's 2006 quarter final staged?
22 Which game in Germany 2006 saw 16 yellow cards and four reds?
23 Who was coach of the 2006 FIFA World Cup winners?
24 Who was top scorer in Germany 2006?
25 What number was Wayne Rooney wearing when red carded v. Portugal?
26 Who scored the final penalty in the 2006 Final shoot-out?
27 Which side became the first to be eliminated in a finals without letting in a goal?
28 Who managed South Korea to their success in 2002?
29 Who hit the shoot-out penalty to send England packing in 2006?
30 Excluding shoot-outs, how many goals did England score in Germany 2006?

Answers | Pot Luck 40 *(see Quiz 86)*

1 Paris. 2 December. 3 Apple. 4 Poland. 5 Beans. 6 Head/shoulder. 7 Annie Lennox (2004). 8 Evangeline Booth. 9 Whitney Houston. 10 Mike Gatting. 11 Sweet Charity. 12 Space. 13 Ashanti. 14 Omelette. 15 British Prime Minister. 16 Three. 17 Petits Fours. 18 Presidential Partner. 19 Grapefruit. 20 Prince of Wales. 21 Quinine. 22 Freckles. 23 Cleo Laine. 24 Blue. 25 Bette Davis. 26 Beverley Unwin. 27 None. 28 Roma. 29 Etna. 30 Burnley.

1 Which airport had a major luggage delivery backlog over Xmas 2006?
2 Where in Europe are Partu and Tartu airports to be found?
3 Hopkins Airport is in which US state?
4 Which is further east – Gatwick or Heathrow?
5 Which US president gives his name to an airport in La Paz, Bolivia?
6 The planes hitting the World Trade Center on 9/11 were scheduled to fly to which city?
7 In which country is Yellowknife airport?
8 Which city in Austria is near the Blue Danube airport?
9 Which B is an airport situated in the Hebrides?
10 Santa Ana airport in the US takes the name of which legendary movie hero?
11 Willie Walsh was chief executive of which airline?
12 Which is further north – Aberdeen or Glasgow airport?
13 The plane involved in the Lockerbie bombing was travelling to which US city?
14 Which of Aarborg, Aarhous and Amborovy airports is not in Denmark?
15 In which country is Fornebu airport?
16 The Ben Apps airport in the US has the name of which European city?
17 Liverpool airport was renamed after which pop celebrity?
18 In which country is Linate airport?
19 The Concorde crashing in 2000 in France had taken off from which airport?
20 Which is further south – Bristol or Norwich airport?
21 In which country is Santander airport?
22 In which English county is Stanstead airport?
23 The Robert Bradshaw airport is located on which group of islands?
24 Which explorer gives his name to an airport in Venice?
25 On 9/11 2001, the ill-fated Flight 93 took off from which Washington airport?
26 In which US city is Tacoma airport?
27 Is Peretol airport in Argentina, Italy or Paraguay?
28 The regally named Prince George and Prince Rupert airports are in which country?
29 What was the main cause of the many cancellations from Heathrow, December 2006?
30 In which country is Vaasa airport?

Answers	Andrew Lloyd-Webber *(see Quiz 91)*

1 1940s. 2 How Do You Solve a Problem Like Maria?. 3 Cello. 4 Sarah. 5 Jesus Christ Superstar 6 Evita. 7 Ayckbourn. 8 Dr Barnardo. 9 Mary Magdalen. 10 Christine. 11 Prince Edward. 12 Boyzone. 13 Sunset Boulevard. 14 Tell Me on a Sunday. 15 Joseph and the Amazing Technicolor Dreamcoat. 16 Michael Crawford. 17 Phantom of the Opera. 18 Jeeves. 19 Bombay Dreams. 20 Ball. 21 Phantom of the Opera. 22 Evita. 23 Barbara Dickson. 24 Northern Ireland. 25 Lesley Garrett. 26 Palace. 27 Cats. 28 Roger Moore. 29 1990s. 30 Any Dream Will Do.

Quiz 90 | Pot Luck 41

Answers – page 216

1 David Marks and Julia Barfield designed which modern London landmark?
2 In what year was AIDS officially recognised?
3 In which country did Sven Goran Eriksson first coach outside Sweden?
4 Which character did Meryl Streep play in the movie "The Devil Wears Prada"?
5 What is the first name of George Harrison's widow?
6 Who told Tony Blair in the Commons in 2005, "You were the future once"?
7 What was the first independent trade union in the former Eastern bloc?
8 After ten years of hits, who had an album called "Never Gone"?
9 Which club returned to the Football League this century, 44 years after resigning?
10 Which Michael became head of Ryanair?
11 The 2003 album "Final Straw" proved to be anything but for which band?
12 When did Vodafone start to sponsor the England cricket team – 1997, 2000 or 2004?
13 In Spain, who or what is El Gordo?
14 Who chose the celestial objects for the set of six stamps issued in February 2007?
15 In what year were the first Olympics held behind the Iron Curtain opened?
16 "Endless Wire" was the first studio album in 24 years made by which band?
17 Who became the first woman speaker of the USA's House of Representatives?
18 "Dreamgirls" actress Jennifer Hudson was discovered on which US talent show?
19 Which 60-plus singer Tom was knighted in 2006?
20 How many Von Trapp children are there in "The Sound of Music"?
21 The death of which musician moved Don McLean to write "American Pie"?
22 Which actress played the character Nana in "The Royle Family"?
23 Which celebrity chef appeared in "Rachel's Favourite Food"?
24 Which country hosted the first Eurovision Song Contest?
25 Did the national daily paper "Today" cease publication in 1985, 1995 or 2005?
26 Which Ethan starred in "Explorer" before his 20th birthday?
27 Who was the first King of the Belgians?
28 Which comedian wrote "Tim the Tiny Horse"?
29 Shane Filan was a member of which chart-busting boy band?
30 Darfur is a province of which country?

Answers | Pot Luck 42 *(see Quiz 92)*

1 Pakistan. 2 Vogue. 3 Stereophonics. 4 Drugs. 5 Witney. 6 New York. 7 Celebrity Big Brother. 8 Darling. 9 RSPB. 10 Damien Martyn. 11 MSC Napoli. 12 James Morrison. 13 Dog. 14 Costello Music. 15 Panama. 16 Dido. 17 Bruce Willis. 18 Rosamunde Pilcher. 19 Feyenoord. 20 Il Divo. 21 Def Leppard. 22 Jimmy Carter. 23 Harrison Ford. 24 Piano. 25 Publishing. 26 Pink. 27 Long playing records. 28 Juliette Binoche. 29 Chris Cornell. 30 Little Chef.

1 In which decade was Lloyd-Webber born?
2 In which 2006 talent show was he an adjudicator?
3 Which musical instrument does his brother Julian play?
4 Which first name is shared by two of his wives?
5 Which musical based on a Bible story followed "Joseph"?
6 Which of his musicals saw Elaine Paige shoot to stardom?
7 With which playwright Alan did he collaborate on the flop "Jeeves"?
8 His musical "The Likes of Us" was based on which children's benefactor?
9 In "Superstar" which character sings "I Don't Know How to Love Him"?
10 Who did the then Mrs Lloyd-Webber play in "The Phantom of the Opera"?
11 Which Royal once worked for his Really Useful Company?
12 Which boy band recorded "No Matter What" from "Whistle Down the Wind"?
13 Which musical was about Norma Desmond?
14 Which1980s song cycle was subtitled "An English Girl in America"?
15 Which of his musicals first opened at the Colet Court School in 1968?
16 Who was the original but short-lived Fosco in "The Woman in White"?
17 Which of his musicals was based on Gaston Leroux's gothic novel?
18 What was his shortest-lived musical of the 20th century?
19 Which Bollywood musical did he present in 2002?
20 Which future superstar Michael starred as Alex in "Aspects of Love"?
21 Which of his musicals was made into a movie in 2004?
22 For which movie did he win his first Oscar?
23 Which Barbara sang on the original recording of "Evita"?
24 "The Beautiful Game" was about sectarian conflict where?
25 Which opera star played the Mother Abbess in his 2006 revival of "The Sound of Music"?
26 Which theatre with a "royal" link was the first which he bought?
27 In which musical did "Memory" feature?
28 Which former 007 dropped out of "Aspects of Love" a month before opening night?
29 In which decade was he knighted and made a life peer?
30 What was the title of the talent show when it was announced it would find the stars of Joseph?

Answers | Airports *(see Quiz 89)*

1 Heathrow. 2 Estonia. 3 Ohio. 4 Gatwick. 5 JF Kennedy. 6 Los Angeles. 7 Canada. 8 Linz. 9 Benbecula. 10 John Wayne. 11 British Airways. 12 Aberdeen. 13 New York. 14 Amborovy. 15 Norway. 16 Athens. 17 John Lennon. 18 Italy. 19 Charles de Gaulle. 20 Bristol. 21 Spain. 22 Essex. 23 West Indies (St Kitts). 24 Marco Polo. 25 Dulles International. 26 Seattle. 27 Italy. 28 Canada. 29 Fog. 30 Finland.

1 Angelina Jolie's movie "A Mighty Heart" was set in which country?
2 Which glossy magazine celebrated its 90th anniversary with the December 2006 edition?
3 Which top-selling band featured Kelly Jones on vocals?
4 Shire is one of Britain's leading makers of what?
5 Was David Cameron returned as MP for Windsor, Witney or Woking?
6 Michael Bloomberg was mayor of which famous city?
7 In January 2007 Carphone Warehouse withdrew sponsorship for which reality TV show?
8 What was the name of Kylie's perfume launched in London, January 2007?
9 Which organisation launched Operation Lapwing in 2007?
10 Who retired from international cricket with Australia 2-0 up in the 2006–07 Ashes?
11 Items from which container ship were washed up in Cornwall in January 2007?
12 Who made the 2006 hit album "Undiscovered"?
13 In a New Year tragedy, what killed young Ellie Lawrence?
14 Fratellis featured what sort of music in the title of the 2006 hit album?
15 Which country has the international car registration code PA?
16 Florian Cloud de Bounevialle Armstrong is better known under which name?
17 Which actor played the psychiatrist in the movie "The Sixth Sense"?
18 Which Rosamunde wrote the novel "The Shell Seekers"?
19 Which Dutch club was disqualified from the 2006–07 Uefa Cup following crowd trouble?
20 Who took "Ancora" to the top of the album charts?
21 Joe Elliot was vocalist with which heavy metal band?
22 Which US President announced that the USA would not take part in the Moscow Olympics?
23 In the 1980s, who starred in three "Indiana Jones" and two "Star Wars" movies?
24 Which instrument is associated with musician Stephen Hough?
25 John Wiley is a US company dealing in which market?
26 Who declared "I'm Not Dead" in the title of her 2006 hit album?
27 What used to go round at 33 and a third r.p.m.?
28 Which French actress and artist was Oscar nominated for "Chocolat"?
29 Who was a singer with Soundgarden and Audioslave?
30 Which chain of roadside restaurants was in danger of closure in 2006?

Answers | Pot Luck 41 *(see Quiz 90)*

1 London Eye. 2 1981. 3 Portugal. 4 Miranda Priestly. 5 Olivia. 6 David Cameron. 7 Solidarity. 8 Backstreet Boys. 9 Accrington Stanley. 10 Michael O'Leary. 11 Snow Patrol. 12 1997. 13 Spanish lottery. 14 Sir Patrick Moore. 15 1980. 16 The Who. 17 Nancy Pelosi. 18 American Idol. 19 Tom Jones. 20 Seven. 21 Buddy Holly. 22 Liz Smith. 23 Rachel Allen. 24 Switzerland. 25 1995. 26 Hawke. 27 Leopold I. 28 Harry Hill. 29 Westlife. 30 Sudan.

1 Which imprint was behind the JK Rowling series of books?

2 Which Patricia wrote the 2006 novel "Predator"?

3 What is the last name of "Unfortunate Events" writer Lemony?

4 Which Fortress featured in the title of a Dan Brown book?

5 Who died aged 44 leaving his novel "The Last Tycoon" unfinished?

6 Who created the character of diary-writing Bridget Jones?

7 Who wrote about the Spanish Civil War in "For Whom the Bell Tolls"?

8 Which pop celebrity from the 1960s wrote "Be My Baby"?

9 Which character appeared in all of Raymond Chandler's novels?

10 Who penned the classic sci-fi story "I Robot"?

11 How did the barrister Rumpole refer to his wife Hilda?

12 In the Morse books as opposed to the TV series, where did Lewis come from?

13 Who won a Booker Prize for "Midnight's Children"?

14 In which decade of the 20th century did HG Wells die?

15 Under which name did American author Samuel Langhorne Clemens write?

16 Who created the most filmed horror character of the 20th C?

17 Whose sports-based novels of the 90s include "Comeback" and "To the Hilt"?

18 Aunt Agatha and Bingo Little feature in the escapades of which man about town?

19 Which writer Stephen was a pioneer in pay as you read on the Internet?

20 In which decade was "The Lord of the Rings" first published?

21 Who is Frank Richards' most famous creation?

22 Who penned the airport lounge best seller titled "Airport"?

23 Which writer wrote about his rural upbringing in Slad, Gloucestershire?

24 In 1917 which Joseph endowed an annual literary prize in America?

25 David John Cornwell wrote spy stories under which name?

26 Which fictional detective refers to using the little grey cells?

27 Georges Simenon created which character known by one name?

28 What was the first name of New Zealand novelist Ms Marsh?

29 Which American novelist with an English place surname wrote "White Fang"?

30 Who wrote the children's classic "Swallows and Amazons"?

Answers | Pop Places *(see Quiz 95)*

1 The River Thames. 2 Cambodia. 3 California. 4 San Francisco. 5 Amsterdam. 6 Japan. 7 Dionne Warwick. 8 New York. 9 Toto. 10 Tina Turner. 11 Roger Whittaker. 12 Glen Campbell. 13 American Idiot. 14 Moscow. 15 Caribbean. 16 Bon Jovi. 17 Philadelphia. 18 Tahiti. 19 Mississippi. 20 Mott the Hoople. 21 The Clash. 22 Twenty-four. 23 Tony Christie. 24 Dakota. 25 Barbados. 26 Liverpool. 27 Madonna. 28 Elton John. 29 Georgia. 30 Bruce Springsteen.

1 What did the Kyoto Protocol intend to curb the emission of?
2 The London NYC Hotel, Manhattan, was the first US restaurant of which UK chef?
3 Who did Condoleezza Rice replace as US Secretary of State?
4 What was Craig David's second UK No 1 single?
5 What does the letter C stand for in the acronym NICE?
6 Who is the record-producing son of SIr George Martin?
7 Nicole Kidman and Brittany Murphy did voices for which animated Antarctic film?
8 Which make of watch sponsored the "Unstoppable" Kevin Pietersen?
9 Justin Timberlake featured on which Snoop Dogg hit of 2005?
10 Which city has the constituencies of Blackley and Gorton?
11 Who replaced Antony Worrall Thompson on "Saturday Kitchen"?
12 Kelly Holmes, Helen Mirren and Anita Roddick have all been named as what?
13 Who voiced the eponymous character in Tim Burton's "Corpse Bride"?
14 Who made "Eyes Open", the best-selling album of 2006?
15 In which city was the BBC drama series "Lilies" set?
16 In which animals was foot and mouth first discovered in the 2001 epidemic?
17 In which decade was composer Hans Zimmer born?
18 Who hosted the talent show "When Will I be Famous?" in 2007?
19 Which instrument has 46 or 47 strings?
20 Duncan Bannatyne and Peter Jones were on the panel of which TV show?
21 In which controversial play did Daniel Radcliffe appear in the West End in 2007?
22 Who or what was the Berliner Mauer?
23 "Goldmember" was the third movie romp for Mike Myers as which spy?
24 Which international keeper moved from Sunderland to Arsenal in 2006?
25 Which event caused Lord Nicholas Windsor to renounce his rights to the throne?
26 Which Tim has represented South Suffolk in parliament this century?
27 In which city renowned for its music was "Dreamgirls" set?
28 Who is the mother of James Kerr and Lennon Gallagher?
29 The movie "Jerry Maguire" was about which American sport?
30 "My Dear Country" first featured on which album by Norah Jones?

Answers | Pot Luck 44 *(see Quiz 96)*

1 Le Chiffre. 2 26 tracks. 3 George Carey. 4 Sugababes. 5 King Xerxes. 6 South. 7 Jamie Oliver. 8 Michael Jackson. 9 Will Smith. 10 20. 11 Ricky Gervais. 12 Beatrix Potter. 13 Oil. 14 Elstree. 15 Frank McCourt. 16 Kazakhstan. 17 Attack of the Clones. 18 Respiratory. 19 Naomi Watts. 20 Official census. 21 Dr John Reid. 22 Marquis de Sade. 23 Life Goes On. 24 Fulham. 25 Food. 26 EastEnders. 27 Curriculum. 28 Chelsea. 29 Manchester. 30 Sonia Gandhi.

1 Where is Sixties rock venue Eel Pie Island located?
2 Which Asian country provided Kim Wilde with a 1980s hit?
3 Which US state links with "Dreamin'" and "Girls" in song titles?
4 Which city did Scott McKenzie sing about in the 1967 summer of love?
5 Which city was the title of a Simple Minds EP in 1989?
6 Which geographical group had China, Tokyo and Cantonese in chart titles?
7 Who had a 1960s hit with "Do You Know the Way to San Jose?"?
8 Which city has given hit songs to Frank Sinatra, Gerard Kenny and Sting?
9 Who was in "Africa" in 1983?
10 Which female pop superstar sang about "Nutbush"?
11 Which Roger was "Leavin' Durham Town" in the 1960s?
12 "Wichita Lineman" and "Galveston" provided hits for which Glen?
13 Green Day made the top-selling 2004 album about what kind of "Idiot"?
14 In which Russian city was Michael Jackson a "Stranger" in 1996?
15 Which Queen was a hit for Billy Ocean?
16 Which popular New Jersey band made the popular album "New Jersey"?
17 Which US city links Elton John and Bruce Springsteen in song?
18 Which tropical paradise was the subject of a David Essex hit?
19 Which US state and river was a 1970s hit for Pussycat?
20 Who were "All the Way from Memphis" in 1973?
21 "London Calling" was a hit for which group?
22 How many hours was Gene Pitney away from Tulsa?
23 Which singer did Peter Kay aid on his way to "Amarillo"?
24 Which US state was the title of a Stereophonics 2005 No 1?
25 One-hit wonders Typically Tropical were going to which island?
26 In which city is "Penny Lane"?
27 Who had the 1990s hit version of "Don't Cry for Me Argentina"?
28 Which superstar declared he was "Made in England"?
29 Which G was the state on the mind of the late, great Ray Charles?
30 Who made the mega-selling "Born in the USA"?

Quiz 96 | Pot Luck 44

Answers – page 218

LEVEL 2

1 Mads Mikkelsen played which character in the 2006 movie "Casino Royale"?
2 How many Beatles tracks feature on the "Love" album of 2006?
3 Who was Archbishop of Canterbury when it was decided to ordain women as priests?
4 In which girl group did Heidi Range replace Siobhan Donaghy?
5 The invasion force of which Persian ruler was repulsed by 300 Spartan warriors in 480 BC?
6 Central, East and South – which isn't the name of a parliamentary constituency in Leeds?
7 Which chef was on the first "Top Gear" after Richard Hammond returned after his crash?
8 Which Michael made a first UK stage appearance in nine years in 2006's World Music Awards?
9 Which actor starred with his son in "The Pursuit of Happyness"?
10 How many operas did Mozart write?
11 Who toured with the live stand-up show "Fame"?
12 Which female, featured in a film, married solicitor William Heelis in 1913?
13 Which commodity is exported via the Druzhba, or Friendship, pipeline?
14 The "Big Brother" house is in which Borehamwood studios?
15 Who wrote the novel on which "Angela's Ashes" was based?
16 Alma Ata is the capital of which former Soviet state?
17 What was Star Wars Episode II called?
18 What does R stand for in the medical condition SARS?
19 Which actress starred in the creepy movie "The Ring"?
20 Which ten-yearly event was taken on 29th April 2001 in the UK?
21 The constituency of Airdrie & Shotts returned which MP who became Home Secretary?
22 Which Marquis did Geoffrey Rush play in "Quills"?
23 In song, which line follows "Ob-Lad-Di, Ob-Lad-Da"?
24 Which soccer club has a Hammersmith End and a Putney End?
25 Gael Green is a celebrated US critic of what?
26 In 2007 actor Robert Kazinsky was suspended from which soap?
27 In education, what does C stand for in QCA?
28 Which soccer club launched a Chinese-language website in Beijing in January 2007?
29 What is the home city of boxer Ricky Hatton?
30 In 2004 who won the Indian election but declined to become Prime Minister?

Answers | Pot Luck 43 *(see Quiz 94)*

1 Greenhouse gases. 2 Gordon Ramsay. 3 Colin Powell. 4 7 Days. 5 Clinical. 6 Giles Martin. 7 Happy Feet. 8 Citizen. 9 Signs. 10 Manchester. 11 James Martin. 12 Dames. 13 Helena Bonham Carter. 14 Snow Patrol. 15 Liverpool. 16 Pigs. 17 1950s. 18 Graham Norton. 19 Harp. 20 Dragon's Den. 21 Equus. 22 Berlin Wall. 23 Austin Powers. 24 Mart Poom. 25 Conversion to Roman Catholicism. 26 Tim Yeo. 27 Detroit. 28 Patsy Kensit. 29 American football. 30 Not Too Late.

Quiz 97 | Money Matters

Answers – page 223

1 In which direction does the Queen face on a UK coin?
2 What was the value of a US "greenback"?
3 What is the Australian currency – dollars, pounds or roos?
4 Which group sang "Money, Money, Money"?
5 What is the top source of UK government income?
6 Which soccer club is the world's richest?
7 Which country was the top gold producer of last century?
8 What is the name of Bill Gates' wife?
9 Sir Edward Elgar appeared on which value of banknote?
10 How is Ralph Lifshitz better known?
11 What does GDP stand for?
12 Which country uses shekels as its currency?
13 What was Judas paid with for betraying Jesus?
14 Which country first used paper money?
15 In proverb, the love of money is the root of all what?
16 Were Bank of England pound notes last issued in 1974, 1984 or 1994?
17 In which industry did Rockefeller make his money?
18 Who recorded the album "Money for Nothing"?
19 In which European country could you spend a forint?
20 Charles Darwin's portrait appeared on banknotes of what value?
21 Which country has the world's richest royal family?
22 In which century was the Bank of England founded?
23 In which US state did the first Wal-Mart store open?
24 Which late rock star is the highest-earning celebrity no longer alive?
25 The portrait of which famous architect featured on £50 banknotes?
26 In the US, Diners Club issued the first what?
27 In which decade did both J Paul Getty and Howard Hughes die?
28 Who is the highest-earning British author?
29 In Iran, what do 100 dinars equal?
30 Who appeared on a banknote of higher value – Florence Nightingale or William Shakespeare?

Answers	Schumacher's Circuit *(see Quiz 99)*

1 1960s. 2 Ayrton Senna. 3 Belgium. 4 Seven times. 5 Finland. 6 Corinna. 7 Brazilian. 8 Monaco. 9 Alain Prost. 10 1994. 11 Belgian. 12 No. 13 Benetton. 14 Fourth. 15 French. 16 Damon Hill. 17 Bricklayer. 18 Ross Brawn. 19 Damon Hill. 20 Belgian. 21 Rubens Barrichello. 22 Runner-up. 23 Felipe Massa. 24 Juan Manuel Fangio. 25 Nigel Mansell. 26 Benetton. 27 San Marino. 28 1979. 29 91. 30 121.

Quiz 98 | Bowie

Answers – page 224

1 What is his real surname?
2 What was Bowie's first Top Twenty hit of this century?
3 In which decade was he born?
4 Which word complete the song title ""Rebel Never Gets ___"?
5 Which song contains, "And the papers want to know whose shirts you wear"?
6 In which year did Bowie receive a Lifetime Achievement Grammy?
7 Which album was released first – "Stage" or "Tonight"?
8 Whom did he duet with on "Dancing in the Street"?
9 With which band did he record "Under Pressure"?
10 Whose puppet creations featured in the movie "Labyrinth"?
11 Which planet is named in both an album and single title?
12 What was Bowie's first No 1 album?
13 What name did Bowie's son originally have which rhymed with his surname?
14 What were the first three words of the title of his single with Bing Crosby?
15 What or who was Laughing in an early novelty number?
16 Which hit was the first ever to get to No 1 as a reissue?
17 Bowie wrote "All the Young Dudes" for which act?
18 In 1984 what was his Greatest Hits album called?
19 What followed Black Tie in the title of a 1990s album?
20 Which supermodel did Bowie marry in 1992?
21 Which major space event was "Space Oddity" timed to coincide with in 1969?
22 What was Bowie's first top ten hit of the 1990s?
23 What sort of Dogs featured in the title of a 1970s album?
24 Which album came out first – "Heathen" or "Hours"?
25 Which Rick, now a "Grumpy Old Man" played synthesiser on "Space Oddity"?
26 Who recorded the album "Transformer" which was co-produced by Bowie?
27 In which play did he play John Merrick on Broadway?
28 Which school once attended by Prince Charles did Bowie send his son to?
29 Which Tom co-starred with him in "Merry Christmas Mr Lawrence"?
30 Which song was a sequel to the exploits of Major Tom?

Answers	**Pot Luck 45** *(see Quiz 100)*

1 South Africa. 2 Hamper. 3 Gun ownership. 4 1996. 5 Liverpool. 6 Belorussia. 7 Room on the 3rd Floor. 8 Judi Dench. 9 Steve Hilton. 10 Jessica Simpson. 11 Johnny Briggs. 12 Royal Bank of Scotland. 13 USA. 14 Smash Hits. 15 Baseball. 16 Girls Aloud. 17 Schofield. 18 Jarhead. 19 Electrical fault. 20 Moonlight Sonata. 21 Mike Newell. 22 Man-eating plant. 23 Ireland. 24 Aled Jones. 25 News of the World. 26 Helen Mirren. 27 Mihir Bose. 28 Ant. 29 Nigel Clough. 30 Windows Vista.

1 Was Michael born in the 1960s or the 1970s?

2 Who held the record for pole positions before Schumacher?

3 In which country did he make his first Grand Prix start?

4 How many times was Michael F1 champion?

5 Michael's great rival Mika Hakinnen came from which country?

6 What is the name of Michael's wife?

7 Which 2006 Grand Prix was Schumacher's last?

8 In May 2006 Schumacher was stripped of pole position in which Grand Prix?

9 Who held the record for most victories before Michael?

10 Was Michael first world champion driver in 1992, 1994 or 1996?

11 At which Grand Prix in 1998 was there a collision with David Coulthard?

12 Was Michael ever the youngest F1 world champion?

13 Whom was he driving for when he first became world champion driver?

14 What position did Michael finish in his final race in October 2006?

15 Which Grand Prix did he win for a record eight times?

16 Who was runner-up in Michael's first two seasons as world champion?

17 What was the trade of his father Rolf?

18 Who was Schumacher's technical director at Benetton and at Ferrari?

19 Which Brit was involved in the collision with Michael at Australia in 1994?

20 In which Grand Prix of 2001 did Michael set a new record for victories?

21 Which Brazilian driver and Ferrari team mate was runner-up to Michael in 2002?

22 Where did he finish in the drivers' championship in 2006?

23 Who finished first in Michael's final race in October 2006?

24 Who held the record for winning the drivers' title most times before Michael?

25 In 2002 he broke whose record for winning races in a season?

26 He first won a Grand Prix with which team?

27 In 2006, what was his first victory in his last season?

28 Before Michael, when did Ferrari last claim the drivers' title – 1979, 1989 or 1999?

29 How many career F1 wins did Michael gain?

30 How many points did he gain in his final season of F1 racing in 2006?

1 Who were the opponents in Andy Robinson's last game as England rugby coach?
2 HITA stands for which Industry Trade Association?
3 The Brady Act in the USA imposed some control of what?
4 In which year did Take That have a No 1 single before their 2006 comeback?
5 Which English city was named Capital of Culture for 2008?
6 What was the previous name of Belarus?
7 What was the title of McFly's first No 1 album?
8 Which star of "Iris" played Arabella in "Tea with Mussolini"?
9 Which marketing guru Steve became one of David Cameron's closest advisers?
10 "Employee of the Month" and "Dukes of Hazzard" starred which singer/actress?
11 Who left "Corrie" after 30 years and got an MBE in the 2007 New Year's honours list?
12 What does the RBS logo on Andy Murray's right sleeve stand for?
13 Which country has the most internet users in the world?
14 Which pop magazine closed in 2006 after 30 years of publishing?
15 Which sport does Barry Zito play?
16 Nadine Coyle found fame with which group?
17 Which Phillip presented TV's "Dancing on Ice"?
18 Jake Gyllenhaal and Jamie Foxx starred in which Gulf War film?
19 What was the cause of the fire at Windsor Castle in 1992?
20 How is Beethoven's piano sonata No 14 usually known?
21 Which Luton manager spoke out in 2006 about problems caused by "bungs"?
22 What horror is sold in the shop in the musical "Little Shop of Horrors"?
23 In which country was the drama series "Rough Diamond" set?
24 "You Raise Me Up" was the best-of album from which singer?
25 Andy Coulson stepped down in 2007 from which newspaper?
26 Which famous Helen advertised Virgin Atlantic?
27 Who became BBC sports news editor in 2007, aged 60?
28 Who got married first – Ant or Dec?
29 Who was Burton's manager when they held Man Utd in a 2006 FA Cup tie?
30 Which new version of Windows did Bill Gates launch in 2007?

Answers	Bowie *(see Quiz 98)*

1 Jones. 2 Everyone Says Hi. 3 1940s. 4 Old. 5 Space Oddity. 6 2006. 7 Tonight.
8 Mick Jagger. 9 Queen. 10 Jim Henson. 11 Mars. 12 Aladdin Sane. 13 Zowie.
14 Peace on Earth. 15 Gnome. 16 Space Oddity. 17 Mott the Hoople. 18 Fame and Fashion. 19 White Noise. 20 Iman. 21 Moon landing. 22 Jump They Say. 23 Diamond Dogs. 24 Hours. 25 Wakeman. 26 Lou Reed. 27 The Elephant Man. 28 Gordonstoun. 29 Conti. 30 Ashes to Ashes.

1 Which Bond film was released on the same day as The Beatles' first single?
2 In the first "Toy Story", which child owns the toys?
3 Which film company opened the first ever theme park?
4 Where in Italy did the first film festival take place?
5 Which monster lizard first seen in 1955 was in a 1997 blockbuster?
6 What was the first movie in which Eastwood was Harry Callahan?
7 Which Fay was the first scream queen, in "King Kong"?
8 What was Disney's first feature film – with eight people in the title?
9 Which oriental detective Charlie first appeared on screen in 1926?
10 Where were India's first studios, giving rise to the name Bollywood?
11 What was the first two-colour system used in movie-making?
12 "The Robe" was the first movie with what type of screen?
13 "The Scent of Mystery" was the first movie with sight, sound and what?
14 Which 1995 Story was the first computer-animated film?
15 What was the first major movie about the Vietnam War?
16 Which Dickens' film gave Alec Guinness his major movie debut?
17 Which movie with an all-child cast was Alan Parker's directorial debut?
18 Which Ralph played Steed in the first "Avengers" big-screen movie?
19 In which decade were the Oscars first presented?
20 Which Christmas classic was first heard in "Holiday Inn"?
21 Who was Oscar-nominated for his director debut for "Ordinary People"?
22 Which Brothers made the first talkie?
23 In which movie did Al Jolson say, "You ain't heard nothin' yet"?
24 Which Katharine won the first BAFTA Best Actress award?
25 In which French city was the first movie in Europe shown?
26 Mike Nichols won the first director's BAFTA for which Dustin Hoffman classic?
27 In which movie did Elizabeth Taylor first act with Richard Burton?
28 Glenn Close made her film debut in "The World According to ____"?
29 What was Michael Jackson's first movie?
30 What was Tatum O'Neal's first movie which won her an Oscar?

Quiz 102 | Pot Luck 46

Answers – page 228

1 Auctioned in 2007, who produced the painting "St James, the Greater"?
2 Which ex-US President died the same month as Ray Charles?
3 Released in 2003, which Sugababes album peaked at 3 in the charts?
4 In which square does the famous department store Macy's stand?
5 Who was the first person to beat Roger Federer in a Grand Slam final?
6 What is the last name of US singer Ashanti?
7 Which England soccer midfielder won an MBE in the 2007 New Year's honours list?
8 Which company bought YouTube in 2006?
9 Did the Lib Dems or Tories have more women MPs after 2005's general election?
10 To the nearest year, how long was Diana divorced from Charles before her death?
11 Which Spielberg movie had the ad line, "Whoever saves one life, saves the world entire"?
12 "Billie Jean" was the only No 1 single from which Michael Jackson album?
13 What was the first Grand Slam claimed by Amelie Mauresmo?
14 Which two ex-Prime Ministers were backbenchers between 1990 and 1992?
15 ir. is the internet code for which country?
16 By what method was Timothy McVeigh executed for the Oklahoma City bombing?
17 Which Premiership side signed Greg Halford from Colchester?
18 How many bicycles did Katie Melua sing about?
19 Which constituency returned Jack Straw to parliament?
20 What was responsible for over 19,000 deaths in Gujurat, India in 2001?
21 What goes with "Demons" in the title of a Dan Brown novel?
22 In which country did Berlusconi follow on from Amato as Prime Minister?
23 Who had No 1 singles with "Ignition" and "Wonderful"?
24 Which team were beaten 9-7 by Europe in golf's inaugural Royal Trophy of 2006?
25 In 2001 Barry George was found guilty of the murder of which favourite TV presenter?
26 Which "Syriana" Oscar winner of 2006 played a doctor in "ER" for five years?
27 Who was the first rock superstar to become chairman of a major soccer club?
28 Which US politician was born Madeleine Korbel in 1937 in Czechoslovakia?
29 In which city did Brazil win the 2002 World Cup?
30 Which rock star Rod became a CBE in the 2007 New Year's honours list?

| **Answers** | **Pioneers** *(see Quiz 104)* |

1 Louise. 2 Netherlands. 3 Nestle. 4 Clockwork radio. 5 Colour blindness. 6 Gillette. 7 Thames. 8 C5. 9 The South Pole. 10 Italian. 11 Concorde. 12 Mars. 13 Ceylon. 14 Frying pan. 15 Earl of Sandwich. 16 Shakespeare's Globe. 17 Moon. 18 Television. 19 1980s. 20 Rollerblades. 21 Sony. 22 Sally Ride. 23 Desmond Tutu. 24 Mexican wave. 25 Sweden. 26 Edward Jenner. 27 Boxing . 28 Shorthand. 29 Cambridgeshire. 30 Saxophone.

Quiz 103 | Roger Federer

Answers – page 225

LEVEL 2

1 In which country was he born?
2 In which year did he first became World No 1?
3 Between 2004–06 he won Wimbledon and which other Grand Slam three times?
4 Is he right- or left-handed?
5 What nationality is his mother?
6 In which decade was he born?
7 Which Williams sister was Ladies' Champion when he won his first Wimbledon?
8 In which Olympics was he fourth in 2000?
9 Which was his first Grand Slam title?
10 Which Australian former champion became his coach in 2005?
11 Which Australian did he defeat in his first Wimbledon final?
12 Who beat him in the 2005 French semis and went on to win the title?
13 Which US veteran did he beat in his second US Open Final?
14 In 2004 he became the first since Mats Wilander to win how many Grand Slams in a year?
15 In the 06 Australian Open he beat Marcos Baghdatis who came from where?
16 He is a member of which Davis Cup team?
17 Which Russian lady won Wimbledon when he claimed his second title there?
18 What is his first language?
19 Which country does his arch-rival Nadal come from?
20 Which American did he beat in the final in his first defence of the Wimbledon title?
21 How many Swiss men had won Wimbledon before him?
22 Whom did he beat in his first Australian final?
23 In 2006 which Brit beat Federer in his only straight-sets loss of that year?
24 Which American's 31-match unbeaten Wimbledon run did he end in 2001?
25 What is his official website called?
26 His first visit as a UNICEF Ambassador was to victims of which 2004 disaster?
27 In 2006 which was the only Grand Slam he did not win?
28 Which Australian did he beat to win his first US Open?
29 In 2006 who were the only two players to beat Federer?
30 The Roger Federer Foundation helps children in which country?

Answers | **Famous Movie Firsts** *(see Quiz 101)*

1 Dr No. 2 Andy. 3 Disney. 4 Venice. 5 Godzilla. 6 Dirty Harry. 7 Wray. 8 Snow White & the Seven Dwarfs. 9 Chan. 10 Bombay. 11 Technicolor. 12 Widescreen (Cinemascope). 13 Smell. 14 Toy Story. 15 The Deer Hunter. 16 Great Expectations. 17 Bugsy Malone. 18 Fiennes. 19 1920s. 20 White Christmas. 21 Robert Redford. 22 Warner. 23 The Jazz Singer. 24 Hepburn. 25 Paris. 26 The Graduate. 27 Cleopatra. 28 Garp. 29 The Wiz. 30 Paper Moon.

1 What was the first name of the world's first test tube baby?

2 Which country was the first to legalise voluntary euthanasia?

3 Which Swiss-based company made the first widely used instant coffee?

4 What sort of radio was designed by British inventor Trevor Baylis?

5 The Ishihara Test is a test for what?

6 Which pioneer in men's appearance had the first names King Camp?

7 Air flight pioneer Amy Johnson vanished over which river?

8 What was the name of Clive Sinclair's electric trike?

9 Reaching which place led to the quote, "Great God, this is an awful place"?

10 What was the nationality of Galileo?

11 In 1993 Barbara Harmer became the first woman pilot of which aircraft?

12 Viking was the first probe to send back pictures from which planet?

13 Which country was the first in the world to have a woman Prime Minister?

14 What was the first item of non-stick cookware marketed by Teflon?

15 Which Earl developed a snack where meat was placed between bread slices?

16 Sam Wanamaker was the driving force behind which London theatre?

17 David Scott and James Irwin were the first people to drive where?

18 What had 405 or 625 lines in its early forms?

19 In which decade were camcorders introduced?

20 What was developed by US ice hockey players Scott and Brennan Olson?

21 Which company introduced the first personal stereo?

22 Which Sally was the USA's first spacewoman?

23 Who was the first black archbishop of Cape Town?

24 What sort of wave was seen for the first time at a sporting fixture in 1986?

25 Which Scandinavian country was the first to ban aerosol sprays?

26 Which Edward was a pioneer of vaccination?

27 Jane Couch was the first woman with a professional licence for which sport?

28 Which method of fast writing was developed by Pitman?

29 Specialising in heart surgery, Papworth hospital is in which county?

30 What did the Belgian Adolphe Sax develop?

---

1 What did the Wind cry according to Jimi Hendrix?
2 Which word completes the Yardbirds hit, "Over Under Sideways ____"?
3 Who went "Downtown"?
4 Which song started, "Dirty old river must you keep rolling, Rolling in to the night"?
5 Who first hit the top ten with "Wild Thing"?
6 Which word was the whole of a Mary Hopkin hit and half a Beatles hit?
7 Which group became known as the ones with the girl drummer?
8 Who had a huge hit with "In the Ghetto"?
9 Bob Dylan had what type of "Homesick Blues"?
10 Who sang about a "Swiss Maid"?
11 Which Move hit "sampled" a phrase from the 1812 Overture?
12 Paradoxically, who sang "I Love My Dog"?
13 What other words described Tom Jones' "Funny Forgotten Feelings"?
14 Who were in "Bits and Pieces"?
15 What was the first UK hit for The Supremes?
16 Where did you have to go to find the House of The Rising Sun?
17 "Do You Want to Know a Secret" was a first chart hit for which singer?
18 To whom did the Hollies say Sorry in a 1969 hit?
19 Which Legend gave Dave Dee and the boys a No 1?
20 In a song title what "Has a Thousand Eyes"?
21 Which group invited you all to "F-F-Fade Away"?
22 Who was the biggest-selling artist in the 1967 Summer of Love?
23 What goes before "Yester-You Yesterday"?
24 Which group made a visit to "Atlantis"?
25 What was the name of Manfred Mann's Semi-Detached Suburban character?
26 Which title contained in brackets "Be Sure to Wear Some Flowers in Your Hair"?
27 Who took "Dizzy" to the top?
28 Which vocalist sang "Let the Heartaches Begin"?
29 In song, who took medicinal compounds?
30 Who duetted with Nancy Sinatra on "Something Stupid"?

Quiz 106 Pot Luck 47

Answers – page 232

LEVEL 2

1 In what year was the slave trade abolished in the British Empire?
2 At what number did the Fowler family once live in "EastEnders"?
3 The title of Madonna's 2003 No 1 US and UK album mentioned "American" what?
4 Sonya Thomas was a champion in which American sport?
5 In 2006, Steve Samson of Essex shot himself while cleaning what?
6 Xue Fei Yang is a classical musician specialising in which instrument?
7 Which TV series featured the characters DS Simms and DI Traynor?
8 Which jockey did Catherine Allen marry in the late 1990s?
9 Rafale is the name of a combat aircraft from which country?
10 Which Royal died in the same month as actor John Thaw?
11 Who won the Best Actress Oscar for "Shakespeare in Love"?
12 Which Italian, once soccer's most expensive player, managed Watford?
13 Which Home Secretary in Tony Blair's cabinet was elected by Norwich South?
14 In the Six Nations Rugby tournament which team is first alphabetically?
15 Who wrote the "Little Book of Big Treats" for Comic Relief 2007?
16 Forget Glenbogle but what animal is in the painting "The Monarch of the Glen"?
17 Who was the second American, after Greg LeMond, to win the Tour de France?
18 Where would you find the sequence E, A, D, G, B, E?
19 Who won a Best Song Oscar for "Into the West" as featured in "The Return of the King"?
20 Did Daley Thompson win Olympic gold in the 1970s, 1980s or 1990s?
21 Which theatre director won an Oscar nomination for the movie "Billy Elliot"?
22 Who wrote "Below the Parapet" about her father?
23 Who played opposite Diane Keaton in the movie "Something's Gotta Give"?
24 Which is higher in a standing human frame, the fibula or the patella?
25 The annual Stirling prize is awarded to which professional group of people?
26 Who provided the score for the movie "Notes on a Scandal"?
27 Which group has had an album titled "Chemistry" and a hit single titled "Biology"?
28 In which sport was Blanche Bingley famous?
29 Which son of a famous playwright played Tchaikovsky in the 2007 BBC drama series?
30 Who was Arsenal's top scorer in their final season at Highbury?

Answers | Pot Luck 48 (see Quiz 108)

1 Patsy Kensit. 2 Potatoes. 3 Polonium-210. 4 Iris Murdoch (Iris). 5 118 118. 6 Eddie Murphy. 7 Philippines. 8 Outbreak of foot & mouth. 9 Enron. 10 Craig David. 11 James Joyce. 12 Alec Douglas-Home. 13 Kylie Minogue. 14 Wales. 15 John Major. 16 Evelyn Glennie. 17 Val McDermid. 18 None. 19 Dalziel & Pascoe. 20 Monday. 21 Tony Blair. 22 Sir Thomas More. 23 Who Wants to be a Millionaire? 24 Sugarland Express. 25 Ted Hughes. 26 Scolari. 27 Black. 28 BG. 29 Margaret Beckett. 30 Ian Hislop.

Quiz 107 | Child Stars

Answers – page 229

1 What is Macaulay Culkin's brother called who starred in "Father of the Bride"?
2 Which former child star became Mrs Andre Agassi?
3 Who played the Artful Dodger in the 1960s version of "Oliver!"
4 In which movie, remade in 1998, did Hayley Mills sing "Let's Get Together"?
5 Whose autobiography was called "Little Girl Lost"?
6 Who played the possessed child in "The Exorcist"?
7 Which Oscar winner from "As Good as It Gets" was a US TV child star?
8 In which Bruce Willis movie did Haley Joe Osment star?
9 Mark Lester played the title role in which 60s musical?
10 How many movies had Macaulay Culkin made before "Home Alone"?
11 Was Judy Garland 13, 15 or 17 when she starred in "The Wizard of Oz"?
12 In which 1993 dinosaur film did Joseph Mazello star?
13 Lisa Jakub ended up having her father disguised as nanny in which movie?
14 Rumer Willis appeared with Mum in "Striptease"; who is she?
15 Who appeared in "Mermaids", aged 10, and moved on to "The Ice Storm"?
16 Was Jodie Foster 12, 14 or 16 when she starred in "Taxi Driver"?
17 Who was Macaulay Culkin's first wife?
18 Who said, "I was a 16-year-old boy for 30 years"?
19 Former child star Richard Beymer starred in which 60s musical opposite Natalie Wood?
20 In which country was Deanna Durbin born?
21 Which star of "Chasing Amy" started acting at the age of eight?
22 What was Hayley Mills' first film, in 1959?
23 How many times did Judy Garland marry?
24 Who played two parts in "The Prince and the Pauper" in 1977?
25 Which Mary was the "world's sweetheart" and made her first movie aged 16 in 1909?
26 Young Justin Henry was in which divorce movie with Streep and Hoffman?
27 Which Jackie was immortalised in Chaplin's "The Kid"?
28 Who was the gangster's moll in "Bugsy Malone" and later won Oscars?
29 In which movie did Drew Barrymore find fame as Gertie?
30 Who was asked to "Come Home" in Elizabeth Taylor's 1943 movie?

Answers	Pop Music – the Sixties *(see Quiz 105)*

1 Mary. 2 Down. 3 Petula Clark. 4 Waterloo Sunset. 5 The Troggs. 6 Goodbye. 7 Honeycombs. 8 Elvis Presley. 9 Subterranean. 10 Del Shannon. 11 Night of Fear. 12 Cat Stevens. 13 Familiar. 14 The Dave Clark Five. 15 Where Did Our Love Go?. 16 New Orleans. 17 Billy J Kramer. 18 Suzanne. 19 Xanadu. 20 The Night. 21 The Who. 22 Engelbert Humperdinck. 23 Yester-Me. 24 The Shadows. 25 Mr James. 26 San Francisco. 27 Tommy Roe. 28 Long John Baldry. 29 Lily the Pink. 30 Frank Sinatra.

1 Who took on the role of Faye Morton in "Holby City" in 2007?
2 In December 2006 the government approved plans for trials of which GM crop in Britain?
3 What was the radioactive isotope identified in the death of Alexander Litvinenko?
4 In 2002 Judi Dench won a BAFTA for playing which real person?
5 Which company were the largest provider of telephone directory inquiries in 2005?
6 Who won a Best Supporting Actor Golden Globe for "Dreamgirls"?
7 President Joseph Estrada was forced to resign after protests in which country?
8 What was the cause of widespread closure of rural footpaths in 2001?
9 Which energy-trading conglomerate went bankrupt in December 2001?
10 Who had a big-selling album with "Slicker Than Your Average"?
11 Which Irish novelist opened Dublin's first cinema?
12 Which modern-day PM became Foreign Secretary after he resigned as Premier?
13 Who announced a split from French partner Olivier Martinez in February 2007?
14 In the Six Nations Rugby tournament which team is last alphabetically?
15 Who began his first PM Cabinet meeting with the words, "Well, who'd have thought it?"?
16 Which percussionist was made a Dame in the 2007 New Years Honours list?
17 Which crime writer wrote "The Mermaids Singing"?
18 In 2007 "Casino Royale" was nominated for nine BAFTAS, but how many did it win?
19 Which cop duo were played by Colin Buchanan and Warren Clarke on TV?
20 On which day of the week did England clinch the 2005 Ashes series?
21 Which famous person includes Anthony Charles Lynton in his name?
22 Back in the West End in 2005, a "Man for All Seasons" is about which Thomas?
23 Judith Keppel was the first top prize winner of which TV quiz?
24 Which "Express" was Spielberg's debut as a feature film director?
25 Which Ted was a 1990s Poet Laureate?
26 Which Luis Felipe was the manager of the 2002 World Cup winners Brazil?
27 What was the main colour of the comic character Biffo the Bear?
28 What is the registration for Bulgaria – BA, BG or BUG?
29 Which member of Tony Blair's cabinet represented Derby South?
30 Who was Paul Merton's guest on his final stint on "Room 101"?

Answers	Pot Luck 47 *(see Quiz 106)*

1 1807. 2 No 45. 3 American Life. 4 Competitive eating. 5 A crossbow. 6 Guitarist. 7 Prime Suspect. 8 Frankie Dettori. 9 France. 10 Princess Margaret. 11 Gwyneth Paltrow. 12 Gianlucca Vialli. 13 Charles Clarke. 14 England. 15 Jamie Oliver. 16 A red deer stag. 17 Lance Armstrong. 18 Guitar (six open strings). 19 Annie Lennox. 20 1980s. 21 Stephen Daldry. 22 Carol Thatcher. 23 Jack Nicholson. 24 Patella. 25 Architects. 26 Philip Glass. 27 Girls Aloud. 28 Tennis. 29 Ed Stoppard. 30 Thierry Henry.

1 How many band members were there in the original line-up?
2 What was the first No 1 single?
3 What was the not very original title of their first album?
4 Which band member plays a musical instrument on stage?
5 What was their second album called?
6 Who was the band's first manager?
7 What is Nicky's surname?
8 Who duetted with Westlife on "Against All Odds"?
9 Where do the band hail from in Ireland?
10 "An empty street" is the first line of which of their songs?
11 Including their debut disc, how many consecutive No 1 singles did the boys have?
12 What is Kian's surname?
13 Which Girl was the subject of their March 2001 charity single?
14 Which single was their first not to reach No 1?
15 Bryan McFadden became engaged to which member of Atomic Kitten?
16 Who has a distinctive scar on his right cheek?
17 Which superstar featured on "When You Tell Me that You Love Me"?
18 What was the title of their Greatest Hits Vol 1 collection of 2002?
19 What is Nicky's birth sign – Leo or Libra?
20 What was the first single to have a one-word title?
21 Who left the band in 2004?
22 Which supermodel appeared in the video of "Uptown Girl"?
23 What is the first name of Mr Feehily?
24 Which N was the first English venue for Westlife on their first UK tour?
25 Which album came out first – "Face to Face" or "Turnaround"?
26 The 2003 "Miss You Nights" was originally a 1976 hit for which singer?
27 What is Shane's surname?
28 What was Bryan McFadden's first solo No 1?
29 At Christmas 2006, TV technology allowed Westlife to duet with which late singer?
30 What were the band originally to have been called?

Answers	Codes and Spies (see Quiz 111)

1 40s. 2 Copyright. 3 Hieroglyphics. 4 Enigma. 5 Mole. 6 Tumble drier. 7 Morse. 8 Ring. 9 Ian Fleming. 10 Julius Caesar. 11 8. 12 Stella Rimington. 13 XXV. 14 George. 15 German. 16 Latin. 17 Oddjob. 18 1980s. 19 Red and yellow. 20 Square. 21 Two. 22 Diamonds. 23 Peter Wright. 24 Cold. 25 Semaphore. 26 Black circle. 27 Pig Pen. 28 Anthony Blunt. 29 H. 30 MI5.

1 Who was the third actor to play the Doctor on TV?
2 In which month of the year was "Doctor Who" shown for the very first time?
3 Which planet does the Doctor come from?
4 What is the name of Captain Jack's tiny robots that can treat wounds?
5 What was the name of Rose's mother?
6 Which three words are on the bottom line of the poster on the door of the TARDIS?
7 Daleks were inhabitants of which planet?
8 Who is the creator of Doctor Who?
9 Which MP helped Rose and the Doctor with the Slitheen in control of Downing Street?
10 Which warriors were first seen in the series "The Tenth Planet"?
11 What colour is the Moxx of Balhoon?
12 Which ex-Dr Who is the father of actress Georgia Moffett?
13 Which race used high-tech broadcasting in the year 200,000 to brainwash humans?
14 What does the letter R stand for in TARDIS?
15 Which actor played travelling companion Steven Taylor?
16 In which city did the Doctor find Charles Dickens under threat from the walking dead?
17 Which planet did the Ice Warriors come from?
18 The Doctor challenged the Sycorax leader to what sort of fight?
19 Which surname has been shared by two actors to portray the Doctor?
20 Who was the billionaire collector who held a Dalek in his vault at Utah?
21 What was the registration of the Doctor's car as owned by Jon Pertwee?
22 In which year did Rose's father die?
23 What had been Sarah Jane Smith's job before time travelling?
24 In which year was the Earth destroyed?
25 John Leeson and David Brierly have both supplied the voice to which character?
26 Which real-life historical figure was involved with a werewolf and Warrior Monks?
27 What was the surname of Jamie as portrayed by Fraser Hines?
28 In 18th-century France, where did the court come under attack from the clockwork killers?
29 Which sport did the Doctor like, as portrayed by Peter Davison?
30 Which year will mark the 50th anniversary of the first programme?

| **Answers** | **Pot Luck 49** *(see Quiz 112)* |

1 Scotland. 2 Kensal Green. 3 Cliff Richard. 4 ITV. 5 QI. 6 Congo. 7 Gareth Gates. 8 Trevor Francis. 9 New Zealand. 10 Kofi Annan. 11 Variety Club of Great Britain. 12 Harriet Harman. 13 All You Need is Love. 14 Korea. 15 Lost in Translation. 16 Sheffield. 17 Jeremy Clarkson. 18 Joyce Smith. 19 King Albert II. 20 Chelsea. 21 Smoking. 22 Roald Dahl. 23 Ronald Reagan. 24 The Goblet of Fire. 25 James Dyson. 26 Graham Rix. 27 History. 28 Confetti. 29 Snooker. 30 Postal charges.

1 Was Alexander Litvinenko in his 30s, 40s or 50s when he was poisoned?
2 What does a letter c enclosed in a circle stand for?
3 What was the picture language of Ancient Egypt know as?
4 What word links an Elgar work and a movie about code cracking in the war?
5 A spy in a position of trust with the enemy is known as a what?
6 On clothing labels, what does a circle inside a square stand for?
7 Which code is based on dots and dashes?
8 What term links a mobile phone tone and a network of spies?
9 Who created the most famous double agent of them all – James Bond?
10 Who devised an alphabet code – Julius Caesar or Richard the Lionheart?
11 On a standard keyboard the star sign shares a key with which number?
12 Which Stella became head of MI5?
13 How is the number 25 written in Roman numerals?
14 What was the first name of Smiley created by John Le Carré?
15 Runes developed from which language?
16 The English word code derives from the word codex from which language?
17 Which villain did Bond face in "Goldfinger"?
18 In which decade did the double agent Kim Philby die in Russia?
19 What are the normal colours on a semaphore flag?
20 In Ancient Greece, Polybius made a letter cipher that took which shape?
21 How many dots show on an iron to indicate warm?
22 In playing cards, which suit symbol contains four angles?
23 Who wrote "Spycatcher" the controversial 1980s book about the workings of M15?
24 In meteorology what front is shown by triangles pointing up?
25 Depillon, Popham and Paisley all developed which system?
26 In astronomy what is the sign for a new moon?
27 In the 16thC the Freemasons used a diagram code known as which "Pen"?
28 In 1979 which Anthony was revealed as a spy and stripped of his knighthood?
29 In Morse Code which letter is represented by four dots?
30 In which organisation did Martin Furnival Jones replace Roger Hollis?

Answers	**Westlife (see Quiz 109)**

1 Five. 2 Swear It Again. 3 Westlife. 4 None of them does. 5 Coast to Coast. 6 Ronan Keating. 7 Byrne. 8 Mariah Carey. 9 Sligo. 10 My Love. 11 Seven. 12 Egan. 13 Uptown Girl. 14 What Makes a Man. 15 Kerry Katona. 16 Kian. 17 Diana Ross. 18 Unbreakable. 19 Libra. 20 Mandy. 21 Bryan McFadden. 22 Claudia Schiffer. 23 Mark. 24 Newcastle. 25 Turnaround. 26 Cliff Richard. 27 Filan. 28 Real to Me. 29 Roy Orbison. 30 Westside.

1 After 2003, Jonny Wilkinson's next international was in 2007 against which side?

2 Near which London tube station was Tom ap Rhys Pryce murdered?

3 Whose 100th single was called "The Best of Me"?

4 Charles Allen was the chief executive who left which media group in August 2006?

5 "The Book of General Ignorance" was linked to which TV quiz show?

6 What was Zaire renamed in 1997?

7 Whose second album was "Go Your Own Way"?

8 Steve Bruce took over from which soccer manager at Birmingham?

9 In which Southern Hemisphere country was "Lord of the Rings" partly made?

10 Who succeeded Boutros Boutros Ghali as UN Secretary General?

11 Which club has members called Barkers?

12 Which lady became Solicitor General in Tony Blair's government in 2001?

13 In the days before sampling, which No 1 began with the French National anthem?

14 In 2005, which North & South countries agreed on a joint team for Olympics 2008?

15 Scarlett Johansson starred in which Tokyo-set film of 2004?

16 Which city has the constituencies of Hallam and Heeley?

17 Which Jeremy wrote the big-selling book "I Know You Got Soul"?

18 Which lady from the UK won the first two London Marathons?

19 Who was the King of the Belgians at the start of the 21st century?

20 Damian Duff first played in a Premiership-winning side at which club?

21 What became illegal in 1984 on the London Underground?

22 Which children's author wrote the screenplay for "You Only Live Twice"?

23 Who was the first US President to have been divorced?

24 What was the first "Harry Potter" film in which Katie Leung appeared?

25 Which English inventor James created the bagless cyclone vacuum cleaner?

26 Which Graham got the sack as head coach of Hearts in 2006?

27 Bob Geldof was a spearhead of the campaign to Make Poverty what?

28 Which 2006 movie followed three couples trying to hold unusual weddings?

29 Shaun Murphy has won a World Championship in which sport?

30 Which everyday charges were changed to be based on size and shape from September 2006?

Answers | George W Bush *(see Quiz 115)*

1 Walker. 2 Al Gore. 3 Jeb. 4 John Kerry. 5 Yo, Blair! 6 Iran, Iraq & North Korea. 7 Colin Powell. 8 Florida. 9 Condoleezza Rice. 10 Texas. 11 Dick Cheney. 12 Afghanistan. 13 Jenna & Barbara. 14 9/11. 15 Dubya. 16 Donald Rumsfeld. 17 Marathon. 18 43rd. 19 Katrina. 20 Fahrenheit 9/11. 21 St Petersburg. 22 60th. 23 March. 24 Connecticut. 25 One. 26 Yale. 27 Baseball. 28 George & Barbara. 29 Robert Gates. 30 Oil.

1 What was Slade's first No 1 single?
2 Which group went on a "Teenage Rampage"?
3 Who had a 1970s No 1 with "Oh Boy"?
4 Which Barry was "(Dancin') on a Saturday Night"?
5 What was Alvin Stardust's name when he charted in the 60s?
6 Which Gary Glitter song was in Parts 1 & 2?
7 Who penned the T.Rex hits?
8 Who came alive down in "Devilgate Drive?"
9 Who was the leader of Wizzard?
10 Which group had a Noddy as singer?
11 Who was Chapman's song-writing partner?
12 Which Bowie No 1 was a reissue of his song that charted in 1969?
13 Which group had a hit with "Angel Face"?
14 Which song has the chorus line "Bang a gong"?
15 Brian Connolly was lead singer with which group?
16 Who played bass guitar in Suzi Quatro's group?
17 Mott the Hoople recorded Bowie's "All the Young" what?
18 Who recorded "Children of the Revolution"?
19 What was Mud's first top ten hit?
20 Which Micky was producer for the Suzi Quatro hits?
21 Who wished that it could be Christmas everyday?
22 And who was "Lonely This Christmas"?
23 Who was born Mark Feld?
24 Which Midlands town did Slade come from?
25 Which Alvin Stardust hit was one word repeated three times?
26 According to Sweet, "It's, it's a ballroom" what?
27 What words in brackets complete the title of "I'm the Leader of the Gang"?
28 What dance was Wizzard's baby doing in the title of a No 1 hit?
29 Which song features the words, "Do the fairies keep him sober for a day"?
30 Who was the lead singer with the original Mud?

| **Answers** | Pot Luck 50 *(see Quiz 114)* |

1 Simon Cowell. 2 Luiz Felipe Scolari. 3 Martin Campbell. 4 Alexander Litvinenko. 5 192. 6 Atlanta. 7 Yorks. 8 Foot & mouth outbreak. 9 I Want It That Way. 10 Shaun Udal. 11 Liverpool. 12 Rural Affairs. 13 Frank. 14 Isle of Wight. 15 Hans Zimmer. 16 Villarreal. 17 Ralf Little. 18 Fabio Copella. 19 Australia. 20 Japan. 21 Light. 22 Austria. 23 Aston Villa. 24 The Return of the King. 25 November (1990). 26 James Martin. 27 Snooker. 28 Wonderland. 29 JM Barrie. 30 Australian Open 2007.

1 Who launched the classically trained singers known as Il Divo?
2 Who cited press intrusion for his pulling out as a potential England soccer boss in 2006?
3 Who directed the 2006 movie "Casino Royale"?
4 In 2006, Mario Scaramella met up with which ex-spy shortly before his death?
5 What was the BT directory enquiry service number prior to deregulation?
6 Where were the Centennial Modern Olympics held?
7 In 1996 which Royals were divorced first, the Yorks or the Waleses?
8 Which crisis led to Tony Blair postponing the 20001 General Election?
9 What was the first UK No 1 for the Backstreet Boys?
10 Which veteran off-spinner Shaun made England's tour of India in 2006?
11 Which city has the constituencies of Garston and Walton?
12 What do the letters R and A stand for in DEFRA?
13 What was the title of Amy Winehouse's debut album?
14 On which Isle was Jeremy Irons born?
15 Who links music from the "Da Vinci Code" and "Pirates of the Caribbean: Dead Man's Chest"?
16 Which Spanish side did Arsenal beat to reach their first Championship League Final?
17 Which actor played Antony Royle in "The Royle Family"?
18 Who was Real Madrid coach when Beckham announced his move to the USA?
19 Richard Farleigh of "Dragon's Den" fame comes from which country?
20 The massage technique shiatsu developed in which country?
21 What do you fear if you suffer from photophobia?
22 Which country has the alphabet's first letter as its international vehicle registration code?
23 Which soccer club has Witton Road and Trinity Road around the stadium?
24 Which film won eleven awards at the 2004 Academy Awards?
25 In which month did Thatcher leave Downing Street for the last time as PM?
26 Which celebrity chef wrote "Great British Winter?
27 Which sport is associated with Graeme Dott?
28 What was McFly's second No 1 album called?
29 Johnny Depp played which writer in "Finding Neverland"?
30 What was the first Grand Slam that Roger Federer won without dropping a set?

Answers | Dr Who *(see Quiz 110)*

1 Jon Pertwee. 2 November. 3 Gallifrey. 4 Nanogenes. 5 Jackie. 6 Pull to Open. 7 Skaro. 8 Sydney Newman. 9 Harriet Jones. 10 Cybermen. 11 Blue. 12 Peter Davison. 13 Jagrafess. 14 Relative. 15 Peter Purves. 16 Cardiff. 17 Mars. 18 Swordfight. 19 Baker. 20 Henry Van Statten. 21 WHO 1. 22 1987. 23 Journalist. 24 5.5/Apple/26. 25 K9. 26 Queen Victoria. 27 McCrimmon. 28 Versailles. 29 Cricket. 30 2013.

1 What does the W stand for in Bush's middle name?
2 Who did Bush defeat to become President for the first time?
3 What is the first name of Bush's brother, who was Governor of Florida?
4 Who did Bush beat to be President in 2004?
5 How did George W Bush say he greeted Tony Blair when they met in private?
6 Which countries did he call the "axis of evil"?
7 Who was Bush's first Secretary of State?
8 In which state was Bush at the time of the first 9/11 attack?
9 Who replaced Colin Powell as Secretary of State?
10 Where was Bush Governor before he became President?
11 Who was his first Vice President?
12 Bush ordered the invasion of which country in October 2001?
13 What are his twin daughters called?
14 "The Pearl Harbor of the 21st century took place today", related to which event?
15 Which of his nicknames is based on the pronunciation of his middle initial?
16 Who was his first Secretary of Defense?
17 Which sporting race did he run in 1993, the first US President to do so?
18 Bush became what number of President of the USA?
19 Which major hurricane hit the US shortly into Bush's second term?
20 Which 2004 Michael Moore movie was critical of Bush?
21 Where was the G8 summit when Bush said "Yo Blair"?
22 Which milestone birthday did he celebrate in 2006?
23 In which month of 2003 did he order the invasion of Iraq?
24 Brought up in Texas, in which state was he born?
25 How many sisters does he have?
26 He graduated with a history degree from which university in 1968?
27 What game do the Texas Rangers play, a team Bush had a share in?
28 What are the name of his parents?
29 Who replaced Rumsfeld as Secretary of Defense?
30 He worked for Spectrum 7 and Arbusto Energy which dealt in what?

Answers	Pop – Glam Rock *(see Quiz 113)*

1 Coz I Luv You. 2 The Sweet. 3 Mud. 4 Blue. 5 Shane Fenton. 6 Rock and Roll.
7 Marc Bolan. 8 Suzi Quatro. 9 Roy Wood. 10 Slade. 11 Chinn. 12 Space Oddity.
13 The Glitter Band. 14 Get It On. 15 The Sweet. 16 Suzi Quatro. 17 Dudes.
18 T. Rex. 19 Dyna-Mite. 20 Most. 21 Wizzard. 22 Mud. 23 Marc Bolan. 24
Wolverhampton. 25 You, You, You. 26 Blitz. 27 I Am. 28 Jive. 29 Merry Xmas
Everybody. 30 Les Gray.

Hard Questions

Ah yes, the hard questions. Cackle fiendishly, and take just a moment to stroke your white, diamond-collared cat before rubbing your hands together gleefully, because these questions are the real McCoy. The posers in this selection will sort the men out from the boys, and no mistake. If you do find any boys in the public bar by the way, be sure to let the landlord know, so he can give them a packet of crisps and a bottle of coke and send them outside. The quizzes in this section will make even the most dedicated trivia hound quake with fear. No one is going to get many of them correct, so if someone turns out an incredible score on these questions, search their coat for a copy of this book.

When you're setting a quiz, use these questions sparingly, like hot chilli powder. Even for teams, they're going to be decidedly tricky. You'll need to allow plenty of time for people to think about each question. What you don't want to do is make an entire night's quizzing out of this section, because you'll only make people feel stupid, and everyone hates a smart aleck who makes them look dumb. A few of these questions, strategically placed, can go a long way.

1 Which charity was given the first shorn fleece of Dolly the cloned sheep?
2 The Prometheus was the first of which type of kitchen equipment?
3 Which US state was acquired from the Badsen Purchase?
4 Where was "God Save the King" first sung in public?
5 Who was the first British Foreign Secretary to visit Iran after the fall of the Shah?
6 Who founded Amazon.com?
7 In 1992 Don Hollister and Don Pelazzo were responsible for developing what?
8 Who was Germany's longest-serving post-war Chancellor?
9 When did the first Page Three girl appear in the "The Sun"?
10 Which distress signal did SOS replace?
11 Where was the first gold rush in Western Australia in 1885?
12 In which country was Hrant Dink murdered?
13 In 2000 how many sovereign countries were there in the world?
14 Which was the first regiment to wear khaki?
15 What is the world's largest conservation charity?
16 How was the first balloon to circumnavigate the globe non-stop named?
17 Who became chairman of the KGB in 1967?
18 What date was the first Penguin book published – the same date that England won the World Cup 31 years later?
19 Who was Hitler's propaganda chief?
20 When was PAYE Income Tax introduced?
21 What did laser surgery, pioneered by Ludwig Demling, first destroy?
22 Which politician was accused of possessing "Stalinist ruthlessness" by a former top civil servant in March 2007?
23 At which golf club was the Jack Nicklaus Online Golf Championship played in December 1999?
24 Which leader of the Progressive Unionist Party died in January 2007?
25 Who took part in the USA's first manned orbital flight?
26 Where was the tanker registered, which spilt millions of gallons of oil off the French coast in March 1978?
27 Where was the on-line bookstore Amazon first based?
28 John F Kennedy said the Apollo programme would land a man on the Moon and what else?
29 Who was the first elected President of Argentina after the Falklands War?
30 Dying in December 2006, who was the last surviving Briton to see active service in the First and Second World Wars?

Answers   TV Soaps *(see Quiz 3)*

1 Twice. 2 Hairdresser. 3 Maggie (ER). 4 Sharon Maughan. 5 Luke. 6 Melrose Place. 7 Viv Martell. 8 Five. 9 Dennis. 10 Black Forest Clinic. 11 Ricky Tomlinson. 12 Derek Thompson. 13 Fallon. 14 Julie Goodyear. 15 Meadowcroft. 16 Leonard Swindley. 17 QE2. 18 Conundrum. 19 Tara King. 20 Mal Young. 21 Lucy-Jo Hudson. 22 Dynasty. 23 Carol Boswell. 24 The Brothers. 25 Liam. 26 Hathaway. 27 Thomas. 28 Compact. 29 Dynasty. 30 Debbie Travers-Macy.

1 Who was the first US President to ride in a car?

2 The drink Kir was named after the mayor of which town?

3 Where was the SALT II treaty signed?

4 Who was the leader of the Taliban at the beginning of the raids on Afghanistan in October 2001?

5 In which country was the first double hand transplant carried out?

6 In the US what were "swift walkers"?

7 Where was the first sugar beet extraction factory built?

8 In which city was Britain's Independent Labour Party founded?

9 Which Oscar-winning actor links "Tomb Raider" and "Pearl Harbor"?

10 In what year were dog licences abolished in the UK?

11 Of the three top names in the US's Ivy League which is the middle one alphabetically?

12 On which river is the state capital of Mississippi?

13 Which Pope excommunicated Martin Luther?

14 Who made jasperware?

15 To three, how many games did Sven Goran Eriksson's England draw?

16 Which future party leader was the then youngest-ever government minister when he became Under-Secretary to the Navy on his 30th birthday?

17 During which months did Jack the Ripper kill five prostitutes?

18 Jatakas are stories of the previous lives of whom?

19 Which US President pardoned the first US President to have resigned from office?

20 Which monarch knighted Isaac Newton?

21 Which state is to the south west of Rajashan in India?

22 What colour is the head and neck of the jabiru?

23 Which rock star died two years to the day after the death of Rolling Stone Brian Jones?

24 Where was Europe's oldest university founded?

25 Where were emeralds first mined?

26 Which dams in the Ruhr were hit by the Dam Busters in 1943?

27 In which city was Chop Suey invented?

28 Where was the world's first electric power station?

29 A strophium was an early prototype of which garment?

30 A car from where can display the letters WAG?

Answers	Plants *(see Quiz 4)*

1 Alaska. 2 Chlorophyll. 3 Dead matter. 4 New Zealand. 5 0.9%. 6 Barley. 7 Lamina. 8 Gymnosperm. 9 Hollies. 10 Epiphyte. 11 Cork. 12 Forget Me Not. 13 Small stalk. 14 Myrtle sprig. 15 Honesty. 16 Azalea. 17 Pink. 18 Autumn crocus. 19 Rosa gallica. 20 Carnations. 21 Saffron. 22 Glory of the snow. 23 South Africa. 24 Sap. 25 Boston. 26 Root. 27 Aubretia. 28 Parsley. 29 Daffodil. 30 Flemish.

1 How many times a week was "Coronation Street" originally broadcast?

2 Which profession did Helen Shapiro's character play in "Albion Market"?

3 For which character did Sally Field win an Emmy in 2000?

4 Which ex-"Holby City" star is the mother of actress Alice Eve?

5 What was "Nora Batty's" surname in the revival of "Crossroads"?

6 What was the spin-off of "Beverly Hills 90210"?

7 Which character did the barmaid from "Only Fools and Horses" play in "The Bill"?

8 How many members of the family were there which was created on "Soapstars"?

9 In "Coronation Street" who was Elsie Tanner's son?

10 Which overseas soap had the character Klaus Brinkmann?

11 In "Brookside" which actor who had been a striker in real life played a builder on strike?

12 Which member of the "Casualty" cast played an IRA terrorist in "The Long Good Friday"?

13 In "The Colbys" who shared her name with a youngster in "The Archers"?

14 Which "Coronation Street" barmaid was given an OBE?

15 What was the original title of "Brookside" to have been?

16 "Pardon the Expression" was a spin-off series about which "Coronation Street" character?

17 In "Crossroads", where was Meg when the motel burned down?

18 What was the final episode of "Dallas" called?

19 Which character did "Emmerdale"'s Rosemary King play in "The Avengers"?

20 Which producer of "Brookside" took over the same year that the set expanded to include the shopping centre?

21 Which ex-Corrie star played Hayley Mills' granddaughter in "Wild at Heart"?

22 In which soap did the voice of Charlie in "Charlie's Angels" appear?

23 Which character did "Emmerdale"'s Diane Sugden play in "The Liver Birds"?

24 Which soap/drama centred on Hammond Transport Services?

25 Whom did Bianca leave "EastEnders" with?

26 In "The Archers" what was Siobhan's surname when she lived in Ambridge?

27 What was Sinbad's real name?

28 Which magazine soap had "Crossroads" creators previously created?

29 Which soap boasted appearances by Gerald Ford and Henry Kissinger?

30 Which role did the 2007 Olivier Award Best Actress play in "The Archers"?

Answers	Newsworthy (see Quiz 1)

1 Cystic Fibrosis Fund. 2 Electric kettle. 3 Arizona. 4 Theatre Royal Drury Lane. 5 Jack Straw. 6 Jeff Bezos. 7 High tech light bulb. 8 Helmut Kohl. 9 1970. 10 CQD. 11 Halls Creek. 12 Turkey. 13 192. 14 Oxford Light Infantry. 15 World Wildlife Fund. 16 Breitling Orbiter. 17 Yuri Andropov. 18 30th July. 19 Josef Goebbels. 20 1944. 21 Gallstones. 22 Gordon Brown. 23 Pelican Hill. 24 David Ervine. 25 John Glenn. 26 Cyprus (Amoco Cadiz). 27 Seattle. 28 Return him safely to Earth. 29 Raul Alfonsin. 30 Captain Kenneth Cummins.

1 In which US state is the Tongass National Forest?
2 Which of the following do algae have – chlorophyll, roots and stems?
3 What does a saphrophyte feed on?
4 Urtica ferox is a deadly tree nettle native to where?
5 How much chlorophyll does spinach have – 0.9%, 0.12% or 0.17%?
6 Which of the following originated in the Middle East – barley, maize or millet?
7 What is another name for the blade of a plant?
8 What name is given to a plant whose seed is not enclosed in an ovary?
9 Which of the following are in the Aquilfoliacae group – conifers, hollies or ivies?
10 What name is given to a plant which grows on another without damaging it?
11 The Whistler Tree is what type of tree?
12 Myosotis is another name for which flower?
13 What is a funicle?
14 According to legend which plant did Adam take from the Garden of Eden?
15 How is lunaria biennis better known?
16 What type of plant is a Silver Slipper?
17 What colour are the blooms of the Zephirine Drouhin?
18 What is another name for the meadow saffron?
19 What is the rose of Lancaster also called?
20 What are Alice Forbes and Bailey's Delight?
21 What is crocus sativus?
22 How is chionodoxa also known?
23 The agapanthus is native to where?
24 Which part of asafoetida is used?
25 The borlotti bean also takes its name from which city?
26 Which part of a mooli is edible?
27 How is rock cress better known?
28 Which herb reputedly travels seven times to the devil before it will emerge?
29 The amaryllis is related to which popular spring flower?
30 What is the nationality of the man who gave his name to the plant Lobelia?

Answers	Pot Luck 1 *(see Quiz 2)*

1 Teddy Roosevelt. 2 Dijon. 3 Vienna. 4 Mullah Mohammed Omar. 5 Spain. 6 Bicycles. 7 Silesia. 8 Bradford. 9 Jon Voight. 10 1984. 11 Princeton. 12 Pearl. 13 Leo X. 14 Wedgwood. 15 17 games. 16 David Owen. 17 August–November (1888). 18 Buddha. 19 Gerald Ford pardoned Richard Nixon. 20 Queen Anne. 21 Gujarat. 22 Blue. 23 Jim Morrison. 24 Salerno, Italy. 25 Egypt. 26 Hohne & Eder. 27 New York. 28 Godalming. 29 Bra. 30 Gambia.

1 Which John won the Best Director Oscar for the movie "The Informer"?
2 The world's first known drilling for oil took place in which US state?
3 At which London club did Bill Wyman have his 70th birthday bash?
4 The Kate Bush album "Never for Ever" featured a song about which classical composer?
5 On which special day was William the Conqueror crowned King of England?
6 Which day of the week was dubbed the "Black" day of the 1929 Wall Street Crash?
7 The first kindergarten was established in which country?
8 Ingemar Johansson became Sweden's first champion in which sport?
9 Roger Moore played 007 in how many films?
10 Matching the date of the French Revolution, how many steps are there to the top of the Eiffel Tower?
11 In which US state was John Travolta born?
12 Which security item was Joseph Farwell Glidden's patent in 1873?
13 In which city was the first Model T Ford produced in Britain?
14 In which country would you watch Jazz Pori play a home soccer match?
15 Which England cricket captain was born in Italy?
16 King Michael abdicated which European throne in 1947?
17 Which Mr Smith was the main character of the novel "1984"?
18 "A Man for All Seasons" was set in the 16th century but was written in which century?
19 The first prime minister of Australia shared his surname with which fictional detective?
20 Which country did 1990s group Whale come from?
21 Who was the first Scot to appear on an English bank note?
22 If 12 January falls on a Friday, on what day does 12 February fall?
23 John Street and Cherry Street go past the soccer stadium of which club?
24 How many hurdles are there in total in a six-lane 400-metre hurdle race?
25 Which paper did Superman work on?
26 In which year did Shirley Bassey, the Tigress of Tiger Bay, first have a Top Ten single?
27 The first heart transplant patient survived for how long after the operation?
28 Which actor links the movies "Sliding Doors" and "Pandaemonium"?
29 In which country is the city of Londrina?
30 What is the first word of "My Heart Will Go On"?

Answers | **Pot Luck 3** *(see Quiz 7)*

1 Prince Edward. 2 Body Shop. 3 Doug Mountjoy. 4 Friendship 7. 5 Charles Blondin.
6 Painting. 7 Portugal. 8 46 years. 9 Argentine. 10 Sued. 11 Pink. 12 Farce. 13 Fulham. 14 Vanbrugh. 15 Belgium. 16 Henry. 17 The Forfarshire. 18 Tonga. 19 White Town. 20 Pope. 21 Bruton Street. 22 Norway. 23 Soccer club. 24 Paddington. 25 Brazil. 26 Frank Coraci. 27 France. 28 Coca Cola. 29 Brazil. 30 Pointer Sisters.

1 Who was the only American lady to have a million-seller in the UK in the 1980s?

2 Who directed Michael Jackson's best-selling album?

3 Whose album of "Love Songs" was the top-selling album of 1982?

4 Who was the first country artist to have two UK No 1s?

5 What was Blondie's third single from the "Eat to the Beat" album?

6 Who wrote the first double A side of the 1980s to debut at No 1?

7 What were the Detroit Spinners called in the UK before using this name?

8 Which song was at No 1 when Prince Charles & Diana married?

9 The writer of Kelly Marie's "Feels Like I'm in Love" was a member of which 1970s band?

10 Who was the last Australian with a UK No 1 before Men at Work's first No 1?

11 What was the only song from "Thriller" to reach No 1 in the UK?

12 The brother of the writer of "True" starred in which TV soap?

13 Who was Billy Joel's 1983 No 1 dedicated to?

14 Which album did Lionel Richie's first No 1 of 1984 come from?

15 Who co-wrote and produced Blondie's "Call Me"?

16 Who was the only American man to have a million-seller in the UK in the 1980s?

17 Which top-selling hit of 1985 was a hit for a Canadian singer in the 1990s?

18 Which movie gave ELO their only UK No 1?

19 What colour shirt is Michael Jackson wearing on the cover of "Thriller"?

20 Which record of John Lennon's went to No 1 almost immediately after his murder?

21 What was the fourth British Eurovision Song Contest winner, which charted in this decade?

22 Which song did Smokey Robinson release to celebrate his silver anniversary in show business?

23 Under what name did Mary Sandeman have a 1980s No 1?

24 Who was the first white singer to have No 1 on the Motown label?

25 Where did Paul McCartney and Stevie Wonder record their No 1 duet?

26 Which big 1980s band were once called In Praise of Lemmings?

27 What was the first single to be at No 1 in the 80s?

28 Who directed the video for the Pet Shop Boys' second No 1?

29 Which band topped the charts in the 1980s, as well as the 1960s and 1970s?

30 What was the surname of the singer who sang "Orinoco Flow"?

Answers	**UK Travel** *(see Quiz 8)*

1 Canada. 2 32. 3 Gentlemen's toilet. 4 Aberystwyth. 5 Christchurch. 6 Kessock.
7 Victoria. 8 Caernarvon. 9 Pratt. 10 603. 11 Powys. 12 Widnes. 13 Dorset. 14
Dover. 15 Anne. 16 John Christie. 17 Lincoln Cathedral. 18 Bedford. 19 Llantrisant.
20 220 miles. 21 Angus. 22 1988. 23 Stour. 24 Granta. 25 1940. 26 Book dealer.
27 Berkshire. 28 Caerphilly. 29 Gillespie Road. 30 Brighton.

1 Who was Prince Andrew's best man for his wedding to Sarah Ferguson?
2 What did L'Oréal buy for £652 million in 2006?
3 Who did Steve Davis beat to win his first World Snooker Championship?
4 John Glenn orbited the Earth in 1962 in which craft?
5 How did daredevil stuntman Jean Francois Gravelet become known?
6 John Sell Cotman became famous for doing what?
7 In which country is the Penina golf course?
8 How long was the Nazi Rudolf Hess in prison?
9 What was the nationality of Cuban revolutionary leader Che Guevara?
10 Satirical editor Richard Ingrams suggested his motto should be "Publish and be" what?
11 What colour is the flesh of a dragon fruit?
12 What kind of theatrical play was the speciality of Brian Rix?
13 In his second Anfield spell, Robbie Fowler first scored against which side?
14 Which Sir John was the designer of Castle Howard and Blenheim Palace?
15 Albert became a king of which country in 1993?
16 What is Warren Beatty's other Christian name?
17 The crew of which boat were saved by the heroics of Grace Darling?
18 In which country did Queen Salote Tupou III rule for nearly 50 years?
19 Under which name did producer Jyoti Mishra have a No 1 hit?
20 Nicholas Breakspear was the first British what?
21 In which London Street is the residence where Princess Elizabeth – later Elizabeth II – was born?
22 In which country would you watch Tromso playing Molde at soccer?
23 What was the setting of the 1960s soap "United!"?
24 Michael Hordern provided the voiceover for which TV bear?
25 Djalma Santos played soccer 100 times for which country?
26 Who directed the movie "The Wedding Singer"?
27 After abdicating, in which country did the former Edward VIII marry?
28 Dr John Pemberton invented which world-famous drink?
29 In which country is the city of Recife?
30 How were June, Anita, Ruth and Bonnie known collectively?

Answers	Pot Luck 2 (see Quiz 5)

1 John Ford. 2 Pennsylvania. 3 Ronnie Scott's. 4 Delius. 5 Christmas Day. 6 Thursday. 7 Switzerland. 8 Boxing. 9 Seven. 10 1789. 11 New Jersey. 12 Barbed wire. 13 Manchester. 14 Finland. 15 Ted Dexter. 16 Romania. 17 Winston Smith. 18 20th. 19 Barton. 20 Sweden. 21 Adam Smith. 22 Monday. 23 Sheffield Utd. 24 60. 25 Daily Planet. 26 1957. 27 18 days. 28 John Hannah. 29 Brazil. 30 Every.

1 In which Square is the UK's highest building?
2 How many capsules or pods does the London Eye have?
3 What did the Theatre of Small Convenience in Malvern used to be?
4 Where is the National Library of Wales?
5 Where does the Avon flow into what the French call La Manche?
6 Which Bridge spans the Beauly Firth?
7 What was London's first new underground railway line to open in the second half of the 20th century?
8 Which Welsh city is near the old Roman fort of Segontium?
9 What was Lord Camden's name before he became a Lord and before the London borough was named after him?
10 How many miles is it from Land's End to John O'Groats?
11 Which county is to the west of Hereford & Worcester?
12 At which northern railway station did Paul Simon write "Homeward Bound"?
13 In which county is the Cerne Giant?
14 Which of the Cinque Ports is nearest the beginning of the alphabet?
15 One of the founders of Fortnum and Mason was a footman in the service of which monarch?
16 Who inaugurated the Glyndebourne Festival?
17 Which is the UK's tallest structure built before the 20th century?
18 Where is the Cranfield Institute of Technology?
19 Where in Wales is the Royal Mint?
20 How long is Britain's longest river?
21 Which county is the largest to the east of Perth & Kinross?
22 When were the Broads designated a National Park?
23 Constable country is along which river?
24 What is the local name of the river which runs through Cambridge?
25 In what year were marriages at the famous blacksmith's shop in southern Scotland made illegal?
26 The founder of Guy's Hospital followed which profession?
27 Which county is to the south of Oxfordshire?
28 Where is the second largest castle in England and Wales?
29 What was Arsenal tube station called before it was called Arsenal?
30 Where did Britain's first nudist beach open in 1979?

Answers	**Sounds of the Eighties** *(see Quiz 6)*

1 Jennifer Rush. 2 Quincey Jones. 3 Barbra Streisand. 4 Kenny Rogers. 5 Atomic. 6 Paul Weller. 7 Motown Spinners. 8 Ghost Town – The Specials. 9 Mungo Jerry. 10 Rolf Harris. 11 Billie Jean. 12 EastEnders (the Kemps). 13 Christie Brinkley. 14 Can't Slow Down. 15 Giorgio Moroder. 16 Stevie Wonder. 17 The Power of Love. 18 Xanadu. 19 Cream. 20 (Just Like) Starting Over. 21 Making Your Mind Up. 22 Being with you. 23 Aneka. 24 Charlene. 25 Montserrat. 26 Culture Club. 27 Another Brick in the Wall. 28 Derek Jarman. 29 Bee Gees. 30 Brennan.

Quiz 9 Pot Luck 4

Answers – page 251

LEVEL 3

1 Chester Carlson invented a machine that produces what?
2 Jobs and Wozniak pioneered development in which field?
3 In which country would you watch Karpaty playing Krivbas at soccer?
4 One language is spoken in more countries of the world than any other – which is it?
5 General Choi Hong Hi developed which martial art?
6 What position does the canoeist adopt in Canadian canoeing?
7 What did Wilhelm Rontgen discover to help medical science?
8 Which movement did George Williams found in 1844?
9 How is St Kentigern, patron saint of Glasgow, also known?
10 Brigham Young was a leader of which religious movement?
11 In 2006 how many million people used the internet in China, according to state sources?
12 In 1989, who became the first US male tennis player in over 30 years to win the French Open?
13 Iwao Takamoto created the design of which popular cartoon dog?
14 In 1987 Lindy Chamberlain said her baby had been snatched by what?
15 How many track races are included in the decathlon?
16 Who was the last boxer to fight Muhammad Ali?
17 Which film soundtrack topped the first classified UK album chart?
18 Who was convicted of murdering nanny Sandra Rivett?
19 In which country is the city of San Cristobal?
20 Who was the first US President not to be elected into office and who subsequently failed to win a presidential election?
21 Polly Nicholas was the first victim of which killer?
22 2007 marked the 150th anniversary of which British-born classical composer?
23 Who composed the opera "Adelaide di Borgogna"?
24 France, Great Britain and which other country competed in every Winter Olympic Games of the 20th century?
25 William Kemmler was the first man to die in what?
26 What is Japan's highest peak?
27 Who won the Best Actress Oscar for the movie "Blue Sky"?
28 The Galapagos Islands belong to which country?
29 What was the only top ten hit for West End featuring Sybil?
30 What was the name of Franco's fascist party in Spain?

Answers | Pot Luck 5 *(see Quiz 11)*

1 25 March. 2 Dixie Dean. 3 Harold Macmillan. 4 1994. 5 Hi-De-Hi!. 6 Norwegian. 7 1914. 8 Armani. 9 Henry I. 10 Half-marathon. 11 Godzilla. 12 Colchester. 13 John Adams. 14 Bay. 15 Ajax. 16 Normal. 17 Voice over Internet Protocol. 18 144. 19 Unchained. 20 Transformer. 21 Alexander. 22 Swimming. 23 British Empire Exhibition. 24 Rievaulx. 25 21. 26 Julie Walters (2000). 27 Abstract Expressionism. 28 20 mins. 29 Silk screen. 30 Blythe Danner.

1 Who beat Costa Rica in Germany 2006 to make the second round for the first time?

2 In the penultimate World Cup Final of last century, what was the score at 90 minutes?

3 Which of FIFA's original member came nearest the end of the alphabet?

4 Why did India pull out of the fourth World Cup?

5 When did West Germany win their second European Championship ?

6 Which was the most northerly club Peter Shilton played for?

7 In July 2000 which club owned the world's most expensive footballer?

8 Which was the first indoor arena used in a World Cup Final?

9 Liverpool signed defender Daniel Agger from which club?

10 For how much did the first hat trick scorer in a World Cup final sell his shirt in 2000?

11 In which 2001 movie did Pele make an appearance?

12 Whose World Cup medal was sold for almost £125,000 in 2001?

13 For how many years was the League Cup the Rumbelows League Cup?

14 The Football League Cup was a two-legged final until which year?

15 Who won the FA Cup the year Prince William was born?

16 The world's second most expensive goalie at the beginning of 2001 had been transferred from which club?

17 Who won the first post-WWII Scottish FA Cup?

18 In which country did West Germany win their first World Cup?

19 Roy Keane made his Celtic debut in a Scottish Cup game against which team?

20 Who were the first runners-up of the Milk Cup?

21 Which was the first country to have players who scored more than once in a World Cup Final?

22 Who was Tommy Lawton playing for when he scored his first League hat trick?

23 Who was the first man to score twice in a European Championships final?

24 The first Yorkshire side to win the Fairs Cup in the 1960s beat which side in the final?

25 Which was the first side to win the UEFA Cup on penalties?

26 Who were runners-up in the first FA Cup final played at Wembley?

27 Who were the last runners-up of the old First Division?

28 At the end of the millennium who was the world's most expensive goalkeeper?

29 In which stadium was the sixth World Cup final held?

30 In the last World Cup final of the 20th century played outside Europe, what colour shirts did the winners wear?

Answers	The Royals (see Quiz 12)

1 Edward VII. 2 Lord Provost of Scotland. 3 Princess Victoria. 4 32. 5 Prince of Wales (later Edward VIII). 6 George VI. 7 Prince Andrew. 8 Philip. 9 One. 10 Rania. 11 Chelsea Hospital. 12 Princess Beatrice. 13 Diana Spencer. 14 The Queen, his grandmother. 15 The Archers. 16 December. 17 Chris Evert. 18 Frederick. 19 Switzerland. 20 Kent. 21 Blood transfusion. 22 Trinity. 23 Peter. 24 Beatrice. 25 Eloise Taylor. 26 Ian Ball. 27 Bryan Organ. 28 Diana. 29 Saudi Arabian. 30 Windsor Castle.

Quiz 11 | Pot Luck 5 | Answers – page 249

1 Before the Calendar Act of of 1752 what date was New Year's Day?
2 Which English goal scorer had the first names William Ralph?
3 Who described Margaret Thatcher's privatisation policy as "selling the family silver"?
4 In which year did Ayrton Senna die in a Grand Prix accident?
5 Crimpton-on-Sea was the location for which sitcom?
6 What was the nationality of the first team to reach the South Pole?
7 When was the Panama Canal opened?
8 Which designer made clothes for younger people under the Emporio label?
9 Which monarch was responsible for founding the first English zoo?
10 Haile Gebrselassie set a 2006 sporting world record in which event?
11 In which monster movie film did the character Dr Niko Tatopoulos appear?
12 Which city was known as Camulodunum in Roman times?
13 Who was the first president to live in the White House?
14 What was the official colour of legendary racehorse Arkle?
15 Which soccer team from Holland is named after a mythological Greek figure?
16 Where is the University of Illinois?
17 What does the BT service VoIP stand for?
18 How many tiles are there in a game of mah-jong?
19 Which 1955 movie used "Unchained Melody" as its theme tune?
20 No 1 in the 1990s, "Perfect Day" first appeared on which early 1970s album?
21 What was Cary Grant's middle name?
22 Which sport follows FINA rules?
23 The original Wembley Stadium was costructed for which event?
24 Harold Wilson became Baron of where when he was made a peer?
25 After "The Flapper Vote" in 1928, women over what age could vote in an election?
26 Who was 50 first – Ruby Wax, Julie Walters or Kim Basinger?
27 What school of painting does Mark Rothko belong to?
28 In the silent days of cinema how long would a "two-reeler" last?
29 Serigraphy is also known as what type of printing?
30 Who is Gwyneth Paltrow's mother?

Answers	**Pot Luck 4** *(see Quiz 9)*

1 Photocopies. 2 Computers. 3 Ukraine. 4 English. 5 Taekwondo. 6 Kneeling. 7 X-rays. 8 YMCA. 9 St Mungo. 10 Mormons. 11 132 million. 12 Michael Chang. 13 Scooby-Doo. 14 A dingo. 15 Four. 16 Trevor Berbick. 17 South Pacific. 18 Lord Lucan. 19 Venezuela. 20 Gerald Ford. 21 Jack the Ripper. 22 Elgar. 23 Gioachino Rossini. 24 Switzerland. 25 An electric chair. 26 Fujiyama. 27 Jessica Lange. 28 Ecuador. 29 "The Love I Lost". 30 Falange.

1 Who was the last person to be born first in line to the British throne?
2 Whom did the Queen make the first STD call to?
3 Which Royal's wedding saw the first performance of Mendelssohn's Wedding March?
4 How old was Prince Charles on his engagement to Lady Diana Spencer?
5 Who in 1934 said, "I can see no reason why women should not wear shorts"?
6 Who was the first British monarch to eat a hot dog?
7 Who was the last Royal of the 20th century to serve in the armed forces in a war zone?
8 What is Prince William's penultimate Christian name?
9 How many interviews did the Queen Mother give in the 20th century?
10 Which Queen of Jordan succeeded Queen Noor?
11 From where did the Duke & Duchess of York leave for honeymoon by helicopter?
12 Which Royal celebrated her 18th birthday in August 2006?
13 Who was the first royal bride to include her family's motto on her personal coat of arms?
14 Who was Reviewing Officer at Harry's passing out parade at Sandhurst?
15 On which soap did cast members "visit" Duchy Home Farm?
16 In which month did Edward VIII cease to be Edward VIII?
17 Who won the Ladies' Singles at Wimbledon just before Charles and Diana married?
18 Which Prince of Wales considered marrying a Lady Diana Spencer before Prince Charles?
19 Where did the Duke and Duchess of York consider having their daughters educated until there was a scandal about that school's principal?
20 Sir William Worsley was the father of which Duchess?
21 Medically, what did the Queen Mother receive just before her 101st birthday?
22 At which Cambridge college was Prince Charles educated?
23 What was the name of Diana, Princess of Wales' stepfather?
24 Who is the Queen's second oldest granddaughter?
25 In order of succession, who is higher – Eloise Taylor or Estella Taylor?
26 Who attempted to kidnap Princess Anne in 1974?
27 Whose portrait of Lady Diana Spencer was damaged in the National Portrait Gallery shortly after her wedding to Prince Charles?
28 Who was the first Royal bride to omit the word "obey" in her marriage vows?
29 Which royal family is the richest in the world?
30 Where is Queen Mary's Dolls' House on permanent display?

Answers	Soccer *(see Quiz 10)*

1 Ecudaor. 2 0–0. 3 Switzerland. 4 They had to wear boots. 5 1980. 6 Bolton Wanderers. 7 Real Madrid. 8 Pontiac Silverdome, Detroit. 9 Brondby. 10 £91,750. 11 Mike Bassett: England Manager. 12 Gordon Banks. 13 Two. 14 1966. 15 Tottenham Hotspur. 16 Monaco (Barthez to Manchester United). 17 Aberdeen. 18 Switzerland. 19 Clyde. 20 Tottenham Hotspur. 21 Italy. 22 Burnley. 23 Gerd Müller. 24 Ferencvaros. 25 Tottenham Hotspur. 26 West Ham. 27 Manchester United. 28 Angelo Peruzzi. 29 Rasunda (Stockholm). 30 Yellow.

1 Alex James and Dave Rowntree played in which band?
2 The Olympic Games were first televised by the BBC in which year?
3 Where in suburbia was the sitcom "The Good Life" set?
4 In India what was Suttee?
5 Constantine, Liberius and Sissinius are names of what?
6 What was Abba's only single to make No 1 in the USA?
7 On a keyboard all the letters from F to L are in alphabetical order apart from which one?
8 Who was the Foreign Secretary who lost his seat in the 1997 British General Election?
9 Which retail company was founded by Donald Fisher?
10 Willie Park became the first winner of which sporting trophy?
11 Jane Wyman was the first wife of which famous American?
12 What colour separates the black, red and green bands on the Kenyan flag?
13 If you are misocapnic what do you dislike?
14 Whose first solo album after leaving a chart-topping group was "All Things Must Pass"?
15 Which year marked the 200th anniversary of Hans Christian Andersen's birth?
16 In which year did the first kidney transplant take place?
17 Which first name is derived from Greek for rock or stone?
18 What was Il Divo's third album called?
19 How many episodes of "Fawlty Towers" were made in total?
20 Which country was the first to retain soccer's World Cup?
21 How long does the French presidential term in office last?
22 Bruce Willis was born in which country?
23 What was the number of the Earl of Derby who gave his name to the Classic horse race the Derby?
24 In which country is the city of Panshan?
25 In which century was Robbie Burns born?
26 Who links the groups Slik, Visage and Ultravox?
27 Which element has the atomic number one?
28 Solo round-the-world yachtsman Francis Chichester sailed in which craft?
29 Which famous person was born on Feb 5th, 1948, in Torsby?
30 Esperanto actually means one who does what?

Answers	The 20th Century (1900–1950) *(see Quiz 15)*

1 Humpty Dumpty Store, Oklahoma. 2 Paris Observatory. 3 1946. 4 Pluto. 5 Little Boy. 6 First on National Health. 7 Stockings. 8 July. 9 Folkestone. 10 1900. 11 Popov. 12 Policewomen. 13 Hull. 14 League of German Maidens. 15 13. 16 Japan. 17 Banting & Best. 18 Ernest. 19 Plymouth. 20 Italy. 21 Bao Dai. 22 Bateman. 23 Beaverbrook. 24 Begin. 25 Abercrombie. 26 Balfour. 27 Gertrude Bell. 28 Poland (Ben Gurion). 29 Virginia Woolf. 30 1,100.

1 Which company won a Special Oscar for producing "the pioneer outstanding talking picture"?

2 Which movie classic was remade in the 1950s as "You Can't Run Away from It"?

3 Who won the first ever posthumous Oscar for "Gone with the Wind"?

4 Which studio made the original "King Kong"?

5 Which dance was Fred Astaire and Ginger Rogers' first together on screen?

6 For which movie did James Stewart receive his first Oscar nomination?

7 Which song was Oscar-nominated in the Fred Astaire/Ginger Rogers musical of 1935?

8 Which gossip columnist asked for the withdrawal of the movie "Citizen Kane" because its main character bore a passing resemblance to her boss?

9 Which category of censorship did "The Outlaw" have on its UK release?

10 Who was the prostitute played by Ingrid Bergman in "Dr Jekyll & Mr Hyde"?

11 In which movie did Bogart say, "I'm the only cause I'm interested in"?

12 To which studio did George M Cohan sell the movie rights of his life story?

13 Which piece of music ends the movie "Mrs Miniver"?

14 To the nearest 10 minutes how long did "The Wizard of Oz" last?

15 Which leader banned the Marx Brothers' "Duck Soup"?

16 Who plays Judy Garland's mother in "Meet Me in St Louis"?

17 Where is the setting for Lauren Bacall's screen debut?

18 Whose music accompanied Mickey's broomstick dance in "Fantasia"?

19 Who was the voice of Snow White in Disney's classic?

20 To whom or what did Cary Grant sing "I Can't Give You Anything but Love" in "Bringing Up Baby"?

21 Why does Trevor Howard first assist Celia Johnson in "Brief Encounter"?

22 Where does the climax of the UK's first talkie take place?

23 Who won the only Oscar for "Key Largo"?

24 What was Hitchcock's favourite of his British movies?

25 Which skier was the third screen Tarzan?

26 Who was the fuddy duddy professor in the film which made Dietrich a star?

27 Whose play was the movie "Harvey" based on?

28 Who was Charlie Chaplin's co-star in his last silent movie?

29 Who was Katharine Hepburn's character in "The African Queen"?

30 How old was Elizabeth Taylor when she first kissed Montgomery Clift on screen?

Answers | Pot Luck 7 *(see Quiz 16)*

1 2005. 2 Haltemprice. 3 Pink Floyd. 4 Warner Brothers. 5 59.4. 6 Everton.
7 Freshwater angling. 8 Canada. 9 Scottish. 10 DDT. 11 Crazy. 12 1972.
13 Cabaret. 14 Jim Davidson. 15 Joanna Lumley. 16 Tim Henman. 17 Japan.
18 Grapes. 19 David Dundas. 20 Winston Churchill. 21 23 wickets. 22 Canada/USA.
23 Venus. 24 The Accidental Tourist. 25 Hans Wegner. 26 Jack Nicklaus. 27 Sir
Thomas Cullinan, superintendent at Premier Mine. 28 Paris. 29 IMF. 30 Tipp-Ex.

1 Which store inaugurated supermarket trolleys in 1937?
2 Where was the first speaking clock revealed?
3 In which year did the World Bank open?
4 What was discovered by Clyde Tombaugh?
5 What was the codename of the bomb which was dropped on Hiroshima?
6 Why was Jean Murray's birth near Wigan in 1948 memorable?
7 In 1942 women were allowed to enter the Vatican without wearing what?
8 In which month was the "Beano" first published?
9 In which UK resort was the first international beauty contest held?
10 When did Coca Cola go on sale in Britain?
11 What was the name of the first pilot killed in warfare?
12 In 1914 Miss Allen and Miss Harburn became the first what?
13 Where was Britain's first crematorium opened?
14 What was the female equivalent of the Hitler Youth called?
15 Which lifeboat did "Titanic" survivor Millvina Dean take when she escaped from the doomed ship aged nine weeks?
16 Who joined the Axis Powers after signing the Anti Comintern Pact?
17 Who first isolated insulin?
18 What was the first name of the Duchess of Windsor's second husband?
19 Britain's first woman MP represented which constituency?
20 The Hoare Laval pact allowed the annexation of which country?
21 Who abdicated as Vietnamese Emperor at the end of WWII?
22 Who developed the The Man Who ... cartoons?
23 Who was Minister of Aircraft Production in Winston Churchill's wartime Cabinet?
24 Who was the first head of Israel's Herut Party?
25 Which pioneer town planner drew up plans for green belts in the Great London Plan of 1935?
26 Who was Foreign Secretary during WWI?
27 Who in her capacity as Oriental Secretary to the British High Commissioner helped negotiate the independence of Iraq in the early 1920s?
28 Where was Israel's first Prime Minister born?
29 Who was Vanessa Bell's famous younger sister?
30 Dying in 1931, how many inventions had Thomas Edison patented in his lifetime?

Answers	Pot Luck 6 *(see Quiz 13)*

1 Blur. 2 1948. 3 Surbiton. 4 Widow sacrifice. 5 Popes. 6 Dancing Queen. 7 I. 8 Malcolm Rifkind. 9 GAP. 10 Golf's British Open. 11 Ronald Reagan. 12 White. 13 Tobacco smoke. 14 George Harrison. 15 2005. 16 1950. 17 Peter. 18 Siempre. 19 12. 20 Italy. 21 Seven years. 22 West Germany. 23 12th. 24 China. 25 18th. 26 Midge Ure. 27 Hydrogen. 28 Gipsy Moth IV. 29 Sven Goran Eriksson. 30 Hopes.

1 YouTube was founded in which year?
2 Which constituency did MP Alan B'Stard's represent in TV's "The New Statesman"?
3 "Atom Heart Mother" was the first album to top the UK charts by which long-lasting group?
4 Which film studio released the first talking film?
5 Roger Bannister's first sub-four-minute mile was recorded at 3 minutes and how many seconds?
6 Which club did Mark Hughes join when he left Chelsea?
7 In which sport has Bob Nudd been world champion?
8 Which Commonwealth country was the first to issue a special Christmas stamp?
9 What was the nationality of the first manager to win the European Cup with an English club?
10 Which initials are linked to the discovery by Paul Muller?
11 What was the first top ten hit for Seal?
12 When was the last manned moon landing of the last century?
13 Which musical is based on the writing of Christopher Isherwood?
14 TV presenter Alison Holloway became the third wife of which comic?
15 "Stare Back and Smile" was the autobiography of which actress?
16 Who was the first winner on Wimbledon's new No 1 court in the 1990s?
17 In which country is the city of Nara?
18 Concord and Louise Bonne are both types of what?
19 Whose one and only UK top ten hit was "Jeans On"?
20 Who was Queen Elizabeth II's first Prime Minister?
21 How many wickets did Shane Warne take in his final Test series?
22 Which two countries share the world's longest frontier?
23 Which planet's day is actually longer than its year?
24 For which film did Geena Davis first win an Oscar?
25 Which renowned Danish furniture designer engaged in a lifelong quest to design the perfect chair?
26 Which former golfer shares a birthday with opera star Placido Domingo?
27 Who or what was the fabulous Cullinan Diamond named after?
28 The first solo transatlantic flight started in New York but where did it finish?
29 Usually known by its initials, what was set up at the Bretton Wood Agreement of 1944?
30 Which office item was registered by Wolfgang Dabisch in 1962?

Answers	**Movie Classics** *(see Quiz 14)*

1 Warner Bros. 2 It Happened One Night. 3 Writer Sidney Howard. 4 RKO. 5 Carioca. 6 Mr Smith Goes to Washington. 7 Cheek to Cheek (Top Hat). 8 Louella Parsons. 9 U. 10 Ivy Patterson. 11 Casablanca. 12 Warner Bros. 13 Land of Hope & Glory. 14 101. 15 Benito Mussolini. 16 Mary Astor. 17 Martinique (To Have & Have Not). 18 Paul Dukas. 19 Adriana Caselotti. 20 Katharine Hepburn's pet leopard. 21 She has grit in her eye. 22 British Museum (Blackmail). 23 Claire Trevor. 24 39 Steps. 25 Lex Barker. 26 Emil Jannings. 27 Mary Chase. 28 Paulette Goddard. 29 Rose Sayer. 30 17.

1 What was the last answer Judith Keppel gave to win a million on "Who Wants to be a Millionaire?"?

2 Who was "The Flying Gardener"?

3 What was the name of Amanda Holden's character in "EastEnders"?

4 How many World Cups had there been before the first one was broadcast in colour?

5 Who presented the BBC's "10 O'Clock News" on September 11th 2001?

6 In which series did Tricky Woo appear?

7 In what type of programmes does Charlotte Uhlenbroek mainly appear?

8 What was the first, unsuccessful, spin-off of "Baywatch"?

9 Who was the first woman sports presenter on Independent Television?

10 Who was Channel 4's chief executive during the "Celebrity Big Brother" Shilpa Shetty storm?

11 In 1999 who had a TV special called "Just for You"?

12 Which famous football commentator died the same day that England had their memorable World Cup qualifying win over Germany?

13 At which surgery did Will Preston and Jack Kerruish work?

14 With which celebrity golfer did Tiger Woods appear on US TV aged two?

15 Who was the first US President to be interviewed by Barbara Walters?

16 Which husband and wife presented the Channel 4 programme, "Top Ten TV Lovers"?

17 How long did the Saturday-morning show "Live & Kicking" run?

18 Which Derbyshire Hall became Thornfield in the 2006 BBC "Jane Eyre"?

19 In which year was "Life on Mars" set?

20 Which of Dennis Potter's dramas was the first he directed himself?

21 What was Britain's first daily TV quiz?

22 Who was in Dictionary Corner in Des O'Connor's first week as "Countdown" host?

23 About which series did a cast member say, "When the show got to No 1, I decided it could only be because none of us wears a bra"?

24 Who were the first Dalziel & Pascoe on TV?

25 What was the name of the company in the US comedy "Designing Women"?

26 What did Richard Arnold look at on GMTV?

27 Which show received the first National Television Award for Comedy?

28 Who wrote the novels on which "Lloyd & Hill" was based?

29 Which actress played Annie Blackburn in "Twin Peaks"?

30 Who launched the first Pay TV system?

1 What is another name for tungsten?
2 In the Watergate scandal, the Republican Committee to Re elect the President was known as what?
3 Which city was capital of Spain before Madrid?
4 What does a herpetologist study?
5 What type of fruit features in the title of a Chekhov play?
6 Coffee is named after the city of Kaffa in which country?
7 Against orders, what is Epimethius supposed to have opened?
8 Which present-day place in the East of England was the centre of the ancient kingdom of Lindsey?
9 Who sailed in "Lively Lady"?
10 What did John Speke and James Grant discover in the 19th century?
11 In Da Vinci's masterpiece the Mona Lisa in which direction is the lady looking?
12 How many titles did Jimmy Connors win in his tennis career?
13 What is the most number of letters in the name of any one calendar month?
14 How many storeys are there in the Empire State Building?
15 Who was the world's richest self-made millionaire at the end of the old millennium?
16 Which country did Scotsman Robert Louis Stevenson die in?
17 In which country would you watch Brann playing Bryne at soccer?
18 In the stage farce, where did Charley's Aunt come from?
19 Which of The Beatles has the same name as the patentor of the dental drill?
20 Who wrote "An Accidental MP"?
21 Which referee sent off Wayne Rooney against Portugal in 2006?
22 In 1984 WPC Yvonne Fletcher was shot outside which London Embassy?
23 Who was the first US President to make a visit to China?
24 The first rugby union player to score 50 international tries played for which country?
25 ANDi was the first genetically modified what?
26 What was the first album to make its debut at No 1 in the UK chart?
27 Who was the last British Royal to visit Hong Kong while it was under British rule?
28 Who did Mehmet Ali Agca try to assassinate in 1981?
29 What was the first top ten hit for Simple Minds?
30 In which city did the original Wallace and Gromit models get mislaid in the 1990s?

Answers	**Music Charts** *(see Quiz 20)*

1 The Way I am. **2** Never Had a Dream Come True. **3** Bills, Bills, Bills. **4** Oasis. **5** Written in the Stars. **6** Summertime of Our Lives. **7** Wishing I was Lucky. **8** Arsenal. **9** One week. **10** Deeper Shade of Blue. **11** Bohemian Rhapsody. **12** War of Nerves. **13** Five and Queen. **14** Hercules. **15** Billie. **16** Madison Avenue. **17** Samantha Fox. **18** Gangster Trippin'. **19** E-17. **20** Tsunami. **21** Six. **22** Rolf Harris. **23** Westlife. **24** Des O'Connor. **25** Fairytale of New York. **26** Six. **27** Manchester United. **28** 12. **29** Even After All. **30** When Doves Cry.

Quiz 19 | Animals

Answers – page 257

LEVEL 3

1 What is the second largest species of fish?
2 What type of animals were space travellers Sam and Miss Sam?
3 Which animals spends the largest amount of time asleep?
4 Who first named the gorilla?
5 Which usually weighs the most – a bison, a moose or a polar bear?
6 What are Pacific leatherbacks and Atlantic leatherbacks?
7 Which of these swims the fastest – marlin, sailfish or swordfish?
8 Kittis's hognosed bat is native to which country?
9 What is Rhincodon typus?
10 The devil's hole pupfish restricts its habitat to an isolated part of which US state?
11 What is a Ruppell's griffon?
12 What has the highest reproductive rate of all marsupials?
13 What is another name for the colugo?
14 Approximately how many domestic breeds of dog are there?
15 What is the most socially organised member of the cat family?
16 Which is the largest – giant African snail, giant clam or giant squid?
17 Which creature is unique in its ability to penetrate the quills of a porcupine?
18 What is the only truly amphibious member of the weasel family?
19 The skunk is a major carrier of which disease?
20 The greatest number of feathers counted on a bird was on a what?
21 Which is the largest of the toothed whales?
22 What is the smallest of the Ratitae order?
23 Which flies the fastest – mallard, pintail or teal?
24 Which sense does the Old World vulture lack?
25 What is the most beautiful part of the bulbul?
26 What does the tuatara have on top of its head?
27 What is the only marsupial which specialises in burrowing?
28 Where is the Bolson tortoise native to?
29 What is the San Joaquin leopard lizard also known as?
30 What is the largest living rodent?

Answers	TV Trivia *(see Quiz 17)*

1 Henry II. 2 Chris Beardshaw. 3 Carmen. 4 Eight. 5 Peter Sissons. 6 All Creatures Great and Small. 7 Wildlife. 8 Baywatch Nights. 9 Rachel Heyhoe-Flint. 10 Andy Duncan. 11 Boyzone. 12 Brian Moore. 13 The Beeches. 14 Bob Hope. 15 Richard Nixon. 16 Paul Daniels and Debbie McGee. 17 8 years. 18 Haddon Hall. 19 1973. 20 Blackeyes. 21 Blockbusters. 22 Tom O'Connor. 23 Charlie's Angels. 24 Hale & Pace. 25 Sugarbakers. 26 TV. 27 Men Behaving Badly. 28 Jill McGown. 29 Heather Graham 30 Zenith Radio Corp.

Quiz 20 | Music Charts

Answers – page 258

LEVEL 3

1 What was Eminem's chart success between his first two UK No 1s?
2 What was SClub7's second No 1 which went straight to the top spot?
3 What was Beyonce Knowles' band's first US No 1?
4 Which chart-topping band's line-up has included Tony McCarroll and Gem Archer?
5 What was LeAnn Rimes' first UK hit with another artist?
6 What was A1's follow-up to their UK chart debut?
7 Their biggest hit was "Love is All Around" in 1994, what was their first?
8 Which soccer side charted with "Hot Stuff"?
9 For how long was the NME chart a Top 25?
10 What was Steps' first Top Ten hit of the new millennium?
11 Which classic single topped the chart when Mel C was born?
12 What was All Saints' last hit of the 1990s?
13 With whom did "We Will Rock You" first chart?
14 From which movie was Stephen Gately's solo chart debut?
15 Who was the first lady to top the charts three times before being able to vote in the UK?
16 How are chart toppers Andy Van Dorsselaer and Cheyne Coates better known?
17 Who was the only British female to have three US & UK Top Ten singles in the 1980s?
18 What was Fatboy Slim's second single to enter the UK Top Ten?
19 What did Brian Harvey's band change their name to on their return to the charts in 1998?
20 What was the Manic Street Preachers' last hit of the 1990s?
21 What was Mansun's last 1990s hit to have a number in the title?
22 Who had the final chart topper of the 1960s?
23 Which was the first band to have four UK No 1's in a single year?
24 Who had a Top Twenty hit in 1969 with "Dick a Dum Dum"?
25 What was the Pogues' follow-up to their first Top Ten hit?
26 How many Top Ten hits did Ocean Colour Scene have in a row in the 1990s?
27 Whose last hit of the 1990s was "Move Move Move"?
28 How many successive Top Twenty singles did Prodigy have by the end of the millennium?
29 What was Finley Quaye's first Top Ten single?
30 Which single was Prince's most successful before "Purple Rain"?

Answers	Pot Luck 8 *(see Quiz 18)*

1 Wolfram. 2 CREEP. 3 Valladolid. 4 Reptiles. 5 Cherry. 6 Ethiopia. 7 Pandora's box. 8 Lincoln. 9 Alec Rose. 10 Source of the Nile. 11 To her right. 12 109. 13 Nine. 14 102. 15 Bill Gates. 16 Samoa. 17 Norway. 18 Brazil. 19 George Harrison. 20 Martin Bell. 21 Horacio Elizondo. 22 Libyan. 23 Nixon. 24 Australia. 25 Monkey. 26 Help!. 27 Prince Charles. 28 The Pope. 29 Don't You (Forget About Me). 30 New York.

Quiz 21 | Pot Luck 9

Answers – page 263

LEVEL 3

1 What is named after Benjamin Hall?
2 Who wrote "I'm a Believer" for The Monkees?
3 What is the name for a sentence containing all the letters of the alphabet?
4 How many of the first five letters of Singapore appear on the international car index mark for a car from that country?
5 The time it takes a planet to orbit the sun is called what?
6 In 2007 which company unveiled "Plan A", to become carbon neutral in five years?
7 In which decade of last century did Fiji leave the Commonwealth?
8 Which US state has a capital bearing the name of 15th-century explorer Christopher?
9 "Girls on Film" was the first Top Ten hit for which group?
10 A fear of dust is known as what?
11 Which Marc Bolan song features on the soundtrack of "Moulin Rouge"?
12 Who did Justine Henin-Hardenne beat to claim her third French Open title?
13 What does the musical notation "pesante" mean – heavy and ponderous, unaffected or lively?
14 Who was the Greek goddess of victory?
15 In which month is Canada Day celebrated?
16 Which agoraphobic won the Costa prize for "The Tenderness of Wolves"?
17 In which city did the first Cruft's dog show take place?
18 To the nearest ten, how many minutes did the audience have to scream during the first "Scream" movie?
19 What did Melville Bissell patent in 1881?
20 What was the first Tom Cruise/Nicole Kidman film after their marriage?
21 In which decade was the Brazilian Grand Prix first held?
22 Who coined the name vaccination?
23 Which European leader was executed with his wife in December 1989?
24 On which label did Vengaboys first make No 1 – Positiva, Outpost or Skint?
25 The old London Bridge was dismantled, transported and rebuilt in which US state?
26 As a fully grown male which weighs the most – a baboon, a mandrill or a proboscis monkey?
27 Which Elvis Presley movie featured the song "Return to Sender"?
28 What was the occupation of John Dunlop of tyre fame?
29 In song lyrics, what – according to Buggles – "Killed the Radio Star"?
30 The owner of the Cleveland Browns took over which Premiership club?

Answers	Pot Luck 10 *(see Quiz 23)*

1 Dr Crippen. 2 Google. 3 Henrik Stenson. 4 Norman Tebbit. 5 Simon. 6 Tenerife. 7 Winchester. 8 Blue Peter. 9 Shropshire. 10 200m and 800m. 11 Three. 12 20. 13 Bohemian Rhapsody. 14 Face Value. 15 DeForest. 16 Venezuela. 17 Goodbye Yellow Brick Road. 18 1975. 19 Katharine Hepburn. 20 Simian Films. 21 1666. 22 Kenya. 23 Madonna. 24 Belgium. 25 Nobel prizes. 26 Harry James. 27 Jack Ruby. 28 Italy. 29 1974. 30 Vincent.

1 Which is the largest province of the country which has Madrid as its capital?
2 Which building houses the Bayeux Tapestry?
3 France, Italy, Sweden – which does not have an internet code made up of its first two letters?
4 In which department of Basse Normandie is the village where the famous soft cheese is made?
5 Where are the Bakony Mountains?
6 Where is Switzerland's oldest university?
7 What is Europe's most southerly point?
8 Which country is to the immediate north of the Ukraine?
9 In which Sea are Gotland and Oland?
10 Which language is Euskara?
11 Which city is the burial place of William the Conqueror and Beau Brummel?
12 Which Austrian city was known as Thermae Helveticae to the Romans?
13 Anjou is now part of which French departement?
14 In Austria what is the Fohn?
15 The Campine coalfield is to the east of which country?
16 Which country is to the immediate south of Croatia?
17 Where is the Jotunheimen range of mountains?
18 Which Italian port takes its name from the Greek for elbow?
19 Which language is spoken in Wallonia?
20 What is the capital of Brabant?
21 How many countries border the Federal Republic of Germany?
22 In which country is the city of Esztergom?
23 What is the currency of Slovenia?
24 What is the capital of the German province to the south of Brandenburg?
25 What is the capital of the province to the west of Abruzzio?
26 In which country are the Pripet Marshes?
27 Which river bisects Andorra?
28 Who designed the Finlandia Concert Hall in Helsinki?
29 In which mountain range is Europe's highest peak?
30 Of the ten largest cities in Europe which three were once part of the Soviet Union?

Answers	Unforgettables *(see Quiz 24)*

1 Brian Jones and Jim Morrison. 2 Lake Tanganyika. 3 13 years. 4 331. 5 Somalia. 6 Montserrat Caballe. 7 Hotel de la Reine. 8 Martha Washington. 9 Victor Gollancz. 10 John Reed. 11 Mrs Ronald Reagan. 12 Bernard Herrmann. 13 Dashiel Hammett. 14 Rex Harrison. 15 Alexander Graham Bell. 16 Ian Richardson. 17 19 May. 18 Three. 19 Agatha Christie. 20 Elizabeth Arden. 21 Clement Attlee. 22 Doctor. 23 Giles Gilbert Scott. 24 Leonard. 25 Bertrand Russell. 26 Jennifer Jones. 27 Where's the Bourbon?. 28 John Paul II. 29 Alfred Hitchcock. 30 Frankie Howerd.

1 Which villain had a mistress called Ethel Le Neve?
2 Which company bought YouTube in 2006?
3 Who holed the winning shot in the 2006 Ryder Cup?
4 Which Norman said his father "got on his bike and looked for work"?
5 Who was named as being in The Chipmunks along with Alvin and Theodore?
6 On which island were 583 people killed in a 1970s air disaster?
7 Where is Britain's longest cathedral?
8 Leila Williams was the first female presenter of which long-running TV show?
9 In which English county was the world's first iron bridge built?
10 100m hurdles and which two other track events are included in the World Championship women's heptathlon?
11 How many of Henry VIII's children followed him to the throne?
12 How old was Mike Tyson when he became boxing's youngest ever heavyweight world champion?
13 Which hit was the first single to be No 1 over two separate Christmases?
14 What was the first solo No 1 album for Phil Collins?
15 What was the middle name of Humphrey Bogart?
16 In which country is the city of Maracay?
17 Elton John's original "Candle in the Wind" first featured on which album?
18 In what year did Charlie Chaplin eventually receive a knighthood?
19 Ludlow Ogden married which famous Hollywood actress?
20 Which production company was set up by Hugh Grant and Liz Hurley?
21 In which year was fire insurance first pioneered in London – was it 1666, 1812 or 1914?
22 In which country was Mau Mau a nationalist movement?
23 Stephen Bray and Patrick Leonard have both co-written No 1 singles with which solo singer?
24 In which country did the Battle of Passchendaele take place?
25 Which prizes were first awarded in 1901?
26 Which bandleader did Betty Grable marry in 1943?
27 Involved in a famous 20th-century murder how was Jacob Rubinstein better known?
28 Who held the wooden spoon at the start of the 2007 Six Nations Rugby tournament?
29 In which year was Juan Peron – of "Evita" fame – last in office as President of Argentina?
30 Don McLean's "American Pie" album featured which song that he took to No 1 as a UK single?

Quiz 24 | Unforgettables | Answers – page 262

1 Which two major rock stars died on 3 July, one in 1969 one in 1971?
2 Where did Henry Stanley say, "Dr Livingstone I presume"?
3 For how long were Napoleon and Josephine married?
4 How many weekly radio addresses did Ronald Reagan make?
5 Which country did Audrey Hepburn visit as a UNICEF Ambassador shortly before her death?
6 Which opera star was born on the late Maria Callas's 10th birthday?
7 In which hotel did John Lennon and Yoko Ono have their famous "bed in"?
8 Who was the first First Lady of the USA – although the actual phrase had yet to be coined?
9 Which publisher founded the charity War on Want?
10 Who was the first American to be buried in the Kremlin?
11 What was the actress born Anne Frances Robbins' most famous married name?
12 To whom did Martin Scorsese dedicate "Taxi Driver"?
13 Which novelist investigated the Fatty Arbuckle assault case when working for the Pinkerton Detective Agency?
14 Who edited the anthology of romantic poems "If Love be Love"?
15 Who said on 10th March 1876, "Come here, Watson, I want you"?
16 Which actor played Sir Epicure Mammon in "The Alchemist" at the National, 2006?
17 On what date did Marilyn Monroe famously sing "Happy Birthday" to John F Kennedy?
18 How many No 1 singles did Roy Orbison achieve in the UK during his lifetime?
19 Mary Westmacott is also known as whom?
20 How is cosmetics queen Florence Nightingale Graham better known?
21 Who was the first Labour PM to have an absolute majority in House of Commons?
22 What was the occupation of the first independent President of Malawi?
23 Who designed Battersea Power Station?
24 What was the first name of Baron Callaghan of Cardiff?
25 Who was the first president of CND?
26 Who was the widow of the producer of "Gone with the Wind"?
27 What was Marilyn Monroe's only line of dialogue in the scene which took 59 takes in "Some Like It Hot"?
28 Who was the youngest Pope of the 20th century?
29 Which film director married Alma Reville?
30 Which late comedian's autobiography was called "On My Way I Lost It"?

Answers | European Travel *(see Quiz 22)*

1 Badajoz. 2 William the Conqueror Cultural Centre. 3 Sweden. 4 Orne. 5 Hungary.
6 Basle. 7 Tarifa Point. 8 Belarus. 9 Baltic. 10 Basque. 11 Caen. 12 Baden.
13 Maine et Loire. 14 Wind. 15 Belgium. 16 Bosnia Herzegovina. 17 Norway.
18 Ancona. 19 French. 20 Brussels. 21 Nine. 22 Poland. 23 Jolar. 24 Dresden.
25 Rome. 26 Belarus. 27 Valira. 28 Alvar Aalto. 29 Caucasus. 30 Moscow, St Petersburg and Kiev.

Quiz 25 | Pot Luck 11

Answers – page 267

LEVEL 3

1 Who wrote Blondie's 1999 chart topper "Maria"?
2 "Tenko" was a popular TV series but what does Tenko mean?
3 The first ever programme of "Top of the Pops" was broadcast from which city?
4 Ed Koch is a former mayor of which American city?
5 What is the nationality of actor William Shatner famous as Captain Kirk?
6 What's the job of Jack Nicholson's character in the movie "Wolf"?
7 In which country is the city of Sorocaba?
8 What was the first top ten hit for Wilson Phillips?
9 On which special day did Dirty Den serve divorce papers on Angie in "EastEnders"?
10 In which department did TV MP Jim Hacker first become a minister?
11 In 1995 which visiting side became the first team in 22 years to win a Test series in the West Indies?
12 What did the letter K stand for in the film company name RKO?
13 What was the first name of the late classically trained actor John Gielgud?
14 Joseph Merlin invented what kind of sporting footwear?
15 Who as a youngster was brought up in disguise in Smallville, USA?
16 In which county did the Great Train Robbery take place?
17 How many neck bones does a giraffe have?
18 Who presented the Rugby World Cup to Francois Pienaar in 1995?
19 Which religious movement was founded by Mary Baker Eddy?
20 What was singer songwriter Hoagy Carmichael's real first name?
21 Who was head coach of Los Angeles Galaxy when the Beckham deal was announced?
22 What four nationalities make up the members of Il Divo?
23 Kim Campbell was the first woman PM of which country?
24 According to a Henry Kissinger quote what was "the ultimate aphrodisiac"?
25 Elizabeth Garrett Anderson is recognised as being the first British woman to carry out which profession?
26 Which Mike broke Bob Beaman's 23-year long jump record in 1992?
27 Which boxer coached actor Daniel Day-Lewis for his role in "The Boxer"?
28 Which Indian Prime Minister resigned in the same month that Saddam Hussein became president of Iraq?
29 Johann Christophe Denner invented which musical instrument?
30 In which year did Yasser Arafat become PLO chairman?

Answers	Pot Luck 12 *(see Quiz 27)*

1 Dundalk. 2 May. 3 Invincible (adamas). 4 Cello. 5 Root. 6 Isabella Rossellini.
7 Cuban missile. 8 Ibadan. 9 Fidel Castro. 10 Stephen Dorrell. 11 The Blue Room.
12 University College. 13 The Absinthe Fairy. 14 Private Lives. 15 Sweden (5 points).
16 Leprosy. 17 Texas. 18 Iberus (hence Iberia) 19 Capricorn. 20 William Rodgers.
21 New Zealand. 22 His mother (Statue of Liberty). 23 Iraq. 24 Steven Spielberg.
25 Margot. 26 Valerie. 27 What hath God wrought?. 28 Platform shoes. 29 Nancy
Griffith. 30 Royal Exchange.

1 To whom did Helen Mirren dedicate her 2007 movie BAFTA?
2 Which wife of Robert De Niro appeared in "New York New York"?
3 What is the real name of the actress who played the title role in "Octopussy"?
4 Which role did Lorraine Bracco play in "Goodfellas"?
5 Which pseudonym did Kim Basinger use when she performed as a solo singer in her early career?
6 For which of his movies did Nicolas Cage reputedly swallow a live cockroach?
7 Who was the fourth movie "Batman"?
8 Who traditionally sings the US National Anthem at each season's first home game of baseball team the New York Mets?
9 Who was Oscar nominated for playing Olive in "Little Miss Sunshine"?
10 Who was the big screen's first nude Lady Macbeth?
11 Who was known in France as "le sacre monstre"?
12 Which character did Hugh Grant play in "Music and Lyrics"?
13 Which actress was president of Actors Equity in the US from 1982 to 1985?
14 What was Disney's last hand-painted movie?
15 Which star of "Drugstore Cowboy" is a grand-nephew of the creator of Flash Gordon?
16 Which profession did the director of "If" play in "Chariots of Fire"?
17 What was Daniel Day Lewis's very first movie at the age of 14?
18 Who set up a production company called Tribeca Films?
19 Whose production company was called Memorial Enterprises?
20 Who was Carrie Fisher's first stepmother?
21 Who directed the second "Bridget Jones" movie?
22 Which leader did Anthony Hopkins play in "Victory at Entebbe"?
23 What was Jodie Foster's second movie as director?
24 Who prefaced his first book with, "This book is for people who like movies"?
25 John Huston died during the making of which film, due to be directed by his son?
26 Who did Kirstie Alley play in her debut movie?
27 Which star of "The Exorcist" competed in equestrian events as Martha McDonald?
28 What was Bob Hoskins' next film after his first Oscar nomination?
29 Joel and Ethan Coen are said to have written "Raising Arizona" with which actress in mind?
30 Famous daughter Anjelica Huston played opposite the son of which General in "A Walk with Love and Death"?

| **Answers** | Sporting Legends (see Quiz 28) |

1 Seven. 2 Reggie Jackson. 3 24. 4 Arnold Palmer. 5 13. 6 Elizabeth Ryan. 7 1966. 8 Horacio Elizondo. 9 Backstroke. 10 Philippe Sella. 11 112. 12 Tiger Woods. 13 Bruce Sheldon. 14 Gary Player. 15 Natalie Tauziat. 16 Tuberculosis. 17 1959. 18 Brooklyn Dodgers. 19 Merlin Olsen. 20 Tracey Edwards. 21 Wimbledon. 22 Liz McColgan. 23 Seamus McDonagh. 24 Billie Jean King. 25 Marvin Hart. 26 Huddersfield. 27 Sabatini. 28 Jack Brabham. 29 Melbourne. 30 Knocked overboard on his yacht.

Quiz 27 | Pot Luck 12 | Answers – page 265

1 Which town do The Corrs hail from?
2 In which month was Britain's first official bank holiday?
3 The word diamond comes from a Greek word meaning what?
4 Which musical instrument does Han-Na Chang play?
5 What part of the plant does phylloxera vitifoliae attack?
6 Which actress lost her Lancome contract around her 40th birthday?
7 During which crisis did a US politician comment, "We're eyeball to eyeball and I think the other fellow just blinked"?
8 What is the second largest city of Nigeria?
9 Which world leader was excommunicated in 1962?
10 Who was health secretary when the link between BSE and CJD was first admitted?
11 In which play did Elle Macpherson make her stage debut?
12 What is the oldest Oxford college?
13 Which role did the singer of the No 1 "Can't Get You Out of My Head" play in "Moulin Rouge"?
14 In which play did Noel Coward write, "Very flat, Norfolk"?
15 Which team topped the 2002 World Cup Group stage with fewest points?
16 What is another name for Hansen's disease?
17 Alaska replaced which state as the USA's largest?
18 What was the Roman name for the River Ebro?
19 What is Mel Gibson's star sign?
20 Which male founder of the SDP had the surname nearest the end of the alphabet?
21 Where did Jim Bulger form a coalition government in December 1996?
22 Who did FA-Bartholdi use as a model for his most famous sculpture?
23 The ancient civilisation of Sumeria is now in which country?
24 Who directed the movie about Gigolo Joe, a robot boy and his teddy bear?
25 What was Anne Frank's older sister called?
26 What was the first name of TS Eliot's widow?
27 What was the first message transmitted by telegraph?
28 What were buskins?
29 Who made the album "Clock without Hands"?
30 What was the Stock Exchange called when it was first founded?

| **Answers** | **Pot Luck 11** *(see Quiz 25)* |

1 Jimmy Destri. 2 Roll call. 3 Manchester. 4 New York. 5 Canadian. 6 Book editor. 7 Brazil. 8 Hold On. 9 Christmas Day. 10 Administrative Affairs. 11 Australia. 12 Keith. 13 Arthur. 14 Roller skate. 15 Superman. 16 Bedfordshire. 17 Seven. 18 Nelson Mandela. 19 Christian Science. 20 Hoagland. 21 Frank Yallop. 22 French, Swiss, Spanish & American. 23 Canada. 24 Power. 25 Doctor. 26 Powell. 27 Barry McGuigan. 28 Morarji Desai. 29 Clarinet. 30 1968.

1 How many times did Jaden Gil Agassi's mum win Wimbledon?
2 Who was the second man, after Babe Ruth, to hit three home runs in one baseball World Series game?
3 For how many years was Matt Busby boss of Manchester United?
4 Who won golf's British Open in its centenary year?
5 How many conversions were among the 35 points Jonny Wilkinson scored at Twickenham in February 2001?
6 Who died on the day that Billie Jean King beat her Wimbledon title record?
7 When did Jack Nicklaus win his third US Masters?
8 Which referee sent off Zinedine Zidane against Italy in the World Cup Final?
9 Which of backstroke, butterfly or freestyle did Mark Spitz not swim at Munich in 1972?
10 Who won a record 111 international caps for Rugby between 1982 and 1995?
11 How many games were played in Wimbledon's longest match?
12 Whom did Nick Faldo hand a green jacket to in April 1997 in Georgia?
13 Whom did Mike Tyson beat to win his third world heavyweight title?
14 Who was the first US Open golf winner to be neither British nor American?
15 Against whom did Jana Novotna play her third Wimbledon Singles Final?
16 Harry Vardon won two British Open golf titles after contracting which illness?
17 Which was Pele's most successful individual year as a goalscorer?
18 Against whom did New York Yankees pitcher Don Larson pitch a World Series perfect game?
19 Who completed the Los Angeles Rams' "Fearsome Foursome" along with Deacon Jones, Lamarr Lundy and Roosevelt Grier?
20 In the Whitbread Round the World Race who skippered "Maiden"?
21 Of her 24 Grand Slam titles which did Margaret Court win the least?
22 Who was the only female BBC Sports Personality of the Year in the 1990s?
23 Who did Evander Holyfield beat in his first win by a knockout in the 1990s?
24 Who was the first president of the WTA?
25 Who won the first 20th-century heavyweight boxing championship to be stopped?
26 For which team did Albert Rosenfield score his record 80 Rugby League tries in 1914?
27 Who did Steffi Graf beat to win her first 1990s Wimbledon Singles title?
28 Who was the first man to win the world F1 championship in his own car?
29 Where did Shane Warne take his 700th Test wicket?
30 How did Eric Tabarly meet his death?

Answers	**Movies Who's Who?** *(see Quiz 26)*

1 Ian Richardson. 2 Diahnne Abbott. 3 Maude Wikstrum. 4 Karen Hill. 5 Chelsea. 6 Vampire's Kiss. 7 George Clooney. 8 Glenn Close. 9 Abigail Breslin. 10 Francesca Annis. 11 Charles Bronson. 12 Alex Fletcher. 13 Ellen Burstyn. 14 The Little Mermaid. 15 Matt Dillon. 16 Schoolmaster (Lindsay Anderson). 17 Sunday Bloody Sunday. 18 Robert De Niro. 19 Albert Finney. 20 Elizabeth Taylor. 21 Beeban Kidron. 22 Yitzhak Rabin. 23 Home for the Holidays. 24 Leslie Halliwell. 25 Mr North. 26 Lt Saavik (Star Trek II). 27 Linda Blair. 28 A Prayer for the Dying. 29 Holly Hunter. 30 Dayan.

Quiz 29 | Pot Luck 13

1 Which film director said, "Not only is there no God, try getting a plumber at weekends"?
2 What was the first building in England to be lit by incandescent light?
3 Who accompanied Dr Michael Stroud on the first unsupported crossing of the Antarctic?
4 Which name is the Hebrew for trickster or supplanter?
5 What was the name of the first nuclear submarine to circumnavigate the world underwater?
6 Who was the first British monarch to visit China?
7 Which were the last two imperial territories in Africa?
8 In which city was the premiere of Orson Welles' first film?
9 In India, which is furthest south, Bombay, Calcutta, or Hyderabad?
10 Who developed the computer language Java?
11 Which magazine did Charles Russell found?
12 The original Globe Theatre burned down during which Shakespeare play?
13 What did the middle initial stand for in the name of the author who wrote "Three Men in a Boat"?
14 In the UK what was the first speed limit for cars in the country as opposed to town?
15 Which 1960s Norman Jewison film won five Oscars?
16 What does the Arabic word jihad mean?
17 Which island did Columbus call St Iago?
18 Which 19th-century Prime Minister was the subject of a biography written by Baron Jenkins of Hillhead after he left Parliament?
19 In Germany 2006, who got a four-game ban for elbowing USA's Brian McBride?
20 Which Henry James novel was the subject of an opera by Benjamin Britten?
21 Who wrote the TV series "Clocking Off" and "Linda Green"?
22 With which architect did Gertrude Jekyll work?
23 Who was the first president of Iran?
24 Which monarch knighted Sir Winston Churchill?
25 In which US state is the George Rogers Clark National Historical Park?
26 Who reputedly said, "Die my dear doctor. That's the last thing I shall do"?
27 Which Pope excommunicated King John and declared the Magna Carta void?
28 In cars, what was the Procon Ten?
29 What did the island of Hispaniola later become?
30 Among his first five consecutive Tour de France wins, in which year did Miguel Indurain set the record for the fastest average speed?

1 Vermouth (Wermut). 2 Carolyn Murphy. 3 Rachel Portman. 4 Elena Xanthoudakis. 5 Rio Ferdinand. 6 Madonna. 7 Pam Warren. 8 Nevada. 9 Return of Apollo 11 from the Moon. 10 Herbert Marcuse. 11 Jo Moore. 12 Rome. 13 Diamonds are a Girl's Best Friend. 14 Kirov. 15 Terry Venables. 16 Scott Walker. 17 Thomas Gresham. 18 Chris Smith. 19 Wasp. 20 Resolution. 21 Claire Danes. 22 Over the Moon. 23 Noel Coward. 24 Cairo. 25 Martin Campbell. 26 Dith Pran. 27 Billy Crystal. 28 Albert Camus & TS Eliot. 29 The Cochran. 30 Jim Davidson.

1 Whom did Major run against to become Tory Party leader and PM?
2 Who was the first man to be General Secretary and President of the USSR?
3 Who was Chairman of the Republican National Committee during the Watergate scandal?
4 What was Hosni Mubarak's profession before entering politics?
5 Jacques Santer became president of the European Commission after Britain's veto of whom?
6 What was the name of the autobiography of the first woman leader of a British political party?
7 Who succeeded Willy Brandt as Chancellor of West Germany?
8 Which US president won the Pulitzer Prize for "Profiles in Courage"?
9 Who was Albania's second Prime Minister in 1997?
10 Who was the first President of a united post-WWII Germany?
11 Who became Israel's acting PM after the assassination of Rabin?
12 Gro Harlem Brundtland was the first woman PM in which country?
13 Which Conservative Canadian politician served between Pierre Trudeau's two terms of office?
14 Who was the first British President of the EU?
15 Before becoming Pope Karol Jozef Wojtyia was Archbishop of where?
16 At which educational institution did Bill Clinton meet Hillary Rodham?
17 Which then leader won the 1969 Hobart Ocean race?
18 How was Prince Ras Tafari Makonnen better known?
19 Who was the first living ex-PM of Australia not to accept the Companion to the Order of Australia after he left politics?
20 Who was President of Chile during the Falklands conflict?
21 How long after becoming German Chancellor did Hitler assume the title of Führer?
22 Who was the longest-serving US President of the 1970s?
23 Which Austrian president was a former Secretary General to the UN?
24 Winston Churchill became Chancellor of the Exchequer under which PM?
25 Who succeeded Chairman Mao as Chairman of China's ruling Communist Party?
26 What was Tony Blair's first responsibility in Labour's Shadow Cabinet?
27 Who did Ronald Reagan defeat the second time he became US president?
28 Who was the last King of Greece in the 20th century?
29 Who was the second President of France's Fifth Republic?
30 Who was the first and last Executive President of the USSR?

Answers	TV Adverts *(see Quiz 32)*

1 Nationwide. 2 Mir. 3 Labi Siffre. 4 Fly Away. 5 Michael Jackson. 6 Peter O'Toole. 7 The Joker. 8 Schwartz. 9 Frank Muir. 10 Elgar's Cello Concerto in E Minor. 11 Halifax. 12 (Auto) Windscreens. 13 Benylin. 14 Meg Smith. 15 Penelope Keith. 16 Benecol. 17 David Ginola. 18 Paul Dukas. 19 Giuseppe Verdi. 20 Peter Sellers. 21 Optivita. 22 Trevor Eve. 23 Sainsbury's. 24 Lesley Dunlop. 25 Mr Oizo. 26 Specsavers. 27 Pastoral Symphony. 28 Advertising Standards Authority. 29 Junk food adverts. 30 Gibbs SR.

1 Which wine takes its name from the German for wormwood, an early ingredient?

2 Who replaced Liz Hurley as the face of Estée Lauder?

3 Who won an Oscar for the score of "Emma"?

4 Which soprano won the 2006 International Mozart Competition?

5 Which player played all of Sven's first and last games as England boss?

6 Which superstar had a Max Factor cosmetics contract for just one year?

7 Which co-winner of the Woman of the Year 2001 was a survivor of the Paddington rail crash?

8 Where in the US were atomic bombs first tested?

9 What did Richard Nixon describe as, "The greatest week in the history of the world since the Creation"?

10 Who wrote "One Dimensional Man"?

11 Who sent an e mail saying it would be a good day to bury bad news the day the World Trade Center was hit?

12 Which was the world's largest city at the end of the first millennium?

13 Which song has the line, "We all lose our charms in the end"?

14 Which ballet company was called the Maryinsky until 1935?

15 Which former England football manager shares a birthday with cricketer Kapil Dev?

16 Which 60s/70 star produced Pulp's "We Love Life"?

17 Who founded what was to become the Stock Exchange?

18 Who did Tessa Jowell replace in Tony Blair's Cabinet after the 2001 election?

19 What is an ichneumon fly?

20 What was the name of the first ship to cross the Antarctic Circle?

21 Who was the voice of Princess Mononoke in the "Studio Ghibli" movie?

22 In which play did a 65+ Joan Collins star in skimpy underwear in 2001?

23 Who said, "Work is much more fun than fun"?

24 Where did the last Shah of Iran die?

25 Who directed Pierce Brosnan's first outing as 007?

26 Who is the central character in "The Killing Fields"?

27 Who produced and co-wrote the 2001 movie where Julia Roberts and Catherine Zeta Jones played sisters?

28 Which two winners of a Nobel Prize for Literature both died on 4th January, one in 1960 and one in 1965?

29 What was the name of the first dishwasher?

30 Whose autobiography was called "Close to the Edge"?

Answers | Pot Luck 13 *(see Quiz 29)*

1 Woody Allen. 2 Gateshead Town Hall. 3 Ranulph Fiennes. 4 Jacob. 5 Triton. 6 Elizabeth II. 7 Mozambique & Angola. 8 New York (Citizen Kane). 9 Hyderabad. 10 Sun Microsystems. 11 The Watchtower. 12 Henry VIII. 13 Klapka. 14 4 mph. 15 In the Heat of the Night. 16 Holy War/Struggle. 17 Jamaica. 18 William Gladstone. 19 Daniele de Rossi. 20 The Turn of the Screw. 21 Paul Abbott. 22 Edwin Lutyens. 23 Abolhassan Bani Sadr. 24 Elizabeth II. 25 Indiana. 26 Lord Palmerston. 27 Innocent III. 28 Collapsible steering wheel. 29 Haiti. 30 His second win, 1992.

1 Which Building Society boasts that it is "proud to be different"?
2 Where was the first TV ad filmed in space actually filmed?
3 Who sang the song for the 2001 ad for the Peugeot 307?
4 In 1999 which song was the first advert No 1 for three years?
5 Who was the first artist to appear in a Pepsi ad?
6 Which veteran actor appeared in the ad for Zurich insurance?
7 Which Steve Miller Band song advertised jeans?
8 Who sponsored "Richard & Judy" on their Channel 4 return at the beginning of 2007?
9 Which writer advertised Cadbury's Fruit & Nut accompanied by music by Tchaikovsky?
10 Which music used in "Hilary & Jackie" encouraged the drinking of Buxton Spring Water?
11 Which building society fell foul of Equity for using its own employees in an ad?
12 Which part of a car is connected with the "Toreador's Song" from "Carmen"?
13 Which cough mixture was Pavarotti's "theme song" used to advertise?
14 What was the name of the first woman to appear in a UK TV ad?
15 Which ex-"Good Life" cast member became the voice behind Lurpak butter?
16 "Countdown"'s statistician extolled the virtues of which margarine?
17 Which footballer was "worth it"?
18 Who wrote the "Sorcerer's Apprentice", used in an ad for round tea bags?
19 Whose "Requiem Mass" accompanied the virtues of Irn Bru?
20 Who was the first voice of the PG Tips chimps?
21 Which oat cereal was advertised by Ray Winstone?
22 Which actor's wife was in the famous long-running Gold Blend coffee ad?
23 Which supermarket chain employs the Naked Chef?
24 Which "Where the Heart is" star passed around the Kleenex tissues?
25 Who recorded the seventh No 1 hit to be associated with Levi jeans?
26 Who sponsored "Countdown" at the time Des O'Connor took over?
27 Which Beethoven Symphony advertised Blue Band margarine?
28 Which organisation makes sure that all advertising meets certain codes of practice?
29 In November 2006, Ofcom announced a ban on what during programmes targeted at under-16s?
30 Toothpaste was the first product advertised on UK TV – but which brand?

Answers	**World Leaders** *(see Quiz 30)*

1 Michael Heseltine and Douglas Hurd. 2 Leonid Brezhnev. 3 George Bush Sr. 4 Pilot. 5 Jean Luc Dehaene. 6 Margaret Thatcher: The Downing Street Years. 7 Helmut Schmidt. 8 JF Kennedy. 9 Bashkim Fino. 10 Richard Von Weizsacker. 11 Shimon Peres. 12 Norway. 13 Joseph Clark. 14 Roy Jenkins. 15 Cracow. 15 Yale Law School. 17 Edward Heath. 18 Haile Selassie. 19 Paul Keating. 20 Augusto Pinochet. 21 A year. 22 Richard Nixon. 23 Kurt Waldheim. 24 Stanley Baldwin. 25 Hua Guofeng. 26 Energy. 27 Walter Mondale. 28 Constantine II. 29 Georges Pompidou. 30 Mikael Gorbachev.

1 At which meeting was the establishing of an International Monetary Fund proposed?

2 How is Iran's Dasht e Kavir also known?

3 Which is farthest north – Kerry, Limerick or Munster?

4 Which famous car did Issigonis design as well as the Mini?

5 WG Grace died on which future England captain's 15th birthday?

6 Where was the first permanent English settlement in the New World?

7 The lady born Sheila Gilhooly wrote the second part of whose autobiography?

8 Who described Herbert Von Karajan as "a kind of musical Malcolm Sargent"?

9 What does M stand for in HTML?

10 In 1994 Johannesburg was made capital of which region?

11 Which painter, and sister of a famous painter was the model and mistress of Rodin?

12 What is the southernmost city of New Zealand?

13 Who is the heroine of "Fear of Flying"?

14 Who made his debut in "The Wise Little Hen" in 1934?

15 Which classic did Kylie Minogue sing when she starred in the show which opened the Fox Studios in Sydney in 1999?

16 On which Channel is Alaska's capital?

17 Who broke the solo flight record to Cape Town in 1932?

18 What was the speed limit raised to when it no longer required a person with a red flag to walk in front of a motor vehicle?

19 Where did "The Mousetrap" have its first night in the West End?

20 Which newspaper published the first crossword?

21 Where is Yupik or Yuk spoken?

22 How are the Sandwich Islands now known?

23 Which UN Secretary General negotiated peace in the Iran–Iraq War?

24 Who did Helmut Kohl overtake as Germany's longest serving Chancellor in 1995?

25 What was Prince Philip's military rank when he married Princess Elizabeth?

26 Which Great Britain forward was sacked by Leeds Rhinos in January 2006?

27 What is the English title of the play "La Cantatrice Chauve"?

28 "Whom the Gods Would Destroy" was an episode in a series about which TV detective?

29 In which city did Tchaikovsky die?

30 In which month did Margaret Thatcher announce her resignation as Prime Minister?

Answers	Pot Luck 16 *(see Quiz 35)*

1 Australian Open (2007). 2 The Colosseum in Rome. 3 David Scarboro. 4 Wrigley's Chewing Gum. 5 Likeness. 6 Rue Cambon. 7 Jordan. 8 Alexander Korda. 9 Michelle. 10 Appendix. 11 Kuwait City. 12 Margarine. 13 WH Auden. 14 Under a Blackpool tram. 15 Cramp. 16 Grover Cleveland. 17 1400. 18 Millais. 19 Thomas Jefferson's. 20 The Catcher in the Rye. 21 US Open. 22 Sweden. 23 Southwark. 24 2 mph. 25 Idaho. 26 Lambeth. 27 Lanzarote. 28 Pall Mall. 29 Hamburg. 30 John F Kennedy.

1 What was the name of the first storm to be given a name?
2 Which volcanic rock is named after a mountain range in South America?
3 What is our Solar System's nearest stellar neighbour?
4 Which Asian country has the greatest area of inland water?
5 What is the highest waterfall in Norway?
6 What is the next largest body in the Solar System after Venus?
7 What is the largest lake in the UK after Neagh?
8 In which US state is the Mammoth cave system?
9 What is V4641 Sgr?
10 What was the first asteroid to be discovered?
11 Where was the meteorite Hoba West found?
12 What is the world's highest island after New Guinea?
13 What is the name of the nearest planetary nebula to the Earth?
14 What percentage of the sky does the smallest constellation take up?
15 Which of the following is the brightest – Rigel, Sirius or Vega?
16 What was the second planet to have been visited by a spacecraft?
17 On which island is the Aceh province that was devastated by the 2004 tsunami?
18 Which state along with Texas and Nebraska is known as Tornado Alley?
19 About how many million years did the longest ice age last?
20 Which planet has the longest day in the solar system?
21 Which element discovered in 1931 is the rarest on Earth?
22 What is the defined visibility of a sea fog?
23 Which nebula is brightest in the night sky?
24 In which constellation is Procyon?
25 In which constellation is the Hyades cluster?
26 At which university is the McDonald Observatory?
27 Where was the meteorite Rowton found?
28 Which Asian Sea is the deepest?
29 From which country was the Andromeda Galaxy first observed?
30 After Pluto which is the next furthest body from the Sun?

1 In which Grand Slam final did a woman first umpire a Men's Final?
2 Which landmark was called the Flavian Amphitheatre when it opened?
3 Who played Mark Fowler in "EastEnders" before Todd Carty?
4 What was the first recorded purchase using a bar code?
5 The word icon comes from a Greek word meaning what?
6 In which street did Coco Chanel found her fashion house?
7 What is pop star Gabrielle's son called?
8 Who founded London Film Productions in 1932?
9 What is Cameron Diaz's middle name?
10 In 1885, Mary Gartside was the first person to have which part of the body successfully removed?
11 The industrial suburb of Shuwaikh is in which city?
12 Which food item was patented by Hippolyte Mege Mouries?
13 Which poet's centenary took place on 21st February 2007?
14 In "Coronation Street", how did Alan Bradley meet his death?
15 What is the result if lactic acid accumulates in the muscles during exercise?
16 Who was the first US President to marry while in office?
17 How many kilometres are there from Great Britain's most south-westerly tip to its northernmost one?
18 Who painted the picture which gave Lillie Langtry her nickname of the Jersey Lily?
19 Which President's grandchild was the first baby to be born in the White House?
20 Which book was John Lennon's murderer carrying when he killed the rock star?
21 What was golfer Geoff Ogilvy's first major?
22 What was the first European country to issue banknotes?
23 In which part of London is the Menier Chocolate Factory theatre?
24 In the UK what was the first speed limit for cars in town?
25 What is the USA's Spud State as it produces over a quarter of the country's potato crop?
26 In which London borough is the cricket ground owned by the Duchy of Cornwall?
27 What is the most easterly of the Canary Islands?
28 What was the first street in the world to be lit by gas lamps?
29 The first hour of "Tomorrow Never Dies" is set in which European city?
30 Who, when asked how he became a war hero said, "they sank my boat"?

Answers | Pot Luck 15 (see Quiz 33)

1 Bretton Woods Conference. 2 Great Salt Desert. 3 Limerick. 4 Morris Minor. 5 Douglas Jardine. 6 Jamestown. 7 John Peel's. 8 Thomas Beecham. 9 Mark up. 10 Gauteng. 11 Gwen John. 12 Invercargill. 13 Isadora Wing. 14 Donald Duck. 15 Diamonds are a Girl's Best Friend. 16 Gastineau. 17 Amy Johnson. 18 14 mph. 19 Ambassadors Theatre. 20 New York World. 21 Southern Alaska/Siberia. 22 Hawaii. 23 Perez De Cuellar. 24 Konrad Adenauer. 25 Lieutenant. 26 Danny Ward. 27 The Bald Prima Donna. 28 Lewis. 29 St Petersburg. 30 November.

1 Which band was formed by Anthony Kiedis and Michael Balzary?
2 Which single gave The Spice Girls their ninth No 1?
3 At which Sheffield pub did the Arctic Monkeys perform their first gig?
4 On which label did Jamiroquai release their first single?
5 Which top-selling performer was born in Louisiana on 2nd December 1981?
6 Who directed the video of Michael Jackson's best-selling album?
7 How is Eileen Edwards better known?
8 For which 1980s movie did the oldest woman to have a UK No 1 win an Oscar?
9 How was Chris Hamill better known?
10 Which actress directed the video of Belinda Carlisle's first No 1?
11 Who was the first band to top both the singles and album charts with their debut releases?
12 Who sang "I Don't Like Mondays" with Bob Geldof in a Wembley Stadium concert in 1995?
13 Who appeared as the character Mimi Clifton in "Midsomer Murders"?
14 Who won the Best New Act Grammy of 1983?
15 How was Hilary Lester known on the single "Save Your Love"?
16 Who was the first British female to top the charts on both sides of the Atlantic with the same single?
17 Which soccer star provided rap contributions to "World in Motion"?
18 Who had the original hit with Bombalurina's biggest 1990 hit?
19 Who sang Bart's lines on The Simpsons' first No 1 hit in the UK?
20 Who was the oldest lady Eric Clapton was singing with on his first No 1?
21 Who was the first non-Briton to represent the UK in the Eurovision Song Contest?
22 Which singer's brother was drummer with Billy J Kramer's backing band?
23 Who released the album "Organic" in 1996?
24 Who had a 1990s No 1 from the West End show in which he was starring?
25 Rozonda Thomas was a member of which trio?
26 Who made the album "Almost Naked", with appropriate sleeve, in 1996?
27 "Still D.R.E." was the first Top Ten hit for which artist?
28 Which late singer wrote the musical "Apples" in 1989?
29 The bands Garden Wall and Anon amalgamated to form who?
30 Who collaborated with Elvis Costello on "Painted from Memory"?

Answers	Natural Phenomena *(see Quiz 34)*

1 Carol. 2 Andesite. 3 Proxima centauri. 4 India. 5 Utigard. 6 Mars. 7 Erne. 8 Kentucky. 9 Black hole. 10 Ceres. 11 Namibia. 12 Akutan. 13 Helix. 14 0.16%. 15 Sirius. 16 Venus. 17 Sumatra. 18 Iowa. 19 70. 20 Venus. 21 Astatine. 22 1000 yds. 23 Orion. 24 Canis minor. 25 Taurus. 26 Texas. 27 Shropshire. 28 South China. 29 Germany. 30 Neptune.

Quiz 37 | Pot Luck 17

Answers – page 279

1 The first Top Ten hit for Sash! had a title in which language?
2 In which decade was the Italian Grand Prix first held?
3 How long is the rope at the start of a water-skiing competition?
4 Kate Winslet was nominated for a BAFTA in 2007 for which movie?
5 What contained a poleyn and a pauldron?
6 In which country is the city of Cali?
7 Apart from in America, in which country is the city of Salem found?
8 Which Bananarama star went on to join Shakespear's Sister?
9 In which TV series did Johnny Depp play a character named Tom Hanson?
10 How is TV comic Cyril John Mead better known?
11 In which century was Leonardo da Vinci born?
12 In what type of car did James Dean meet his death?
13 How many rivers are there in the United Arab Emirates?
14 In which avenue is the White House situated?
15 How is French Somaliland now known?
16 What was the first Top Ten hit for Nightcrawlers?
17 Where is Hellgate Bridge?
18 Mt Godwin-Austen is also known by which letter and number?
19 Who was Education Secretary, Home Secretary and Chancellor of the Exchequer in the 1990s?
20 How many James Bond films were released during the lifetime of creator Ian Fleming?
21 In which year will Alcoholics Anonymous celebrate their centenary?
22 In which Chinese Year was Beyonce born?
23 What common factor links children of Cheryl Baker and children of Mollie Sugden?
24 Who played Ron Jenkins in "Coronation Street"?
25 Which hit got to No 2 simultaneously in November 1995 with two separate groups?
26 Who in Gilbert and Sullivan is "a dealer in magic and spells"?
27 Which country do the Aleutian Islands belong to?
28 What does the Arabic word intifada mean?
29 In which ocean are the Maldives?
30 In which London borough was the first cash dispenser installed?

Answers	Celebs *(see Quiz 39)*

1 Catherine Zeta Jones. 2 Kate Middleton. 3 Nino Cerruti. 4 Richmond upon Thames.
5 Moses & Dylan. 6 Kate Capshaw. 7 Jean Paul Gaultier. 8 Lauren. 9 Miranda
Priestly. 10 Elizabeth Taylor. 11 Languages. 12 Burt Reynolds. 13 Transplant patient.
14 Ian Hislop. 15 Neil Cunningham. 16 Politicians' wives. 17 19. 18 Grays, Essex.
19 Custard pie. 20 2006. 21 Robbie Williams. 22 Wilnelia. 23 Lawson. 24 Elton
John. 25 Renny Harlin. 26 Meg. 27 18 years. 28 Advertiser's logo. 29 1958. 30
Elton John.

1 Which is further north – St Lucia or St Vincent?
2 Where was the world's largest shopping centre opened in 1985?
3 In 1990, in which country was the world's largest McDonald's?
4 Which Tower in Hong Kong is 100 storeys high?
5 In which country did fashion designer Cabeen launch his men's range of clothes?
6 What is Ecuador's largest Pacific seaport?
7 Where is the Seacon Square shopping centre?
8 Which is further south – Atlanta or Dallas?
9 Which country has the internet code .lk?
10 Where was the first state-subsidised theatre in the English-speaking world opened?
11 Which Canal links the Ebrie Lagoon and the Gulf of Guinea?
12 Which of these islands is the largest – Great Britain, Java or Sumatra?
13 What does the Mississippi-Missouri eventually flow into?
14 Which of these deserts is the smallest – Great Basin, Great Sandy or Great Victoria?
15 Why is Amarillo, Texas, so called?
16 On which river is Jordan's capital?
17 The capital of Maryland is on which river?
18 Which of these Seas is the largest – Arabian, Coral or South China?
19 The Appalachian mountains end in the centre of which state?
20 On which island does the Otira Rail Tunnel run?
21 Which of the following Australian cities is the most southerly – Melbourne, Perth or Sydney?
22 What is the Great Slave?
23 What was Brazil's first planned city?
24 What is the principal language of Andhra Pradesh?
25 Palmerston, Mangaia and Rarotonga are among which islands?
26 In which sea do the so-called ABC islands lie?
27 Which town is closest to the Everest base camp – Kathmandu, Namche or Sagarmatha?
28 In 2000 which was the largest city in the world by population?
29 Where is the "Leap the Dips" roller coaster?
30 The Dogon are inhabitants of where?

Answers	Pot Luck 18 *(see Quiz 40)*

1 Marie Antoinette. 2 Hamish Macbeth. 3 Anne Reid. 4 Wine. 5 Kandy. 6 Texas. 7 Benjamin Netanyahu. 8 Ruth Ellis (last woman to be hanged in Britain). 9 Sicily. 10 Felix Unger. 11 Sandie Shaw. 12 A Bridge Too Far. 13 Vincent Price. 14 Give It Away. 15 Hattie McDaniel. 16 Hit by a cricket ball. 17 Dr No. 18 Liberia and Ethiopia. 19 Nigeria. 20 Dwight Eisenhower. 21 Austin, Minnesota. 22 England (2 goals). 23 Springfield, Illinois. 24 Comédie Française. 25 Sulby. 26 Busta Rhymes. 27 1988. 28 Momofuku Ando. 29 Grand National. 30 Uranus.

1 Who was the highest-placed mother in "Celebrity Bodies" magazine poll of autumn 2001?

2 In February 2007, who was voted top natural beauty in a poll commissioned by a biscuit company?

3 For which fashion house did Armani first work?

4 The older Attenborough brother is Baron of where?

5 What were the names of Woody Allen's adopted children with Mia Farrow?

6 Who was Mrs Spielberg after Amy Irving?

7 Who designed the dress Nicole Kidman wore when she won her first Oscar?

8 Which designer's real surname is Lifschitz?

9 Which character did Meryl Streep play in "The Devil Wears Prada"?

10 Who hosted "Victoria's Secret Fashion Show" in Cannes in 2000 with Elton John?

11 What did chef Antonio Carluccio study in Vienna?

12 Who was the first male centrefold in "Playgirl" magazine?

13 In 1997 Baebhen Schuttke became Britain's youngest what?

14 Who said, after losing a libel case, "If this is justice, I'm a banana"?

15 Who designed Ffion Hague's wedding dress?

16 Linda McDougal wrote a book about which group of women?

17 How old was Lady Diana Spencer when she became engaged?

18 Which town in which county does Russell Brand hail from?

19 What was Bill Gates hit in the face with on a trip to Belgium in 1998?

20 Which year marked the 50th anniversary of the Prince Rainier/Grace Kelly marriage?

21 Which celeb's parents ran the Red Lion pub in Burslem?

22 What is Mrs Bruce Forsyth called?

23 What was Twiggy's surname when she was a presenter of "This Morning"?

24 Who is the famous partner of David Furnish?

25 Who was Geena Davis's third husband?

26 What was the first name of the first Mrs Noel Gallagher?

27 For how many years did Andrew Lloyd Webber's show on roller skates run in the West End?

28 In 1987 Luis Reina became the first matador in the bull ring to wear what?

29 In which year were Michael Jackson, Madonna and Prince all born?

30 Which pop star received a knighthood in the same honours list as Tom Finney?

---

1 Jason Schwartzmann featured in which 2006 film directed by Sofia Coppola?
2 Which series took place in Lochdubh?
3 Which ex-"Corrie" star played Catherine Tate's mother in "The Bad Mother's Handbook"?
4 What would stum be added to, to give it more strength?
5 How is the sacred city of Senkadagala now known?
6 Odessa is found in Washington and which other US state?
7 Who beat Simon Peres in the Israeli elections of 1996?
8 "Dance with the Stranger" was about whom?
9 Marsala wine is produced on which island?
10 Which character did Jack Lemmon play in "The Odd Couple"?
11 Who was the first British female soloist to have a hat trick of chart No 1 hits?
12 In which war film did the character Major General Roy Urquhart appear?
13 Known for his spooky voice, which actor voices over on Michael Jackson's video "Thriller"?
14 What was the first Top Ten hit for Red Hot Chili Peppers?
15 Who was the first black actress to win an Oscar?
16 In what unusual circumstances did George II's eldest son die?
17 Which Bond movie dealing with world-threatening scenarios opened during the Cuban missile crisis?
18 Who were the only independent nations in Africa at the outbreak of WWI?
19 In which country was Lassa fever first identified?
20 Who was the first US President to appear on colour television?
21 Where is there a Spam Museum?
22 Which team qualified from the 2002 World Cup Group stage with fewest goals?
23 Which town in which state was the home of Abraham Lincoln?
24 What was the world's first national theatre?
25 What is the longest river of the island which has a Parliament called Tynwald?
26 Trevor Smith became known as which rapper?
27 In which year did the £1 note cease to be legal tender in England?
28 Which Taiwanese-Japanese entrepreneur is credited with creating the craze for Pot Noodles?
29 Which Grand event was first broadcast live on BBC television in 1960?
30 Which planet was the first to be discovered by use of a telescope?

| **Answers** | **World Travel** *(see Quiz 38)* |

1 St Lucia. 2 Alberta, Canada. 3 Russia. 4 Nina. 5 China. 6 Guayaquil. 7 Bangkok. 8 Dallas. 9 Sri Lanka. 10 Dublin. 11 Vridi. 12 Sumatra. 13 Gulf of Mexico. 14 Great Sandy. 15 Yellow colour of a creek bank. 16 Zarqa. 17 Severn. 18 Coral. 19 Alabama. 20 South island, New Zealand. 21 Perth. 22 Lake. 23 Aracaju. 24 Telugu. 25 Cook Islands. 26 Caribbean. 27 Namche. 28 Tokyo. 29 Lakemont Park, Pennsylvania. 30 Mali.

1 Who sang the title song of a movie for which Marvin Hamlisch won two 1974 Oscars?

2 Who did Betty Hutton replace in "Annie Get Your Gun"?

3 "Fiddler on the Roof" and which other big musical did Norman Jewison direct in the 1970s?

4 Who was Gene Kelly's co-star in his Hollywood debut?

5 Which character did Debbie Allen play in the movie and TV show about Manhattan's High School for the Performing Arts?

6 For which song from "Lady be Good" did Oscar Hammerstein II win an Oscar?

7 Which novelist, when a Pinkerton detective in real life, investigated the gambling affairs of the man Barbra Streisand married in "Funny Girl"?

8 What was the Hollywood debut of the man born Harold Leek?

9 Who directed Nicole Kidman's first movie after divorcing Tom Cruise?

10 Whom did Miss Olsen fall in love with in the 1970s movie?

11 Where does Tony Manero do his day job in a big 1970s musical?

12 In which city is the song "Do Re Mi" sung in a musical?

13 Who wrote the music for the last Best Oscar-winning song of the 1990s?

14 Who played the male lead in the musical which included "Let's Hear It for the Boy"?

15 Who said, "I am simple, complex, generous, selfish, unattractive, beautiful, lazy, driven"?

16 In which musical do teenagers tune in to Wolfman Jack's rock 'n' roll show?

17 What is the name of the flower shop owner in "Little Shop of Horrors"?

18 Where is the 1983 musical with Jennifer Beals and Michael Nouri set?

19 Who plays the angry young intellectual in "Fiddler on the Roof"?

20 Who played Janet in the musical movie with the song "Dammit Janet"?

21 Who directed and choreographed the original production of "West Side Story" on stage before being involved in the movie?

22 In which state is the movie based on the life of Loretta Lynn set?

23 Which was the first Disney musical of the 1990s to win Best Song Oscar?

24 Who sang "Honeysuckle Rose" in "New York New York"?

25 What won the Best Song Oscar in Julie Andrews' first Oscar-winning film?

26 For which movie did Howard Ashman win his last Oscar in his own lifetime?

27 Which musical film included a psychopathic agricultural worker called Fry?

28 Who directed "Spiceworld: The Movie"?

29 What was Olivia Newton John's surname in "Grease"?

30 What was Jennifer Beals studying while she was making "Flashdance"?

Answers | Horse Racing *(see Quiz 43)*

1 Limerick, Ireland. 2 Lovely Cottage. 3 Willie Carson. 4 Lammtarra. 5 Vodaphone. 6 Lord Huntingdon. 7 Pat Eddery. 8 Jean Luc Lagardere. 9 Melling Chase. 10 Esha Ness. 11 Eleanor. 12 Durbar II. 13 Cape Verdi. 14 Mr Frisk. 15 Entrepreneur. 16 Gay Trip. 17 Olivier Peslier. 18 Athens Wood. 19 Greville Starkey. 20 Prince Charles. 21 Golden Fleece. 22 Party Politics. 23 Humble Duty. 24 Lester Piggott. 25 1945. 26 Royal Tan. 27 Powerstown Park. 28 Las Meninas. 29 Victory Note. 30 Kahyasi.

Quiz 42 | Pot Luck 19 | Answers – page 284

1 Mr Ashwell of Herne Hill patented which famous sign?
2 How many of the five 2006–07 Ashes Tests made it to the fifth day?
3 Junta is the Spanish word for what?
4 What was usually the penultimate word in an episode of "The Two Ronnies"?
5 Which world leader was executed on Christmas Day 1989?
6 Which 1960s classic song had the line, "Nobody knows where my Johnny has gone"?
7 "Infamous" starred Toby Jones as which writer?
8 Which favourite sitcom star played Jeremy Parsons QC in Crown Court?
9 What did Radovan Karadzic practise before founding the Serbian Democratic Party?
10 Grace Stafford was the voice of which cartoon character?
11 Which father of an ex-"Coronation Street" star wrote over 100 episodes of the soap including one of Elsie Tanner's weddings?
12 What was the name of the evacuation operation which created the artificial Lake Kariba?
13 To the nearest 20 degrees centigrade what is the melting point of iron?
14 Which Emperor was responsible for building the Great Wall of China?
15 What in London was originally called Nottingham House?
16 Which Florida port and tourist city used to be known as Cayo Hueso or Bone Island?
17 What was the name of the first kibbutz?
18 When did "The Star Spangled Banner" become the US National Anthem?
19 Who wrote the novel on which Quentin Tarantino's follow-up to "Pulp Fiction" was based?
20 With which club did Mike Tindall begin his professional rugby career?
21 The phrase "iron curtain" was first used by Churchill but who is credited with the idea behind it?
22 What is the oldest lead and zinc mining town in Zambia?
23 Elizabeth Taylor's second divorce was from whom?
24 In which game reserve are the Kapachira Falls?
25 What is the Burmese name for the main river of Myanmar?
26 Who wrote a poem about the Tay Bridge Disaster of 1879?
27 Who wrote the book "Palestine: Peace Not Apartheid"?
28 Where was the first purpose-built music hall built?
29 Which was the last navy to scrap the daily rum ration?
30 In which Bond film did Toby Stephens play Gustav Graves?

Answers	21st Century Headlines (see Quiz 44)

1 Michel Desjoyeaux. 2 15. 3 New York. 4 I Love You. 5 Brooklands. 6 Dennis Tito. 7 Selby. 8 MacPherson. 9 60%. 10 Douro. 11 Australian. 12 Peter Tachell. 13 Poole. 14 Georgia. 15 Mahzer Mahmood. 16 30th Dec. 17 Refused to use metric measures. 18 Vandevelde. 19 NBC. 20 Kursk. 21 Chesterfield. 22 Barak. 23 His TV set. 24 PY Gerbeau. 25 Alun Michael. 26 Chappaqua. 27 Croatia. 28 Australian Labor Party. 29 Freedom Party. 30 110.

1 In which county was the first steeplechase held?
2 Which horse won the first post-WWII Grand National?
3 Which jockey rode the 2,000 Guineas-winner four times between 1972 and 1989?
4 Which horse ran the fastest Epsom Derby of the 1990s?
5 Who sponsored the Derby at the turn of the century?
6 Who resigned as the Queen's trainer towards the end of the 1990s?
7 Who was the first jockey in the 1990s to ride 200 winners?
8 Who owned Sagamix when he won the Prix de l'Arc de Triomphe in 1998?
9 The steeplechaser One Man had to be put down after being injured in which race?
10 Which horse finished first in the last Grand National of the millennium to be abandoned?
11 What was the first filly to win the Derby?
12 Which horse won the Derby the year WWI began?
13 What was Frankie Dettori's first 1000 Guineas win of the 1990s?
14 Which horse ran the fastest Grand National of the 1990s?
15 What was Mick Kinane's second 2000 Guineas win of the 1990s?
16 Which horse won the Grand National the year that Nijinsky won the Derby?
17 Which jockey won his third successive Prix de l'Arc de Triomphe in 1998?
18 Which horse won the St Leger the year that Mill Reef won the Derby?
19 Who rode the only Derby winner with Shirley in its name?
20 Which member of the Royal family got married the year Aldaniti won the National?
21 Which horse won the Derby the year after the legendary Shergar?
22 Which horse won the Grand National the year of the first 1990s General Election?
23 What was Lester Piggott's first 1000 Guineas winner in the second half of the 20th century?
24 Rodrigo de Triano was which jockey's thirtieth Classic winner?
25 What was the last year before 1993 that the Grand National was not run?
26 Before Royal Athlete what was the last Grand National winner to have Royal in its name?
27 In which park is Ireland's Clonmel Racecourse?
28 What was the first 1000 Guineas winner of the 1990s to have two words in its name?
29 Which was the fastest of the first four British horses in the 1998 French 2000 Guineas?
30 Which horse ran the fastest Epsom Derby of the 1980s?

Answers	Musical Movies *(see Quiz 41)*

1 Barbra Streisand. 2 Judy Garland. 3 Jesus Christ Superstar. 4 Judy Garland. 5 Lydia. 6 The Last Time I Saw Paris. 7 Dashiel Hammett. 8 Annie Get Your Gun. 9 Baz Luhrmann. 10 Danny Zuko. 11 DIY store. 12 Salzburg. 13 Phil Collins. 14 Kevin Bacon. 15 Barbra Streisand. 16 American Graffiti. 17 Mr Mushnik. 18 Pittsburgh. 19 Paul Michael Glaser. 20 Susan Sarandon. 21 Jerome Robbins. 22 Kentucky. 23 Beauty & the Beast. 24 Diahnne Abbott. 25 Chim Chim Cheree. 26 Beauty & the Beast. 27 Oklahoma! 28 Bob Spiers. 29 Olsen. 30 US Literature.

1 Who beat Ellen MacArthur in the Vendee Globe race 2000–001?
2 How many naval personnel were taken into custody by Iran in March 2007?
3 The plane involved in the first supersonic air crash was heading for where?
4 Which computer virus was first detected in Hong Kong in May 2000?
5 From which airfield did Jennifer Murray begin and end her helicopter circumnavigation of the world solo in 2000?
6 Who was the first private individual to make a journey into space?
7 Where in England was there a major rail crash in March 2001?
8 What was the name of the inquiry into the death of Stephen Lawrence?
9 Around what percentage of the electorate voted in the January 2005 Iraq elections?
10 Over which river did a bridge collapse in 2001 causing the resignation of that country's minister of public works?
11 At which 2001 Grand Prix was a marshal killed after he was struck by a wheel?
12 Who tried to make a citizen's arrest on Robert Mugabe in Brussels in 2001?
13 Which judge presided over the first Lee Bowyer and Jonathan Woodgate trial?
14 Zurab Zhvania who died in 2005 was Prime Minister of which country?
15 Which reporter set up the "Sophiegate" scam?
16 On which date was Sadaam Hussein hanged in 2006?
17 How did Steve Thoburn hit the headlines?
18 What was the name of the Belgian that M & S appointed to turn around the company's ailing fortunes?
19 Which station aired Anne Robinson's ruthless quiz show in the US?
20 Which Russian nuclear submarine sank in 2000?
21 Towards the end of the 2000–01 football season which side was docked three points for financial irregularities?
22 Who did Ariel Sharon replace as Israeli PM in February 2001?
23 Mitch Hallen hit the headlines as he married what?
24 Who succeeded Jennie Page as chief executive of the Millennium Dome?
25 Who did Rhodri Morgan replace as First Secretary of the Welsh Assembly?
26 Where did Hillary Clinton buy a home before announcing she would run for the Senate?
27 Stipe Mesic was elected President of where?
28 In 2005 Mark Latham resigned as leader of which political party?
29 Which political party did Jorg Haider head?
30 How many storeys did the twin towers of the World Trade Center have?

Answers	Pot Luck 19 *(see Quiz 42)*

1 Vacant/Engaged toilet sign. 2 Three. 3 Join. 4 Him. 5 Ceausescu. 6 It's My Party. 7 Truman Capote. 8 Richard Wilson. 9 Psychiatry. 10 Woody Woodpecker. 11 Geoffrey Lancashire (father of Sarah). 12 Noah. 13 1535°. 14 Shih Huang Ti. 15 Kensington Palace. 16 Key West. 17 Deganya. 18 1931. 19 Elmore Leonard (Jackie Brown). 20 Bath. 21 Josef Goebbels, in Das Reich. 22 Kabwe. 23 Michael Wilding. 24 Majete. 25 Ayeyarwady. 26 William McGonagall. 27 Jimmy Carter. 28 Bolton. 29 New Zealand. 30 Die Another Day.

1 Which French region incorporates the city of Paris?
2 "Ruby" and "Boxing Champ" featured on which album?
3 Which Betty Marsden character's catchphrase was, "Many many times," in the radio classic "Round the Horne"?
4 What was Kazuo Ishiguro's next novel after "Artist of the Floating World" which won the Booker Prize?
5 Which Beatles song was recorded as "Sie liebt dich" in West Germany?
6 What was the codename of the bomb which was dropped on Nagasaki?
7 Which port is Italy's chief naval station?
8 Who did Robin Givens divorce in 1989?
9 Which DH Lawrence novel was set in Mexico?
10 Who spent more years as Chancellor of the Exchequer in the 1980s than anyone else?
11 On which river is the Yorkshire city which hosts a piano competition every three years?
12 The movie "Starter for Ten" was based on a book by which writer?
13 What do the Greeks call Nicosia?
14 In which church is JS Bach buried?
15 Which was the last European power to have imperial territories in Africa?
16 Who was chief photographer of "Rolling Stone" magazine from 1973 to 1983?
17 In which country is the city of Tetouan?
18 EAT is the tasty sound code for which country?
19 What type of wine is described by the term frizzante?
20 Which country did the group Rednex come from?
21 Which movie great had his final TV role as Daniel Reece in "Dynasty"?
22 In which country is the city of Brasov?
23 Kim Basinger lost a multi-million-pound lawsuit after pulling out of which movie?
24 In which decade was the Mexican Grand Prix first held?
25 Who played Sir Arthur Sullivan in "Topsy Turvy"?
26 In which London borough is Sadlers' Wells Theatre?
27 In which key is Schubert's "Unfinished Symphony"?
28 Which leaders signed the SALT II treaty?
29 The Silk Road ran from Shanghai to which Sea?
30 Which actor manager was born Henry Brodribb?

Answers | Pot Luck 21 *(see Quiz 47)*

1 Cambodia. 2 H. 3 Minder. 4 Kandahar. 5 1920s. 6 Lemur. 7 David Wasco.
8 Ben Hur. 9 Gambia. 10 Goldeneye. 11 The Bangles. 12 Mayor of Casterbridge.
13 Blood Diamond. 14 The Return of the Native. 15 Heart-Shaped Box. 16 Gladys
Aylward. 17 William IV. 18 Cissy Houston. 19 Argentina. 20 Bond movie. 21 Bolivia.
22 The Flintstones. 23 Sherlock Holmes. 24 Barbara Bach. 25 Venezuela. 26 Bryn
Terfel. 27 Ronnie Barker. 28 Tarsiers. 29 Ten players. 30 Angell.

1 In which month in 1966 was "Star Trek" first broadcast?
2 Which Briton won an Emmy as Best Supporting Actress in 1971?
3 Who directed the series "7 Up" and its sequels, about the lives and aspirations of a group of children?
4 Which studio was the first "Blue Peter" filmed from?
5 Whose music was used for the series "Light of Experience"?
6 Who was known as "The Switchboard Girl"?
7 The first TV broadcast of "Alice in Wonderland" was under which banner?
8 What was the name of the very first programme designed for children of school age?
9 Who presented "Cookery Lesson" in the 1950s?
10 In which year was the first General Election results broadcast production?
11 Who was the creator of Mr Pastry?
12 Which town was shown on the first cross-Channel broadcast?
13 Which children's title replaced "Watch with Mother"?
14 Who replaced Eamonn Andrews on "What's My Line"?
15 At what time was the first BBC TV news broadcast put on air?
16 Which Olympics was "Sportsview" the first to cover?
17 Who was the first presenter of "Sunday Night at the London Palladium"?
18 What was the UK version of "Tic Tac Dough"?
19 Which series's spin-off was called "Oxbridge 2000"?
20 How long had "Grandstand" been running before a regular Sunday programme was introduced?
21 On which day of the week did "Juke Box Jury" begin?
22 In which series did Chief Supt Lockhart appear?
23 The Ponderosa Ranch was near which City?
24 Which puppet series featured Tex Tucker?
25 Which "Dad's Army" regular appeared in "It's a Square World"?
26 Ian Hendry played which crime-buster alongside Patrick Macnee in "The Avengers"?
27 Which astronomer created "A for Andromeda"?
28 Which Prime Minister appeared with "Morecambe & Wise"?
29 Who wrote "Brothers in Law"?
30 In what year did "Top of the Pops" celebrate its 2000th show?

Answers	Science *(see Quiz 48)*

1 Star sailor. 2 Charles Kowal. 3 Mars. 4 Kentucky. 5 Kodak. 6 Czechoslovakia. 7 Humerus. 8 Calcium hydroxide. 9 Tanzania. 10 Orion. 11 Tibia. 12 Vomiting. 13 Titan. 14 Dialysis machine. 15 Five. 16 90+. 17 Neptune. 18 Therapeutics plc. 19 Lungs. 20 Jupiter. 21 1880s. 22 John Russell Hind. 23 iPhone. 24 Carbon. 25 Titan. 26 Benthos. 27 Lakes. 28 13. 29 Triton. 30 Heavy water.

1 Which country has the internet code .kh?
2 On a computer keyboard what letter is below and between Y and U?
3 Which TV series featured a pub called the Winchester?
4 What was the first capital of Afghanistan after it became independent?
5 In which decade was the Monaco Grand Prix first held?
6 Which creature is also known as the aye-aye?
7 Who co-wrote the screenplay of "Pulp Fiction" along with Quentin Tarantino?
8 Which 1950s film cost $4million, double the maximum spend of the time?
9 In which country is the city of Banjul?
10 Xenia Onatopp was the villain in which movie?
11 The girl band once known as The Colours made the charts using which name?
12 In fiction, what position did Michael Henchard rise to?
13 Jennifer Connelly and Djimon Honsou starred in which 2007 film?
14 Which Thomas Hardy novel starts with a brooding description of Egdon Heath?
15 What was the last Top Ten hit for Nirvana?
16 Whose story was told in "Inn of the Sixth Happiness" with Ingrid Bergman?
17 Who was the first British monarch to be born in Buckingham Palace?
18 Who recorded the original "Midnight Train to Georgia" before Gladys Knight had the big international hit?
19 Falabellas are native to which country?
20 Rowan Atkinson made his big-screen debut in a movie in which series of films?
21 In which country were Butch Cassidy and Sundance finally tracked down?
22 On TV which family read "The Daily Slate"?
23 Who in London had 221B as part of his address?
24 Which Bond girl married a Beatle?
25 Barcelona is found in Spain and which other country?
26 Who made the albums "Some Enchanted Evening" and "We'll Keep a Welcome"?
27 Gerald Wiley was an assumed name of which TV comedy writer?
28 The term monkey includes all the primates except man, apes and what else?
29 How many Italian players scored the 12 goals in open play in Germany 2006?
30 What was Zoe's name before her marriage to Alec in "May to December"?

1 What did the word astronaut originally mean?
2 Who discovered the mystery object Chiron?
3 What was the third planet to have been visited by a spacecraft?
4 In which US state is the Fisher Ridge cave system?
5 Which company introduced Photo CD?
6 What was the third country to have a man in space?
7 Which is the longest bone in the arm?
8 What is another name for slaked lime?
9 Where was the meteorite Mbosi found?
10 In which constellation is Rigel?
11 Which bone is named after the Italian for flute?
12 What is emetophobia a fear of?
13 What is Saturn's biggest moon?
14 Willem Johan Kolff devised which item of equipment, a pioneer in medicine and health?
15 How much faster does the strongest wind blow on Neptune than on Earth?
16 How many miles below the Earth' surface do diamonds form?
17 What is the next largest body in the Solar System after Uranus?
18 Which company created Dolly the Sheep?
19 What is the next largest human organ after the brain?
20 Asteroids usually appear between the orbits of Mars and which other planet?
21 In which decade were contact lenses first devised?
22 Who discovered the asteroid Flora?
23 Which device did Apple CEO Steve Jobs say would "reinvent" telecommunications in 2007?
24 What is the most common element in the human body after oxygen?
25 Which satellite has the thickest atmosphere?
26 What name is given to the animal and plant life which lives at the bottom of the sea?
27 What does a limnologist study?
28 How many people were in space on 14th March 1995, a then record?
29 What is Neptune's largest moon?
30 What is D_2O?

Answers	TV Classics (see Quiz 46)

1 September. 2 Jenny Agutter (The Snow Goose). 3 Michael Apted. 4 Lime Grove. 5 Gheorge Zamfir. 6 Joan Miller. 7 Theatre Parade. 8 For the Children. 9 Philip Harben. 10 1940. 11 Richard Hearne. 12 Calais. 13 See Saw. 14 David Jacobs. 15 7.30pm. 16 Melbourne (1956). 17 Tommy Trinder. 18 Criss Cross Quiz. 19 Emergency Ward 10. 20 23 years. 21 Monday. 22 No Hiding Place. 23 Virginia City. 24 Four Feather Falls. 25 Clive Dunn. 26 Dr Keel. 27 Fred Hoyle. 28 Harold Wilson. 29 Frank Muir and Denis Norden. 30 2001.

1 "Titanic" overtook which movie as the most costly ever made?

2 Which animal is linked with the US state of Minnesota?

3 In which American city sharing its name with a European city were R.E.M. formed?

4 In which month did the Japanese launch the 1941 attack on Pearl Harbor?

5 Who or what is a merlon?

6 The unlikely-sounding writing duo Ham and Evans penned which song that made No 1 for two different artists?

7 Who wrote the book on which 101 Dalmatians was based?

8 England led Australia by what score at half time in the 2003 rugby World Cup Final?

9 How long was the run of Arthur Miller's first Broadway play?

10 What was the creature-named publishing company set up by Paul Hamlyn?

11 What was the occupation of Louis Washkansky, the first heart transplant recipient?

12 Who played Ava Gardner in the movie "The Aviator"?

13 What was Eternal's first single not to make the Top Ten?

14 Who drew the caricature sequences at the start of TV's "Yes Minister"?

15 Which character did Jim Davidson play in "Up the Elephant and Round the Castle"?

16 In 1824 William Buckland named the first what?

17 What was the middle name of sub-four-minute-miler Roger Bannister?

18 Which creatures were wild in the title of a Jung Chang novel?

19 In which royal residence did Queen Victoria die?

20 To which Olympic thrower was runner Mary Decker married?

21 What was the first – and only – Top Ten hit for Silver Convention?

22 What celestial body is portrayed in the seventh movement of Gustav Holst's "Planet Suite"?

23 From which play was the movie "Casablanca" adapted?

24 "June is Bustin' Out All Over" features in which musical?

25 Which horse was the first ever winner of the Derby?

26 In which country is the city of Kumasi?

27 Which player scored the first penalty in the 2006 FIFA World Cup Final shoot-out?

28 How many Motown acts recorded "I Heard It Through the Grapevine" before Marvin Gaye?

29 Laennec is credited with inventing which medical aid?

30 What percentage of zebras have exactly the same pattern of stripes?

Answers	Pot Luck 23 *(see Quiz 51)*

1 Order of discovery. 2 The Man without a Face. 3 Iran. 4 One by One. 5 Janice Long. 6 Anaemia. 7 Samuels. 8 Giacomo Puccini. 9 Influenza. 10 Benson. 11 2000 Guineas. 12 Zimbabwe. 13 Mariah Carey. 14 Richard III. 15 David Copperfield. 16 Nicholas Lyndhurst. 17 Dulwich College. 18 Peru. 19 Angela Rippon. 20 Snodgrass. 21 Gall bladder. 22 South Africa. 23 Malcolm Bradbury. 24 Sally Phillips. 25 JCB. 26 Nigel West. 27 Nancy Sinatra. 28 1951. 29 Uncle. 30 Alphabetical order.

1 On the soundtrack of "Bridget Jones's Diary" who sang the only song with Miss Jones in the title?

2 "Virtual Insanity" originally appeared on which album?

3 Who sang "I could be violet sky"?

4 Which duo was the duo with the best-selling single of the 1990s in the UK?

5 Whose No 1 had the line, "You're about as easy as a nuclear war"?

6 In which year was the album "1" the best-seller in over six countries despite only being released in the November?

7 What was the second of Motown's first two consecutive No 1s?

8 Who wrote the Spanish lyrics "Volver A Empezar" to a Cole Porter classic?

9 Survivor were commissioned to write which song for the third "Rocky" film?

10 Which famous writing team wrote Phil Collins' first solo No 1?

11 With which single did Whitney Houston's husband top the chart in the 1980s when part of a band?

12 What was the Freddie Mercury song on "Five Live" EP?

13 Who penned Michael Jackson's "You are Not Alone"?

14 Who was Guiot, a provider of words and music on Shakespear's Sister's "Stay"?

15 Which single topped the charts in the US after being used in a movie based on a 1970s TV series?

16 What was the first German Eurovision winner to top the UK charts?

17 What was the name of the third single written to raise funds for Comic Relief?

18 Who wrote Take That's first No 1?

19 Which Motown star co-wrote Paul Young's first No 1?

20 What was The Jam's last single before disbanding?

21 Who was the first person to write five No 1 singles as sole composer?

22 Who joined Skinner & Baddiel as writer of the Euro 96 anthem?

23 From which album was The Fugees' second No 1 single taken?

24 What was the first No 1 of the 21st century to have a boy's name in the title?

25 What was Oasis's first No 1 with Noel Gallagher as writer and lead vocals?

26 How did Bucks Fizz's second No 1 finish?

27 In which song did Terry meet Julie every Friday night?

28 In Nelly Furtado's song which line goes after "Flames to dust"?

29 The Bluebells' 1993 hit was used to advertise what?

30 What was the shortest title on the compilation EP Abba-esque?

Answers | Transport *(see Quiz 52)*

1 Jahre Viking. 2 Chicago. 3 Farringdon. 4 Volkswagen Beetle. 5 Imperial Airways. 6 General Motors. 7 Little Piece of Coal. 8 Czechoslovakia. 9 District. 10 Maggiore. 11 Helicopter. 12 2003. 13 Jeantaud. 14 Honda. 15 Tractor. 16 Nissan Sunny. 17 Finland. 18 Seven. 19 Ice. 20 Wilbur Wright. 21 Central. 22 Russia. 23 Honda. 24 1948. 25 Jeep. 26 St Petersburg. 27 Buick. 28 Fire engine. 29 Lada Riva. 30 Blackbird.

1 Which order is the system of numbering asteroids?
2 In which 1993 movie did Mel Gibson direct himself?
3 In which country is the city of Qom?
4 What was Cher's last Top Ten hit before the massive No 1 "Believe"?
5 Who was the only female presenter at the Live Aid concert?
6 Which blood disorder is caused by a lack of folic acid?
7 Which surname does Janet Leigh's character use when signing in to the Bates Motel?
8 Who wrote the operatic comedy "Gianni Schicchi"?
9 John Huxham coined the name for which common illness?
10 What was the surname of Cherie Lunghi's character Gabriella in "The Manageress"?
11 In 1998 which race did Aiden O'Brien not win – the Ascot Gold Cup, King George VI and Queen Elizabeth Stakes or the 2000 Guineas?
12 Alphabetically, which team was last in the 2007 Cricket World Cup?
13 Who became the first solo female singer to enter the UK charts at No 1?
14 The bones of which king were thrown in the River Soar after his grave was desecrated?
15 In fiction, whose first wife was called Dora Spenlove?
16 Who played Ronnie Barker's son Raymond in "Going Straight"?
17 PG Wodehouse and Raymond Chandler both went to which English school?
18 In which country is the city of Chiclayo?
19 Who was the first female to present TV's "Top Gear"?
20 Which Carrie featured in Clint Eastwood's "Pale Rider"?
21 Which part of his anatomy did Jim Carrey have removed following the making of the movie "The Mask"?
22 In which country did Harold Macmillan deliver his famous "Wind of Change" speech?
23 Who dramatised Tom Sharpe's "Porterhouse Blue" for television?
24 Who played Shazza in "Bridget Jones's Diary"?
25 What were the initials of Mr Bamford who gave his name to a heavy vehicle?
26 Under what name is one-time MP Rupert Allason known as an author?
27 Which 60-plus performer was featured in a 2005 hit for Audio Bullys?
28 In what year was the first colour TV programme transmitted in America?
29 In motor racing, what relation was Emerson to Christian Fittipaldi?
30 Earth comes first of the planets in order of what?

Answers	**Pot Luck 22** *(see Quiz 49)*

1 Waterworld. 2 Gopher. 3 Athens. 4 December. 5 Part of a parapet. 6 Without You. 7 Dodie Smith. 8 14-5. 9 One week. 10 Octopus. 11 Dentist. 12 Kate Beckinsale. 13 So Good. 14 Gerald Scarfe. 15 Jim London. 16 Dinosaur. 17 Gilbert. 18 Swans. 19 Osborne House. 20 Bob Slaney. 21 Get Up and Boogie. 22 Neptune. 23 Everybody Comes to Rick's. 24 Carousel. 25 Diomed. 26 Ghana. 27 Pirlo. 28 Two. 29 Stethoscope. 30 None.

1 In 2000 what was the world's largest ship?
2 Where did the first car hire company start, in 1918?
3 The first Underground railway ran from Paddington to which Street?
4 In the 1970s which vehicle became the most constructed car of all time?
5 Which airline served the first cooked meals on a scheduled flight?
6 Which was the largest Internet advertiser in 2000?
7 What was the meaning of the name of the dog Ugolek who was a space traveller in the 1960s?
8 Which was the first country to make seat belts compulsory?
9 What was London's second underground railway line?
10 On which Lake was the first hydrofoil tested?
11 What is a Mil Mi 26?
12 In which year were Concorde supersonic airlines finally withdrawn?
13 Which car held the first land speed record?
14 Of the following, which make of motor cycle was made first – Honda, Suzuki or Yamaha?
15 What was Henry Ford's Fordson?
16 Which of the following was produced first – Ford Escort, Ford Orion or Nissan Sunny?
17 The cruise ship "Explorer of the Seas" was built in which country?
18 How many people died in the space shuttle tragedy of 2003?
19 On what surface did Henry Ford set a land speed record in 1904?
20 Who piloted the first flight of over one hour with a passenger?
21 Bethnal Green tube station is on which London Underground line?
22 Which country has the most submarines?
23 Which company produced the first zero-level-emission engine?
24 Which year saw the arrival of the Land Rover and the 2CV?
25 Which vehicle was known as the Bantam, the Gnat and the Peep before its final name stuck?
26 Which Russian city has the most comprehensive tramway system?
27 What was the make of the first car to have front and rear flashing indicators?
28 What type of vehicle is a Hawaiian Eagle?
29 Which of the following was produced last – Lada Riva, Nissan Pulsar or Renault 4?
30 Which reconnaissance aircraft is the world's fastest?

Quiz 53 | Villains

Answers – page 295

1 Which right-hand man of Slobodan Milosevic was arrested in March 2001?

2 Which country does Osama Bin Laden hail from?

3 In 1998 General Pinochet was arrested in the UK pending extradition to where?

4 What was the job of Anthony Blunt when he was stripped of his knighthood?

5 Michael Barratt was not the last person to be hanged in the UK but why was he a famous "last"?

6 Where was the murderer of 10 Rillington Place executed?

7 Which villain died on the same date as Freddie Mercury but almost 30 years earlier?

8 How many patients was Harold Shipman originally convicted of killing?

9 Which celebrity surname did Barry George use?

10 Timothy McVeigh was executed for which bombing?

11 On what date did Lord Lucan disappear?

12 Which father of a famous novelist played the villain Captain Hook in the first production of Peter Pan?

13 Volkert van der Graaf was sentenced for the murder of which person?

14 What was the nickname of Protestant paramilitary leader Billy Wright?

15 Who was the first woman to be executed in Texas in the 20th century?

16 Ta Mok was a successor to which leader?

17 On TV what was the surname of the Weatherfield One?

18 In 1902 Harry Jackson was the first person convicted on the basis of what evidence?

19 How was Illich Ramirez Sanchez better known?

20 Which Oscar-nominated film of 2007 was about a former dictator of Uganda?

21 What was the name of Jack the Ripper's final victim?

22 The book "Cried Unheard" was about which convicted killer?

23 Which movie was about pardoned murderer Derek Bentley?

24 Who did James Earl Ray shoot?

25 Where did Michael Ryan carry out his murders?

26 How did Great Train Robber Charles Wilson meet his death?

27 Which group captured hostages John McCarthy, Brian Keenan and Frank Reed in Lebanon?

28 Which of the three men in the Guinness scandal received an 18-month jail sentence?

29 Who was the first person to be executed by lethal injection in the USA?

30 How old was Ian Huntley when he was convicted of the Soham murders?

Answers	Olympics *(see Quiz 55)*

1 Paris. 2 Donovan Bailey. 3 Sinclair. 4 Spiridon Louis. 5 London. 6 Sergey Belov. 7 1916. 8 Averoff. 9 Upton Park FC. 10 John Boland. 11 Luigi Carrozza. 12 80. 13 1 May 2001. 14 Birgit Fischer (nee Schmidt). 15 Gymnastics (Nikolai Andrianov). 16 Norway. 17 Al Oerter. 18 Italy. 19 Miroslav Mecir. 20 Moscow. 21 Ornskoldsvik, Sweden. 22 Equatorial Guinea. 23 Toronto. 24 10. 25 1960s. 26 Millie. 27 1500 metres. 28 Steve Redgrave. 29 Montreal. 30 1940/1944.

Quiz 54 | Pot Luck 24

Answers – page 296

LEVEL 3

1 In which decade did mountain biking become an Olympic event?
2 What was the occupation of the Jack Russell who gave his name to a breed of dog?
3 "The Meltdown" was the sequel to which movie?
4 Which was the first country to give women the vote?
5 On average, how many times does an adult heart beat a minute?
6 Who had a No 1 hit with Bryan Adams and also with Lisa Lopes?
7 Quarter, quell, quote – which of these words is made from letters on the top row of a keyboard?
8 In "Just Good Friends", what were the first names of Vince Pinner's parents?
9 In which country would you watch Polonia play a home soccer match?
10 In the Bible what is the name of John the Baptist's mother?
11 Which country did Martina Hingis represent when she first won Wimbledon?
12 Who directed Jamie Bell's major debut movie?
13 Collectively, who were Bobby Farrell, Marcia Barrett, Liz Mitchell and Maisie Williams?
14 What does the Archbishop of York signs himself as?
15 Burt Reynolds was born in which American state?
16 How is vichyssoise soup usually served?
17 What type of "Schoolboy" appears in the title of a John Le Carre novel?
18 Delft pottery is usually which colours?
19 Which Hill is the highest point in the Cotswolds?
20 Which song begins, "I see trees of green, Red roses too"?
21 Who was 50 first, Carrie Fisher, Mel Gibson or Kevin Costner?
22 In which decade of last century was Andy Warhol born?
23 What was held at Mount Tremblant, Mosport and Montreal at different years in the 1970s?
24 What was the name of Steptoe and Son's horse?
25 In which country did the Russian revolutionary Leon Trotsky die?
26 What was the first Top Ten hit for Go West?
27 In 1919 the Curzon Line divided Poland on what basis?
28 What was founded following the Dumbarton Oaks Conference of the 1940s?
29 Which present-day county goes with White to name the favourite horse of the monarch Richard III?
30 Who did Cassius Clay beat when he first became world heavyweight champion?

Answers | Pot Luck 25 *(see Quiz 56)*

1 Church. 2 10. 3 India. 4 Danish. 5 Glass. 6 The New York Dolls. 7 December. 8 Mary Carillo. 9 Annapurna. 10 British Honduras. 11 28. 12 Harness racing cart. 13 Basketball. 14 Sorry Seems to be the Hardest Word. 15 Polio. 16 When I Need You. 17 Arms and hands. 18 50. 19 Gloucester Cathedral. 20 30. 21 Waterloo Bridge. 22 Blackburn Rovers. 23 Charles the Mad. 24 Portugal. 25 Pointed. 26 Eva Green. 27 Jimmy Young. 28 Elizabeth. 29 1930s. 30 86 minutes.

294

Quiz 55 | Olympics

Answers – page 293

LEVEL 3

1 Where did the first man to win five gold medals in one Games win them?
2 Who lowered Carl Lewis's Olympic 100m record in Atlanta?
3 What was the middle name of the athlete disqualified from the 100m in Seoul?
4 Who won the first Marathon of the Modern Olympics?
5 Of the first three Marathons of the Modern Olympics which had the longest course?
6 Who scored the winning basket in the 1972 Olympic basketball final?
7 Which Olympics were cancelled due to WWI?
8 In which stadium were the first Modern Olympics held?
9 Who represented Britain the first time soccer was included in the Olympics?
10 Who won the first men's singles tennis final of the modern Olympics?
11 In 20th-century Olympics, who made the highest batting average in baseball?
12 In the 2000 Olympics how many different countries won medals?
13 On which date was the first Briton to win five consecutive gold medals knighted?
14 Which woman won four gold medals in successive games starting in Seoul?
15 Which discipline was practised by the man who won 15 Olympic medals between 1972 and 1980?
16 In the 20th century which country won most medals at the Winter Olympics?
17 Who first won four consecutive individual titles in the same event?
18 Who were the silver medallists in basketball the year of the US boycott?
19 Who won the first Olympic gold for the men's singles in tennis after it was reinstated after 60 years?
20 In which city was it announced that Beijing would host the 2008 Olympics?
21 Where were the first Winter Paralympics held?
22 From which country does the competitor nicknamed Eric the Eel come from?
23 Which city in the Americas was beaten by Beijing to host the 2008 Olympics?
24 By winning the dressage in Sydney, Germany made it a total of how many team golds in this event?
25 In which decade were the first Summer Paralympics held?
26 Which creature went with Syd and Olly in the Sydney Olympics?
27 In Sydney, which discipline did Dean Macey compete in last?
28 Which Olympic gold medallist was a member of the team which won the British four-man bobsleigh championship in 1989?
29 Where did the first Olympic women's basketball tournament take place?
30 Which Olympics were cancelled due to WWII?

Answers	**Villains** *(see Quiz 53)*

1 Markovic. 2 Saudi Arabia. 3 Spain. 4 Surveyor of the Queen's Pictures. 5 Last man to be hanged in public. 6 Pentonville. 7 Lee Harvey Oswald. 8 15. 9 Bulsara. 10 Oklahoma. 11 7 November. 12 Gerald Du Maurier. 13 Pim Fortuyn. 14 King Rat. 15 Karla Faye Tucker. 16 Pol Pot. 17 Rachid. 18 Fingerprints. 19 Carlos the Jackal. 20 The Last King of Scotland 21 Marie Kelly. 22 Mary Bell. 23 Let Him Have It. 24 Martin Luther King. 25 Hungerford. 26 Shot in Spain. 27 Hezbollah. 28 Tony Parnes. 29 Charles Brooks. 30 29 years old.

Quiz 56 | Pot Luck 25 | Answers – page 294

1 In what type of building would a dossal be hung?
2 Shergar won the 1981 Derby by a record how many lengths?
3 In which country is the city of Meerut?
4 What is the nationality of speedway champion Hans Hollen Nielsen?
5 Nelophobia is the fear of what?
6 As a teenager Morrissey ran a fan club for which American band?
7 In which month of 2003 was Saddam Hussein captured?
8 Who was John McEnroe's partner in his first Grand Slam title, a mixed doubles win in the French Open?
9 Maurice Herzog was the first person to conquer which mountain?
10 Belize changed its name from what?
11 How many dominoes are there in a double six set?
12 Who or what is a sulky?
13 In the mid-1970s the NBA and the ABA merged in which sport?
14 What was Elton John's first solo hit on his own Rocket label?
15 The Salk vaccine was developed in the fight against which disease?
16 Which Leo Sayer hit gave the Chrysalis label their first No 1?
17 In sepek takrow you can hit the ball with any part of the body except which?
18 How old was James Herriot when he began writing books?
19 In which cathedral was King Henry III crowned?
20 How old was Eric Cantona when he retired from soccer?
21 What was Vivien Leigh's first movie after Gone with the Wind?
22 Which British club was Sven Goran Eriksson reported to be joining in 1996?
23 How was Charles II King of Spain unkindly known?
24 Which country joined the European Union in the same year as Spain?
25 What shape is the top of a lancet window?
26 "The Dreamers" starred which future Bond girl?
27 Who had the first UK No 1 with "Unchained Melody"?
28 What is Julie Andrews' middle name?
29 In which decade of last century was the first Archery World Championship held?
30 In minutes, how brief was the movie "Brief Encounter"?

Answers | **Pot Luck 24** *(see Quiz 54)*

1 1990s. 2 Clergyman. 3 Ice Age. 4 New Zealand. 5 60–80. 6 Melanie C. 7 Quote. 8 Rita & Les. 9 Poland. 10 Elizabeth. 11 Switzerland. 12 Stephen Daldry. 13 Boney M. 14 Ebor. 15 Georgia. 16 Cold. 17 Honourable. 18 Blue and white. 19 Cleeve Hill. 20 What a Wonderful World. 21 Kevin Costner (2005). 22 1930s. 23 Canadian Grand Prix. 24 Hercules. 25 Mexico. 26 We Close Our Eyes. 27 Language. 28 United Nations. 29 White Surrey. 30 Sonny Liston.

Quiz 57 | Movie Legends

Answers – page 299

LEVEL 3

1 Who was the male star of the first film to have a Royal Command Performance?
2 Which first name was Harpo Marx born with?
3 What was Woody Allen's first film with Mia Farrow?
4 Which actress wrote an autobiography called "Every Frenchman Has One"?
5 Lauren Bacall was "discovered" when she appeared on the cover of which magazine?
6 What was Ingrid Bergman's final film for the big screen?
7 On which ship was Humphrey Bogart injured in WWI?
8 On which island was Yul Brynner born?
9 Who was the mother of Cary Grant's only child?
10 Which director fired Bette Davis on her very first professional engagement?
11 Ann Margret's screen debut was as which Hollywood legend's daughter?
12 What did Walt Disney do in WWI?
13 What was Robert Donat's last word on screen in the last film before his death?
14 Who played jazz piano in "In the Line of Fire"?
15 Whose debut movie "Every Sunday" also featured the star born Frances Gumm?
16 How was Paulette Goddard billed when she was a Ziegfeld Girl?
17 At the age of 13 Sam Goldwyn was apprenticed as a maker of what?
18 In which movie did the first Mrs Charlie Chaplin play Dorothy?
19 What was the British title of the movie where Alfred Hitchcock made his first cameo appearance?
20 Who played Judy Holliday's tutor in the 1950 film directed by George Cukor?
21 In which year between 1941 and 1953 was Bob Hope not in the Top Ten Hollywood money-making stars?
22 Which Hollywood gossip columnist was born Elda Furry?
23 Who played the title role in the movie about the greatest escapologist of all time?
24 Which movie gave Trevor Howard his first Oscar nomination?
25 What was Rock Hudson's debut movie?
26 Which Howard Hughes movie launched the career of Jean Harlow?
27 Who in the movie industry was knighted by King Olav V in 1979?
28 Who did Susan Hayward play in the penultimate film for which she was Oscar-nominated?
29 Who was introduced to the public in "Orphan's Benefit"?
30 Irving Berlin could only write music in which key?

Answers | Crime (see Quiz 59)

1 Identikit. 2 Louisiana. 3 Argentina. 4 Little war. 5 The Nuremberg Files. 6 Texas. 7 Auburn. 8 Lanarkshire. 9 Washington Sniper. 10 Arkansas. 11 Louise Woodward. 12 Anna Lindh. 13 21st July. 14 Festina. 15 Dar es Salaam. 16 Market Street. 17 Strangeways. 18 Jerusalem. 19 Pickles. 20 Iraq. 21 Thailand. 22 Young offenders. 23 Eastbourne. 24 Luxor. 25 Bit opponent's ear. 26 Selling beef on the bone. 27 Bletchley Park Museum. 28 Norfolk & Norwich. 29 Beverly Hills. 30 Armley.

1 David Bryant became the first world champion in which sport?
2 In which country is the city of Karaj?
3 Which silent movie comic turned director used the pseudonym William Goodrich?
4 In which decade of the last century did women's hockey become an Olympic event?
5 In the 1997 Tory leadership election, who finished third?
6 Who first took Led Zeppelin's "Stairway to Heaven" into the singles charts?
7 A terrorist bomb outside Paddy's Bar took place in 2002 on which holiday island?
8 Which Briton held the record number of Grand Prix victories before Alain Prost set a new record?
9 Which animated film was Walt Disney working on at the time of his death?
10 "GoldenEye" was named after Ian Fleming's home in which country?
11 Who found more success after leaving his band King Crabbs?
12 Which character does James Stewart play in the movie classic Harvey?
13 In which country is the port of Lobito?
14 What was the first Top Ten hit for Morrissey?
15 Which MP's father-in-law was played by Sean Connery in "A Bridge Too Far"?
16 What was the first movie that the Marx Brothers made for MGM?
17 Which English king was nicknamed because of his red face?
18 How many Oscars did composer Tim Rice win during the 1990s?
19 In which movie did the character Kimberly Wells feature?
20 Jim Clark spent all his racing career with which team?
21 Who plays the older detective in TV's Dalziel and Pascoe?
22 Which team did defending champions Brazil play in their Germany 2006 opener?
23 Who was the first PM to move to 10 Downing Street?
24 How many chapters are there in the first book of the Old Testament?
25 Which Dickens novel featured Jerry Cruncher?
26 Which team won the first University Boat Race?
27 Who starred as Isadora Duncan in the movie "Isadora"?
28 A barrico is a type of small what?
29 The 1930s movie classic "It Happened One Night" was originally called what?
30 Which Patty was the first woman to win golf's British and US Opens in the same year?

Answers	Pot Luck 27 *(see Quiz 60)*

1 Frederick. 2 Hamburg. 3 Boynton. 4 Brunei. 5 Veronica Guerin. 6 Lord Byron.
7 Parsec. 8 Athenia. 9 Georgia. 10 Gary Busey. 11 151. 12 East. 13 Ten. 14
A library. 15 Wyoming. 16 Alan Lancaster. 17 France. 18 Year of the Dragon. 19
1920s. 20 Wet Wet Wet. 21 Iceland. 22 John Lennon. 23 Luise Rainer. 24 London
Stock Exchange. 25 Dinner jacket. 26 John Lewis Partnership. 27 Cecil Beaton. 28
Bon Jovi. 29 Wiseguy. 30 Spain.

1 Guy Trebert was the first person apprehended due to what?
2 In which state were Bonnie & Clyde arrested?
3 In 1960 in which country was Adolf Eichmann apprehended?
4 What does the word guerrilla mean?
5 What was the name of the Internet site used by US anti-abortionists which resulted in a massive fine for them?
6 Where is the USA's Ellis II prison unit?
7 In which prison was the electric chair first used?
8 In which county is Schotts prison?
9 Arrested in October 2002, John Allen Muhammed was known as what?
10 In 1998 two schoolboys were tried in which state for shootings at Westside Middle School?
11 Elaine Whitfield Sharp was a chief defence lawyer in whose trial?
12 Which Swedish Foreign Minister died of stab wounds in September 2003?
13 In 2005, what was the date of the failed terrorist attack on the London transport system?
14 Which team was suspended from the Tour de France over drug allegations in 1998?
15 Other than Nairobi where was a US embassy attacked at the end of the 1990s?
16 In which Street was the Omagh bomb detonated?
17 Which British prison was the scene of a major riot in 1990?
18 In which city was Yitzhak Rabin shot?
19 Which Judge in the early 1990s famously imprisoned a teenage shoplifter and her baby?
20 Farzad Bazoft was convicted and executed for spying where?
21 In which country were Karen Smith and Patricia Cahill accused of smuggling heroin in 1990?
22 What type of institution is Glenochil – remand centre, women's prison or young offenders?
23 Ian Gow was MP for where when he was killed by an IRA bomb?
24 Where in Egypt was there a massacre of tourists in 1997?
25 Why was Kevin Yates given a six-month suspension by the rugby union in 1998?
26 Jim Sutherland was the first man to be convicted of which crime?
27 Where was the Enigma coding machine stolen from in 2000?
28 In which hospital did Reggie Kray receive his final treatment before his death?
29 Where in America was George Michael arrested in 1998?
30 What is the name of the famous prison in Yorkshire's major city?

Answers	**Movie Legends** *(see Quiz 57)*

1 David Niven. 2 Adolf. 3 Midsummer Night's Sex Comedy. 4 Olivia De Havilland. 5 Harper's Bazaar. 6 Autumn Sonata. 7 Leviathan. 8 Sakhalin. 9 Dyan Cannon. 10 George Cukor. 11 Bette Davis. 12 Drove a Red Cross Ambulance. 13 Farewell. 14 Clint Eastwood. 15 Deanna Durbin. 16 Peaches. 17 Gloves. 18 The Patchwork Girl of Oz. 19 The Lodger. 20 William Holden (Born Yesterday). 21 1948. 22 Hedda Hopper. 23 Tony Curtis. 24 Sons & Lovers. 25 Fighter Squadron. 26 Hell's Angels. 27 Celeste Holm. 28 Lilian Roth. 29 Donald Duck. 30 F sharp.

Quiz 60 | Pot Luck 27

Answers – page 298

1 In "The Pirates of Penzance" who was born on the 29th of February?
2 Where was Monica Seles playing when she was stabbed during a tennis match in 1993?
3 What does the B stand for in JB Priestley's name?
4 Bandar Seri Begawan is the capital of where?
5 Which Irish journalist inspired the story of the movie "When the Sky Falls"?
6 Who said,"I awoke one morning and found myself famous"?
7 Which unit of measurement equals 3.2616 light years?
8 Which British liner was the first to be sunk by a U-boat on the first day of the Second World War?
9 Which state is Otis Redding's home in the lyrics of "On the Dock of the Bay"?
10 Who played Buddy in the 1970s movie "The Buddy Holly Story"?
11 What is the next prime number after 149?
12 Manhattan lies between the Hudson and which river?
13 To the nearest million, what is the population of Portugal?
14 Where do tragic lovers Jenny and Oliver meet for the first time in "Love Story"?
15 In which US state was the first National Park established?
16 Who was Francis Rossi's school mate and long-time bass player in Status Quo?
17 Which was the first country in the world to introduce national conscription?
18 In which Chinese Year was Sharon Osbourne born?
19 In which decade was the surgeon Christiaan Barnard born?
20 Who were the first Scottish group to have three No 1 singles?
21 USA's Reagan and Russia's Gorbachev first met in which country?
22 Which prominent figure did Mark Chapman murder?
23 Who was the first winner of consecutive best actress Oscars?
24 In 1973 Susan Shaw became the first woman to work on the floor where?
25 Which item of evening wear for men was created by Griswold Louillard?
26 "Never knowingly undersold" was the slogan of which chain store?
27 Which designer created the Ascot scene costumes for the film "My Fair Lady"?
28 Tico Torres was drummer with which globally successful band?
29 The movie "Goodfellas" was based on which novel?
30 In which country is the city of Murcia?

Answers | Pot Luck 26 *(see Quiz 58)*

1 Bowls. 2 Iran. 3 Fatty Arbuckle. 4 1980s. 5 John Redwood. 6 Far Corporation. 7 Bali. 8 Jackie Stewart. 9 The Jungle Book. 10 Jamaica. 11 Jimmy Nail. 12 Elwood P Dowd. 13 Angola. 14 Suedehead. 15 Menzies Campbell. 16 A Night at the Opera. 17 William II, Rufus. 18 Three. 19 The China Syndrome. 20 Lotus. 21 Warren Clarke. 22 Croatia. 23 Hugh Walpole. 24 50. 25 A Tale of Two Cities. 26 Oxford. 27 Vanessa Redgrave. 28 Barrel. 29 Night Bus. 30 Sheehan.

Quiz 61 | TV Sitcoms

1 Which star of a classic sitcom is the son of the actor born Alphonso Giuseppe Giovanni Roberto d'Abruzzo?

2 In which show did "Star Wars" Luke Skywalker make his professional debut?

3 Which series did "The Offer" become?

4 Who played Hamish the restaurant critic in "Absolutely Fabulous"?

5 How many couples were "Coupling"?

6 What make of car was Bo & Luke Hazzard's "General Lee"?

7 In what type of establishment was "Desmonds" set?

8 Who said, "I have been complimented on my gestures by the chief psychiatrist of Broadmoor"?

9 In which month and year was the last episode of "Seinfeld" first broadcast in the US?

10 Which sitcom started life as "The Bishop Rides Again"?

11 Who was married to Ben in "My Family"?

12 Which actress/dancer is the elder sister of "The Cosby Show" regular Phylicia Rashad?

13 What was the last screen work of the actor who played Mainwaring in "Dad's Army"?

14 Which gay German officer in "Allo Allo" spent an episode disguised as a flamenco dancer?

15 Who were initially called Bobby and Billy?

16 For which firm did Samantha's husband work in "Bewitched"?

17 Which writer on "Birds of a Feather" also played Tracey's husband on the show?

18 Which "Blackadder" series covered the Regency period?

19 For which character did Kirstie Alley win an Emmy in 1991?

20 Whom did the creator of "Ally McBeal" model his main character on?

21 In "Bread" what was the name of the vicar Aveline married?

22 Who sang the theme song to "Brush Strokes"?

23 What type of coat did Wolfie Smith wear?

24 Which character in "Cheers" was the sister in real life of the show's early producer?

25 What was the address of the Huxtables?

26 Which "Dad's Army" regular had written almost 40 plays?

27 In "The Day Today" who appeared under his own name?

28 Who played the Devil in the 2001 "Absolutely Fabulous"?

29 Where was the US version of "Till Death Us Do Part" set?

30 What is the real name of the actor who played George Constanza in "Seinfeld"?

Answers	Music Legends (see Quiz 63)

1 Satisfaction. 2 Stephen King. 3 John Lennon's. 4 Five. 5 Barbra Streisand. 6 Liberace. 7 Malcolm Arnold. 8 1971. 9 Patsy Cline. 11 Kay Starr. 10 Elvis Presley (Surrender). 12 Cathy's Clown. 13 The Searchers. 14 1990s. 15 Lennon & McCartney. 16 Shirley Bassey. 17 Jerry Lee Lewis. 18 Frankie Laine. 19 Bee Gees. 20 Dreamboat (Alma Cogan). 21 Tony Bennett. 22 Ray Charles. 23 Doris Day. 24 Berwick Street (London). 25 Connie Francis. 26 Mantovani (Moulin Rouge). 27 Status Quo. 28 Dusty Springfield. 29 Winifred Atwell. 30 Reg Presley.

1 Holly Hunter and Craig T Nelson provided voices for which animated family?
2 Which TV Mr was Richard Hearne?
3 In which country would you watch Boavista play a home soccer match?
4 Which herb goes into a bearnaise sauce along with tarragon?
5 What was the first Top Ten hit for 911?
6 What was the surname of the first Peter to be a presenter on "Blue Peter"?
7 Which singer with No 1's in his own right wrote the Buddy Holly classic "It Doesn't Matter Anymore?
8 Who was murdered in the first ever episode of "EastEnders"?
9 Which black and white cat was for many years on the cover of the "Dandy" comic?
10 Who was the longest reigning British King?
11 Mesclun is a type of what?
12 Made back in 1950, what was Marlon Brando's first film?
13 Who was the first Prime Minister to use Chequers?
14 What is a Dorset Blue Vinney?
15 Which character did Drew Barrymore play in "Music and Lyrics"?
16 What is the name of the alter ego of Turner Prize-winning potter Grayson Perry?
17 How many different Olympic Games did Tessa Sanderson compete in?
18 Who visited Kirrin Island?
19 What does a palmiped possess?
20 Chronos was the Greek god of what?
21 Which original Rolling Stone was eligible for a bus pass in October 2001?
22 What is Ted's middle name in the movie "Bill & Ted's Excellent Adventure"?
23 A natatorium is another name for a what?
24 How is comedian Robert Harper better known?
25 In which city were Haagen-Dazs ice creams first sold?
26 Sue Barker and Penelope Keith both married husbands following which career?
27 What is the collective noun for a flock of larks?
28 What was the first Top Ten hit for 2 Unlimited?
29 In Mexican cookery what is a quesadilla?
30 How old was Prince Charles when he was invested as Prince of Wales?

| **Answers** | **Pot Luck 29** *(see Quiz 64)* |

1 Dolly Parton. 2 The English Channel. 3 K7. 4 Bastian Schweinsteiger. 5 £20 note. 6 Fletcher Christian. 7 Egypt. 8 H5N1. 9 Otis Redding. 10 George V. 11 Release Me. 12 Ice cream. 13 Original. 14 Pakistan. 15 50 pence. 16 Mr Loud. 17 A wind which blows from Morocco to Spain. 18 Go. 19 Paris. 20 Delia Smith. 21 Italy. 22 Sunday in the Park with George. 23 The Beagle. 24 Rio Lobos. 25 Windsurfing. 26 Emma Bunton. 27 Iggy Pop. 28 Big Jazza. 29 Rob Bowman. 30 Apiphobia.

1 Which single did The Rolling Stones release on the day The Beatles received their MBEs?

2 Michael Jackson's longest music video was the concept of whom?

3 Whose piano was bought by George Michael for £1.45 million in London in 2000?

4 What was the highest UK chart position of "My Way"?

5 Who released the album "Timeless – Live in Concert" in 2000?

6 Which pianist had the real first names Wladziu Valentino?

7 Who wrote the music for the classic movie "Bridge on the River Kwai"?

8 Before "Supernatural" in 1999 in which year did Santana last have a US No 1 album?

9 Who died in the same crash as Hawkshaw Hawkins and Cowboy Copas?

10 Which 1950s chart topper was born Katherine Starks?

11 Who recorded the English lyrics version of "Torna A Sorrento" in 1961?

12 What was the Everly Brothers' first hit on both sides of the Atlantic?

13 Which Mersey band was the first to top the charts not managed by Brian Epstein?

14 In which decade has Tom Jones had least Top Ten hits?

15 Which songwriters gave The Overlanders their only hit?

16 Who made a "Diamond Tour" in 1998?

17 Whose autobiography was entitled "Killer"?

18 Who was No 1 when Queen Elizabeth II was crowned?

19 Which trio were the subject of "The South Bank Show" in March 1997?

20 What was the only No 1 for the girl with "the giggle in her voice"?

21 Who won a Grammy for "For the Ladies"?

22 Who sang "Ol' Man River" at Frank Sinatra's 80th birthday party?

23 Who won the Best Song Oscar in 1953, in a movie she starred in?

24 Which street features on the cover of Oasis's "(What's the Story) Morning Glory"?

25 Who recorded "Something Stupid" with the lead singer of Culture Club?

26 Which orchestra leader had a hit from a film with the same title as a 2001 blockbuster?

27 Who celebrated their 30th anniversary in the music business with the album "Don't Stop"?

28 Who sang the theme song about the movie on the Profumo Affair?

29 Which 1954 chart topper was, according to the man himself, a huge influence on Elton John?

30 Which composer of Wet Wet Wet's biggest hit is an expert on crop circles?

Answers	TV Sitcoms *(see Quiz 61)*

1 Alan Alda. 2 The Cosby Show. 3 Steptoe & Son. 4 Adrian Edmondson. 5 Three. 6 Dodge Charger. 7 Barber's shop. 8 John Cleese. 9 May 1998. 10 All Gas and Gaiters. 11 Susan. 12 Debbie Allen. 13 AJ Wentworth BA. 14 Gruber. 15 Beavis & Butt Head. 16 McMann & Tate. 17 Alun Lewis. 18 Blackadder the Third. 19 Rebecca Howe. 20 Michelle Pfeiffer. 21 Oswald. 22 Dexy's Midnight Runners. 23 Afghan. 24 Carla Tortelli (Rhea Perlman). 25 10 Stigwood Avenue. 26 Arnold Ridley. 27 Christopher Morris. 28 Anita Pallenberg. 29 New York. 30 Jay Scott Greenspan.

1 Which singer/actress was Mrs Carl Dean?
2 Harriet Quimby was the first woman to fly over what?
3 The 1990s hit "Come Baby Come" was the first Top Ten appearance for which act?
4 Who scored twice for Germany as they finished 2006's third-place match?
5 Scientist Michael Faraday died in 1867 but where was his face much seen late in the 20th century?
6 Clark Gable, Marlon Brando and Mel Gibson have all played which screen role?
7 In which country is the city of Tanta?
8 Which strain of bird flu was involved in the outbreak in Suffolk in February 2007?
9 Who wrote Aretha Franklin's first UK hit "Respect"?
10 Who became the first British monarch to make a broadcast on Christmas Day?
11 Which 1967 No 1 recorded the longest-ever stay in the UK Top 50?
12 A dessert served "a la mode" in America would include what?
13 Under what name did Everett Bradley and Walter Taieb make the charts in the 1990s?
14 Who won the first ever World Cup in hockey?
15 What was Britain's first issued decimal coin?
16 Who – aptly enough – patented the first upright piano?
17 What is leveche, and where does it come from?
18 What was the first Top Ten hit for Moby?
19 The world's first speaking clock service started in which city?
20 Whom is editor and publisher Michael Wynn-Jones married to?
21 Umberto II was the last king of which country?
22 Which musical won five awards at the 2007 Olivier Awards?
23 What was the animal name of Charles Darwin's survey ship?
24 Which movie was John Wayne making when he won his Oscar for "True Grit"?
25 Stephan van den Berg was the first Olympic gold winner in which water sport?
26 Which ex-Spice Girl shares a birthday with actor Martin Shaw?
27 James Jewel Osterberg became better known under which name?
28 Which role did Robbie Coltrane play in "Tutti Frutti"?
29 Who directed the movie "The X Files"?
30 What is a phobia about bees known as?

1 Which book received the greatest publisher's advance in the 20th century?
2 Whose "Decline and Fall" is described in Evelyn Waugh's first novel?
3 Who won the Booker Prize the year after Paddy Clarke first won in the 1990s?
4 Who provided the "Four Words" at the start of "The Book of General Ignorance"?
5 Which zoo was founded by the author of "The Overloaded Ark"?
6 Who are the two sisters in the novel subtitled "The Sacred and Profane Memories of Captain Charles Ryder"?
7 Where is Michael Ondaatje's "In the Skin of a Lion" set?
8 Which book has the cover line "Three Secrets, Two Women, One Grail"?
9 In which village does the hero of George Eliot's first full-length novel live?
10 Whose diary opens Bram Stoker's most famous novel?
11 Who wrote the novel about the WWII drama brought to the small screen by Steven Spielberg and Tom Hanks?
12 "One Flew Over the Cuckoo's Nest" is told from whose standpoint?
13 What is Charles Dickens' only other work of historical fiction along with "A Tale of Two Cities"?
14 In "Animal Farm" what is the name of the animal seen as Trotsky?
15 Which painting did Donald Sassoon write about?
16 What is the title of journalist John Simpson's "Tales from a Traveller's Life"?
17 What was the first novel in which PD James' Cordelia Gray appeared?
18 Which poet is the official biographer of Philip Larkin?
19 Which sportsman's autobiography was called "A Season in Paradise"?
20 Which Award did "A Stitch in Time" win?
21 Who was the youngest of the "Little Women"?
22 Who is the subject of "Dear Tom"?
23 Approximately how many books per year did Barbara Cartland write during the last 20 years of her life?
24 From which Shakespeare play does the title of "Brave New World" come?
25 Which novel by "The Snowman"'s author was about a nuclear attack?
26 Which novel did the author of "Akenfield" write in 1960?
27 What is "Barchester Towers" the sequel to?
28 What was the title of the 2001 bestseller by the writer who had achieved 20th-century success with "The Day of the Jackal" and "The Odessa File"?
29 What was the first novel in which Hercule Poirot appeared?
30 "Killing Dragons" is about the conquering of what?

Answers	Famous Names *(see Quiz 67)*

1 Zak Starkey and Stella McCartney. 2 Jack Ryan. 3 Desperate Dan. 4 Alan Shepherd. 5 Jelly Roll Morton. 6 Elzie Sagar. 7 George W Bush & Tony Blair. 8 Mariel Hemingway. 9 Francis Ford Coppola. 10 Stella Rimington. 11 Bill Hudson and Goldie Hawn. 12 Columbia. 13 Patricia Highsmith. 14 Alfred Butts. 15 Ernie Wise. 16 Jackie Coogan. 17 Sam Wanamaker. 18 Harry Secombe and Peter Sellers. 19 Eric Idle. 20 L'Oreal. 21 Swimmer. 22 Kennedy. 23 Tyra Banks. 24 Harvard. 25 Kate Greenaway. 26 Stevens. 27 Medicine. 28 Bernard. 29 Astronomer Royal. 30 Trent.

1 In motor racing, who was the first driver to be sacked twice by Benetton?
2 Who was the first "Coronation Street" actress to be awarded an OBE?
3 A brochette is another name for what type of food?
4 Who adapted "The Cider House Rules" into a movie?
5 In which country is the city of Makeyevka?
6 What does a lapidary deal in?
7 On 19th February 2007, Notting Hill, Kensington, Westminster became subjected to what?
8 Which group had 1970 top ten hits with "Sunny", "Belfast" and "Painter Man"?
9 What did D stand for in Franklin D Roosevelt's name?
10 In which 1980s movie did Mr & Mrs Harvey Keitel star?
11 Victor Emmanuel was the first King of which European country?
12 Leander is the oldest club in the world in which sport?
13 In 2007 who won the Orange Rising Star Award at the BAFTAS?
14 What is Sebastian Coe's middle name?
15 Which 1990s English soccer champions have a ground with the Darwen End?
16 Where in the US was the first artificial turf soccer pitch?
17 What was the first Top Ten single for Iron Maiden?
18 Which city hosts the oldest modern-day marathon race?
19 Whose wives included Helen Menken and Mary Philips?
20 On TV for many years Michael Miles invited contestants to do what?
21 Paris and which other capital city were the first to be linked by telephone?
22 What was Gary Cooper's job before he became an actor?
23 The Strathcona Cup is competed for in which sport?
24 What was the first Top Ten single for James?
25 Which folk singer and writer who inspired Dylan, passed away in February 2007?
26 Who dropped out of "The Godfather, Part III", allowing Sofia Coppola to play the role?
27 Michael Fagan made the headlines when he broke into where?
28 In which film did a pilot named Klaatu appear?
29 How does Roger Peterson fit into the history of pop music?
30 Geraldine Rees was the first woman jockey to finish which race?

| **Answers** | Pot Luck 31 *(see Quiz 68)* |

1 Long jump and high jump. 2 Max Bygraves. 3 The Queen. 4 Mark Lawson. 5 Stuart Gray. 6 Tony McCoy. 7 Tom Stoppard. 8 One. 9 Kate Long. 10 Boat Race. 11 200m. 12 Irvin Kershner. 13 Mexico. 14 Colin Clive. 15 Jersey Joe Walcott. 16 Greece. 17 Lincoln. 18 The Old Bailey. 19 Germany. 20 Two. 21 Drowned. 22 Shoes. 23 Charly. 24 Place it was first detected. 25 Pilot's licence. 26 Algeria. 27 Germany & Japan. 28 Global Challenger. 29 May. 30 Mats Wilander.

1 Which two Beatles children had the same birthday?
2 Who invented the Barbie doll?
3 Which fictional Dan first put in an appearance in 1937?
4 Who was the first person to hit a golf ball on the Moon?
5 How was Ferdinand Joseph Lamothe better known?
6 Who created Popeye?
7 Which famous names expressed they used the same toothpaste in 2001?
8 Which member of a famous film and writing family owned Sam's Restaurant in Manhattan?
9 Which film director is the son of a former first flute of the New York Symphony Orchestra under Toscanini?
10 Who wrote an autobiography called "Open Secret"?
11 Who are Kate Hudson's parents?
12 Which university awarded the Prize named after publisher Pulitzer?
13 How is Patricia Plangman better known?
14 Who invented Scrabble?
15 Which late comedian's autobiography was called "Still on My Way to Hollywood"?
16 Who was the first movie child to earn a million dollars?
17 The rebuilding of the Globe Theatre on the south bank of the Thames was the brainchild of whom?
18 Which two Goons had the same birthday?
19 Which member of the Monty Python team wrote "The Rutland Dirty Weekend Book"?
20 Liliane Bettencourt is heiress to which company's fortune?
21 What type of sports person tested the first Rolex Oyster watch?
22 Which father of a future President was executive producer on many Gloria Swanson movies?
23 Who was the first African-American to be featured on the cover of "Sports Illustrated"'s swimsuit issue?
24 Dr Lawrence Summers stood down in 2005 as president of which university?
25 Which author has a prize for children's book illustration named after her?
26 Who owned the original yacht after whom the Americas Cup was named?
27 What did Giorgio Armani study at university?
28 What was the first name of "Mr Laura Ashley"?
29 Which position was held by Sir Martin Rees at the turn of the century?
30 Jesse Boot, of Boots fame, was which Lord when he died in 1931?

Answers | **Books** (see Quiz 65)

1 Without Remorse. 2 Paul Pennyfeather. 3 James Kelman. 4 Alan Davies. 5 Jersey. 6 Julia and Cordelia. 7 Toronto. 8 Labyrinth. 9 Hayslope. 10 Jonathan Harker. 11 Stephen Ambrose. 12 Bromden. 13 Barnaby Rudge. 14 Snowball. 15 Mona Lisa. 16 A Mad World, My Masters. 17 An Unsuitable Job for a Woman. 18 Andrew Motion. 19 Henrik Larsson. 20 Whitbread. 21 Amy. 22 Tom Courtenay. 23 23. 24 The Tempest. 25 When the Wind Blows. 26 A Treasonable Growth. 27 The Warden. 28 The Veteran. 29 The Mysterious Affair at Styles. 30 The Alps.

1 At the 1948 Olympics in which two events did Fanny Blankers Koen choose not to compete despite holding the world record in both?

2 Who was the only British male to feature in the first ever UK album chart?

3 For which movie did Helen Mirren win her first movie BAFTA?

4 Which former politician's son became a regular presenter of Radio 4's "Front Row"?

5 Who was Southampton manager for 113 days in 2001?

6 In 2001 which jockey was the fastest to ride 100 winners in a season?

7 Which well-known literary figure wrote the screenplay for the movie "Billy Bathgate"?

8 How many women had been a Prime Minister before Indira Gandhi took office?

9 Catherine Tate played Karen Cooper in a TV series based on whose novel?

10 Susan Brown was the first woman to compete in which race?

11 What was Carl Lewis's third Olympic gold among the four he won in Los Angeles?

12 Who directed the movie "The Empire Strikes Back"?

13 In which country is the city of Culiacan?

14 Who played the part of Frankenstein in the 1930s classic movie?

15 Before losing to Rocky Marciano who said, "If I can't beat this bum take my name off the record books"?

16 In which country did malmsey wine originate?

17 Which US President patented a type of lifebelt?

18 In London what was built on the site of Newgate prison?

19 In which country were post codes first introduced?

20 How many "Die Hard" movies were made before Samuel L Jackson was introduced as Bruce Willis's sidekick?

21 Australian prime minister Harold Holt died in what circumstances?

22 Imelda Marcos had hundreds of pairs of what?

23 What was the first Top Ten hit for Prodigy?

24 Lassa Fever was named after whom or what?

25 Lord Brabazon was the first Briton to receive which type of licence?

26 In which country was the first HQ of the French Foreign Legion?

27 Which two countries concluded the Anti-Comintern Pact in 1936?

28 What was Tony Bullimore's craft when he capsized in the 1996 Vendee Globe?

29 Which month of the year was part of the name of a Bond girl?

30 Who did Yannick Noah beat to become the first Frenchman to win the French Open tennis champion for 37 years?

Answers | Pot Luck 30 *(see Quiz 66)*

1 Johnny Herbert. 2 Violet Carson. 3 Kebab. 4 John Irving. 5 Ukraine. 6 Gemstones. 7 Congestion charge. 8 Boney M. 9 Delano. 10 The Naples Connection. 11 Italy. 12 Rowing. 13 Eva Green. 14 Newbold. 15 Blackburn Rovers. 16 Houston. 17 Run to the Hills. 18 Boston. 19 Humphrey Bogart. 20 Take Your Pick. 21 Brussels. 22 Cartoonist/illustrator. 23 Curling. 24 Sit Down. 25 Eric von Schmidt. 26 Winona Ryder. 27 Buckingham Palace. 28 The Day the Earth Stood Still. 29 In charge of the flight that claimed the life of Buddy Holly. 30 Grand National.

1 Who took 107 international wickets in 1998?
2 How many different countries had won the ICC World Cup before 2007?
3 Who won the County Championship in 1966?
4 By how many wickets did Middlesex win the last Gillette Cup?
5 In the 1970s which NatWest Trophy winner had the shortest name?
6 Which humorous writer said October was a strange month for the real cricket fan as it was then he discovered his wife had left him in May?
7 Which was the more northerly County to share the title in 1977?
8 Who captained the first South African side after the fall of apartheid?
9 Against whom did Sachin Tendulkar score his 18th ODI century?
10 Against which country did Trevor Chappell bowl an underarm delivery?
11 Who took eight wickets for England in the first ever Test match?
12 Where did Brian Lara score 390 runs in one day in June 1994?
13 Who was man of the match after taking a Test hat-trick against the West Indies in 1995?
14 How was Mansur Ali Khan better known?
15 Who was the first Pakistan cricketer to score 1000 runs and take 100 wickets in a year twice?
16 Which captain won every toss against South Africa in 1960?
17 Who was the first player to score 2000 first-class runs in a season without scoring a century?
18 Who played for Australia in the 1980s and for South Africa in 1991?
19 Which then Lancashire soccer club did EH "Patsy" Hendren play for?
20 Where was the first Oxford and Cambridge match played?
21 How many balls did Adam Gilchrist need to reach an 2006–07 Ashes ton at Perth?
22 Who took all 10 wickets against Pakistan in February 1999?
23 Which football club employed ex-England captain Rachael Heyhoe Flint?
24 Which Englishman overtook the Englishman who overtook Geoff Boycott's record of runs scored in Test cricket?
25 Why was Geoff Boycott banned from Test cricket in 1982?
26 To the nearest 20, how many record-breaking Test runs did Viv Richards make in one calendar year in 1976?
27 Which was the first city to have four Test grounds?
28 How many runs did Jim Laker concede in his 19-wicket haul in a 1956 Test?
29 Who won the County Championship for seven consecutive years in the 1950s?
30 Where did Brian Lara score 375 runs against England in April 1994?

1 Which Saw movie was released in 2006?

2 Who scored the injury-time penalty by which Italy beat Australia in Germany 2006?

3 At which university did Anthony Minghella teach before becoming an Oscar winner?

4 Balti is the Indian word for what?

5 Who won an Oscar for the song "Three Coins in the Fountain"?

6 Frank McCourt's memoirs were set in which Irish county?

7 Which Elvis single made him the first artist to have three consecutive British No 1s?

8 Hanepoot is a type of what?

9 What was named after Buck's Club in London?

10 Which food item comes from the Turkish for rotating?

11 Kummel is a Russian liqueur extracted from what?

12 Which country has a wine-growing area called O'Higgins?

13 Which rays did Ernest Rutherford discover?

14 What subject did TV cook Sophie Grigson study at university?

15 What is added to an omelette to make an Omelette Argenteuil?

16 After winning the world title, who was Jack Dempsey's first opponent where the fight went to the full distance?

17 Who did Tottenham Hotspur beat in the final to become FA Cup and League Champions for the first time?

18 Which No 1 single mentions Jackie – Madame – Onassis?

19 Who was the first professional to captain England at cricket?

20 In 1952 at the Chateau de Chambord what type of display was first shown?

21 In which country did the card game canasta originate?

22 What did the Tower Commission investigate in the US in the 1980s?

23 Which band's vocalists have included Blaze Bayley and Bruce Dickinson?

24 On TV, who had a house featuring a dog, cat and a frog?

25 In which city did Kurt Cobain die?

26 How is writer Salvatore Lombino better known?

27 Radium has the atomic number of which bingo call?

28 How is comedian Edward McGinnis better known?

29 Cocose is a butter made from what?

30 Which was the first US state to abolish slavery?

Answers | Pot Luck 33 *(see Quiz 72)*

1 Savage Garden. 2 Gary Oldman. 3 Have a heart transplant. 4 Bertie Mee. 5 Giles Foden. 6 Angling. 7 Texas. 8 Hampton Court maze. 9 Harmonica. 10 Do They Know It's Christmas?. 11 Lacrosse. 12 Peru. 13 Boxing. 14 House. 15 Rudolph. 16 Degerfos. 17 Boisterous. 18 Irene Nemirosvsky. 19 Elizabeth Taylor. 20 Iowa. 21 Kenya. 22 Gandhi. 23 Roper. 24 Handkerchief. 25 Wilhelm. 26 Pack horse. 27 Germany. 28 Jack Ryan. 29 Symptoms of disease. 30 Connie Francis.

1 Who named Hollywood?

2 What was the first film of the actor married to Debra Winger from 1986 to 1990?

3 Helen Hunt's fourth movie shares its name with which later musical?

4 What was music composer James Horner's first Oscar nomination of the 1990s?

5 Who used the pseudonym William Goodrich when Hollywood turned his back on him after a scandal?

6 Humphrey Bogart underwent surgery for cancer of the oesophagus after making which film?

7 In which 1953 film did Oscar Hammerstein II appear as himself?

8 Which studio gave Lauren Bacall her film debut?

9 Which movie was based on the life of John Belushi?

10 Who portrayed the author of "The Maltese Falcon" in "Julia"?

11 His directorial debut was "That Thing You Do", but what was his first movie as an actor?

12 What type of screen animal was Rhubarb?

13 Which Lillian Hellman novel became the movie "Julia", starring Jane Fonda?

14 Which company did William Randolph Hearst found with the express purpose of making his mistress Marion Davies a star?

15 Which MGM movie did Katharine Hepburn make directly after "The Philadelphia Story"?

16 What was Woody Allen's last film with United Artists?

17 Which Hollywood star was co-owner of the Mount Kenya Safari Club?

18 What was Gene Kelly's solo directing debut?

19 Who played Commodus in Russell Crowe's Oscar-winning movie?

20 "Deeper Underground" was written for which Hollywood movie?

21 Which Hollywood legend did Charles Dance play in "Good Morning Babylon"?

22 Who co-wrote "Heaven Can Wait" with Warren Beatty?

23 What was Whitney Houston's follow-up to her on-screen debut?

24 Who was the first non-Swede to star in an Ingmar Bergman movie?

25 Which mother and daughter appeared in "Carrie"?

26 Who played opposite Anthony Hopkins in the follow-up to "Silence of the Lambs"?

27 What was Robert De Niro's directorial debut?

28 How many Golden Globes did "Dreamgirls" win?

29 Which role did Spottiswoode Aitken play in "Birth of a Nation"?

30 Who wrote and directed "The Sixth Sense"?

Answers | Cricket *(see Quiz 69)*

1 Allan Donald. 2 Five. 3 Yorkshire. 4 Seven. 5 Kent. 6 Denis Norden. 7 Middlesex. 8 Kepler Wessels. 9 Zimbabwe. 10 New Zealand. 11 Alfred Shaw. 12 Edgbaston. 13 Dominic Cork. 14 The Nawab of Pataudi. 15 Imran Khan. 16 Colin Cowdrey. 17 David Green, Lancashire. 18 Kepler Wessels. 19 Manchester City. 20 Lord's. 21 57 balls. 22 Anil Kumble. 23 Wolves. 24 Graham Gooch passed David Gower. 25 Went on a rebel tour to South Africa. 26 1710. 27 Colombo. 28 90. 29 Surrey. 30 Recreation Ground, St John's Antigua.

1 Daniel Jones and Darren Hayes made the pop charts under what name?
2 To whom was Uma Thurman married before Ethan Hawke?
3 Philip Blaiberg was the second person to do what?
4 Which double-winning soccer manager died in October 2001?
5 On whose book was the movie "The Last King of Scotland" based?
6 CIPS is the body which regulates which sport?
7 The gigantic nightclub Gilley's Club is in which US state?
8 London and Wise designed which famous much-visited feature?
9 Charles Wheatstone is the creator of what?
10 Which debut single became the first to enter the charts straight at No 1?
11 Baggataway developed into which game?
12 In which country is the city of Callao?
13 What was the first sport screened on ITV?
14 What name is given to the circular target in curling?
15 What is the middle name of former US President Gerald Ford?
16 Sven Goran Eriksson first coached at which club in the late 1970s?
17 What does the musical term strepitoso mean – boisterous, in military style or in strict tempo?
18 Who wrote the besteller "Suite Française"?
19 Who has been married to Larry Fortensky, John Warner and Nicky Hilton?
20 Which state in America is known as the Hawkeye State?
21 Princess Elizabeth was visiting which country at the time that she become Queen Elizabeth II?
22 "No man's life can be encompassed in one telling" are the opening words of which epic movie?
23 What was the surname of sitcom marrieds George and Mildred?
24 Richard II is said to have popularised the use of which everyday item?
25 What is Leonardo Di Caprio's middle name?
26 Who or what is a sumpter?
27 In which country is the city of Wuppertal?
28 Who was Zsa Zsa Gabor's sixth husband?
29 What is semeiology the study of?
30 Concetta Franconero took old standard songs back into the pop charts under which name?

---

1 In which US state is the Jewel cave system?
2 The largest man-made excavation in the world mines which element?
3 Which animal weighs the most – grizzly bear, polar bear or a walrus?
4 What is Europe's largest island which is not a country in its own right?
5 Which desert is on the US–Mexico border?
6 What is the most common element in the earth's crust after oxygen?
7 Which planet orbits the Sun fastest?
8 Acid rain results due to a pollution of the atmosphere with oxides of nitrogen and what?
9 What is another name for a tsunami?
10 What colour is apatite?
11 Where was the meteorite High Possil found?
12 Where is the highest waterfall outside South America?
13 What is the world's highest island?
14 How many states does Lake Michigan cover?
15 Which planet has the hottest surface?
16 Orogenesis is concerned with the formation of what?
17 Which unit measures distances beyond the solar system?
18 Where was the meteorite Armanty found on Earth?
19 Actinobiology studies the effect of what on living organisms?
20 Cryogenics studies materials under what conditions?
21 Of the five largest glaciers in the world which is the only one not in Antarctica?
22 Which part of planet Earth would a pedologist observe?
23 The Appleton layer plays a role in what – heat control, sifting of toxic gases or radio communication?
24 It isn't a sea, but what is the Afsluidijk Sea?
25 How many countries does the Mekong river flow through?
26 What is the most common element in the universe after hydrogen?
27 Which planet is the lightest?
28 Which scale measures the hardness of substances?
29 How many light years is Alpha Centauri from the Earth?
30 What substance is around 90% of the Earth's core made from?

Answers	TV Drama *(see Quiz 75)*

1 Hearts & Bones. 2 DCI Tom Barnaby. 3 William Boyd. 4 Ian Rankin. 5 Mersey Beat. 6 Sherlock Holmes. 7 Ken Loach. 8 Band of Brothers. 9 Arthur Parker. 10 Holding On. 11 Victoria & Albert. 12 Peak Practice. 13 Hamish Macbeth. 14 James Nesbitt. 15 Sabbach. 16 Chicago. 17 The Final Cut. 18 The Way We Live Now. 19 Warren Clarke. 20 Hamble. 21 John Sullivan. 22 Masterpiece Theater. 23 Anthony Minghella. 24 Colin Bateman. 25 Alan Davies. 26 Jewel in the Crown. 27 Chris Kelly. 28 Pharmaceutical. 29 Sir Godber Evans. 30 Telly Savalas (Kojak).

1 Which country is directly south of the southern area of Morocco?
2 Which band has had Briana Corrigan and Jacqui Abbot among its vocalists?
3 To the nearest ten, how many minutes did the original "Planet of the Apes" movie last?
4 Which Elton John song mentions a "man who sells potions"?
5 Who wrote the screenplay for the phenomenally successful movie "The Bodyguard"?
6 In which country is the city of Chiba?
7 The song "Secret Love" came from which movie?
8 In which country is the city of Constanta?
9 Which Offenbach composition was used to advertise Bailey's Irish Cream?
10 TV's popular sitcom "To the Manor Born" was set in which village?
11 Who is Postman Pat's wife?
12 Pete Townshend's first No 1 as a producer was for which group?
13 Who was the first non-African to win the Olympic 5000m after Lasse Viren in Canada?
14 How did James Wight become better known to the reading world?
15 Dao wine comes from which country?
16 Who received an Oscar nomination for the original score for "The Talented Mr Ripley"?
17 What is the name of the state-of-the-art, super-bright light generator located in south Oxfordshire?
18 Sibbald's rorqual is also known as what?
19 A passata is made from which vegetable?
20 Who got the fastest individual goal of Japan and South Korea's 2002 tournament?
21 Who won the Best Director Oscar for the movie "Cavalcade"?
22 Which country borders Argentina, Brazil and Bolivia?
23 Who conducted the Three Tenors in their Italia 90 concert?
24 Which Springsteen song was a hit for Manfred Mann's Earth Band?
25 Who directed the first "Terminator" film?
26 In which country is the city of Campos?
27 Which poet wrote "Sea Fever"?
28 Who became Sudanese president in 1993?
29 What was the third line on the London Underground?
30 A maxwell unit is a measure of what?

Answers | **Pot Luck 35** *(see Quiz 76)*

1 17th October. 2 Spit. 3 Space Shuttle launch. 4 Angus Deayton. 5 Ticket to Ride. 6 Oenology. 7 Valentino Rossi. 8 Roberta Flack. 9 Jean Terrell. 10 Jürgen Hingsen. 11 Private Godfrey. 12 Michinomiya. 13 Crescent-shaped. 14 Princess. 15 William. 16 Azerbaijan. 17 Bryan Robson. 18 Poles. 19 Daniel Day-Lewis. 20 James Naughtie. 21 Bernard Herrmann. 22 Sandwich. 23 Multiplex. 24 India. 25 Twin Peaks. 26 2061. 27 Three. 28 Maurice Jarre. 29 Betty Stove. 30 The Phil Silvers Show.

1 In which drama did Rich, Emma, Annie and Sam share a surname?
2 Who was Sgt Gavin Troy's boss?
3 Who wrote the novel on which "Armadillo" was based?
4 Whose novels were used as the basis for the drama series "Rebus"?
5 In which series did Supt Susan Blake take charge?
6 "Murder Rooms" was a drama series about which detective?
7 Which veteran film maker wrote "Navigators" about the break-up of the rail network?
8 Which series was about Easy Company, a unit of paratroopers?
9 What was the name of the songsheet salesman in "Pennies from Heaven"?
10 Which 1990s Tony Marchant series about life in London starred Phil Daniels?
11 Which famous couple were portrayed by Jonathan Firth and Victoria Hamilton in a 2001 drama?
12 In which series did character Erica Matthews replace Beth Glover?
13 Which detective was played on TV by the star of "The Full Monty" and "Angela's Ashes"?
14 Who played Adam in "Cold Feet"?
15 Where was the German-made series "Heimat" based?
16 The outside scenes for "Hill Street Blues" were filmed in which city?
17 What was the last part of the trilogy which began with "House of Cards"?
18 In which series was Auguste Melmotte a central character?
19 Who played Faith's husband in "Down to Earth"?
20 Alongside which river was "Howard's Way" set?
21 Who wrote the David Jason series based on an infamous Dickens character?
22 Under what label was "I Claudius" broadcast in the USA?
23 Which early writer of "Morse" went on to write the movie "Truly Madly Deeply"?
24 Who wrote "Murphy's Law" for James Nesbitt?
25 If Lesley Sharp played Rose, who played Bob in 2001?
26 Which epic won the 1984 International Emmy for Best Drama?
27 Which one-time food show presenter produced "Kavanagh QC"?
28 Swallow was about which industry?
29 Who did Ian Richardson play in "Porterhouse Blue"?
30 Which actor who played a TV cop won a Purple Heart in Korea in real life?

1 In 2006, what was the date of the One Day in History project?
2 Which dog did Chris Tarrant have to contend with on "TISWAS"?
3 John Young was the commander on which notable flight?
4 Who played Mike Channel in "KYTV"?
5 What was the first No 1 single from The Beatles' film "Help!"?
6 What is the study of wine known as?
7 Which motor cyclist took his 10th win of the 2001 season in the Malaysian Grand Prix?
8 Who sang the title song in "Someone to Watch Over Me" with Sting and Gene Ammons?
9 Who replaced Diana Ross when she left The Supremes?
10 Who was world record holder when Daley Thompson won Olympic gold in 1984?
11 In sitcom, which character had sisters called Dolly & Cissy?
12 What was the first name of Japan's Emperor Hirohito?
13 What shape is a roll if it is rugelach?
14 "Say I'm Your Number One" was the only Top Ten hit for which act?
15 What was Clark Gable's real first name?
16 In which country is the city of Baku?
17 Who else hit a hat-trick for England during the time that Gary Lineker was notching his five hat-tricks?
18 What did the initial P stand for in the name of writer LP Hartley?
19 Julia Roberts turned down "Shakespeare in Love" because which actor of her choice did not get to play Shakespeare?
20 Which newsman replaced Richard Baker as the presenter of the Proms on BBC?
21 Who scored the music for the famous shower scene in "Psycho"?
22 Which food item was linked to Colin in the title of a Mel Smith sitcom series?
23 Who were the building firm working on the new Wembley Stadium?
24 In which country is the city of Guntur?
25 As well as being an ex-US President, Harry S Truman was a sheriff in which TV series?
26 When is Halley's Comet predicted to make its next visit in Earth's vicinity?
27 How many books were there in Mervyn Peake's "Gormenghast" series?
28 Who produced the stirring movie music for "Lawrence of Arabia"?
29 Who won the first set in the last Wimbledon Ladies' Singles final to have a British competitor?
30 Which sitcom was first called "You'll Never Get Rich" in the US?

Answers | Pot Luck 34 *(see Quiz 74)*

1 Mauritania. 2 Beautiful South. 3 120. 4 Your Song. 5 Lawrence Kasdan. 6 Japan. 7 Calamity Jane. 8 Romania. 9 Barcarolle. 10 Cricket St Thomas. 11 Sarah. 12 Thunderclap Newman. 13 Dieter Baumann. 14 James Herriot. 15 Portugal. 16 Gabriel Yared. 17 Diamond Synchotron. 18 Blue whale. 19 Tomatoes. 20 Hakan Sukur. 21 Frank Lloyd. 22 Paraguay. 23 Zubin Mehta. 24 Blinded by the Light. 25 James Cameron. 26 Brazil. 27 John Masefield. 28 Omar al-Bashir. 29 Piccadilly line. 30 Magnetic flux.

1 Which tribe did Rwanda's majority tribe try to wipe out in the 1990s?
2 On which day of the week in 1953 was Everest conquered?
3 Which Apollo mission saw the fastest human speed record?
4 In 1990 who was granted a US patent for an energy-saving double filament light bulb?
5 The Clean Air Act was introduced after which year when 4,000 people died in London's worst recorded smog?
6 Where did Francisco Bahamonde rule?
7 Radio Caroline first began broadcasting five miles off which port?
8 Who commanded the first nuclear submarine under the North Pole?
9 On which day of the week was the Channel Tunnel opened?
10 How old was Spain's General Franco when he died?
11 Which country first had a postcode made up of letters and numbers?
12 What was the "Queen Elizabeth" being used as when sabotaged in Hong Kong harbour?
13 Which US President during the height of the Cold War, said there would be no Soviet domination of Eastern Europe?
14 In which city was the first Cadillac made?
15 In 1951's general election where was Margaret Roberts (later Thatcher) defeated?
16 For how many years in World War II were the lights in Piccadilly Circus blacked out?
17 Who was the first centre spread in "Playboy"?
18 Jacqueline Cochrane was the first woman to break what?
19 Who was the first cartoon character to appear on a US postage stamp?
20 Who or what were Able and Baker, the first pair of their kind to return from space?
21 Who devised transparent solar panels which can be used as windows and as a means of producing solar power?
22 Che Guevara was killed while training guerrillas against which government?
23 In which hospital was the world's first test tube baby born?
24 Who was the youngest winner of the Nobel Peace Prize in 1964?
25 Which charity began as a newspaper appeal "The Forgotten Prisoners"?
26 In what year was the first phone card issued in Japan?
27 Which play first won five of the awards named after Antoinette Perry?
28 In 1997 which country saw the largest and most numerous forest fires?
29 Which company's pesticide plant in Bhopal had a tragic chemical leak?
30 In which game did Nintendo's Mario character first appear?

Answers	Music – Solo Performers *(see Quiz 79)*

1 Microsoft Network. 2 Marian Anderson. 3 Feels Like Home. 4 Tears on My Pillow.
5 Anita Harris. 6 Mary Hopkin. 7 Jilted John. 8 Courtney Love. 9 Barry Gibb. 10 Frozen. 11 Liza Minnelli. 12 Kylie Minogue. 13 Prince. 14 Suzi Quatro. 15 Greetings From Asbury Park. 16 Alvin Stardust. 17 Brentford. 18 Evergreen. 19 Smokey Robinson. 20 Barry Manilow. 21 Apple. 22 Marty Wilde. 23 Paul Simon. 24 58. 25 Jewel of the Nile. 26 Peter Asher. 27 Sinead O'Connor. 28 Don McLean. 29 Eartha Kitt. 30 Carole King.

Quiz 78 | Pot Luck 36

Answers – page 320

LEVEL 3

1 Who broke the world 200m record at the Atlanta Olympics?
2 Who composed the musical score for "On the Town"?
3 What was Orlando Bloom's occupation in "Elizabethtown"?
4 Dzongkha is the official language of which monarchy?
5 Which Spice Girl wrote "Girl Power" by her signature on the cover notes of the album "Spice"?
6 What's the number of HAL the computer in Kubrick's movie "2001"?
7 Which capital is furthest north – Addis Ababa, Kampala, Khartoum or Nairobi?
8 Which Premiership club was helped out by Russian businessman Alexandre Gaydamak?
9 What was the final Bond film in which Lois Maxwell played Miss Moneypenny?
10 In which country is the city of Las?
11 Nice ads, but which make of car were Papa and Nicole advertising?
12 Who was the first female presenter of TV's "Grandstand"?
13 Which Rod Stewart No 1 was originally the flip side of "Reason to Believe"?
14 The man who broke Sebastian Coe's 800m world record was running for which country?
15 Who was the first jockey to win the Derby in three consecutive races?
16 Mungo Park, the explorer of the River Niger, came from which country?
17 In sitcom, which vehicle was connected with Stan Butler?
18 Ambergris obtained from which sea creature?
19 "You'll Never Find Another Love Like Mine" was the only Top Ten hit for which singer?
20 Which screen tough guy made his debut as a mugger in Woody Allen's "Bananas"?
21 On a computer keyboard where is the letter B in relation to V?
22 Which group still meeting up for reunions included Peter Tork and Michael Nesmith?
23 In round figures, what was Irving Berlin's output of writing popular songs?
24 In which decade was the Argentinian Grand Prix first held?
25 Who gave Stock/Aitken/Waterman their first No1 hit?
26 On which atoll was the US's first hydrogen bomb detonated?
27 In fiction which detective married Harriet Vane?
28 Which country can have the letters NO added to its name to name its currency?
29 Which cereal is polenta made from?
30 Who was the first woman to lecture at the Sorbonne?

| **Answers** | **Pot Luck 37** *(see Quiz 80)* |

1 Franklin. 2 Neil Young. 3 Dear John. 4 Swimming. 5 Skin. 6 Springfield. 7 Uruguay. 8 George C Scott. 9 The Addams Family. 10 Ty Hardin. 11 Bing Crosby. 12 Po. 13 Shopping. 14 Elizabeth Taylor. 15 Australia. 16 The weather. 17 Jeanie Linders. 18 Cilla Black. 19 Laser. 20 Ohio. 21 Address unknown. 22 Potassium. 23 Whitney Houston. 24 The Mikado. 25 Fosco. 26 Hockey. 27 Can fly backwards. 28 Three Men and a Baby. 29 Trouser leg. 30 All I Wanna Do.

1 Which on-line company broadcast Madonna's Brixton Academy concert live on the Internet?

2 Who was the first black performer to sing at the New York Metropolitan Opera?

3 What was the title of the second No 1 album for Norah Jones?

4 What was Kylie Minogue's last No 1 produced by Stock, Aitken and Waterman?

5 Which solo performer promoted Slendertone keep fit equipment in 1997?

6 Which solo singer married record producer Tony Visconti?

7 How did Graham Fellows aka John Shuttleworth appear in the UK charts in 1978?

8 Which singer's daughter by a controversial performer was called Frances Bean?

9 Who produced Lulu's album which included the tracks "Every Woman Knows" and "How 'Bout Us"?

10 What did Madonna sing on her first live UK TV show for 15 years in 1998?

11 Which music and musical star deputised for Julie Andrews on Broadway in Victor/Victoria in the mid-1990s?

12 Who was about to release an album called "Impossible Princess" in 1997 but changed the title after the death of Princess Diana?

13 Who married Mayte Garcia in 1996?

14 Which singer appeared as Leather Tuscadero in "Happy Days"?

15 What was "The Boss's" debut album?

16 Which singer has appeared in "Hollyoaks" and was Gaston in "Beauty & The Beast" in the West End?

17 Which club gave a teenage Roderick David Stewart a soccer trial?

18 For what did Barbra Streisand win an Oscar for Best Song?

19 Which singer had children called Berry and Tamla?

20 Whose musical Harmony opened on Broadway in 1998?

21 Which company released James Taylor's debut album?

22 Which 1950s star wrote Status Quo's "Ice in the Sun"?

23 Which singer wrote the then biggest musical flop in New York history in 1998?

24 How many albums had Cliff Richard made by his 40th year in show business?

25 From which movie soundtrack was Billy Ocean's biggest hit?

26 Which 1964 chart topper won the Producer of the Year Grammy in 1977?

27 Whose debut album was "The Lion and the Cobra"?

28 Who was the subject of the song "Killing Me Softly"?

29 Which vocalist who recorded with Bronski Beat in the the late 1980s was described by Orson Welles as "the most exciting woman in the world"?

30 To which singer was the album "Tapestry Revisited" dedicated?

1 Who designed the first lightning conductor?
2 The soundtrack of the movie "Philadelphia" featured songs by Bruce Springsteen and who else?
3 Which sitcom introduced viewers to the 1-2-1 Club?
4 The trudgen is a movement in which sport?
5 Where are denticles found on a shark?
6 Where in Illinois in 2007 did Barack Obama announce he was running for the Presidency?
7 Which country is home to the airline Pluna?
8 Who was the first actor ever to refuse an Oscar?
9 Who lived at Cemetery Ridge?
10 Under which name did Orson Whipple Hungerford III become an actor riding across our screens?
11 Who described himself as "an average guy who could carry a tune"?
12 Who is the smallest Teletubby?
13 What was Jude Law's first film?
14 Which movie great set up the American Foundation for AIDS Research?
15 The Kakadu National Park is located in which country?
16 What could Sean Connery's character change in "The Avengers"?
17 Who wrote "Menopause the Musical"?
18 Which TV star is mum to Robert, Ben and Jack Willis?
19 Charles Townes pioneered what?
20 Where in America was Alcoholics Anonymous founded?
21 In the Elvis song, which two words follow "Return to sender"?
22 Kalium is an alternative name for which element?
23 What was the title of Whitney Houston's first album?
24 Which musical work for the stage is set in the town of Titipu?
25 Which Count is the villain in "The Woman in White" by Wilkie Collins?
26 John Potter became the most capped English player in which sport?
27 What is the unique about the flight of a hummingbird?
28 Which film comedy was "Trois Hommes et Un Couffin" in French?
29 Calzone, a folded pizza dough dish, takes its name from what in Italian?
30 What was the first Top Ten hit for Sheryl Crow?

Answers	Pot Luck 36 *(see Quiz 78)*

1 Michael Johnson. 2 Leonard Bernstein. 3 Shoe designer. 4 Bhutan. 5 Geri. 6 9000. 7 Khartoum. 8 Portsmouth. 9 A View To A Kill. 10 Romania. 11 Renault. 12 Helen Rollason. 13 Maggie May. 14 Denmark (Wilson Kipketer). 15 Steve Donoghue. 16 Scotland. 17 Bus. 18 Sperm whale. 19 Lou Rawls. 20 Sylvester Stallone. 21 Right. 22 The Monkees. 23 900. 24 1940s. 25 Mel and Kim. 26 Eniwetok. 27 Lord Peter Wimsey. 28 Bolivia. 29 Maize. 30 Marie Curie.

1 What culinary item is produced by Filippo Berio?
2 What type of milk was first processed in 1899?
3 In which year did Bird's Eye Fish Fingers first go on sale in the UK?
4 Which drink had the first registered British trademark?
5 Which French city is famous for Cointreau?
6 Which author of "La Bonne Chère" ran the French Pavilion at Disneyworld, Orlando?
7 Which type of pasta lends it name to a type of chocolate decoration?
8 Who created vichysoisse?
9 Who founded the restaurant with Rose Gray where Jamie Oliver was "discovered"?
10 Which area is the only one not to grow a Muscat which is sweet?
11 The Chardonnay grape is a native of where?
12 Which food or drink was named after American John McAdam?
13 Where did Balti cooking originate?
14 In wine making what is another name for tartrate?
15 What are the most common herbs in a bearnaise sauce?
16 Which herb is used in gremolata?
17 When were pressure cookers invented – 1891, 1905 or1933?
18 Where was Anton Mosimann's first post as chef in the UK?
19 Which size of wine bottle is the equivalent of 12 standard bottles?
20 Which monk was responsible for putting the liqueur Chartreuse on sale?
21 Which nuts are usually used in a pesto sauce?
22 Which food item comes form the Hindi meaning pounded meat?
23 Pyrex was made originally to be used where?
24 What is arborio?
25 Auslese is usually made from which grape?
26 Which food comes from the Tamil word meaning pepper water?
27 Dom Bernardo Vincelli devised which drink?
28 Who opened the Miller Howe restaurant in 1971?
29 Fitou is made from which grape?
30 What is unusual about the harvesting of Spätlese grapes?

1 Kubrick's movie "Eyes Wide Shut" used the music of Jazz Suite No 2 by which composer?
2 In which country is the city of Joao Pessoa?
3 On a computer keyboard what letter is below and between G and H?
4 Which English palace was used for the Kenneth Branagh's movie version of "Hamlet"?
5 What was the first name of owner Mr Maplin in the sitcom "Hi De Hi!"?
6 "Cathy" and "Claudette" appear in No 1's for which artists?
7 What is the opponent's goal called in shinty?
8 Whose Divenire Tour took place in 2007?
9 On a computer keyboard what letter is below and between J and K?
10 Which agony aunt shares a birthday with actor John Hurt?
11 Which warrior ruler had a horse called Bucephalus?
12 What species of sea creature is a "Mesonychotenthis hamiltoni"?
13 Eric Oliver was the first world champion in what?
14 What did the second A stand for in ANZAC?
15 What was Cliff Richard's first million seller?
16 Which term indicates the amount of wine by which a container falls short of being full?
17 King Edward VII's father in law was king of which country?
18 In which country is the city of Hermosilla?
19 In the Bond movie what was Goldfinger's first name?
20 When was "The Highway Code" first published?
21 On which horse did Gordon Richards have his only Derby triumph?
22 Which cards were not included in a pack of cards until 1857?
23 Which number followed NCC on the side of the "Starship Enterprise"?
24 What did Harry Brearley invent in 1913 to revolutionise kitchens?
25 In movies, what is the first name of Ralph Fiennes' character in "Schindler's List"?
26 What is Madame Harel credited with creating around 1790?
27 Whose play was turned into the movie "Shadowlands"?
28 Romana Barrack is better known as a TV playwright under which name?
29 Which English club had most players represented in Germany 2006?
30 With which record label did Norah Jones sign in 2002?

Answers	Pot Luck 39 *(see Quiz 84)*

1 1905. 2 The Duke. 3 Ranging. 4 Queen Anne. 5 France. 6 Raquel Welch.
7 Windsor. 8 Roberto di Matteo. 9 A toilet. 10 Cyprus. 11 Evelyn Waugh. 12 Clydesdale. 13 Orbital. 14 Happy Valley. 15 Mount McKinley. 16 Guildford. 17 1981. 18 Warm. 19 Stoller. 20 Stabiliser. 21 Mick McCarthy. 22 Smarty Pants. 23 Spa Francorchamps. 24 Aberdeen. 25 Darwin. 26 Nurse. 27 Luxembourg. 28 Iran. 29 Ian "H" Watkins. 30 Separate Lives (Julian Fellowes).

Quiz 83 | The Oscars | Answers – page 321

1 Which movie shared the Palme d'Or with "Farewell My Concubine"?
2 How many Oscar nominations did "Little Miss Sunshine" receive?
3 Who was Burt Bacharach's lyricist on the song which won an Oscar for "Arthur"?
4 For which film did Richard Harris receive his first nomination?
5 In which movie did Dan Aykroyd play Jessica Tandy's son?
6 Which future Oscar-winner won the Australian Film Institute Award as Best Supporting Actor for "Proof"?
7 Which character did Willem Dafoe play in "Platoon"?
8 Which Oscar-winning actress is the daughter of stage actress Blythe Danner?
9 How many years did Robert Donat age in his 1939 Oscar-winning movie?
10 Which movie led to Sally Field's "You like me. You really like me," speech?
11 What was Morgan Freeman's second Oscar nomination?
12 Who was the first person to win three Oscars in one night?
13 Which Oscar did Woody Allen win when Michael Caine also won for the same movie?
14 For which movie was Rex Harrison nominated a year before his first win?
15 How many films had Goldie Hawn made before she had her first nomination for Best Supporting Actress?
16 In which category did "The Piano"'s director win an Oscar?
17 Lauren Bacall won her first Oscar nomination playing whose mother?
18 For which movie did "Cheers" Woody receive his first nomination?
19 Susan Hayward received five nominations; which movie was her third?
20 Audrey Hepburn won her first nomination for a role opposite whom?
21 Who was the youngest performer ever to be nominated for an Oscar?
22 How many years were there between Julie Andrews' second and third nominations?
23 Who played the husband in the movie for which Pauline Collins was nominated?
24 Who played opposite Joan Fontaine when she won her Oscar for a Hitchcock movie?
25 Who first hosted the Oscar ceremony in 1940?
26 For which Mike Nichols' film was Ann Margret nominated for an Oscar?
27 For which movie did Wendy Hiller win between her nominations for "Pygmalion" and "A Man for All Seasons"?
28 For which 1981 film was the husband of Penelope Wilton nominated?
29 How many Special Academy Awards did Bob Hope win?
30 For which film did Dustin Hoffman have his third nomination?

Answers	**Food and Drink** *(see Quiz 81)*

1 Olive oil. 2 Evaporated milk. 3 1955. 4 Bass Pale Ale. 5 Angers. 6 Paul Bocuse. 7 Vermicelli. 8 Louis Diat. 9 Ruth Rogers. 10 Alsace. 11 Burgundy. 12 Macadamia nuts. 13 Britain. 14 Argol. 15 Tarragon & chervil. 16 Parsley. 17 1905. 18 Dorchester. 19 Salmanazar. 20 Jerome Maubee. 21 Pine nuts. 22 Kofta. 23 Railroad kitchens. 24 Rice. 25 Riesling. 26 Mulligatawny. 27 Benedictine. 28 John Tovey. 29 Carignan. 30 Harvested late.

1 To ten years when was the Rotary Club founded?
2 Which horse with a John Wayne link won the first Grand National?
3 What does the second R stand for in the acronym RADAR?
4 Which monarch attended the very first Royal Ascot?
5 Which country was the first to introduce vehicle registration plates?
6 Jo-Raquel Tejad become known as which movie actress?
7 What is the largest castle in England?
8 Who scored the quickest ever FA Cup Final goal?
9 What was George II supposedly sitting on at the time of his death?
10 EOKA was an active terrorist organisation on which island?
11 Who wrote the novel "The Ordeal of Gilbert Pinfold"?
12 A cross between a Scottish draught horse and a Flemish horse produced which breed?
13 Under what name did Paul and Phil Hartnoll have hit records?
14 What is the name of the Royal Hong Kong Jockey Club's racecourse?
15 How is Denali in Alaska also known?
16 Which place used to form part of The Stranglers' name?
17 In which year did Bernhard Langer first play in a Ryder Cup?
18 What is the usual general temperature requirements for serving sake?
19 Who combined with Leiber to write the rock classic "Jailhouse Rock"?
20 Which food additive prevents fat and water separating out?
21 Who was Republic of Ireland boss when Sven was appointed?
22 What was the only Top Ten hit for US female group First Choice?
23 At which track did Michael Schumacher achieve his record-breaking 52nd career win?
24 Dyce Airport serves which city?
25 Who was born first, Albert Einstein or Charles Darwin?
26 In "Penny Lane", what is the occupation of the person selling poppies from a tray?
27 Alan Shearer scored his only England hat trick against which team?
28 In which country is the city of Tabris?
29 Which former member of Steps featured in "Celebrity Big Brother" in 2007?
30 What was the directorial debut of the screenwriter of "Gosford Park"?

Answers	Pot Luck 38 *(see Quiz 82)*

1 Shostakovich. 2 Brazil. 3 B. 4 Blenheim. 5 Joe. 6 Everly Brothers. 7 Hail. 8 Ludovico Einaudi. 9 M. 10 Claire Rayner. 11 Alexander the Great. 12 Squid. 13 Sidecar. 14 Army. 15 Living Doll. 16 Ullage. 17 Denmark. 18 Mexico. 19 Auric. 20 1931. 21 Pinza. 22 Jokers. 23 1701. 24 Stainless steel. 25 Amon. 26 Camembert cheese. 27 William Nicholson. 28 Carla Lane. 29 Arsenal (15 players). 30 Blue Note.

Quiz 85 | Sporting Who's Who? | Answers – page 327

1 Who were the first fully professional team of baseball players?
2 Who was runner-up when a Dutchman won Wimbledon's Men's Singles in the 1990s?
3 Which actress named her son after baseball pitcher Satchel Paige?
4 Which country won the baseball silver medal at the 2000 Olympic Games?
5 The last time they won Olympic gold in ice hockey in the 20th century the USSR team was known by what name?
6 How old was Jack Nicklaus when he became the oldest US Masters winner?
7 Who won the longest match in a Grand Slam in the 1990s?
8 Which motor sport team did the then record holder for Grand Prix victories buy in 1997 before giving it his own name a year later?
9 Who were the second winners of the NBA in the US?
10 Which side did Martin Corry play for when he made his England debut?
11 Which English-born footballer was picked to play for Scotland during the time his father managed for Wales?
12 When did Karine Ruby's sport become an Olympic event?
13 Who did the older Williams sister beat in her second Wimbledon final?
14 Where did Linford Christie win his fastest 100m?
15 In the 1990s who was the fastest winner of the New York City Marathon?
16 Who was the oldest winner of the singles at the French Open Tennis?
17 Who was the first non-European to run a mile in under four minutes?
18 Where did Carl Lewis set his personal best in the long jump?
19 In 1998 which team's player set a new baseball record for most home runs in a season?
20 What nationality was the youngest Wimbledon Men's Singles winner?
21 How many gold medals did Carl Lewis win at his second Olympics?
22 Who won the first London Marathon of the new millennium?
23 Which country was the second to play Test cricket against England?
24 Who holds the record as the biggest money earner between 1993 and 2001 in women's golf?
25 How many world records did Sergey Bubka break before the end of 1999?
26 Who, in December 1993, was the fastest European woman in the world?
27 On which make of motor cycle was the fastest world championship of the 1970s raced?
28 Who became the youngest man to end the year as World No 1 in 2001?
29 Which European won most US Open Men's Singles titles in the 1990s?
30 Which name was added in the 1990s to the side which has won the Challenge Cup most times in Rugby League?

Answers | Movie Firsts (see Quiz 87)

1 Otto Preminger's The Moon is Blue. 2 A Matter of Life and Death. 3 Imperial Airways.
4 40. 5 Fury. 6 Schumann's Scenes from Childhood. 7 Point Blank. 8 Marlon
Brando. 9 White Christmas. 10 Behind the Great Wall. 11 Taking Off. 12 Nosferatu.
13 Earthquake. 14 The Replacement Killers. 15 Cimarron. 16 Love Finds Andy Hardy.
17 Little Lord Fauntleroy. 18 Richard Gere. 19 The Last Emperor. 20 Trouble with
Harry. 21 Rope. 22 Al Jolson. 23 The Lost World. 24 The Robe. 25 Photoplay. 26
Blackmail. 27 Birth of a Nation. 28 Mike Nichols. 29 DW Griffith. 30 Hayley Mills.

Quiz 86 | Pot Luck 40

Answers – page 328

LEVEL 3

1 Matthew Fisher won a 2006 court case for part copyright of which 1960s song?
2 Which Dutch-based broadcaster agreed to buy worldwide rights to "Who Wants to be a Millionaire?"?
3 "Tory Idol" was first staged to select a candidate in which constituency?
4 How many points did England score in Andy Robinson's last game as rugby coach?
5 Nick Carter was in which best-selling boy band?
6 Which programme won a BAFTA in 2006 for best "situation comedy"?
7 In which US state did "Enron: The Musical" open in 2006?
8 What was the name of the first daughter of Katie Holmes and Tom Cruise?
9 Which club side did the late Ferenc Puskas take to a European Cup Final?
10 Which 1970's T. Rex drummer was still playing in a Christian band 30 years on?
11 Who did Martina Hingis beat to claim her first WTA Tour title in her 2006 comeback?
12 At the time of his death Ian Richardson was due to play in which TV series?
13 What was the name of Martin Luther King's widow who died in 2006?
14 Justin King became chief executive of which supermarket group in 2004?
15 Veronica Donovan and Fernando Sucre featured in which US drama series?
16 Who became Andy Roddick's tennis coach in 2006?
17 Who quit Motherwell to move to warmer climes as Sydney FC soccer boss in 2006?
18 Roman Abramovich was governor of which region in north-east Russia?
19 In which year was Shirley Bassey 70?
20 What type of entertainment was George M Cohan famous for?
21 In January 2007 who became the youngest person to sail across the Atlantic single-handed?
22 In which city did Tony Blair deliver his final conference speech to the Labour Party?
23 Clinton Woods was an IBF world title holder at which weight?
24 Which "Sunday Mirror" columnist appeared in "Celebrity Big Brother" in 2007?
25 Steve Culp played which character in "Desperate Housewives"?
26 Which soccer club has Cattell Road and Tilton Road around the stadium?
27 Who was born John Beverley and would have celebrated his 50th birthday in 2007?
28 Where is the volcanic Mount Metrap?
29 The right-wing political action group the Moral Majority was founded where?
30 Who wrote the play "Bent" revived with Alan Cumming in 2006?

| **Answers** | 1980s Pop *(see Quiz 88)* |

1 Soft Cell. 2 Joe Jackson. 3 Virgin. 4 Madonna. 5 New Edition. 6 Birmingham. 7 Steve Winwood. 8 Respect Yourself. 9 Coco Hernandez. 10 Red Red Wine. 11 Nothing Has Been Proved. 12 David Bowie. 13 Scotland. 14 Mad World. 15 OMD. 16 1988. 17 Zenyatta Mondatta. 18 Giorgio Moroder. 19 Santa Claus. 20 Ultravox. 21 I Want to Know What Love is. 22 Germany. 23 Odyssey. 24 Eye of the Tiger. 25 Living in a Box. 26 Karma Chameleon. 27 Super Trouper. 28 Joe Dolce. 29 Two Tribes. 30 Kelly Marie.

1 What was the first mainstream film to use the word "virgin"?
2 What was the first Royal Command Performance film?
3 Which airline showed the first in flight movie?
4 How old was Mae West when she made her movie debut?
5 What was Fritz Lang's first Hollywood film?
6 What did Kevin Kline play on the piano in his first movie "Sophie's Choice"?
7 What was John Boorman's US directing debut?
8 Who was the first actor to receive $1 million for a single picture?
9 VistaVision was first used in which classic movie?
10 What was the first movie shown in Aromarama?
11 What was Milos Forman's first US movie?
12 What was the first movie to feature Dracula?
13 Which movie was the first to have Sensurround?
14 In which movie did Chow Yun-Fat make his US debut?
15 What was the first western to win an Oscar for best film?
16 What was the first movie which teamed Mickey Rooney and Judy Garland?
17 What was Selznick's first movie from his own independent company?
18 Who was the first American to join the Young Vic company on an American tour?
19 What was the first production from the west allowed in Bejing's Forbidden City?
20 What was Shirley MacLaine's first movie?
21 What was Hitchcock's first film for an independent producer?
22 Who was the first US singer/actor to entertain the troops in Korea?
23 What was the first in-flight movie?
24 What was the first movie shown in Cinemascope?
25 "Motion Picture Story Magazine" and which other title were the US's first film magazines?
26 What was Hitchcock's first talkie?
27 What was the first movie shown at the White House?
28 "Who's Afraid of Virginia Woolf" was the movie debut of which director?
29 Which movie pioneer said, "I moved the whole world on to a 20 foot screen"?
30 Whose screen debut was aged 13 with father John in "Tiger Bay"?

Answers	**Sporting Who's Who?** *(see Quiz 85)*

1 Cincinnati Red Stockings. 2 Malavai Washington. 3 Mia Farrow. 4 Cuba. 5 Unified Team. 6 46. 7 Alex Corretja. 8 Ligier (Alain Prost). 9 Baltimore Bullets. 10 Bristol. 11 Jonathan Gould. 12 1998 (Snowboarding). 13 Justine Henin. 14 Stuttgart. 15 John Kagwe. 16 Andres Gimeno. 17 John Landy. 18 Tokyo. 19 St Louis Cardinals. 20 West German (Boris Becker). 21 Two. 22 Antonio Pinto. 23 South Africa. 24 Annika Sorenstam. 25 35. 26 Christine Arron. 27 Suzuki (Barry Sheene). 28 Lleyton Hewitt. 29 Stefan Edberg. 30 Warriors.

1 Dave Ball was part of which hit-making combination?
2 Who had 80s hits with "It's Different for Girls" and "Steppin' Out"?
3 Which label did Culture Club record on?
4 Patrick Leonard co-wrote and produced No 1 hits for which artist?
5 Which group met at school at Roxbury, Massachusetts?
6 Duran Duran got together in which city?
7 "Roll with It" and "Higher Love" were US No 1s for which British artist?
8 What was the first top ten hit for Bruce Willis?
9 What was the name of the Irene Cara character in Alan Parker's "Fame"?
10 What was the first No 1 single for UB40?
11 What gave Dusty Springfield a solo Top Twenty hit after a twenty-year gap?
12 Who went on a Serious Moonlight Tour?
13 Which country did Aneka, the singer of "Japanese Boy", come from?
14 What was the first Top Ten hit for Tears for Fears?
15 Andy McCluskey provided vocals and synthesiser for which outfit?
16 In which year did U2 first make it to No 1?
17 The Police's "Don't Stand so Close to Me" was from which album?
18 Who wrote and produced Berlin's "Take My Breath Away"?
19 Who was "On the Dole" in a song from the Spitting Image team?
20 Warren Cann and Chris Cross were part of which group?
21 The New Jersey Mass Choir appear on which 80s No 1?
22 Nicole's No 1 won the Eurovision Song Contest for which country?
23 Who were Tony Reynolds and Louise and Lillian Lopez?
24 Which No 1 was linked to the movie "Rocky III"?
25 Who had hits with "Blow the House Down" and "Room in Your Heart"?
26 Which was the first 80s No 1 to be top for six weeks?
27 Abba's "The Winner Takes It All" track came from which album?
28 Who followed up a No 1 with the unsuccessful "Reggae Matilda"?
29 Which single spent most weeks at No 1 in the 80s?
30 Under what name did Jacqueline McKinnon make No 1?

Quiz 89 Iron Curtain

Answers – page 331

1 Who first popularised the expression "Iron Curtain"?
2 Which newspaper used "Iron Curtain" earlier in the sense of protection?
3 What was the official name of the Soviet Union?
4 What name, meaning speaking aloud, was given to Gorbachev's new approach?
5 What was the communist economic association called?
6 Which Treaty Organisation was set up as a communist counterpart to NATO?
7 Which Eastern European country was the only one to maintain close relations with China?
8 What was East Germany's official name?
9 Which communist country remained outside the military alliance of Eastern Bloc countries in 1955?
10 In which country were the AVF the security police?
11 Who succeeded Stalin as Communist Party leader?
12 What was the period of liberalisation in Czechoslovakia in 1968 called?
13 Which General introduced martial law in Poland in 1981?
14 What was the Czech Charter 77 protesting about in 1977?
15 In which year was the Berlin Wall built?
16 What name was given to the state of tension between the communist states and the west after World War II?
17 What name was given to the reconstruction of Soviet society through Gorbachev's reforms?
18 Who was East Germany's last Chairman of the Council of State?
19 Where in Gdansk was Solidarity founded?
20 What were the KGB in the Soviet Union?
21 Which former head of the KGB became General Party Secretary in 1982?
22 Who was the first Russian to be General Secretary and President simultaneously?
23 What does the T stand for in the acronym SALT?
24 Astana replaced Almaty as the capital city of which former Soviet state?
25 Which communist state was ruled by the Volkskammer?
26 Who was the leading architect of East Germany in the 50s and 60s?
27 Who was the East German leader tried for high treason in 1993?
28 Which Hungarian army major fled his homeland after the Soviet invasion and died a world-revered sportsman in 2006?
29 Which Soviet foreign minister formulated the Sinatra doctrine?
30 Why was the Sinatra doctrine so called?

Answers	Premiership Relegation (see Quiz 91)

1 Jermaine Pennant. 2 Paul Sturrock. 3 Derby. 4 Kevin Ball. 5 42 points. 6 Jamie Clapham. 7 Ipswich 1995. 8 Barnsley. 9 Gary Megson. 10 21 goals. 11 No. 12 Gabor Kiraly. 13 Coventry. 14 Norwich. 15 Dave Bassett. 16 Kanu. 17 Sunderland. 18 Chris Sutton. 19 Peter Crouch. 20 Charlton. 21 Norwich. 22 Chris Kirkland. 23 Jim Jeffers. 24 21 goals. 25 Derby. 26 Barnsley, Blackburn, Bradford. 27 Hermann Hreidarsson. 28 Man Utd. 29 Ian Pearce. 30 Bolton.

1 What did Rachel Lowe try and market to the "Dragon's Den" team?
2 Where in London did ex-Russian spy Alexander Litvinenko live prior to his murder?
3 Which Prime Minister was dubbed Finland's sexiest man in 2006 tabloids?
4 Barry George was convicted of the murder of which TV presenter?
5 Sherron Watkins was vice president of which famous company?
6 Eto'o and Belletti scored Champions League Final goals for which club?
7 Sarah Alexander, Jack Davenport and Ben Miles starred in which TV comedy?
8 Stuart Rose took over as chief executive of which major company in 2004?
9 The debut album from The Arctic Monkeys appeared on which record label?
10 In 2007, Dr Drew Faust became first female president of which institution?
11 Which England player bowled just one over in the 2006–07 Ashes series?
12 Which famous economist, a former adviser to JF Kennedy, died in 2006, aged 97?
13 Who wrote the novel "Melted into AIr"?
14 Hans Horrevoets was swept overboard and died in which 2006 sporting event?
15 The track "Chasing Cars" appeared on which top-selling album?
16 Which book beat the "Beano" to be top-selling annual around Xmas 2006?
17 Which year marks the 100th anniversary of the Ryder Cup?
18 Which much-used item was invented by Douglas Engelbardt?
19 Which single gave Geri Halliwell her third No 1 solo hit?
20 Michael Sinnott made movies in the USA under which name?
21 Who left Leeds to become director of rugby at Llanelli in 2006?
22 In which month of the year did Britain have its first woman Prime Minister?
23 Where was author Jean Rhys born?
24 Emily Blunt and Bill Nighy won Golden Globes for their roles in which drama?
25 Aged 16, David Howell, of Sussex, became the UK's youngest what?
26 Billie Joe Armstrong was vocalist for which top-selling band?
27 Who played "Leatherface" in the film "The Texas Chain Saw Massacre"?
28 Who were the opponents as Ronaldo set a new individual World Cup finals tally?
29 In 2006, Steve McClaren became England coach on a contract for how many years?
30 American journalist Daniel Pearl was kidnapped and killed in which country in 2002?

| **Answers** | Pot Luck 42 *(see Quiz 92)* |

1 Spain. 2 Wigan. 3 Reconstruction. 4 Steps. 5 Riverbank. 6 Paediatrician. 7 Sibelius. 8 Hungary. 9 Mexico. 10 Selma Bouvier. 11 Jeremy Paxman (2000). 12 The Tide is High. 13 Snowdon. 14 2008. 15 Germany. 16 1500m freestyle. 17 Stephen Spielberg. 18 Reblochon. 19 Saint Swithin. 20 MP. 21 Mafia. 22 Fron Male Voice Choir. 23 Walter Winterbottom. 24 Pim Fortuyn. 25 Lord of the Rings: The Return of the King. 26 Northern Rock. 27 Changeling. 28 Google. 29 Beirut. 30 Badminton.

1 Who played most games for Birmingham as they went down in 2006?
2 Who started the 2004–05 season as Southampton boss?
3 Colin Todd and John Gregory managed which team on the way down?
4 In 2006, who replaced Mick McCarthy as interim manager at Sunderland?
5 Going down in 2003 – did West Ham have 33, 37 or 42 points?
6 Which Jamie suffered relegation with Ipswich and Birmingham?
7 Which team set the record of 29 Premiership defeats in 42 games?
8 Which team did boss Danny Wilson take into and out of the Premiership?
9 Who was boss of the Baggies when they went down in 2003?
10 In 2003 Sunderland set a fewest goals in a season record of how many?
11 Did Alan Shearer ever play for a team in a relegation season?
12 Who was Palace's regular keeper in the 2005 relegation season?
13 At which club did Craig Bellamy first experience Premiership relegation?
14 Craig Fleming played every game as which team went down?
15 Which manager Dave got Sheff Utd into and out of the the top flight in the 90s?
16 Nathan Ellington and who else were WBA's 2006 joint top scorers with 5 goals?
17 Which team ended the season with an unlucky for some 13 straight defeats?
18 Which Chris played for Blackburn and Birmingham in relegation seasons?
19 Who was top scorer when Southampton left the top flight in 2005?
20 Which club were the last side to be relegated from the Premiership last century?
21 Ashton, Francis and McKenzie were joint top scorers as which team went down?
22 Who played most games in goal in Coventry's 2001 relegation season?
23 Who was boss as Bradford City left the Premiership in 2001?
24 How many goals did Andy Johnson hit as Palace went down in 2005?
25 Veterans Barton and Lee left Newcastle for which club that went down in 2002?
26 Ashley Ward was relegated with which three B teams?
27 Which defender went down with Wimbledon in 2000 and Ipswich in 2002?
28 In 2006, Sunderland were relegated after holding which title chasers to a 0-0 draw?
29 Who won the Premiership with Blackburn and went down with West Ham in 2003?
30 Per Frandsen was an ever present in the season which northern club went down?

1 In 2006 ScottishPower agreed a takeover by a company from which country?
2 Peter Crouch's first Liverpool Premiership goal was against which team?
3 In SIGIR, the second I stands for Iraq – what does the R stand for?
4 Which pop quintet featured Claire Richards and Lee Latchford-Evans?
5 Which LS Lowry painting did Bury Council auction for over £1 million in November 2006?
6 Sir Roy Meadow gave evidence in court cases in what expert capacity?
7 Who wrote the theme music that has been used for "The Sky at Night"?
8 Theo Walcott made his international debut against which country?
9 Felipe Calderon became President of which country in 2006?
10 Who in "The Simpsons" owned an iguana named Jub-Jub?
11 Who was 50 first – Jimmy Nail, Jeremy Paxman or Victoria Wood?
12 What was the third UK No 1 for Atomic Kitten?
13 Who photographed the cover of Renee Fleming's CD "Homage"?
14 Which year celebrates 50 years of parking meters in London?
15 In which country was a killer brown bear known as JJ put down in 2006?
16 In 2006, David Davies became Commonwealth Games swimming champ in which event?
17 Who produced the creepy movie "Poltergeist"?
18 Which creamy cheese comes from the Haute Savoie?
19 Which Saint has 15th July as his Feast Day?
20 Diane Abbot became Britain's first black woman to serve as what?
21 Carmine Galante was reputedly the boss of what when he was shot in New York in 1979?
22 Which male voice choir had classical success with "Voices of the Valley"?
23 Which ex-England soccer manager died in the same month as Spike Milligan?
24 Which Dutch politician was assassinated by an animal rights campaigner in 2002?
25 What was the third film to win 11 Oscars?
26 Which sponsor's name was on Alan Shearer's shirt in his final Premiership game?
27 What was the autobiography of Mike Oldfield called?
28 What did Sergey Brin and Larry Page launch in 1998?
29 Rafik Hariri was killed in a bomb attack in which city?
30 Nathan Robertson and Gail Emms formed a winning partnership in which sport?

Answers	**Pot Luck 41** *(see Quiz 90)*

1 Board games. 2 Muswell Hill. 3 Matti Vanhanen. 4 Jill Dando. 5 Enron. 6 Barcelona. 7 Coupling. 8 Marks & Spencer. 9 Domino. 10 Harvard University. 11 Ian Bell. 12 JK Galbraith. 13 Sandy Toksvig. 14 Volvo Open Race. 15 Eyes Open (Snow Patrol). 16 Dr Who Annual. 17 2027. 18 Mouse (Computers). 19 Bag It Up. 20 Mack Sennett. 21 Phil Davies. 22 June (1979). 23 West Indies. 24 Gideon's Daughter. 25 Chess grandmaster. 26 Green Day. 27 Gunner Hansen. 28 Ghana. 29 Four. 30 Pakistan.

1 "Santa Claus is Comin' to Town" was on the other side of "My Hometown" in 1985 for whom?

2 Which residents of Home Hill had a Xmastime No 1 in 1997?

3 Which Welsh performer topped the charts in 1985 with "Merry Christmas Everyone"?

4 Who duetted with Cliff Richard on "Whenever God Shines His Light" in December 1989?

5 Which Mel was "Rockin Around the Christmas Tree" with Kim Wilde?

6 Who sang "All I Want for Christmas is You" in 1994?

7 Which song of the 1980s featured boy soprano Peter Auty?

8 Which weatherman was in the title of a song during the Xmas period in 1988?

9 What was Wham!'s classic Christmas hit?

10 Which duo's song was knocked off the top spot by Michael Jackson's "Earth Song" in 1995?

11 Which group featured Bono, Katie Melua and Snow Patrol?

12 Who was the first non-human Xmas No 1?

13 Who pleaded "Please Come Home for Christmas" in 1994?

14 Which pop classic has the line, "Well here it is, Merry Christmas"?

15 Which ex-Beatle had an Xmas hit with "Wonderful Christmas Time"?

16 Which female took "Christmas Through Your Eyes" to No 8 in 1992?

17 Which much-played hit has the words, "When the snowman brings the snow"?

18 Who had three consecutive Xmas No 1s in the later half of the 90s?

19 Which David duetted with Bing Crosby in 1982?

20 Which Jive Bunny single was a Xmas No 1 in 1989?

21 Which minor hit was a Xmas follow-up to the Xmas No 1 "Mr Blobby"?

22 Which George Michael hit replaced "Earth Song" after Xmas 1995?

23 Who had a Xmas No 1 with "Saviour's Day" in 1990?

24 Which Chris's classic is "Driving Home for Christmas"?

25 Which duo had "Merry Christmas Darling" in the 1990 charts?

26 In which year did John and Yoko's "Happy Xmas (War is Over)" first hit the charts?

27 The voice of Gary Jules featured on which Xmas No 1?

28 What was the first Xmas No 1 for Girls Aloud?

29 Who had the last Xmas No 1 of last century?

30 Which actress had a hit with Ewan McGregor before an Xmas No 1 duet?

Answers	US Presidents *(see Quiz 95)*

1 Roosevelt. 2 Hubert Humphrey. 3 60%. 4 Warren Harding. 5 Friday. 6 Truman. 7 William Taft. 8 2001. 9 Leon Czolgosz. 10 Jimmy Carter. 11 Kennedy. 12 USA. 13 Roosevelt. 14 Jack Kemp. 15 Florida. 16 George Bush (Snr). 17 Lincoln. 18 Earl. 19 Tennessee. 20 24 years old. 21 FD Roosevelt. 22 Richard the Lionheart. 23 Woodrow Wilson. 24 Jackie Oh!. 25 Jimmy Carter. 26 George W Bush (Jnr). 27 Harry S Truman. 28 Ronald Reagan. 29 Adams. 30 Andrew Jackson.

1 On which day of the week was Prince Harry born?
2 What is William's second Christian name?
3 In 2006 the princes announced which date for a "Concert for Diana"?
4 In which subject did William get his highest A-level grade?
5 What is the name of their stepbrother?
6 How tall is William?
7 Where were the princes staying when they heard of their mother's death?
8 On which Royal's birthday was William christened?
9 What is their stepsister's married name?
10 In which country did William carry out his first official duties representing the Queen?
11 Whom did William succeed as President of the FA?
12 Which surname did William use when he was at university?
13 Where was Harry baptised?
14 Which portrait painter was one of Harry's godfathers?
15 In which subject did Harry achieve his higher A-level result?
16 Where in Africa did Harry spend part of his gap year?
17 What is the meaning of "Sentebale", the charity Harry set up in Lesotho?
18 It was announced in 2006 that Harry would join which Household Cavalry regiment?
19 In a 18th-birthday interview William said he would miss which Eton house master?
20 When William gave his 18th-birthday interview, who or what was Widgeon?
21 How old was William when his father remarried?
22 What was the first name of their maternal grandfather?
23 Which Archbishop of Canterbury christened both princes?
24 As a child William expressed support for which football club?
25 Which two Berkshire schools did both princes attend?
26 In autumn 2005 William took a work placement with which bank?
27 William became Vice Royal Patron of which Union from February 2007?
28 Which high-profile event did Kate Middleton first attend as William's guest?
29 If William used his first name when king what would his title be?
30 Which was the first charity William became patron of?

Answers	Pot Luck 43 *(see Quiz 96)*

1 Highland Spring. 2 Turkey. 3 Newcastle. 4 £12,100. 5 Bobby Robson. 6 Durian. 7 Danny Grewcock. 8 Nottm Forest. 9 Michael Johnson. 10 Clouds. 11 Horatio Nelson. 12 Forth & Clyde canal. 13 Les Misérables. 14 Dundrum Castle. 15 Look at Me. 16 St Petersburg. 17 Transformer. 18 27 points. 19 Houses of Parliament. 20 2012. 21 Swimming. 22 1994. 23 The Final Act. 24 118 minutes. 25 Crosswords. 26 141. 27 Films. 28 If Tomorrow Never Comes. 29 Teague Sparrow. 30 John Tusa.

1 Which US President did Guiseppe Zangara attempt to assassinate?

2 Who was vice president directly before Spiro Agnew?

3 What percentage of voters turned out when George W Bush was re-elected in 2004?

4 Which US President had the middle name Gamaliel?

5 On which day of the week was Kennedy assassinated?

6 Dean Acheson was US Secretary of State under which President?

7 Which US President was the heaviest?

8 In which year was George Bush Jnr first inaugurated as US President?

9 Who was the first assassin of a US President last century?

10 Who was the first US President to have been born in a hospital?

11 Which President conferred honorary US citizenship on Winston Churchill?

12 What did Ronald Reagan describe as a shining city on a hill?

13 Who said, "A radical is a man with both feet planted firmly in the air"?

14 In 1996 who was Bob Dole's Vice Presidential candidate?

15 Which state was crucial to the outcome of the 2000 election?

16 Who described Ronald Reagan's policies as "Voodoo economics"?

17 What type of car was Kennedy travelling in when he was shot?

18 Which aristocratic title is one of Jimmy Carter's Christian names?

19 Al Gore was Senator of which state before becoming Bill Clinton's Vice President in 1992?

20 How old was John F Kennedy's assassin?

21 Who was the Democrat before Clinton to be elected for a second term?

22 Whom was Richard Nixon named after?

23 Which 20th century US President shared his surname with a 20th century British PM?

24 What was the name of Kitty Kelley's biography of Jackie Kennedy Onassis?

25 Which president's campaign slogan was "Why not the best"?

26 Who became the 43rd US President?

27 Who is credited with the quote, "If you can't stand the heat get out of the kitchen"?

28 Who used the line "Randy, where's the rest of me?" as the title of an early autobiography?

29 The second and sixth President were father and son called what?

30 Which President came first – Andrew Jackson or Abraham Lincoln?

1 Which company producing bottled water set up a £1 million sponsorship deal with Andy Murray?

2 Where did Pope Benedict visit on his first trip to a mainly Muslim nation?

3 In January 2007 Bob Geldof received an honorary degree from which university?

4 To £500, how much did a "Beano" first edition fetch in a new auction record price in 2004?

5 Who was the last previous manager who was boss of England longer than Sven?

6 What was the name of the December 2006 typhoon that devastated central Philippines?

7 Who was sent off for punching Lawrence Dallaglio in a European Challenge Cup final?

8 Colwick Road goes past the soccer stadium of which soccer club?

9 Which man first simultaneously held world records at 200m and 400m?

10 Nephology is the scientific study of what?

11 Whose last words were reputed to be, "Thank God I have done my duty"?

12 On which Scottish waterway is the Falkirk Wheel?

13 Which musical was voted Britain's favourite in a 2005 Radio 2 poll?

14 What is the name of the 12th-century fortress built by John de Courcy in County Down?

15 What was "Ginger" Spice's first solo single after she left The Spice Girls?

16 In 1991 Vladimir Putin became Deputy Mayor of which city?

17 No 1 in the 1990s, "Perfect Day" first appeared on which early 1970s album?

18 How many points did Jonny Wilkinson score on his 2007 England comeback?

19 Brian Haw staged a long-running anti-war protest outside which building?

20 Which year marks the centenary of the death of polar explorer Capt. Scott?

21 Gregor Tait won Commonwealth medal in which sport?

22 In which year was the British National Lottery started?

23 What was the final instalment of "Prime Suspect" called?

24 How many minutes did Michael Owen play in Germany 2006?

25 What did Margery Ruth Crisp produce for many years?

26 How many countries ratified the Kyoto protocol?

27 Awarded a CBE in the 2007 honours, what does Peter Greenaway make?

28 What was the third solo No 1 for Ronan Keating?

29 Which pirate did Keith Richards play in a major movie?

30 Who was managing director of London's Barbican Centre from 1995 to 2007?

Answers | **Princes William and Harry** *(see Quiz 94)*

1 Saturday. 2 Arthur. 3 1st July 2007. 4 Geography. 5 Tom Parker Bowles. 6 6ft 3 inches. 7 Balmoral. 8 Queen Mother's. 9 Laura Lopes. 10 New Zealand. 11 Duke of Kent. 12 Wales. 13 St George's Chapel, Windsor. 14 Bryan Organ. 15 Art. 16 Lesotho. 17 Forget-Me-Not. 18 Blues and Royals. 19 Dr Gailey. 20 His dog. 21 22 years. 22 John. 23 Robert Runcie. 24 Aston Villa. 25 Ludgrove School and Eton College. 26 HSBC. 27 Welsh Rugby Union. 28 Sandhurst passing out parade. 29 William V. 30 Centrepoint.

1 What was Margaret Thatcher's maiden name?

2 As a barrister what did she specialise in?

3 Harold Macmillan described Thatcher's privatisation policy as "selling the family" what?

4 What is the date of Margaret Thatcher's birthday?

5 Which Oxford college did she attend?

6 In which department was Thatcher's first shadow ministerial job?

7 The scrapping of which free school item brought controversy in June 1971?

8 Who was second to Thatcher in the Tory leadership battle in 1975?

9 Which Thatcher aide was killed in 1979 by a bomb in the House of Commons car park?

10 Whom did Thatcher quote on the steps of No 10 on becoming PM?

11 Whom did Thatcher describe as "A man we can do business with"?

12 Over what did she say, "Failure? The possibility does not exist"?

13 Mrs Thatcher was at which Brighton hotel that was bombed in October 1984?

14 Who signed the Anglo-Irish Agreement with Thatcher in 1985?

15 Which major transport project did she give the go-ahead to in January 1986?

16 Michael Heseltine and which other Cabinet member resigned over Westland?

17 How many different Labour leaders did Thatcher beat in General Elections?

18 What did Sir Alan Walters advise Thatcher on?

19 Who was her most famous Press Secretary?

20 Why could Mrs Thatcher have been called Lady Thatcher from 1990?

21 Who replaced Nigel Lawson as Chancellor?

22 Who first challenged Thatcher as party leader when she was PM?

23 What was Geoffrey Howe's Cabinet position when he resigned in 1990?

24 In which town was Margaret Thatcher born?

25 During which rally was Mark Thatcher lost in 1982?

26 In which metal was the Iron Lady's statue cast that was erected in the Houses of Parliament in February 2007?

27 Who did Geoffrey Howe back in the Heseltine/Hurd/Major contest?

28 For her life peerage she became Baroness Thatcher of where?

29 Which sportsman described Thatcher as "nice and cuddly" when he met her?

30 Which seat did Thatcher fight before fighting, and winning Finchley?

Answers | UK Politics *(see Quiz 99)*

1 Thomas Clarke. 2 2005. 3 Dennis Skinner. 4 1983. 5 One (Margaret Thatcher). 6 Crawley. 7 Livingston. 8 Green Party. 9 Asquith. 10 Tyneside North. 11 Normanton. 12 Harold Wilson. 13 Cheadle. 14 28%. 15 Below the Parapet. 16 John Bercow (Buckingham). 17 Brighton. 18 90 years. 19 59%. 20 Cecil Parkinson. 21 Francis Elliott & James Hanning. 22 Elspeth. 23 Tatton. 24 John Major. 25 Harold Wilson's. 26 Aldershot. 27 1992. 28 13,517,911 voters. 29 Seven. 30 David Trimble.

1 Who described James Bond as "a blunt instrument wielded by a government department"?

2 How many official Bond films had been made before Daniel Craig took over?

3 Which Bond film did Deborah Kerr appear in?

4 Who played Pussy Galore in "Goldfinger"?

5 What was the given first name of Bond producer Cubby Broccoli?

6 Which movie's villain was Xenia Onatopp?

7 Which movie first had the toothpaste with plastic explosives?

8 Which was the first Bond movie not to have an action sequence before the credits?

9 In which movie did Rowan Atkinson make his big-screen debut?

10 On which island does Dr No hold Bond and Honeychile Rider?

11 Which 007 backed the restaurant chain the Spy House?

12 Which movie had the electro-magnetic watch with the spinning blade?

13 To fifteen minutes, how long does "You Only Live Twice" last?

14 Which golf course featured in "Goldfinger"?

15 What was the most successful Bond film of the 70s and 80s in terms of cinema admissions?

16 Which character was played by Harold Sakata?

17 May Day was the Bond girl in which film?

18 In the films what replaced the Soviet organisation Smersh which existed in the books?

19 What was Goldfinger's first name?

20 In which movie did Blofeld kidnap US and USSR spaceships to try and gain planetary control?

21 Which quinine-flavoured aperitif did James Bond advocate for a Martini?

22 What is the name of the villain in the movie that preceded "The World is Not Enough"?

23 What was "GoldenEye" named after?

24 What is the motto of the villain in "Tomorrow Never Dies"?

25 What was the last film where Lois Maxwell played Miss Moneypenny?

26 Which film was Roger Moore's last as Bond?

27 Which artists were first to have a US No 1 with a Bond theme?

28 What was the first Bond book that Fleming wrote?

29 In which movie did the silver Aston Martin DB5 appear?

30 Employed by Hugo Drax, who was Dr Holly Goodhead actually working for?

Answers | Pot Luck 44 *(see Quiz 100)*

1 12. 2 Late blight (potato crops). 3 16. 4 University College hospital. 5 Computer graphics. 6 Back to Black. 7 Willie Pep. 8 2010. 9 Million Dollar Baby. 10 38%. 11 I'll Stand by You. 12 116-year-old. 13 Matt Lucas. 14 Speed skating. 15 Italy. 16 John Malkovich. 17 The Mighty Quinn. 18 Nick Barmby. 19 Diner's Club. 20 Quinten Hann. 21 Sir Nicholas Stern. 22 Gary Barlow. 23 Bill Haley. 24 Five. 25 Stern. 26 Claire Connor. 27 2015. 28 Three. 29 Watford. 30 Peter Phillips.

Quiz 99 | UK Politics

Answers – page 337

1 Which Labour MP had the largest majority after 2005's election?

2 In which year did John Major become Sir John Major?

3 Who had a larger majority in 2005 – Gordon Brown or Dennis Skinner?

4 In which year did Tony Blair first become an MP?

5 How many PMs were in office for an entire decade in the last century?

6 Which constituency recorded the smallest majority for an MP in 2005?

7 Which constituency did the late Robin Cook represent?

8 Which political party has had its offices situated at 1a Waterloo Road, London?

9 Alphabetically speaking which PM came first in the 20th century?

10 Which constituency returned Steven Byers to parliament?

11 Ed Balls won which seat to enter parliament?

12 Which ex-PM became Baron of Rievaulx when he was made a peer?

13 Which constituency held the first by-election after the 2005 UK general election?

14 To five, what percentage of Labour MPs were women after 2005's election?

15 What was the name of the book Carol Thatcher wrote about her father?

16 Which Tory MP had the greatest majority at the 2005 general election?

17 Which English place has the constituencies Kemptown and Pavilion?

18 How old was Robert Leakey, the oldest candidate in 2005's election?

19 What percentage of the electorate turned out for the 2001 general election?

20 Who was Tory Party Chairman when Mrs Thatcher won her second term in office?

21 Who wrote "Cameron, the Rise of the New Conservative"?

22 What is the first name of the wife of the Lib Dem leader who succeeded Charles Kennedy?

23 Which seat did former news reader Martin Bell win from Neil Hamilton?

24 Arabella Warburton was PA to which Prime Minister?

25 Whose resignation Honours List was known as the Lavender List?

26 Alphabetically, which constituency comes first in England?

27 In which year did Margaret Thatcher leave parliament as an MP?

28 To half a million, how many people voted Labour as the party took power in 1997?

29 Without hyphenated names, how many Smiths were MPs after the 2005 election?

30 Which well-known political figure lost his seat at Upper Bann in 2005?

Answers	Mrs Thatcher *(see Quiz 97)*

1 Roberts. 2 Taxation law. 3 Silver. 4 13th October. 5 Somerville. 6 Transport. 7 Milk. 8 William Whitelaw. 9 Airey Neave. 10 St Francis of Assisi. 11 Gorbachev. 12 Falklands invasion. 13 Grand Hotel. 14 Dr Garret FitzGerald. 15 Channel Tunnel. 16 Leon Brittan. 17 Three. 18 Economic affairs. 19 Bernard Ingham. 20 Denis Thatcher was knighted. 21 John Major. 22 Sir Anthony Mayer. 23 Deputy Prime Minister. 24 Grantham. 25 Paris Dakar. 26 Bronze. 27 Heseltine. 28 Kesteven. 29 Paul Gascoigne. 30 Dartford.

1 The Rugby World Cup of 2007 was based on how many cities?
2 Phytophthora infestans is reckoned to cost farming some £50m a year – what is it?
3 How many teams played in the 2007 Cricket World Cup finals?
4 At which London hospital did Alexander Litvinenko die in November 2006?
5 Ivan Sutherland is associated with the development of what?
6 "Rehab" and "Just Friends" appeared on which Amy Winehouse album?
7 Which six-times-married featherweight champion boxer died in November 2006, aged 84?
8 Which year marks the 150th anniversary of golf's Open?
9 Which 2004 movie was adapted from "Rope Burns", a book by FX Toole?
10 Library book borrowing fell by how many per cent from 1995 to 2004?
11 What was the second No 1 single for Girls Aloud?
12 How old was the world's oldest woman Elizabeth Bolden when she died in 2006?
13 Kevin McGee shared a civil partnership ceremony with which celeb in December 2006?
14 Enrico Fabris won gold in which Olympic event in February 2006?
15 King Juan Carlos of Spain was born in which country?
16 Who has the double role in "Mary Reilly", based on "Dr Jekyll & Mr Hyde"?
17 Which No 1 has the lines, "Come all without, Come all within"?
18 Which Nick scored in Sven Goran Eriksson's first game in charge for England?
19 Which credit card – first used in restaurants – did Frank McNamara create?
20 Which Australian snooker player was found guilty of match fixing in February 2006?
21 Which ex-World Bank chief economist produced a 2006 report on climate change?
22 Which Take That singer shares a birthday with astronaut Buzz Aldrin?
23 Which major US rock singer died the month before the first London Marathon?
24 How many vessels did the Royal Navy lose in the Falklands War?
25 In which magazine were the fictitious Hitler Diaries published in the 1980s?
26 Who captained English ladies to their cricket series triumph over Australia in 2005?
27 Which year celebrates 50 years since Radio Caroline was established?
28 How many of Joseph Kennedy's sons became Senators?
29 Henrik Larsson first scored in the Premiership against which team?
30 In order of succession, who is nearer to the throne – Peter Phillips or Viscount Linley?

Answers | James Bond *(see Quiz 98)*

1 Ian Fleming. 2 20. 3 Casino Royale. 4 Honor Blackman. 5 Albert. 6 Goldeneye. 7 Licence to Kill. 8 Dr No. 9 Never Say Never Again. 10 Crab Key Island. 11 George Lazenby. 12 Live and Let Die. 13 117 minutes. 14 Stoke Poges. 15 Thunderball. 16 Oddjob. 17 A View to a Kill. 18 Spectre. 19 Auric. 20 You Only Live Twice. 21 Kina Lillet. 22 Carver. 23 Ian Fleming's home in Jamaica. 24 No news is bad news. 25 A View to a Kill. 26 A View to a Kill. 27 Duran Duran. 28 Casino Royale. 29 Goldfinger. 30 CIA.

1 Which great rock guitarist had a daughter named Dandelion?
2 In which London street is there a blue plaque denoting where Jimi Hendrix lived?
3 Peter Buck is in which mega rock band?
4 What did Brian May study at university?
5 Who inspired Eric Clapton to write "Layla"?
6 Which Roy guested on Pink Floyd's "Wish You were Here"?
7 Who made the 60s album "The Twang's the Thang"?
8 Carlos Santa was born in which country?
9 Who made the album "Outrider" in 1988?
10 What was the name of BB King's beloved Gibson guitar?
11 Who awarded Mark Knopfler an honorary music doctorate in 1993?
12 Which heavy metal guitarist said "if it's too loud you're too old"?
13 Which city did the blues guitarist Gary Moore come from?
14 What was Eric Clapton's No 1 album of 1994?
15 Which guitarist's first two names were Brian Robson?
16 Which album did Mark Knopfler release with Chet Atkins in 1990?
17 Which guitarist did Ron Wood replace in The Rolling Stones?
18 Who duetted on "Wonderful Land" on the 1993 "Heart Beat" album?
19 Which British guitarist was instrumental in reuniting the Everly Brothers in the 80s?
20 "Guitar Boogie Shuffle" in 1959 was the only Top Ten hit for which guitarist?
21 Which group included guitarists John Williams and Kevin Peek?
22 What did Brian May reputedly make his first guitar from?
23 What type of guitar did Jimi Hendrix use on the "Are You Experienced?" album?
24 Which two acts took "Cavatina" the theme from "The Deer Hunter" into the Top Ten?
25 Where did Jimi Hendrix take part in a fund-raising "Guitar In" in 1967?
26 Whose career history album was called "Crossroads"?
27 What did Brian May play at the end of the "Concert for Life" at Wembley in 1992?
28 What was Jeff Beck's debut solo album called?
29 What honour did Eric Clapton receive in January 1995?
30 What was the debut album by the Brian May Band?

Answers	**Movie Remakes** *(see Quiz 105)*

1 Alfie. 2 Gore Verbinski. 3 Gérard Dépardieu. 4 Jack Black. 5 Ocean's Eleven. 6 Denzel Washington. 7 The Talented Mr Ripley. 8 High Society. 9 Mary Shelley's Frankenstein. 10 Evergreen. 11 The Look of Love. 12 Mark Wahlberg. 13 Peter Sellers. 14 Eddie Murphy. 15 King Kong. 16 1966 (Alfie). 17 Laurence Olivier. 18 Alan Menken. 19 Four. 20 Arnold Schwarzenegger (California). 21 Kieran Culkin. 22 Graham Greene. 23 Malkovich. 24 Bram Stoker's Dracula. 25 Kenneth Branagh. 26 Psychiatrist. 27 Spencer Tracy. 28 Lewis Milestone. 29 Telly Savalas. 30 Jack Nicholson.

1 Who said he would pursue, "the ultimate goal of ending tyranny in our world"?

2 Who was the first Football Writers' Association player of the year for three times?

3 Keeper Ben Foster made his England debut against which side?

4 In which horror movie did Johnny Depp make his debut?

5 Anna Wintour had been in charge of US and UK editions of which glossy mag?

6 "Harry Potter and the Prisoner of Azkaban" featured which comedian as a shrunken head?

7 English-born Pamela Harriman became US Ambassador to where?

8 Which TV programme was recorded at "Farthings" a cottage in Selsey, Sussex?

9 In which year did a Scot first appear on an English bank note?

10 Hamid Karzai became president in the first free elections in which country?

11 How many England players turned out for all five Tests in Australia 2006–07?

12 Who directed "Miss Potter"?

13 Which cartoonist produced the book "My Vision for a New You"?

14 Tom Koenigs was the diplomat heading a UN mission in which country?

15 Which Beatles No 1 contains the line, "let it out and let it in"?

16 In which state is "Halloween" set?

17 Who played King Theoden of Rohan in the last two parts of the "Lord of the Rings" trilogy?

18 Who was Man Utd's captain in the 1999 European Champions Cup Final?

19 Who was the first black American to win the Nobel Peace prize?

20 England's Peter Nicol won three successive Commonwealth Games golds in which sport?

21 Who wrote the book on which Hitchcock's first Oscar-winning Hollywood film was based?

22 Which British Royals married the year that Spain legalised divorce?

23 When President, Ronald Reagan was shot outside which hotel?

24 Zamora, Konchesky and who else had West Ham penalties saved in 2006's FA Cup Final?

25 Who wrote the novel "Second Honeymoon"?

26 Owen Arthur has been Prime Minister of which Comonwealth country?

27 In which European city did Hannibal Lecter live with his uncle?

28 Who was born first – David Cassidy or Eva Cassidy?

29 Sajid Mahmood made his Test debut in 2006 against which country?

30 Charles Duelfer's report of October 2004 dealt with affairs in which country?

Quiz 103 | John Betjeman

1 His verse autobiography was called "Summoned by" what?
2 The poems "Croydon" and "Westgate on Sea" were in which anthology?
3 John Betjeman succeeded which Poet Laureate?
4 Which poem starts, "She died in the upstairs bedroom"?
5 What was the occupation of Betjeman's father?
6 In which decade was "A Nip in the Air" published?
7 Which Oxford University college did he attend?
8 Where does Betjeman urge the "friendly bombs" to fall?
9 Which popular guide book series did he work on?
10 "I made hay" begins which poem?
11 In which year was Betjeman knighted?
12 Which poem with the name of a county, starts, "How did the Devil come?"?
13 What did he lose from the family name during the First World War?
14 In which year did John Betjeman become Poet Laureate?
15 Whom did Betjeman marry?
16 In which decade did "A Few Late Flowering Chrysanthemums" appear?
17 Which London Underground line featured in a programme made for the BBC?
18 Which poem is "To Randolph Churchill, but not about him"?
19 Who was the longest-serving Poet Laureate of the last century?
20 Which place name ends the line, "Dear, Mary Wilson, this is _____"?
21 In which year did Betjeman die?
22 Which anthology was published in the swinging 60s?
23 What was the name of his daughter born in the 1940s?
24 Who was "burnished by Aldershot sun"?
25 He wrote and did editorial work for which magazine concerned with architecture?
26 "The Costa Blanca" and "Aldershot Crematorium" appear in which collection?
27 Who followed John Betjeman as Poet Laureate?
28 What kind of marmalade is named in "Myfanwy"?
29 Betjeman died in which place?
30 Which poem has the line, "He such a thumping crook"?

Answers	**Guitar Greats** *(see Quiz 101)*

1 Keith Richards. 2 Brook Street. 3 R.E.M. 4 Astronomy. 5 Patti Harrison. 6 Roy Harper. 7 Duane Eddy. 8 Mexico. 9 Jimmy Page. 10 Lucille. 11 Newcastle University. 12 Ted Nugent. 13 Belfast. 14 From the Cradle. 15 Hank Marvin. 16 Neck and Neck. 17 Mick Taylor. 18 Hank Marvin and Mark Knopfler. 19 Albert Lee. 20 Bert Weedon. 21 Sky. 22 19th century fireplace. 23 Stratocaster. 24 The Shadows, John Williams. 25 Royal Festival Hall. 26 Eric Clapton. 27 God Save the Queen. 28 Beck-ola. 29 O.B.E. 30 Live at the Brixton Academy.

1 A limited edition bank note issued in November 2006 featured which person?
2 Katie Holmes and Tom Cruise married in which castle in Italy?
3 When was the BT monopoly of directory enquiry service calls deregulated?
4 Around how many customers did Farepak have at the time of its 2006 collapse?
5 At which ground did Sven Goran Eriksson's England first lose a game?
6 Brian Littrell was in which best-selling boy band?
7 Which commission investigated KGB infiltration in the Italian government?
8 In which state does the action of "The Blair Witch Project" take place?
9 What was on the other side of Elvis' original release of "Little Sister"?
10 Mirza Tahir Hussain spent how many years on death row before his November 2006 pardon?
11 Which country were chosen to host cricket's 2015 World Cup?
12 Gemma Adams and Tania Nicol were victims murdered near which town?
13 How many players did Australia use in the 2006–07 Ashes series?
14 Which Mervyn was Governor of the Bank of England in 2007?
15 Caitlin McClatchey won Commonwealth Gold in which sport?
16 What is the name of the magazine company featured in TV's "Ugly Betty"?
17 Which former "A-Team" actor featured in "Celebrity Big Brother" in 2007?
18 Henrik Larsson missed a penalty against which team in Germany 2006?
19 Which No 1 contained the line, "They're going to crucify me"?
20 What name links a Joseph Conrad novel and the craft in the movie "Alien"?
21 Which year will be the centenary of when Joan of Arc became a Saint?
22 At which West End theatre did "The Woman In White" open?
23 Which middle name is shared by David Beckham and Kevin Keegan?
24 Whose artistic works include "Away from the Flock"?
25 Who shared the 1998 Nobel Peace Prize with David Trimble?
26 In which Jack Nicholson movie did Danny have an imaginary friend called Tony?
27 Who was 50 first – John Kettley, Tony Blair or Richard Madeley?
28 Which country did Asafa Powell run for?
29 Who was the first UK female to have four solo No 1 hit singles?
30 The Rt Rev. David Urquhart became Bishop of where in November 2006?

Answers | **Pot Luck 45** *(see Quiz 102)*

1 George W Bush. 2 Thierry Henry. 3 Spain. 4 A Nightmare on Elm Street. 5 Vogue.
6 Lenny Henry. 7 Paris. 8 The Sky at Night. 9 2007. 10 Afghanistan. 11 Seven.
12 Chris Noonan. 13 Steve Bell. 14 Afghanistan. 15 Hey Jude. 16 Illinois. 17
Bernard Hill. 18 Peter Schmeichel. 19 Ralph Bunche. 20 Squash. 21 Daphne Du
Maurier (Rebecca). 22 Charles & Diana. 23 Washington Hilton. 24 Anton Ferdinand.
25 Joanna Trollope. 26 Barbados. 27 Paris. 28 Eva Cassidy. 29 Sri Lanka. 30 Iraq.

1 Susan Sarandon and Sienna Miller feature in which remake of a 60s movie?
2 Who directed the remake of horror film "The Ring"?
3 Who was the star of the fifth version of "The Count of Monte Cristo"?
4 Who played the character Carl Denham in the 21st-century "King Kong"?
5 George Clooney and Brad Pitt were cast together in which 60s remake?
6 Who was cast as Ben Morro in 2004's "Manchurian Candidate"?
7 What was the 2000 remake of "Purple Moon" called?
8 What was "The Philadelphia Story" called when it was remade into a musical?
9 What was the 1994 Frankenstein movie called, starring Kenneth Branagh?
10 Which song won an Oscar in the 1976 remake of "A Star is Born"?
11 Which song was Oscar-nominated in the pre-Daniel Craig "Casino Royale"?
12 Who played the Michael Caine role in the remake of "The Italian Job"?
13 Which Goon was in the 1979 remake of "The Prisoner of Zenda"?
14 Who played the title role in the remake of "The Nutty Professor"?
15 Fay Wray in the 30s and Jessica Lange in the 70s were in which movie?
16 In which year was the Michael Caine original of a film remade starring Jude Law?
17 Which English Lord was in the remake of the legendary "The Jazz Singer"?
18 Who wrote the music for the animation remake of "The Hunchback of Notre Dame"?
19 How many versions of "Phantom of the Opera" were there in the 20th century?
20 Which actor said "I love doing sequels" when re-elected as Governor on the US?
21 Which brother of the "Home Alone" star was in the remake of "Father of the Bride"?
22 Who wrote "The End of the Affair" remade in 1999?
23 Which John was in the 1990s remake of "Of Mice and Men"?
24 What was the Dracula movie with Gary Oldman and Winona Ryder called?
25 Who directed himself as well as acting in the 1989 remake of "Henry V"?
26 Which profession did Faye Dunaway play in the remake of "The Thomas Crown Affair"?
27 Who starred in the second remake of "Dr Jekyll & Mr Hyde" in 1941?
28 Who directed the 1960 original "Ocean's Eleven"?
29 Which famous TV detective starred in the 1966 remake of "Beau Geste"?
30 Who played the Joker in the second remake of the movie "Batman"?

Answers | **John Betjeman** *(see Quiz 103)*

1 Bells. 2 Mount Zion. 3 Cecil Day-Lewis. 4 Death in Leamington. 5 Cabinet maker. 6 1970s. 7 Magdalen College. 8 On Slough. 9 Shell Guides. 10 The Last Laugh. 11 1969. 12 Norfolk. 13 Letter n (was Betjemann). 14 1972. 15 Penelope Chetwode. 16 1950s. 17 Metropolitan. 18 The Wykehamist. 19 John Masefield. 20 Diss. 21 1984. 22 High and Low. 23 Candida. 24 Joan Hunter Dunn. 25 Architectural Review. 26 A Nip in the Air. 27 Ted Hughes. 28 Robertson's. 29 Trebetherick. 30 In a Bath Teashop.

How to Set Up Your Own
Pub Quiz

It isn't easy, get that right from the start. This isn't going to be easy. Think instead of words like "difficult", "taxing", "infuriating", consider yourself with damp palms and a dry throat and then, when you have concentrated on that, put it out of your mind and think of the recognition you will receive down the local, imagine all the regulars lifting you high upon their shoulders dancing and weaving their way around the pub. It won't help but it's good to dream every once in a while.

What you will need:

- A good selection of Biros (never be tempted to give your own pen up, not even to family members)
- A copy of *The Best Pub Quiz Book Ever! 4*
- A set of answer sheets photocopied from the back of the book
- A good speaking voice and possibly a microphone and an amp
- A pub
- At least one pint inside you
- At least one more on your table
- A table

What to do:

Choose your local to start with; there is no need to get halfway through your first quiz and decide you weren't cut out for all this and then find yourself in the roughest pub in Christendom 30 miles and a long run from home.

Chat it through with the landlord and agree on whether you will be charging or not; if you don't then there is little chance of a prize for the winners other than a free pint each and this is obviously at the landlord's discretion – if you pack his pub to bursting then five free pints won't worry him, but if it's only you and a couple of others then he may be less than unwilling, as publicans tend to be.

If you decide on an entry payment keep it reasonable; you don't want to take the fun out of the quiz; some people will be well aware that they have very little hope of winning and will be reluctant to celebrate the fact by mortgaging their house.

Once location and prize are all sorted then advertising the event is paramount. Get people's attention, sell, sell, sell or, alternatively, stick up a gaudy-looking poster on the door of the bogs. Be sure to specify all the details, time, prize and so on – remember you are selling to people whose tiny attention span is being whittled down to nothing by alcohol.

After this it is time for the big night. If you are holding the event in the "snug" which seats ten or so you can rely on your voice, if not you should get hold of a good microphone and an amplifier so that you can boom out your questions and enunciate the length and breadth of the pub (once again, clear this with the landlord and don't let liquid anywhere near the electrical equipment). Make sure to practise, and get comfortable with the sound of your own voice and relax as much as possible, try not to rely on alcohol too much or "round one" will be followed by "rown' too" which will eventually give way to "runfree". Relax your voice so that you can handle any queries from the teams, and any venomous abuse from the "lively" bar area.

When you enter the pub make sure you take everything listed above. Also, make sure you have a set of tie-break questions and that you instruct everybody who is taking part as to the rules – and be firm. It will only upset people if you start handing out impromptu solutions, and let's face it the wisdom of Solomon is not needed when you are talking pub quiz rules; "no cheating" is a perfectly healthy stance to start with. Keep people happy by double-checking your questions and answers; the last thing you need is a mix-up on the prize-winning question.

Finally, keep the teams to a maximum of five members, hand out your answer papers and pens and, when everybody is good and settled, start the quiz. It might not be easy and it might not propel you to international stardom or pay for a life of luxury but you will enjoy yourself. No, really.

ANSWERS

Level 1

1 _____

2 _____

3 _____

4 _____

5 _____

6 _____

7 _____

8 _____

9 _____

10 _____

11 _____

12 _____

13 _____

14 _____

15 _____

16 _____

17 _____

18 _____

19 _____

20 _____

21 _____

22 _____

23 _____

24 _____

25 _____

26 _____

27 _____

28 _____

29 _____

30 _____

ANSWERS

1 _____

2 _____

3 _____

4 _____

5 _____

6 _____

7 _____

8 _____

9 _____

10 _____

11 _____

12 _____

13 _____

14 _____

15 _____

16 _____

17 _____

18 _____

19 _____

20 _____

21 _____

22 _____

23 _____

24 _____

25 _____

26 _____

27 _____

28 _____

29 _____

30 _____

ANSWERS

Level 3

1 _____

2 _____

3 _____

4 _____

5 _____

6 _____

7 _____

8 _____

9 _____

10 _____

11 _____

12 _____

13 _____

14 _____

15 _____

16 _____

17 _____

18 _____

19 _____

20 _____

21 _____

22 _____

23 _____

24 _____

25 _____

26 _____

27 _____

28 _____

29 _____

30 _____

ANSWERS

Level 3

1 _____

2 _____

3 _____

4 _____

5 _____

6 _____

7 _____

8 _____

9 _____

10 _____

11 _____

12 _____

13 _____

14 _____

15 _____

16 _____

17 _____

18 _____

19 _____

20 _____

21 _____

22 _____

23 _____

24 _____

25 _____

26 _____

27 _____

28 _____

29 _____

30 _____

ISBN 978-1-84442-166-4
£6.99

ISBN 978-1-84442-180-0
£6.99

ISBN 978-1-84442-891-5
£6.99

The Best

Pub Quiz

Books
EVER!

From potluck to Pirates of the Caribbean, over *300* quizzes and *10,000* questions

Challenge yourself with questions on people, places, deeds, inventions, discoveries, disasters, moments of glory. The questions in *The Best Pub Quiz Book Ever!* series have been created to test the quizzer's powers of recall as much as his or her general knowledge.

Topics covered include sport, cinema, pop music, TV, food and drink, history, geography, politics and popular culture. Fully updated to take account of activities of Zinedine Zidane, Beyoncé, the WAGs, Gordon Brown, George W Bush, the contestants of the Big Brother house and all the other the movers and shakers of the 21st century.